DATE DUE

DEMCO 38-296

The Philosophy of Legal Reasoning

*A Collection of Essays by Philosophers
and Legal Scholars*

Series Editor

Scott Brewer
Harvard Law School

A GARLAND SERIES
READINGS IN PHILOSOPHY
ROBERT NOZICK, *ADVISOR*
HARVARD UNIVERSITY

Contents of the Series

Precedents, Statutes, and Analysis of Legal Concepts

Edited with an introduction by

Scott Brewer
Harvard Law School

GARLAND PUBLISHING, INC.
A MEMBER OF THE TAYLOR & FRANCIS GROUP

New York & London
1998

Library of Congress Cataloging-in-Publication Data

Precedents, statutes, and analysis of legal concepts / edited with an
   introduction by Scott Brewer.
          p.   cm. — (The philosophy of legal reasoning ; 2)
       Includes bibliographical references.
       ISBN 0-8153-2656-4 (v. 2 : alk. paper). — ISBN 0-8153-2654-8
   (set : alk. paper)
          1. Law—Interpretation and construction. 2. Judicial process.
       3. Stare decisis. I. Brewer, Scott. II. Series.
       K213.P494 1998 vol. 2
       [K290]
       340'.1 s—dc21   98-5170
       [340]   CIP

Printed on acid-free, 250-year-life paper
Manufactured in the United States of America

Contents

Introduction

This five-volume set contains some of this century's most influential or thought-provoking articles on the subject of legal argument that have appeared in Anglo-American philosophy journals and law reviews. Legal decisions have long been a deeply significant part of the history and life of societies that aspire to satisfy some version of the "rule of law" ideal. These decisions—at least those rendered by a jurisdiction's most prominent courts—are also often accompanied by detailed publicly available statements of the arguments supporting those decisions. For these reasons, among many others, understanding the dynamics of legal argument is of vital interest not only to legal academics, judges, lawyers, and law students, but also to citizens who are subject to law and who vote, directly or indirectly, for the legislators, regulators, and judges who write and interpret laws.

Because of the importance to civil societies of legal decisons and the legal arguments offered to justify them, the subject of legal argument has long been closely studied by scholars and other analysts. These theorists have explicated and criticized the dynamics of legal argument from vastly different perspectives. It is thus not surprising that these theorists have reached strikingly different conclusions, with equally distinct concerns and emphases. Theorists of legal argument have, for example, maintained that legal argument is principally driven by *a priori* legal-cum-moral truths applied to individual cases by formal logical inferences, or that the driving force of legal argument is a more or less thinly veiled imposition of a judge's preferred social or economic policy, or that legal argument is or should be (theorists sometimes blur the line between the descriptive and the prescriptive in their analyses) the incessantly self-critical and self-correcting reasoned elaboration of legal rules and standards that transcend immediate partisan results, or that legal arguments offered by judges are little more than a mystificatory and would-be legitimating veneer covering such darker motives as race, class, or gender bias, or that legal argument is the interpretive effort by judges in the forum of principle to make the law the best it can be from a moral point of view, or is the decision of those legal officials who hold authoritative power by virtue of socially adopted rules.

This set of volumes represents all of the theories just encapsulated, and others as well. As the brief, and certainly incomplete, list in the foregoing paragraph suggests, theorists of legal argument produce what can seem a whelming welter of diverse explanations. Even so, the vast majority of theories of legal argument revolve around two central focal points—rather, perhaps, like the oval-shaped ellipse, which orbits around two fixed foci.

One focus is the role of different *modes of logical inference* in legal argument. There are four basic logical structures that operate in legal argument (indeed, it can be argued plausibly that these are the four that organize all arguments, in all intellectual domains): *deduction, induction, abduction,* and *analogy.* It may help the reader to have a few basic definitions of these terms at the outset—even though by no means all the theorists whose articles are included will use these terms in their analyses. First, the basic term 'argument.' The defining characteristic of *argument,* including legal argument, is the inference of a conclusion from one or more premises. As just noted, all arguments, including legal argument, deploy one or more of four principal and irreducible (though analogical inference is tricky in this regard) modes of logical inference: (i) *deductive inference,* in which the truth of the premises guarantees the truth of the conclusion as long as the conclusion is arrived at by an acceptable deductive inference rule; (ii) *inductive inference,* in which the truth of the premises cannot guarantee the truth of the conclusion, but when the premises are carefully chosen, their truth can warrant belief in the truth of the conclusion to greater or lesser degrees of probability; (iii) *abductive inference,* in which an explanatory hypothesis is inferred as the conclusion of an argument with two distinct types of premise: first, a proposition that describes some event or phenomenon that the abductive reasoner believes stands in need of *explanation,* and second, a proposition to the effect that, *if* the explanatory hypothesis that is inferred ("abducted") were in fact *true* or otherwise warranted, then the explanandum would be sufficiently explained for the reasoner's purposes; and (iv) *analogical inference,* in which a reasoner relies on particular examples to discover (indeed, to "abduce") a rule that states what are the relevant similarities or differences between a less well-known item (the "target" of the analogical inference) and a better known item (the "source" of the analogical inference). The other focal point of theories of legal argument is the role of various types of *norms* in legal argument, including *legal norms* (norms issued by proper legal authorities or endorsed by other social norms—the proper account of legal norms divides "legal positivists" and "natural law" theorists), *moral norms* (norms concerned with right and wrong), *epistemic norms* (norms concerned with true or otherwise warranted beliefs), *linguistic norms* (norms concerned with understanding the meaning of texts), and "instrumental" or "prudential" norms (those nonmoral norms that are "instrumental" to helping a reasoner achieve a goal he or she has chosen to pursue).

Even when they do not explicitly use this exact terminology of "logical inference," "deduction," "induction," "norm," and the like, in one way or another all of the articles in these volumes are within the intellectual gravitational orbit of these two focal points. One hastens to add that, far from being dry and remote "academic" exercises, the inquiries pursued by these articles touch on many of the most pressing and contentious issues in contemporary legal, moral, and political debate—as the list of conclusions of various theories of legal argument in the second paragraph of this introduction clearly indicates.

Several criteria have guided the selection of articles in this set. The broad impact of an article among scholars, judges, and lawyers was certainly a leading criterion, and a great many of the articles satisfy it. But that criterion was by no means the only one. Some of the articles in these volumes are fairly recent, and more time will be needed to assess their enduring impact on the worlds of legal thought and practice. It can be said fairly that even these more recent articles present fresh and thought-provoking claims and insights, worthy of being considered even if only to be ultimately rejected. The criterion of intellectually fertile provocation guided the selection of some of the older articles in the volumes (for example, some of those in volume one), which were chosen neither for fame nor influence but rather because they present an important perspective on an issue that—in this editor's opinion—has received far too little attention in twentieth-century American jurisprudence and legal education: the role of *deductive* inference in legal argument. Even though the role of one or more of the four basic logical inferences is a focus of theories of legal argument, generations of legal academics, judges, and lawyers have tended to ignore or understate the role of deductive inference, largely without understanding enough about what deductive inference is or the many very important ways in which it does guide legal argument. They have been led to this point largely because of the influentially expressed and often parroted sentiment of Justice Oliver Wendell Holmes Jr. and several of his followers, that "[t]he life of the law has not been logic: it has been experience."[1] By 'logic' Holmes meant deductive logic, and his maxim-al hyperbole has done much to encumber the proper understanding of the rational dynamics of legal argument. Several of the articles in these volumes were chosen to help readers rediscover and revivify this important issue and to see its importance for broader political and moral questions.

All in all, I am confident that the articles in these volumes will well repay the attentiveness of readers who wish to think seriously about the nature of significance of legal argument as a vital part of broader legal and political processes, as long as they bring reading minds that are fairly "braced with labor and invention."

Notes

[1] Oliver W. Holmes, *The Common Law*, ed. Mark DeWolfe Howe (Boston: Little, Brown, 1963) p.5.

COLUMBIA LAW REVIEW

| Vol. 47 | MAY, 1947 | No. 4 |

SOME REFLECTIONS ON THE READING OF STATUTES*

FELIX FRANKFURTER[1]

A single volume of 320 octavo pages contains all the laws passed by Congress during its first five years, when measures were devised for getting the new government under way; 26 acts were passed in the 1789 session, 66 in 1790, 94 in 1791, 38 in 1792, 63 in 1793. For the single session of the 70th Congress, to take a pre-depression period, there are 993 enactments in a monstrous volume of 1014 pages—quarto not octavo—with a comparable range of subject matter. Do you wonder that one for whom the Statutes at Large constitute his staple reading should have sympathy, at least in his moments of baying at the moon, with the touching Congressman who not so long ago proposed a "Commission on Centralization" to report whether "the Government has departed from the concept of the founding fathers" and what steps should be taken "to restore the Government to its original purposes and sphere of activity"? Inevitably the work of the Supreme Court reflects the great shift in the center of gravity of law-making. Broadly speaking, the number of cases disposed of by opinions has not changed from term to term. But even as late as 1875 more than 40% of the controversies before the Court were common-law litigation, fifty years later only 5%, while today cases not resting on statutes are reduced almost to zero. It is therefore accurate to say that courts have ceased to be the primary makers of law in the sense in which they "legislated" the common law. It is certainly true of the Supreme Court that almost every case has a statute at its heart or close to it.

This does not mean that every case before the Court involves questions of statutory construction. If only literary perversity or jaundiced partisanship can sponsor a particular rendering of a statute there is no problem. When we talk of statutory construction we have in mind cases in which there is a fair contest between two readings, neither of which comes without respectable title

---

* Sixth Annual Benjamin N. Cardozo Lecture delivered before the Association of the Bar of the City of New York, March 18, 1947. This address is reprinted with permission from 2 THE RECORD OF THE ASS'N OF THE BAR OF THE CITY OF NEW YORK No. 6 (1947).

1. It gives me pleasure to make acknowledgment to my learned friends, Philip Elman, Louis Henkin and Philip Kurland, Esqs. They have no responsibility for what I have said; they are merely subjected to my gratitude.

deeds. A problem in statutory construction can seriously bother courts only when there is a contest between probabilities of meaning.

DIFFICULTIES OF CONSTRUCTION

Though it has its own preoccupations and its own mysteries, and above all its own jargon, judicial construction ought not to be torn from its wider, non-legal context. Anything that is written may present a problem of meaning, and that is the essence of the business of judges in construing legislation. The problem derives from the very nature of words. They are symbols of meaning. But unlike mathematical symbols, the phrasing of a document, especially a complicated enactment, seldom attains more than approximate precision. If individual words are inexact symbols, with shifting variables, their configuration can hardly achieve invariant meaning or assured definiteness. Apart from the ambiguity inherent in its symbols, a statute suffers from dubieties. It is not an equation or a formula representing a clearly marked process, nor is it an expression of individual thought to which is imparted the definiteness a single authorship can give. A statute is an instrument of government partaking of its practical purposes but also of its infirmities and limitations, of its awkward and groping efforts. With one of his flashes of insight, Mr. Justice Johnson called the science of government "the science of experiment."[2] The phrase, uttered a hundred and twenty-five years ago, has a very modern ring, for time has only served to emphasize its accuracy. To be sure, laws can measurably be improved with improvement in the mechanics of legislation, and the need for interpretation is usually in inverse ratio to the care and imagination of draftsmen. The area for judicial construction may be contracted. A large area is bound to remain.

The difficulties are inherent not only in the nature of words, of composition, and of legislation generally. They are often intensified by the subject matter of an enactment. The imagination which can draw an income tax statute to cover the myriad transactions of a society like ours, capable of producing the necessary revenue without producing a flood of litigation, has not yet revealed itself.[3] Moreover, government sometimes solves problems by shelving them temporarily. The legislative process reflects that attitude. Statutes as well as constitutional provisions at times embody purposeful ambiguity or are expressed with a generality for future unfolding. "The prohibition contained in the Fifth Amendment refers to infamous crimes—a term obviously inviting interpretation in harmony with conditions and opinions prevailing from time to time."[4] And Mr. Justice Cardozo once re-

---

2. Anderson v. Dunn, 6 Wheat. 204, 226 (U. S. 1821).
3. 1 REPORT OF INCOME TAX CODIFICATION COMMITTEE, CMD. 5131, pp. 16-19 (England 1936).
4. See Mr. Justice Brandeis in United States v. Moreland, 258 U. S. 433, 451 (1922).

marked, "a great principle of constitutional law is not susceptible of comprehensive statement in an adjective."[5]

The intrinsic difficulties of language and the emergence after enactment of situations not anticipated by the most gifted legislative imagination, reveal doubts and ambiguities in statutes that compel judicial construction. The process of construction, therefore, is not an exercise in logic or dialectic: The aids of formal reasoning are not irrelevant; they may simply be inadequate. The purpose of construction being the ascertainment of meaning, every consideration brought to bear for the solution of that problem must be devoted to that end alone. To speak of it as a practical problem is not to indulge a fashion in words. It must be that, not something else. Not, for instance, an opportunity for a judge to use words as "empty vessels into which he can pour anything he will"—his caprices, fixed notions, even statesmanlike beliefs in a particular policy. Nor, on the other hand, is the process a ritual to be observed by unimaginative adherence to well-worn professional phrases. To be sure, it is inescapably a problem in the keeping of the legal profession and subject to all the limitations of our adversary system of adjudication. When the judge, selected by society to give meaning to what the legislature has done, examines the statute, he does so not in a laboratory or in a classroom. Damage has been done or exactions made, interests are divided, passions have been aroused, sides have been taken. But the judge, if he is worth his salt, must be above the battle. We must assume in him not only personal impartiality but intellectual disinterestedness. In matters of statutory construction also it makes a great deal of difference whether you start with an answer or with a problem.

THE JUDGE'S TASK

Everyone has his own way of phrasing the task confronting judges when the meaning of a statute is in controversy. Judge Learned Hand speaks of the art of interpretation as "the proliferation of purpose." Who am I not to be satisfied with Learned Hand's felicities? And yet that phrase might mislead judges intellectually less disciplined than Judge Hand. It might justify interpretations by judicial libertines, not merely judicial libertarians. My own rephrasing of what we are driving at is probably no more helpful, and is much longer than Judge Hand's epigram. I should say that the troublesome phase of construction is the determination of the extent to which extraneous documentation and external circumstances may be allowed to infiltrate the text on the theory that they were part of it, written in ink discernible to the judicial eye.

---

5. Carter v. Carter Coal Co., 298 U. S. 238, 327 (1936).

Chief Justice White was happily endowed with the gift of finding the answer to problems by merely stating them. Often have I envied him this faculty but never more than in recent years. No matter how one states the problem of statutory construction, for me at least it does not carry its own answer. Though my business throughout most of my professional life has been with statutes, I come to you empty-handed. I bring no answers. I suspect the answers to the problems of an art are in its exercise. Not that one does not inherit, if one is capable of receiving it, the wisdom of the wise. But I confess unashamedly that I do not get much nourishment from books on statutory construction, and I say this after freshly reexamining them all, scores of them.

When one wants to understand or at least get the feeling of great painting, one does not go to books on the art of painting. One goes to the great masters. And so I have gone to great masters to get a sense of their practise of the art of interpretation. However, the art of painting and the art of interpretation are very different arts. Law, Holmes told us, becomes civilized to the extent that it is self-conscious of what it is doing. And so the avowals of great judges regarding their process of interpretation and the considerations that enter into it are of vital importance, though that ultimate something called the judgment upon the avowed factors escapes formulation and often, I suspect, even awareness. Nevertheless, an examination of some 2,000 cases, the bulk of which directly or indirectly involves matters of construction, ought to shed light on the encounter between the judicial and the legislative processes, whether that light be conveyed by hints, by explicit elucidation, or, to mix the metaphor, through the ancient test, by their fruits.

And so I have examined the opinions of Holmes, Brandeis and Cardozo and sought to derive from their treatment of legislation what conclusions I could fairly draw, freed as much as I could be from impressions I had formed in the course of the years.

Holmes came to the Supreme Court before the great flood of recent legislation, while the other two, especially Cardozo, appeared at its full tide. The shift in the nature of the Court's business led to changes in its jurisdiction, resulting in a concentration of cases involving the legislative process. Proportionately to their length of service and the number of opinions, Brandeis and Cardozo had many more statutes to construe. And the statutes presented for their interpretation became increasingly complex, bringing in their train a quantitatively new role for administrative regulations. Nevertheless, the earliest opinions of Holmes on statutory construction, insofar as he reveals himself, cannot be distinguished from Cardozo's last opinion, though the latter's process is more explicit.

4

A judge of marked individuality stamps his individuality on what he writes, no matter what the subject. What is however striking about the opinions of the three Justices in this field is the essential similarity of their attitude and of their appraisal of the relevant. Their opinions do not disclose a private attitude for or against extension of governmental authority by legislation, or towards the policy of particular legislation, which consciously or imperceptibly affected their judicial function in construing laws. It would thus be a shallow judgment that found in Mr. Justice Holmes' dissent in the *Northern Securities* case[6] an expression of his disapproval of the policy behind the Sherman Law. His habit of mind—to be as accurate as one can—had a natural tendency to confine what seemed to him familiar language in a statute to its familiar scope. But the proof of the pudding is that his private feelings did not lead him to invoke the rule of indefiniteness to invalidate legislation of which he strongly disapproved,[7] or to confine language in a constitution within the restrictions which he gave to the same language in a statute.[8]

The reservations I have just made indicate that such differences as emerge in the opinions of the three Justices on statutory construction, are differences that characterize all of their opinions, whether they are concerned with interpretation or constitutionality, with admiralty or patent law. They are differences of style. In the case of each, the style is the man.

If it be suggested that Mr. Justice Holmes is often swift, if not cavalier, in his treatment of statutes, there are those who level the same criticism against his opinions generally. It is merited in the sense that he wrote, as he said, for those learned in the art. I need hardly add that for him "learned" was not a formal term comprehending the whole legal fraternity. When dealing with problems of statutory construction also he illumined whole areas of doubt and darkness with insights enduringly expressed, however briefly. To say "We agree to all the generalities about not supplying criminal laws with what they omit, but there is no canon against using common sense in construing laws as saying what they obviously mean,"[9] is worth more than most of the dreary writing on how to construe penal legislation. Again when he said that "the meaning of a sentence is to be felt rather than to be proved,"[10] he expressed the wholesome truth that the final rendering of the meaning of a statute is an act of judgment. He would shudder at the

---

6. Northern Securities Co. v. United States, 193 U. S. 197, 400 (1904).

7. *Cf.* Nash v. United States, 229 U. S. 373 (1913) and International Harvester Co. v. Kentucky, 234 U. S. 216 (1914).

8. *Cf.* Towne v. Eisner, 245 U. S. 418 (1918) and Eisner v. Macomber, 252 U. S. 189 (1920).

9. Roschen v. Ward, 279 U. S. 337, 339 (1929).

10. United States v. Johnson, 221 U. S. 488, 496 (1911).

5

thought that by such a statement he was giving comfort to the school of visceral jurisprudence. Judgment is not drawn out of the void but is based on the correlation of imponderables all of which need not, because they cannot, be made explicit. He was expressing the humility of the intellectual that he was, whose standards of exactitude distrusted pretensions of certainty, believing that legal controversies that are not frivolous almost always involve matters of degree, and often degree of the nicest sort. Statutory construction implied the exercise of choice, but precluded the notion of capricious choice as much as choice based on private notions of policy. One gets the impression that in interpreting statutes Mr. Justice Holmes reached meaning easily, as was true of most of his results, with emphasis on the language in the totality of the enactment and the felt reasonableness of the chosen construction. He had a lively awareness that a statute was expressive of purpose and policy, but in his reading of it he tended to hug the shores of the statute itself, without much re-enforcement from without.

Mr. Justice Brandeis, on the other hand, in dealing with these problems as with others, would elucidate the judgment he was exercising by proof or detailed argument. In such instances, especially when in dissent, his opinions would draw on the whole arsenal of aids to construction. More often than either Holmes or Cardozo, Brandeis would invoke the additional weight of some "rule" of construction. But he never lost sight of the limited scope and function of such "rules." Occasionally, however, perhaps because of the nature of a particular statute, the minor importance of its incidence, the pressure of judicial business or even the temperament of his law clerk, whom he always treated as a co-worker, Brandeis disposed of a statute even more dogmatically, with less explicit elucidation, than did Holmes.

For Cardozo, statutory construction was an acquired taste. He preferred common law subtleties, having great skill in bending them to modern uses. But he came to realize that problems of statutory construction had their own exciting subtleties and gave ample employment to philosophic and literary talents. Cardozo's elucidation of how meaning is drawn out of a statute gives proof of the wisdom and balance which, combined with his learning, made him a great judge. While the austere style of Brandeis seldom mitigated the dry aspect of so many problems of statutory construction, Cardozo managed to endow even these with the glow and softness of his writing. The differences in the tone and color of their style as well as in the moral intensity of Brandeis and Cardozo made itself felt when they wrote full-dress opinions on problems of statutory construction. Brandeis almost compels by demonstration; Cardozo woos by persuasion.

Scope of the Judicial Function

From the hundreds of cases in which our three Justices construed statutes one thing clearly emerges. The area of free judicial movement is considerable. These three remembered that laws are not abstract propositions. They are expressions of policy arising out of specific situations and addressed to the attainment of particular ends. The difficulty is that the legislative ideas which laws embody are both explicit and immanent. And so the bottom problem is: What is below the surface of the words and yet fairly a part of them? Words in statutes are not unlike words in a foreign language in that they too have "associations, echoes, and overtones."[11] Judges must retain the associations, hear the echoes, and capture the overtones. In one of his very last opinions, dealing with legislation taxing the husband on the basis of the combined income of husband and wife, Holmes wrote: "The statutes are the outcome of a thousand years of history. . . . They form a system with echoes of different moments, none of which is entitled to prevail over the other."[12]

What exactions such a duty of construction places upon judges, and with what freedom it entrusts them! John Chipman Gray was fond of quoting from a sermon by Bishop Hoadley that "Whoever hath an *absolute authority* to *interpret* any written or spoken laws, it is he who is truly the law-giver to all intents and purposes, and not the person who first wrote or spoke them."[13] By admitting that there is some substance to the good Bishop's statement, one does not subscribe to the notion that they are law-givers in any but a very qualified sense.

Even within their area of choice the courts are not at large. They are confined by the nature and scope of the judicial function in its particular exercise in the field of interpretation. They are under the constraints imposed by the judicial function in our democratic society. As a matter of verbal recognition certainly, no one will gainsay that the function in construing a statute is to ascertain the meaning of words used by the legislature. To go beyond it is to usurp a power which our democracy has lodged in its elected legislature. The great judges have constantly admonished their brethren of the need for discipline in observing the limitations. A judge must not rewrite a statute, neither to enlarge nor to contract it. Whatever temptations the statesmanship of policy-making might wisely suggest, construction must eschew interpolation and evisceration. He must not read in by way of creation. He must not read out except to avoid patent nonsense or internal contradiction. "If there is no meaning in it," said Alice's King, "that saves a world of trouble, you know, as

---

11. Barker, The Politics of Aristotle lxiii (1946).
12. Hoeper v. Tax Comm'n, 284 U. S. 206, 219 (1931).
13. Gray, Nature and Sources of the Law 102, 125, 172 (2d ed. 1921).

we needn't try to find any." Legislative words presumably have meaning and so we must try to find it.

This duty of restraint, this humility of function as merely the translator of another's command, is a constant theme of our Justices. It is on the lips of all judges, but seldom, I venture to believe, has the restraint which it expresses, or the duty which it enjoins, been observed with so consistent a realization that its observance depends on self-conscious discipline. Cardozo put it this way: "We do not pause to consider whether a statute differently conceived and framed would yield results more consonant with fairness and reason. We take this statute as we find it."[14]   It was expressed more fully by Mr. Justice Brandeis when the temptation to give what might be called a more liberal interpretation could not have been wanting. "The particularization and detail with which the scope of each provision, the amount of the tax thereby imposed, and the incidence of the tax, were specified, preclude an extension of any provision by implication to any other subject. . . . What the Government asks is not a construction of a statute, but, in effect, an enlargement of it by the court, so that what was omitted, presumably by inadvertence, may be included within its scope."[15]   An omission at the time of enactment, whether careless or calculated, cannot be judicially supplied however much later wisdom may recommend the inclusion.

The vital difference between initiating policy, often involving a decided break with the past, and merely carrying out a formulated policy, indicates the relatively narrow limits within which choice is fairly open to courts and the extent to which interpreting law is inescapably making law. To say that, because of this restricted field of interpretive declaration, courts make law just as do legislatures is to deny essential features in the history of our democracy. It denies that legislation and adjudication have had different lines of growth, serve vitally different purposes, function under different conditions, and bear different responsibilities. The judicial process of dealing with words is not at all Alice in Wonderland's way of dealing with them. Even in matters legal some words and phrases, though very few, approach mathematical symbols and mean substantially the same to all who have occasion to use them. Other law terms like "police power" are not symbols at all but labels for the results of the whole process of adjudication. In between lies a gamut of words with different denotations as well as connotations. There are varying shades of compulsion for judges behind different words, differences that are due to the words themselves, their setting in a text, their setting in history. In short, judges are not unfettered glossators. They are under a special duty not to over-emphasize the episodic aspects of life and not to undervalue its

---

14. Anderson v. Wilson, 289 U. S. 20, 27 (1933).
15. Iselin v. United States, 270 U. S. 245, 250, 251 (1926).

organic processes—its continuities and relationships. For judges at least it is important to remember that continuity with the past is not only a necessity but even a duty.

There are not wanting those who deem naive the notion that judges are expected to refrain from legislating in construing statutes. They may point to cases where even our three Justices apparently supplied an omission or engrafted a limitation. Such an accusation cannot be rebutted or judged in the abstract. In some ways, as Holmes once remarked, every statute is unique. Whether a judge does violence to language in its total context is not always free from doubt. Statutes come out of the past and aim at the future. They may carry implicit residues or mere hints of purpose. Perhaps the most delicate aspect of statutory construction is not to find more residues than are implicit nor purposes beyond the bound of hints. Even for a judge most sensitive to the traditional limitation of his function, this is a matter for judgment not always easy of answer. But a line does exist between omission and what Holmes called "misprision or abbreviation that does not conceal the purpose."[16] Judges may differ as to the point at which the line should be drawn, but the only sure safeguard against crossing the line between adjudication and legislation is an alert recognition of the necessity not to cross it and instinctive, as well as trained, reluctance to do so.

In those realms where judges directly formulate law because the chosen lawmakers have not acted, judges have the duty of adaptation and adjustment of old principles to new conditions. But where policy is expressed by the primary law-making agency in a democracy, that is by the legislature, judges must respect such expressions by adding to or subtracting from the explicit terms which the lawmakers use no more than is called for by the shorthand nature of language. Admonitions like that of Justice Brandeis in the *Iselin* case that courts should leave even desirable enlargement to Congress will not by itself furnish the meaning appropriate for the next statute under scrutiny. But as is true of other important principles, the intensity with which it is believed may be decisive of the outcome.

THE PROCESS OF CONSTRUCTION

Let me descend to some particulars.

The text.—Though we may not end with the words in construing a disputed statute, one certainly begins there. You have a right to think that a hoary platitude, but it is a platitude not acted upon in many arguments. In any event, it may not take you to the end of the road. The Court no doubt must listen to the voice of Congress. But often Congress cannot be heard clearly because its

---

16. St. Louis-San Francisco Ry. v. Middlekamp, 256 U. S. 226, 232 (1921).

speech is muffled. Even when it has spoken, it is as true of Congress as of others that what is said is what the listener hears. Like others, judges too listen with what psychologists used to call the apperception mass, which I take it means in plain English that one listens with what is already in one's head. One more caution is relevant when one is admonished to listen attentively to what a statute says. One must also listen attentively to what it does not say.

We must, no doubt, accord the words the sense in which Congress used them. That is only another way of stating the central problem of decoding the symbols. It will help to determine for whom they were meant. Statutes are not archaeological documents to be studied in a library. They are written to guide the actions of men. As Mr. Justice Holmes remarked upon some Indian legislation "The word was addressed to the Indian mind."[17] If a statute is written for ordinary folk, it would be arbitrary not to assume that Congress intended its words to be read with the minds of ordinary men. If they are addressed to specialists, they must be read by judges with the minds of the specialists.

And so we assume that Congress uses common words in their popular meaning, as used in the common speech of men. The cases speak of the "meaning of common understanding," "the normal and spontaneous meaning of language," "the common and appropriate use," "the natural straightforward and literal sense," and similar variants. In *McBoyle v. United States*,[18] Mr. Justice Holmes had to decide whether an aeroplane is a "motor vehicle" within the meaning of the Motor Vehicle Theft Act. He thus disposed of it: "No doubt etymologically it is possible to use the word to signify a conveyance working on land, water or air, and sometimes legislation extends the use in that direction. . . . But in everyday speech 'vehicles' calls up a picture of a thing moving on land."

Sometimes Congress supplies its own dictionary. It did so in 1871 in a statute defining a limited number of words for use as to all future enactments. It may do so, as in recent legislation, by a section within the statute containing detailed definitions. Or there may be indications from the statute that words in it are the considered language of legislation. "If Congress has been accustomed to use a certain phrase with a more limited meaning than might be attributed to it by common practice, it would be arbitrary to refuse to consider that fact when we come to interpret a statute. But, as we have said, the usage of Congress simply shows that it has spoken with careful precision, that its words mark the exact spot at which it stops."[19] Or words may ac-

---

17. Fleming v. McCurtain, 215 U. S. 56, 60 (1909).
18. 283 U. S. 25, 26 (1931).
19. Boston Sand & Gravel Co. v. United States, 278 U. S. 41, 48 (1928).

quire scope and function from the history of events which they summarize or from the purpose which they serve.

> "However colloquial and uncertain the words had been in the beginning, they had won for themselves finally an acceptance and a definiteness that made them fit to play a part in the legislative process. They came into the statute . . . freighted with the meaning imparted to them by the mischief to be remedied and by contemporaneous discussion. . . . In such conditions history is a teacher that is not to be ignored."[20]

Words of art bring their art with them. They bear the meaning of their habitat whether it be a phrase of technical significance in the scientific or business world, or whether it be loaded with the recondite connotations of feudalism. Holmes made short shrift of a contention by remarking that statutes used "familiar legal expressions in their familiar legal sense."[21] The peculiar idiom of business or of administrative practise often modifies the meaning that ordinary speech assigns to language. And if a word is obviously transplanted from another legal source, whether the common law or other legislation, it brings the old soil with it.

The context.—Legislation is a form of literary composition. But construction is not an abstract process equally valid for every composition, not even for every composition whose meaning must be judicially ascertained. The nature of the composition demands awareness of certain presuppositions. For instance, the words in a constitution may carry different meanings from the same words in a statute precisely because "it is a constitution we are expounding." The reach of this consideration was indicated by Mr. Justice Holmes in language that remains fresh no matter how often repeated:

> "[W]hen we are dealing with words that also are a constituent act, like the Constitution of the United States, we must realize that they have called into life a being the development of which could not have been foreseen completely by the most gifted of its begetters. It was enough for them to realize or to hope that they had created an organism; it has taken a century and has cost their successors much sweat and blood to prove that they created a nation. The case before us must be considered in the light of our whole experience and not merely in that of what was said a hundred years ago."[22]

And so, the significance of an enactment, its antecedents as well as its later history, its relation to other enactments, all may be relevant to the construction of words for one purpose and in one setting but not for another. Some words are confined to their history; some are starting points for history. Words are intellectual and moral currency. They come from the legislative

---

20. Mr. Justice Cardozo in Duparquet Co. v. Evans, 297 U. S. 216, 220, 221 (1936).
21. Henry v. United States, 251 U. S. 393, 395 (1920).
22. Missouri v. Holland, 252 U. S. 416, 433 (1920).

mint with some intrinsic meaning. Sometimes it remains unchanged. Like currency, words sometimes appreciate or depreciate in value.

Frequently the sense of a word cannot be got except by fashioning a mosaic of significance out of the innuendoes of disjointed bits of statute. Cardozo phrased this familiar phenomenon by stating that "the meaning of a statute is to be looked for, not in any single section, but in all the parts together and in their relation to the end in view."[23] And to quote Cardozo once more on this phase of our problem: "There is need to keep in view also the structure of the statute, and the relation, physical and logical, between its several parts."[24]

The generating consideration is that legislation is more than composition. It is an active instrument of government which, for purposes of interpretation, means that laws have ends to be achieved. It is in this connection that Holmes said "words are flexible."[25] Again it was Holmes, the last judge to give quarter to loose thinking or vague yearning, who said that "the general purpose is a more important aid to the meaning than any rule which grammar or formal logic may lay down."[26] And it was Holmes who chided courts for being "apt to err by sticking too closely to the words of a law where those words import a policy that goes beyond them."[27] Note, however, that he found the policy in "those words"!

PROLIFERATION OF PURPOSE

You may have observed that I have not yet used the word "intention." All these years I have avoided speaking of the "legislative intent" and I shall continue to be on my guard against using it. The objection to "intention" was indicated in a letter by Mr. Justice Holmes which the recipient kindly put at my disposal:

> "Only a day or two ago—when counsel talked of the intention of a legislature, I was indiscreet enough to say I don't care what their intention was. I only want to know what the words mean. Of course the phrase often is used to express a conviction not exactly thought out—that you construe a particular clause or expression by considering the whole instrument and any dominant purposes that it may express. In fact intention is a residuary clause intended to gather up whatever other aids there may be to interpretation beside the particular words and the dictionary."

If that is what the term means, it is better to use a less beclouding characterization. Legislation has an aim; it seeks to obviate some mischief, to supply an inadequacy, to effect a change of policy, to formulate a plan of govern-

---

23. Panama Refining Co. v. Ryan, 293 U. S. 388, 433, 439 (1935) (dissenting).
24. Duparquet Co. v. Evans, 297 U. S. 216, 218 (1936).
25. International Stevedoring Co. v. Haverty, 272 U. S. 50, 52 (1926).
26. United States v. Whitridge, 197 U. S. 135, 143 (1905).
27. Olmstead v. United States, 277 U. S. 438, 469 (1928) (dissenting).

rnent. That aim, that policy is not drawn, like nitrogen, out of the air; it is evinced in the language of the statute, as read in the light of other external manifestations of purpose. That is what the judge must seek and effectuate, and he ought not to be led off the trail by tests that have overtones of subjective design. We are not concerned with anything subjective. We do not delve into the mind of legislators or their draftsmen, or committee members. Against what he believed to be such an attempt Cardozo once protested:

> "The judgment of the court, if I interpret the reasoning aright, does not rest upon a ruling that Congress would have gone beyond its power if the purpose that it professed was the purpose truly cherished. The judgment of the court rests upon the ruling that another purpose, not professed, may be read beneath the surface, and by the purpose so imputed the statute is destroyed. Thus the process of psychoanalysis has spread to unaccustomed fields. There is a wise and ancient doctrine that a court will not inquire into the motives of a legislative body. . . ."[28]

The difficulty in many instances where a problem of meaning arises is that the enactment was not directed towards the troubling question. The problem might then be stated, as once it was by Mr. Justice Cardozo, "which choice is it the more likely that Congress would have made?"[29] While in its context the significance and limitations of this question are clear, thus to frame the question too often tempts inquiry into the subjective and might seem to warrant the court in giving answers based on an unmanifested legislative state of mind. But the purpose which a court must effectuate is not that which Congress should have enacted, or would have. It is that which it did enact, however inaptly, because it may fairly be said to be imbedded in the statute, even if a specific manifestation was not thought of, as is often the very reason for casting a statute in very general terms.

Often the purpose or policy that controls is not directly displayed in the particular enactment. Statutes cannot be read intelligently if the eye is closed to considerations evidenced in affiliated statutes, or in the known temper of legislative opinion. Thus, for example, it is not lightly to be presumed that Congress sought to infringe on "very sacred rights."[30] This improbability will be a factor in determining whether language, though it should be so read if standing alone, was used to effect such a drastic change.

More frequently still, in the interpretation of recent regulatory statutes, it becomes important to remember that the judicial task in marking out the extent to which Congress has exercised its constitutional power over commerce, is not that of devising an abstract formula. The task is one of accommodation as between assertions of new federal authority and historic

---

28. United States v. Constantine, 296 U. S. 287, 298, 299 (1936) (dissenting).
29. Burnet v. Guggenheim, 288 U. S. 280, 285 (1933).
30. Milwaukee Social Democrat Publishing Co. v. Burleson, 255 U. S. 407, 438 (1921) (dissenting).

13

functions of the individual states. Federal legislation of this character cannot therefore be construed without regard to the implications of our dual system of government. In such cases, for example, it is not to be assumed as a matter of course that when Congress adopts a new scheme for federal industrial regulation, it deals with all situations falling within the general mischief which gave rise to the legislation. The underlying assumptions of our dual form of government, and the consequent presuppositions of legislative draftsmanship which are expressive of our history and habits, cut across what might otherwise be the implied range of legislation. The history of congressional legislation regulating not only interstate commerce as such but also activities intertwined with it, justify the generalization that, when the Federal Government takes over such local radiations in the vast network of our national economic enterprise and thereby radically readjusts the balance of state and national authority, those charged with the duty of legislating are reasonably explicit and do not entrust its attainment to that retrospective expansion of meaning which properly deserves the stigma of judicial legislation.

Search for Purpose

How then does the purpose which a statute expresses reveal itself, particularly when the path of purpose is not straight and narrow? The English courts say: look at the statute and look at nothing else. Lord Reading so advised the House of Lords when a bill was before it as to which the Attorney General had given an interpretative explanation during its passage in the House of Commons: "Neither the words of the Attorney General nor the words of an ex-Lord Chancellor, spoken in this House, as to the meaning intended to be given to language used in a Bill, have the slightest effect or relevance when the matter comes to be considered by a Court of Law. The one thing which stands out beyond all question is that in a Court of Law you are not allowed to introduce observations made either by the Government or by anybody else, but the Court will only give consideration to the Statute itself. That is elementary, but I think it is necessary to bring it home to your Lordships because I think too much importance can be attached to language which fell from the Attorney General."[31] How narrowly the English courts confine their search for understanding an English enactment is vividly illustrated by the pronouncements of Lord Haldane, surely one of the most broadminded of all modern judges. "My Lords," he said in *Viscountess Rhondda's Claim*,[32] "the only other point made on the construction of the Act was that this Committee might be entitled to look at what passed while the Bill was still a Bill and in the Committee stage in the House.

---

31. 94 H. L. Deb. 232 (5th ser. 1934).
32. [1922] 2 A. C. 339, 383.

It was said that there amendments were moved and discussions took place which indicated that the general words of s. 1 were not regarded by your Lordships' House as covering the title to a seat in it. But even assuming that to be certain, I do not think, sitting as we do with the obligation to administer the principles of the law, that we have the least right to look at what happened while the Bill was being discussed in Committee and before the Act was passed. Decisions of the highest authority show that the interpretation of an Act of Parliament must be collected from the words in which the Sovereign has made into law the words agreed upon by both Houses. The history of previous changes made or discussed cannot be taken to have been known or to have been in view when the Royal assent was given. The contrary was suggested at the Bar, though I do not think the point was pressed, and I hope that it will not be thought that in its decision this Committee has given any countenance to it. To have done so would, I venture to say, have been to introduce confusion into well-settled law. In *Millar v. Taylor* the principle of construction was laid down in words, which have never, so far as I know, been seriously challenged, by Willes J. as long ago as in 1769: 'The sense and meaning of an Act of Parliament must be collected from what it says when passed into a law; and not from the history of changes it underwent in the house where it took its rise. That history is not known to the other house or to the sovereign.' "

These current English rules of construction are simple. They are too simple. If the purpose of construction is the ascertainment of meaning, nothing that is logically relevant should be excluded. The rigidity of English courts in interpreting language merely by reading it disregards the fact that enactments are, as it were, organisms which exist in their environment. One wonders whether English judges are confined psychologically as they purport to be legally. The judges deem themselves limited to reading the words of a statute. But can they really escape placing the words in the context of their minds, which after all are not automata applying legal logic but repositories of all sorts of assumptions and impressions? Such a modest if not mechanical view of the task of construction disregards legal history. In earlier centuries the judges recognized that the exercise of their judicial function to understand and apply legislative policy is not to be hindered by artificial canons and limitations. The well known resolutions in *Heydon's Case*,[33] have the flavor of Elizabethan English but they express the substance of a current volume of U. S. Reports as to the considerations relevant to statutory interpretation. To be sure, early English legislation helped ascertainment of

---

33. 3 Co. 7a, 76 Eng. Rep. 637 (1584).

15

purpose by explicit recitals; at least to the extent of defining the mischief against which the enactment was directed. To take a random instance, an act in the reign of Edward VI reads: " 'Forasmuch as intolerable Hurts and Troubles to the Commonwealth of this Realm doth daily grow and increase through such Abuses and Disorders as are had and used in common Alehouses and other Houses called Tipling houses': (2) it is therefore enacted by the King our Sovereign Lord, etc."[34] Judicial construction certainly became more artificial after the practice of elucidating recitals ceased. It is to be noted that Macaulay, a great legislative draftsman, did not think much of preambles. He believed that too often they are jejune because legislators may agree on what ought to be done, while disagreeing about the reasons for doing it. At the same time he deemed it most important that in some manner governments should give reasons for their legislative course.[35] When not so long ago the Parliamentary mechanism was under scrutiny of the Lord Chancellor's Committee, dissatisfaction was expressed with the prevailing practise of English courts not to go outside the statutes. It was urged that the old practise of preambles be restored or that a memorandum of explanation go with proposed legislation.[36]

At the beginning, the Supreme Court reflected the early English attitude. With characteristic hardheadedness Chief Justice Marshall struck at the core of the matter with the observation "Where the mind labours to discover the design of the legislature, it seizes everything from which aid can be derived."[37] This commonsensical way of dealing with statutes fell into disuse, and more or less catchpenny canons of construction did service instead. To no small degree a more wooden treatment of legislation was due, I suspect, to the fact that the need for keeping vividly in mind the occasions for drawing on all aids in the process of distilling meaning from legislation was comparatively limited. As the area of regulation steadily widened, the impact of the legislative process upon the judicial brought into being, and compelled consideration of, all that convincingly illumines an enactment, instead of merely that which is called, with delusive simplicity, "the end result." Legislatures themselves provided illumination by general definitions, special definitions, explicit recitals of policy, and even directions of attitudes appropriate for judicial construction. Legislative reports were increasingly drawn upon, statements by those in charge of legislation, reports of investigating committees, recommendations of agencies entrusted with the enforcement of laws, etc. When Mr. Justice Holmes came to the Court, the U. S. Re-

---

34. 6 EDW. VI, c. 25 (1552).
35. LORD MACAULAY'S LEGISLATIVE MINUTES 145 *et seq.* (Dharker ed. 1946).
36. Laski, Note to the REPORT OF THE COMMITTEE ON MINISTER'S POWERS, CMD 4060, Annex V, 135 (1932).
37. United States v. Fisher, 2 Cranch 358, 386 (U. S. 1805).

ports were practically barren of references to legislative materials. These swarm in current volumes. And let me say in passing that the importance that such materials play in Supreme Court litigation carry far-reaching implications for bench and bar.

The change I have summarized was gradual. Undue limitations were applied even after courts broke out of the mere language of a law. We find Mr. Justice Holmes saying, "It is a delicate business to base speculations about the purposes or construction of a statute upon the vicissitudes of its passage."[38] And as late as 1925 he referred to earlier bills relating to a statute under review, with the reservation "If it be legitimate to look at them."[39]

Such hesitations and restraints are in limbo. Courts examine the forms rejected in favor of the words chosen. They look at later statutes "considered to throw a cross light" upon an earlier enactment.[40] The consistent construction by an administrative agency charged with effectuating the policy of an enactment carries very considerable weight. While assertion of authority does not demonstrate its existence, long-continued, uncontested assertion is at least evidence that the legislature conveyed the authority. Similarly, while authority conferred does not atrophy by disuse, failure over an extended period to exercise it is some proof that it was not given. And since "a page of history is worth a volume of logic,"[41] courts have looked into the background of statutes, the mischief to be checked and the good that was designed, looking sometimes far afield and taking notice also as judges of what is generally known by men.

Unhappily, there is no table of logarithms for statutory construction. No item of evidence has a fixed or even average weight. One or another may be decisive in one set of circumstances, while of little value elsewhere. A painstaking, detailed report by a Senate Committee bearing directly on the immediate question may settle the matter. A loose statement even by a chairman of a committee, made impromptu in the heat of debate, less informing in cold type than when heard on the floor, will hardly be accorded the weight of an encyclical.

Spurious use of legislative history must not swallow the legislation so as to give point to the quip that only when legislative history is doubtful do you go to the statute. While courts are no longer confined to the language, they are still confined by it. Violence must not be done to the words chosen by the legislature. Unless indeed no doubt can be left that the legislature has in

---

38. Pine Hill Coal Co. v. United States, 259 U. S. 191, 196 (1922).
39. Davis v. Pringle, 268 U. S. 315, 318 (1925).
40. United States v. Aluminum Co. of Amer., 148 F.2d 416, 429 (C. C. A. 2d 1945).
41. New York Trust Co. v. Eisner, 256 U. S. 345, 349 (1921).

fact used a private code, so that what appears to be violence to language is merely respect to special usage. In the end, language and external aids, each accorded the authority deserved in the circumstances, must be weighed in the balance of judicial judgment. Only if its premises are emptied of their human variables, can the process of statutory construction have the precision of a syllogism. We cannot avoid what Mr. Justice Cardozo deemed inherent in the problem of construction, making "a choice between uncertainties. We must be content to choose the lesser."[42] But to the careful and disinterested eye, the scales will hardly escape appearing to tip slightly on the side of a more probable meaning.

CANONS OF CONSTRUCTION

Nor can canons of construction save us from the anguish of judgment. Such canons give an air of abstract intellectual compulsion to what is in fact a delicate judgment, concluding a complicated process of balancing subtle and elusive elements. All our three Justices have at one time or another leaned on the crutch of a canon. But they have done so only rarely, and with a recognition that these rules of construction are not in any true sense rules of law. So far as valid, they are what Mr. Justice Holmes called them, axioms of experience.[43] In many instances, these canons originated as observations in specific cases from which they were abstracted, taken out of the context of actuality, and, as it were, codified in treatises. We owe the first known systematic discussion of statutory interpretation in England to the scholarship of Professor Samuel E. Thorne, Yale's Law Librarian. According to Professor Thorne, it was written probably prior to 1567. The latest American treatise on the subject was published in 1943. It is not unfair to say that in the four intervening centuries not much new wisdom has been garnered. But there has been an enormous quantitative difference in expounding the wisdom. "A Discourse upon the Exposicion & Understandinge of Statutes" is a charming essay of not more than thirty pages. Not even the freest use of words would describe as charming the latest edition of Sutherland's Statutory Construction, with its three volumes of more than 1500 pages.

Insofar as canons of construction are generalizations of experience, they all have worth. In the abstract, they rarely arouse controversy. Difficulties emerge when canons compete in soliciting judgment, because they conflict rather than converge. For the demands of judgment underlying the art of interpretation, there is no vade-mecum.

But even generalized restatements from time to time may not be wholly

---

42. Burnet v. Guggenheim, 288 U. S. 280, 288 (1933).
43. Boston Sand & Gravel Co. v. United States, 278 U. S. 41, 48 (1928).

wasteful. Out of them may come a sharper rephrasing of the conscious factors of interpretation; new instances may make them more vivid but also disclose more clearly their limitations. Thereby we may avoid rigidities which, while they afford more precise formulas, do so at the price of cramping the life of law. To strip the task of judicial reading of statutes of rules that partake of the mysteries of a craft serves to reveal the true elements of our problem. It defines more accurately the nature of the intellectual responsibility of a judge and thereby subjects him to more relevant criteria of criticism. Rigorous analysis also sharpens the respective duties of legislature and courts in relation to the making of laws and to their enforcement.

Fair Construction and Fit Legislation

The quality of legislative organization and procedure is inevitably reflected in the quality of legislative draftsmanship. Representative Monroney told the House last July that "ninety-five percent of all the legislation that becomes law passes the Congress in the shape that it came from our committees. Therefore if our committee work is sloppy, if it is bad, if it is inadequate, our legislation in ninety-five percent of the cases will be bad and inadequate as well."[44] And Representative Lane added that ". . . in the second session of the 78th Congress 953 bills and resolutions were passed, of which only 86 were subject to any real discussion."[45] But what courts do with legislation may in turn deeply affect what Congress will do in the future. Emerson says somewhere that mankind is as lazy as it dares to be. Loose judicial reading makes for loose legislative writing. It encourages the practise illustrated in a recent cartoon in which a senator tells his colleagues "I admit this new bill is too complicated to understand. We'll just have to pass it to find out what it means." A modern Pascal might be tempted at times to say of legislation what Pascal said of students of theology when he charged them with "a looseness of thought and language that would pass nowhere else in making what are professedly very fine distinctions." And it is conceivable that he might go on and speak, as did Pascal, of the "insincerity with which terms are carefully chosen to cover opposite meanings."[46]

But there are more fundamental objections to loose judicial reading. In a democracy the legislative impulse and its expression should come from those popularly chosen to legislate, and equipped to devise policy, as courts are not. The pressure on legislatures to discharge their responsibility with care, understanding and imagination should be stiffened, not relaxed. Above all,

44. 92 Cong. Rec. 10040 (1946).
45. 92 Cong. Rec. 10054 (1946).
46. Pater, *Essay on Pascal* in Miscellaneous Studies 48, 51 (1895).

they must not be encouraged in irresponsible or undisciplined use of language. In the keeping of legislatures perhaps more than any other group is the well-being of their fellow-men. Their responsibility is discharged ultimately by words. They are under a special duty therefore to observe that "Exactness in the use of words is the basis of all serious thinking. You will get nowhere without it. Words are clumsy tools, and it is very easy to cut one's fingers with them, and they need the closest attention in handling; but they are the only tools we have, and imagination itself cannot work without them. You must master the use of them, or you will wander forever guessing at the mercy of mere impulse and unrecognized assumptions and arbitrary associations, carried away with every wind of doctrine."[47]

Perfection of draftsmanship is as unattainable as demonstrable correcness of judicial reading of legislation. Fit legislation and fair adjudication are attainable. The ultimate reliance of society for the proper fulfilment of both these august functions is to entrust them only to those who are equal to their demands.

---

47. Allen, *Essay on Jeremy Bentham* in THE SOCIAL AND POLITICAL IDEAS OF THE REVOLUTIONARY ERA 181, 199 (Hearnshaw ed. 1931).

DETERMINING THE RATIO DECIDENDI OF A CASE

ARTHUR L. GOODHART*

IN discussing the nature of a precedent in English law Sir John Salmond says:

"A precedent, therefore, is a judicial decision which contains in itself a principle. The underlying principle which thus forms its authoritative element is often termed the *ratio decidendi*. The concrete decision is binding between the parties to it, but it is the abstract *ratio decidendi* which alone has the force of law as regards the world at large." [1]

The rule is stated as follows by Professor John Chipman Gray:

"It must be observed that at the Common Law not every opinion expressed by a judge forms a Judicial Precedent. In order that an opinion may have the weight of a precedent, two things must concur: it must be, in the first place, an opinion given by a judge, and, in the second place, it must be an opinion the formation of which is necessary for the decision of a particular case; in other words, it must not be *obiter dictum*." [2]

---

* Fellow and Lecturer in Law, Corpus Christi College, Cambridge, England; editor of the LAW QUARTERLY REVIEW.
[1] SALMOND, JURISPRUDENCE (7th ed. 1924) 201.
[2] GRAY, THE NATURE AND SOURCES OF THE LAW (2d ed. 1921) 261. *Cf.* 2 AUSTIN, JURISPRUDENCE (5th ed. 1885) 627: "It follows from what has preceded, that law made judicially must be found in the general *grounds* (or must be found in the general *reasons*) of judicial decisions or resolutions of specific or particular cases: that is to say, in such *grounds*, or such *reasons*, as detached or abstracted from the specific peculiarities of the decided or resolved cases. Since no two cases are precisely alike, the decision of a specific case may partly turn upon reasons which are suggested to the judge by its specific peculiarities or differences. And that part of the decision which turns on those differences (or that part of the decision which consists of those special reasons), cannot serve as a *precedent* for subsequent decisions, and cannot serve as a rule or guide of conduct.

The general reasons or principles of a judicial decision (as thus abstracted from any peculiarities of the case) are commonly styled, by writers on jurisprudence, the *ratio decidendi*."

Both the learned authors, on reaching this point of safety, stop. Having explained to the student that it is necessary to find the *ratio decidendi* of the case, they make no further attempt to state any rules by which it can be determined. It is true that Salmond says that we must distinguish between the concrete decision and the abstract *ratio decidendi,* and Gray states that the opinion must be a necessary one, but these are only vague generalizations. Whether it is possible to progress along this comparatively untrodden way in a search for more concrete rules of interpretation will be discussed in this paper.[3]

The initial difficulty with which we are faced is the phrase *"ratio decidendi"* itself. With the possible exception of the legal term "malice," it is the most misleading expression in English law, for the reason which the judge gives for his decision is never the binding part of the precedent. The logic of the argument, the analysis of prior cases, the statement of the historical background may all be demonstrably incorrect in a judgment, but the case remain a precedent nevertheless. It would not be difficult to cite a large number of leading cases, both ancient and modern, in which one or more of the reasons given for the decision can be proved to be wrong; but in spite of this these cases contain valid and definite principles which are as binding as if the reasoning on which they are based were correct.

In *Priestley v. Fowler* [4] the famous or infamous doctrine of common employment was first laid down. Of this case it has been well said, "Lord Abinger planted it, Baron Alderson watered it, and the Devil gave it increase." [5] Yet the case is still law in England (although limited in effect by the Employers Liability Act of 1880) in spite of the fact that the two reasons on which Lord Abinger based his judgment are palpably incorrect. The first reason is that any other rule would be "absurd." This argument is always a dangerous one upon which to base a judgment and in this instance, it is, unfortunately, the rule in *Priestly v. Fowler* which has proved to be not only

---

ALLEN, LAW IN THE MAKING (2d ed. 1930) 155: "Any judgment of any Court is authoritative only as to that part of it, called the *ratio decidendi,* which is considered to have been necessary to the decision of the actual issue between the litigants. It is for the Court, of whatever degree, which is called upon to consider the precedent, to determine what the true *ratio decidendi* was."

[3] WAMBAUGH, STUDY OF CASES (2d ed. 1894) is perhaps the leading authority on this subject. On page 29 the learned author gives "The Four Keys to the Discovery of the Doctrine of a Case." They are: (1) the court must decide the very case before it; (2) the court must decide the case in accordance with a general doctrine; (3) the words used by the court are not necessarily the doctrine of the case; (4) the doctrine of the case must be a doctrine that is in the mind of the court.

[4] 3 M. & W. 1 (1837).

[5] Cited in KENNY, CASES ON THE LAW OF TORT (5th ed. 1928) 90.

absurd but also unjust. The second reason given by Lord Abinger is that by his contract of service a servant impliedly consents to run the risk of working with negligent fellow-servants. In fact, of course, a servant does not consent to run the risk; the implication was invented by the judge himself.

In *Hochster v. Delatour* [6] the defendant engaged the plaintiff on April 12 to enter his service on June 1, but on May 11 he wrote to him that his services would not be needed, thus renouncing the agreement. On May 22 the plaintiff brought an action, and the court held that he was not premature in doing so. Lord Campbell, C.J., said: "It is surely much more rational . . . that, after the renunciation of the agreement by the defendant, the plaintiff should be at liberty to consider himself absolved from any future performance of it, retaining his right to sue." [7] But, as Professor Corbin has pointed out, even though this statement is entirely correct, "it does not follow therefrom that the plaintiff should be allowed to sue *before the date fixed for performance* by the defendant".[8] It is clear that, after repudiation, the other party need not perform his part nor remain ready and willing to perform it, but why should he be given the immediate right to sue for damages which will only arise when the threatened breach actually occurs? Lord Campbell's *non sequitur* has not, however, prevented *Hochster v. Delatour* from becoming a leading case in the law of contract, for although the reasoning of the judgment may be at fault, we have no difficulty in finding in it a general rule which will apply to similar cases.

For that matter, by what may seem a strange method to those who do not understand the theory of the Common Law, it is precisely some of those cases which have been decided on incorrect premises or reasoning which have become the most important in the law. New principles, of which their authors were unconscious or which they have misunderstood, have been established by these judgments. Paradoxical as it may sound, the law has frequently owed more to its weak judges than it has to its strong ones. A bad reason may often make good law. Street has put this clearly in his *Foundations of Legal Liability*:

"The dissenting opinion of Coleridge, J., in *Lumley v. Gye* (1853), like the dissenting opinions of Cockburn, C.J., in *Collen v. Wright* (1857), and of Grose, J., in *Pasley v. Freeman* (1789), is exceedingly instructive, for it brings into clear relief the fact that the decision of the majority embodied a radical extension of legal doctrine, not to say an actual departure from former precedents. Nothing better illustrates the process by

---

[6] 2 E. & B. 678 (1853).

[7] *Ibid.* 688.

[8] ANSON, LAW OF CONTRACT (Corbin's 2d ed. 1924) 464.

which the law grows. That situation which to one judge seems to be only a new instance falling under a principle previously recognized, will to another seem to be so entirely new as not to fall under such principle. It will not infrequently be found that the judge of greatest legal acumen, the greatest analyzer, is the very one who resists innovation and extension. This, indeed, is one of the pitfalls of much learning." [9]

Our modern law of torts has been developed to a considerable extent by a series of bad arguments, and our property law is in many instances founded on incorrect history. To state this is not, however, to question the authority of that law. It is clear therefore, that the first rule for discovering the *ratio decidendi* of a case is that it must not be sought in the reasons on which the judge has based his decision.

This view is in conflict with two often-quoted dicta which, by force of repetition, have almost become maxims of the law: "The reason of a resolution is more to be considered than the resolution itself," by Holt, C.J.,[10] and "The reason and spirit of cases make law; not the letter of particular precedents," by Lord Mansfield, C.J.[11] But, however true these dicta may have been of the law at the time they were pronounced, it is clear, as Professor Allen has shown,[12] that they are not in accord with the modern English doctrine of precedent.

Having stated its reasons for reaching a certain conclusion, the court frequently sums up the result in a general statement of the law on the point at issue. Can we find the principle of the case in this proposition of law, this comprehensive expression of the rule involved, which students underline with such enthusiasm in their casebooks? Thus in the chapter on Judgments in Halsbury's *The Laws of England,* the rule is given as follows:

"It may be laid down as a general rule that that part alone of a decision of a court of law is binding upon courts of co-ordinate jurisdiction and inferior courts which consists of the enunciation of the reason or principle upon which the question before the court has really been determined. This underlying principle which forms the only authoritative element of a precedent is often termed the *ratio decidendi*." [13]

Professor Morgan of the Harvard Law School, in his valuable book *The Study of Law,* says:

"Those portions of the opinion setting forth the rules of law applied by the court, the application of which was required

---

[9] 1 STREET, FOUNDATIONS OF LEGAL LIABILITY (1906) 343.

[10] Cage v. Acton, 12 Mod. 288, 294 (1796).

[11] Fisher v. Prince, 3 Burr. 1363, 1364 (1762).

[12] ALLEN, *op. cit. supra* note 2, at 150.

[13] 18 HALSBURY, LAWS OF ENGLAND 210.

for the determination of the issues presented, are to be considered as decision and as primary authority in later cases in
the same jurisdiction." [14]

If these statements are to be understood in their literal sense,
it is respectfully submitted that the words are misleading, for
it is not the rule of law "set forth" by the court, or the rule
"enunciated" as Halsbury puts it, which necessarily constitutes
the principle of the case. There may be no rule of law set forth
in the opinion,[15] or the rule when stated may be too wide or too
narrow. In appellate courts, the rules of law set forth by the
different judges may have no relation to each other. Nevertheless each of these cases contains a principle which can be discovered on proper analysis.

So also a case may be a precedent, involving an important
principle of law, although the court has given judgment without
delivering an opinion. At the present time, although occasionally an appellate court will affirm without opinion a case which
involves an interesting point, we rarely find a case of any importance in which an opinion has not been written. In the past,
however, especially during the Year Book period, we find a
great number of cases in which there were no opinions and in
which the principle therefore must be sought elsewhere.

Of more frequent occurrence in recent cases is the practice
of delivering an opinion, but at the same time being careful not
to state any general principle of law. In the recent case of
Oliver v. Saddler & Co.[16] the House of Lords was faced with a
doubtful and difficult question in the law of torts. It is obvious
that their lordships were anxious to guard themselves against
laying down any general principles; they therefore devoted themselves almost entirely to the facts. The reporter is epually
cautious, for in the headnote he uses the phrases, "in the special
circumstances of the case," and "on the facts." Nevertheless,
the case is an important precedent which, in the future, will
have to be cited in every book on the law of torts.

Again, a case may contain a definite principle, although the
expression of it in the opinion may not be strictly accurate. In

---

[14] MORGAN, THE STUDY OF LAW (1926) 109. In his examination, on the
same page, of the judgments in Dickinson v. Dodds, 2 Ch. D. 463 (1876),
Professor Morgan adopts an entirely different method. He says, "This
case then may be said to be a decision upon three propositions which are
nowhere specifically phrased in it, and to contain only dicta as to three
propositions which may be quoted in the exact language of Lord Justice
Mellish."

[15] In this paper it is convenient to follow the American practice of distinguishing between the opinion, in which the judge states his reasons
for the judgment he is about to give, and the judgment itself. This distinction in terms is not infrequently made in the House of Lords.

[16] [1929] A. C. 584. See note on this case (1930) 46 L. Q. REV. 2.

Rex v. Fenton [17] the prisoner caused the death of a man by wantonly throwing a large stone down a mine. In his charge to the jury Tindal, C.J., said:

> "If death ensues as the consequence of a wrongful act, an act which the party who commits it can neither justify nor excuse, it is not accidental death, but manslaughter." [18]

The principle of the case was correct, although the statement of it was too wide, as was held in the later case of *Regina v. Franklin.*[19] In that case the prisoner threw a box belonging to a refreshment stall keeper into the sea, thereby killing a swimmer. The point at issue was whether, apart from the question of negligence, the prisoner was guilty of manslaughter, his act having been a wrongful one. Field, J., said:

> "We do not think the case cited by the counsel for the prosecution is binding upon us in the facts of this case, and, therefore, the civil wrong against the refreshment-stall keeper is immaterial to this charge of manslaughter." [20]

A striking example of an overstatement of the principle involved in a case may be found in *Riggs v. Palmer.*[21] The court held that a legatee, who had murdered his testator, could not take under the will, because no one shall be permitted "to take advantage of his own wrong, or to found any claim upon his own iniquity, or to acquire property by his own crime." [22] It would, of course, be possible to give a large number of situations in which this statement would be wrong or doubtful. Would it

---

[17] 1 Lew. C. C. 179 (1830).

[18] *Ibid.*

[19] 15 Cox C. C. 163 (1883).

[20] *Ibid.* 165. I have purposely borrowed these two examples from Professor Joseph F. Francis' article, *Three Cases on Possession—Some Further Observations* (1928) 14 St. Louis L. Rev. 11, 16, n. 24a, in which he criticizes very courteously my article *Three Cases on Possession* (1928) 3 Camb. L. J. 195. He, following Professor Oliphant, suggests that the important thing in a case is, "what is in fact *done* by the judges apart from what they have *said.*" He objects to my suggestion that in Bridges v. Hawkesworth, 21 L. J. N. S. 75 (1851), the fact that the notes were found in a shop could not be part of the *ratio decidendi* because the judge had stated that the place where the notes were found was not a material fact. Professor Francis says at page 16, "So I should say that it is not what Patteson, J., said or failed to say that determines what the *Bridges* case decides." To support his contention, the learned author advances the indisputable proposition that a judge's statement of law does not necessarily contain the true *ratio decidendi* of the case. This, however, does not in any way conflict with my view that, in determining the principle of a case, we are bound by the judge's statement of the material facts on which he has based his judgment.

[21] 115 N. Y. 506, 22 N. E. 188 (1889).

[22] *Ibid.* 511, 22 N. E. at 190.

apply, for example, if the legatee had negligently killed the testator in a motor accident? The principle of *Lickbarrow v. Mason* is universally accepted, but the statement of Ashhurst, J., "that wherever one of two innocent persons must suffer by the acts of a third, he who has enabled such third person to occasion the loss must sustain it" [23] is too wide, and has encouraged much vain litigation. As Lord Lindley remarked, "Such a doctrine is far too wide . . . . it cannot be relied upon without considerable qualification." [24]

On the other hand the rule of law may be stated in too narrow a form. In *Barwick v. English Joint Stock Bank* [25] the defendant's bank manager fraudulently induced the plaintiff to accept a valueless guarantee. In delivering the judgment of the court, Willes, J., said:

> "The general rule is, that the master is answerable for every such wrong of the servant or agent as is committed in the course of the service and for the master's benefit, though no express command or privity of the master be proved." [26]

It was generally believed that this statement of the law was correct until, forty-five years later, the House of Lords in *Lloyd v. Grace, Smith & Co.* [27] held that it was too narrow. The words "and for the master's benefit" were merely descriptive of the facts in the *Barwick* case, and not a necessary part of the principle involved. The House of Lords did not disapprove of the principle of the *Barwick* case, but held that "it is . . . a mistake to qualify it by saying that it only applies when the principal has profited by the fraud." [28]

When we consider the appellate courts it becomes even more obvious that the principle of the case cannot necessarily be found in the rule of law enunciated, for it is not infrequent to find that, although the judges may concur in the result, they differ widely in their statements of the law. This is true in particular in England, for in an important case each judge may deliver a separate opinion. In *Hambrook v. Stokes Bros.*,[29] Atkin, L.J., (now Lord Atkin) concurred with Bankes, L.J., that the plaintiff had a good cause of action, but the rule of law he set forth was exceedingly wide while that of Bankes, L. J., was correspondingly narrow. The famous trilogy of conspiracy cases—*Mogul Steamship Co. v. McGregor, Gow & Co.*,[30] *Allen v.*

---

[23] 2 T. R. 63, 70 (1787).
[24] See Farquharson Bros. & Co. v. King & Co., [1902] A. C. 325, 342.
[25] L. R. 2 Ex. 259 (1867).
[26] *Ibid.* 265.
[27] [1912] A. C. 716.
[28] *Ibid.* 736, per Lord Macnaghten.
[29] [1925] 1 K. B. 141.
[30] [1892] A. C. 25.

Flood; [31] *Quinn v. Leathem* [32]—are of peculiar difficulty because of the conflicting statements of the law in the various opinions. As Lord Sumner remarked in *Sorrell v. Smith*:

"I shall not attempt to collect or compare quotations from the opinions delivered in that [*Quinn v. Leathem*] and other cases. They are occasionally expressed in varying terms. In this matter I have not found myself qualified to offer an eirenicon or even an anthology." [33]

Nevertheless these cases cannot be ignored as precedents on the ground that the rules of law set forth cannot be reconciled.

Since, therefore, the principle of the case is not necessarily found in either the reasoning of the court or in the proposition of law set forth, we must seek some other method of determining it. Does this mean that we can ignore the opinion entirely and work out the principle for ourselves from the facts of the case and the judgment reached on those facts? This seems to be the view of a certain American school of legal thought represented by Professor Oliphant. According to him it is what the judge does and not what he says that matters. He writes:

"But there is a constant factor in the cases which is susceptible of sound and satisfying study. The predictable element in it all is what courts have done in response to the stimuli of the facts of the concrete cases before them. Not the judges' opinions, but which way they decide cases, will be the dominant subject matter of any truly scientific study of law." [34]

Undoubtedly this theory has the attractiveness of simplicity. No longer will we have to analyze the sometimes lengthy and difficult opinions of the judges; all that we are concerned with are the facts and the conclusion. The judge who writes an opinion will be wasting both his own time and ours, for it is not what he says but what he does that matters. We can ignore the vocal behaviour of the judge, which sometimes fills many pages, and concentrate upon his nonvocal behaviour which occupies but a few lines. [35]

---

[31] [1898] A. C. 1.

[32] [1901] A. C. 495.

[33] [1925] A. C. 700, 734.

[34] Oliphant, *A Return to Stare Decisis* (1927) HANDBOOK OF THE ASSOCIATION OF AMERICAN LAW SCHOOLS 76. This address is reprinted in (1928) 14 A. B. A. J. 71, 159.

[35] Oliphant, *op. cit. supra* note 34, at 82, 14 A. B. A. J. at 161: "Why has not our study of cases in the past yielded the results now sought? The attempt has been made to show that this is largely due to the fact that we have focused our attention too largely on the *vocal behavior* of judges in deciding cases. A study with more stress on their *nonvocal behavior*, i.e., what the judges actually do when stimulated by the facts of the case before them, is the approach indispensable to exploiting scientifically the wealth of material in the cases."

Unfortunately I believe that there is a fallacy in Professor Oliphant's argument which will prevent our following this convenient course. The fallacy lies in suggesting that the facts of a case are a constant factor, that the judge's conclusion is based upon the fixed premise of a given set of facts. We do not have to be philosophers to realize that facts are not constant but relative. The crucial question is "What facts are we talking about?" The same set of facts may look entirely different to two different persons. The judge founds his conclusions upon a group of facts selected by him as material from among a larger mass of facts, some of which might seem significant to a layman, but which, to a lawyer, are irrelevant. The judge, therefore, reaches a conclusion upon the facts as he sees them. It is on these facts that he bases his judgment, and not on any others. It follows that our task in analyzing a case is not to state the facts and the conclusion, but to state the material facts as seen by the judge and his conclusion based on them. It is by his choice of the material facts that the judge creates law. A congeries of facts is presented to him; he chooses those which he considers material and rejects those which are immaterial, and then bases his conclusion upon the material ones. To ignore his choice is to miss the whole point of the case. Our system of precedent becomes meaningless if we say that we will accept his conclusion but not his view of the facts. His conclusion is based on the material facts as he sees them, and we cannot add or subtract from them by proving that other facts existed in the case. It is, therefore, essential to know what the judge has said about his choice of the facts, for what he does has a meaning for us only when considered in relation to what he has said. A divorce of the conclusion from the material facts on which that conclusion is based is illogical, and must lead to arbitrary and unsound results.

The first and most essential step in the determination of the principle of a case is, therefore, to ascertain the material facts on which the judge has based his conclusion. Are there any rules which will help us in isolating these material facts? It is obvious that none can be found which will invariably give us the desired result, for if this were possible then the interpretation of cases, which is one of the most difficult of the arts, would be comparatively easy. The following tentative suggestions may, however, prove of some aid to the student faced with his first case-book.

If there is no opinion, or if the opinion does not contain a statement of the facts, then we must assume that all the facts given in the report are material except those which on their face are not. Thus the facts of person, time, place, kind, and amount are presumably immaterial unless stated to be material.

As a rule the law is the same for all persons, at all times, and at all places within the jurisdiction of the court. For the purposes of the law a contract made between *A* and *B* in Liverpool on Monday involving the sale of a book worth £10 is identical with a similar contract made between *C* and *D* in London on Friday involving the sale of a painting worth £100,000.

Where there is an opinion but the facts are not stated in it we must examine the report with great care, for the reporter may have left out an essential point. It is for this reason in particular that it is useful to compare the various reports of the same case if there is any doubt as to the principle involved in it. The well known case of *Williams v. Carwardine* has troubled generations of law students because the report usually referred to is the one in 4 Barnewall and Adolphus at page 621. The facts, as given there, merely show that the defendant offered a reward for certain information and that the plaintiff gave the information for motives unconnected with the reward. It is not stated that the plaintiff knew of the offer. But in the report of the case in 5 Carrington and Payne the following colloquy is given at page 574:

"Denman, C.J.—Was any doubt suggested as to whether the plaintiff knew of the handbill at the time of her making the disclosure?

Curwood (for the defendant). She must have known of it, as it was placarded all over Hereford, the place at which she lived."

By omitting a material fact, *viz.*, knowledge of the offer of the reward, the report in Barnewall and Adolphus makes nonsense of the case.[36] This is not infrequent in those cases in which the facts are stated by the reporter, for, either owing to a misunderstanding of the point involved or a zeal for compression, he may have left out an essential fact. At the present time, however, the absence of an opinion, or of an opinion which states the facts, is so infrequent that it is unnecessary to discuss this situation at greater length.

If there is an opinion which gives the facts, the first point to notice is that we cannot go behind the opinion to show that the facts appear to be different in the record. We are bound by the judge's statement of the facts even though it is patent that he has mistated them, for it is on the facts as he, perhaps incorrectly, has seen them that he has based his judgment. The difficulty in the much discussed revocation-of-offer case, *Dickinson v. Dodds*,[37] is due chiefly to the fact that the reporter in his in-

---

[36] In MILES AND BRIERLY, CASES ON THE LAW OF CONTRACT (1923) 6, n. 1, this point is made by the learned editors.
[37] 2 Ch. D. 463 (1876).

troductory statement says, "The plaintiff was informed by a Mr. Berry that Dodds had been offering or agreeing to sell the property to Thomas Allen," [38] while, when we turn to the judgments, we find that James, L.J., says:

"In this case, beyond all question the plaintiff knew that Dodds was no longer minded to sell the property to him as plainly and clearly as if Dodds had told him in so many words, 'I withdraw the offer.' This is evident from the plaintiff's own statement in the bill." [39]

Mellish, L.J., states the facts as follows:

"Then Dickinson is informed by Berry that the property has been sold by Dodds to Allen. Berry does not tell us from whom he heard it, but he says that he did hear it, that he knew it, and that he informed Dickinson of it." [40]

If we take the reporter's facts, the conclusion reached in *Dickinson v. Dodds* is astonishing; if we accept, as we are bound to do, the facts as given in the judgments the conclusion seems a reasonable one.

Two other cases illustrate this point in an interesting manner. In *Smith v. London and South Western Ry.*, Kelly, C.B., Channell, B., and Blackburn, J., each assumed as a fact "that no reasonable man would have foreseen that the fire would get to the plaintiff's cottage." [41] We lose the whole point of their judgments if we attempt to explain them by showing that a reasonable man should have foreseen that the fire might reach the cottage.[42] Similarly in *In Re Polemis and Furness, Withy & Co.*[43] the Court of Appeal was bound by the arbitrators' finding of fact that a reasonable man would not have anticipated that a plank falling into the hold of a steamer filled with petrol vapour might cause an explosion. This finding of fact is probably incorrect, but we cannot ignore it if we are to determine the true principle of the judgments based on it. As has already been said, if we are not bound by the facts as stated by the judge

---

[38] *Ibid.* 464.

[39] *Ibid.* 472. As we do not have the plaintiff's bill, it is obvious that it is impossible to dispute the statement of facts given by James, L.J., even though it is in conflict with that of the reporter.

[40] *Ibid.* 474.

[41] L. R. 6 C. P. 14, 20 (1870). This case is discussed at considerable length in my article *The Unforeseeable Consequences of a Negligent Act* (1930) 39 YALE L. J. 449.

[42] This is what a number of learned American writers have attempted to do. See article cited *supra* note 41. For a similar explanation of the Smith case see Green, *The Palsgraf Case* (1930) 30 Col. L. REV. 789, 792, n. 5a.

[43] [1921] 3 K. B. 560. See article cited *supra* note 41.

it would be wholly illogical to be bound by his conclusion on those facts.

Moreover, such a course would be most inconvenient, for it would then become necessary when citing an important case to go through the record so as to be certain that the facts as given by the court were correct. In view of the vast number of precedents existing on almost any disputed point of law the task of the common law lawyer is sufficiently difficult at the present time; if he must also consult the record in every case to determine the actual facts his work will be overwhelming. The emphasis which American law libraries are now placing on collecting the whole records in the leading cases may prove to be a dangerous one, for such collections tend to encourage a practice which is inconvenient in operation and disastrous in theory.

Although it is comparatively rare to find any real conflict between the facts given in the opinion and those in the record, it is of frequent occurrence to find that the facts in the opinion fail to include some of the facts in the record. Under these circumstances there are two possible explanations of the omission: (1) the fact was considered by the court but was found to be immaterial, or (2) the fact in the record was not considered by the court as it was not called to its attention by counsel or was for some other reason overlooked. Which of the two explanations is the correct one will depend upon the circumstances of the particular case. If counsel have referred to the fact in the course of their arguments this is strong evidence that the fact has not been overlooked but has been purposely omitted. For this reason the practice in the Law Reports of giving a short summary of counsel's speeches is of particular value. But if it is clear that a certain fact, however material it may have been, was not considered by the court, then the case is not a precedent in future cases in which a similar fact appears. Thus in the leading case of *Dunlop Tyre Co. v. Selfridge & Co.*[44] no mention was made by either the judges or counsel of the possible fact that a trust had been created, and Professor Corbin has argued with great force that this case cannot, therefore, be held to be a precedent in any future case in which the fact of a trusteeship is shown to exist.[45] In *Fisher v. Oldham Corporation* McCardie, J., in discussing the *ratio decidendi* of *Bradford Corporation v. Webster*[46] said:

---

[44] [1915] A. C. 847.

[45] Corbin, *Contracts for the Benefit of Third Parties* (1930) 46 L. Q. REV. 12. It may, perhaps, be queried whether the creation of a trust is a question of fact or of law; the answer is that if a set of facts is such that by the application of the appropriate rule of law X is constituted a trustee, then X's trusteeship is itself a fact.

[46] [1920] 2 K. B. 135.

"It is obvious, however, that the point which I am dealing with might there have been raised by the defendants. But, *mirabile dictu*, no such point was even mentioned to the learned Judge . . . . The learned Judge, therefore, never even considered the point that is now before me for decision." [47]

It must be noted however, that the burden of showing that a fact has been overlooked is a heavy one, for as a rule a material fact does not escape the attention of counsel and of the court. [48]

Having, as a first step, determined all the facts of the case as seen by the judge, it is then necessary to discover which of these facts he has found material for his judgment. This is far more difficult than the first step, for the judge may fail to label his facts. It is only the strong judge, one who is clear in his own mind as to the grounds for his decision, [49] who invariably says, "on facts *A* and *B* and on them alone I reach conclusion *X*." Too often the cautious judge will include in his opinion facts which are not essential to his judgment, leaving it for future generations to determine whether or not these facts constitute a part of the *ratio decidendi*. The following guides may,

---

[47] 46 T. L. R. 390 (1930).

[48] An interesting example is the recent case of Vidler v. Sasun, The Times, October 16, 1929. ⟨ This was an action for breach of promise of marriage, the alleged promise having been made by the defendant whilst a convict in prison. The objection that a convict cannot make a contract was not taken until the case reached the Court of Appeal, when that Court held that the point had been raised too late. As the attention of the trial judge was not called to the fact that there was a statute on the subject the case cannot be considered a precedent on this point.

An even more striking example is Rex v. Kynaston, [1927] W. N. 53, in which a doctor was fined for a contravention of the Dangerous Drugs Act (1925), although the Act had not as yet come into operation. See note (1927) 43 L. Q. REV. 155.

In London Street Tramways Co. v. London County Council, [1898] A. C. 375, 380, when discussing the question whether the House of Lords was bound by its own prior judgments, the Earl of Halsbury, L.C., said: "It is said that this House might have omitted to notice an Act of Parliament, or might have acted upon an Act of Parliament which was afterwards found to have been repealed. It seems to me that the answer to that ingenious suggestion is a very manifest one—namely, that that would be a mistake of fact. If the House were under the impression that there was an Act when there was not such an Act as was suggested, of course they would not be bound, when the fact was ascertained that there was not such an Act or that the Act had been repealed, to proceed upon the hypothesis that the Act existed."

[49] It was Jessel, M.R., who said, "I may be wrong, but I never have any doubts." An astounding example of an uncertain judgment is Lord Hatherley's opinion in River Wear Commissioners v. Adamson, 2 App. Cas. 743, 752 (1877). Of this Atkin, L.J., said, in The Mostyn, [1927] P. 25, 37, that he was unable to determine whether Lord Hatherley "was concurring in the appeal being allowed, or the appeal being dismissed, or whether he was concurring in the opinion given by Lord Cairns."

however, be followed in distinguishing between material and immaterial facts.

(1) As was stated above in discussing the principle of a case in which there is no opinion, the facts of person, time, place, kind, and amount are presumably immaterial. This is true to an even greater extent when there is an opinion, for if these facts are held to be material particular emphasis will naturally be placed upon them.

(2) All facts which the court specifically states are immaterial must be considered so. In *People v. Vandewater*[50] the defendant, who was charged with maintaining a public nuisance, kept an illicit drinking place. There was proof that the house was actually disorderly as the evidence showed that persons became intoxicated on the premises and left them in that condition. The majority of the New York Court of Appeals, speaking by Lehman, J., held that the fact that acts of annoyance and disturbance had occurred was immaterial. The learned judge said:

> "It is the disorderly character of the illicit drinking place which constitutes the offense to the public decency. That offense arises from the nature of the acts habitually done upon the premises and the injury to the morals and health of the community which must naturally flow therefrom, apart from the annoyance or disturbance of those persons who might be in the neighborhood."[51]

This case strikingly illustrates the distinction between the view that a case is authority for a proposition based on all its facts, and the view that it is authority for a proposition based on those facts only which were seen by the court as material. If we adopt the first view, then the majority judgment is only a dictum, not binding in any future case in which the facts do not show actual disorder. Under the second view the court has specifically stated that the fact of disorder is immaterial. The case is, therefore, a binding precedent in all future cases in which either orderly or disorderly illicit drinking places are kept. The case can be analyzed as follows:

Facts of the Case

Fact   I. *D* maintained an illicit drinking place.
Fact II. This illicit place was noisy and disorderly.
Conclusion. *D* is guilty of maintaining a nuisance.

Material Facts as seen by the Court

Fact I. *D* maintained an illicit drinking place.
Conclusion. *D* is guilty of maintaining a nuisance.

---

[50] 250 N. Y. 83, 164 N. E. 864 (1928).
[51] *Ibid.* 96, 164 N. E. at 868.

By specifically holding that Fact II was immaterial, the court succeeded in creating a broad principle instead of a narrow one.

(3) All facts which the court impliedly treats as immaterial must be considered immaterial. The difficulty in these cases is to determine whether a court has or has not considered the fact immaterial. Evidence of this implication is found when the court, after having stated the facts generally, then proceeds to choose a smaller number of facts on which it bases its conclusion. The omitted facts are presumably held to be immaterial. In *Rylands v. Fletcher* [52] the defendant employed an independent contractor to make a reservoir on his land. Owing to the contractor's negligence in not filling up some disused mining shafts, the water escaped and flooded the plaintiff's mine. The defendant was held liable. Is the principle of the case that a man who builds a reservoir on his land is liable for the negligence of an independent contractor? Why then is the case invariably cited as laying down the broader doctrine of "absolute liability"? The answer is found in the opinions. After stating the facts as above, the judges thereafter ignored the fact of the contractor's negligence, and based their conclusions on the fact that an artificial reservoir had been constructed. The negligence of the contractor was, therefore, impliedly held to be an immaterial fact. The case can be analyzed as follows:

Facts of the Case
Fact   I. *D* had a reservoir built on his land.
Fact   II. The contractor who built it was negligent.
Fact III. Water escaped and injured *P*.
Conclusion. *D* is liable to *P*

Material Facts as Seen by the Court
Facts   I. *D* had a reservoir built on his land.
Fact III. Water escaped and injured *P*.
Conclusion. *D* is liable to *P*.

By the omission of Fact II, the doctrine of "absolute liability" was established.

It is obvious from the above cases that it is essential to determine what facts have been held to be immaterial, for the principle of a case depends as much on exclusion as it does on inclusion. It is under these circumstances that the reasons given by the judge in his opinion, or his statement of the rule of law which he is following, are of peculiar importance, for they may furnish us with a guide for determining which facts he considered material and which immaterial. His reason may be in-

---

[52] L. R. 3 H. L. 330 (1868).

correct and his statement of the law too wide, but they will indicate to us on what facts he reached his conclusion.

Occasionally, however, we may be misled into believing that a judge has impliedly treated a fact as immaterial when he has not intended to do so. Perhaps the most striking example of this can be found in *Sheffield v. London Joint Stock Bank.*[53] The plaintiff's agent deposited certain negotiable bonds with a money-lender to secure an advance. The money-lender pledged them with the defendant bank for a larger amount, and when he later became bankrupt the bank claimed to hold the bonds as security for all of his debt. In his judgment Lord Halsbury, L.C., said that if the bank had reason to think that the securities "might belong to somebody else, I think they were bound to inquire."[54] Lord Bramwell said, "They [the bank] must have known—I might say, certainly have believed—that the property was not Mozley's [the money-lender] . . . It seems to me, then, that they cannot hold this property except for what the appellant authorized it to be pledged."[55] Lord Macnaghten's opinion reads: "The banks knew that the person who dealt with them as owner was not acting by right of ownership. They took for granted that he had authority, but for some reason or other they did not choose to inquire what that authority was."[56] From these statements it would seem that the material facts of the case were:

Fact   I. *S* pledged certain negotiable securities with *M*.

Fact   II. *M* without authority pledged the securities for a larger sum with the bank.

Fact III. The bank knew or had reason to think that *M* was not the owner of the securities.

Fact IV. The bank failed to inquire what *M*'s authority was.

Conclusion: *S* was entitled to the return of his securities on tendering the amount of the advance made to him by *M*.[57]

Three years later in *Simmons v. London Joint Stock Bank*[58] the facts were as follows. The plaintiff's broker fraudulently

---

[53] 13 App. Cas. 333 (1888).

[54] *Ibid.* 341.

[55] *Ibid.* 346.

[56] *Ibid.* 348.

[57] In his preliminary statement of the facts the reporter said: "In this House, as will be seen from the judgments, their Lordships, being of opinion that the banks either actually knew, or had reason to believe, that the securities did or might belong not to Mozley but to his customers, held that the banks were bound to inquire into the extent of Mozley's authority to pledge the securities." *Ibid.* 334.

[58] [1891] 1 Ch. 270.

pledged with the defendant bank negotiable securities belonging to the plaintiff. The bank knew or had reason to think that the broker was not the owner of the bonds. It made no inquiries as to what his authority was. It is hardly surprising that the trial judge and the Court of Appeal held that they were bound to find for the plaintiff on the authority of the *Sheffield* case, the material facts in both cases being identical. But when the *Simmons* case reached the House of Lords the decision of the Court of Appeal was reversed,[59] their lordships pointing out, with some indignation on the part of Lord Halsbury, L.C., that, "the inferences derived from the business carried on by the money-lender in *Lord Sheffield's Case*, were peculiar to that case. . . ." [60] The fact that Mozley was a moneylender was the all-important one, for his occupation should have given the bank notice that he had only a limited authority to raise money on his client's securities. Unfortunately this material fact was so little stressed in the judgments that its existence completely escaped the notice of a strong Court of Appeal when it was considering the question of a broker's authority in the *Simmons* case. The *Sheffield* case is a warning to us to be careful before assuming that a fact is immaterial merely because it has not been emphasized.[61]

(4) All facts which are specifically stated to be material must be considered material. Such specific statements are usually found in cases in which the judges are afraid of laying

---

[59] London Joint Stock Bank v. Simmons, [1892] A. C. 201.

[60] *Ibid.* 211, Lord Halsbury, L.C., said: "The first observation that I would make is, that if, as I believe, it be accurate that the question is one which is to be determined upon the facts of the case, no one case can be an authority for another." *Ibid.* 208. With all respect, it is difficult to see how any question can be determined except "upon the facts of the case." The true distinction is between facts which can be generalized and those which cannot, or, as Sir John Salmond says, those which can be answered on principle or *in abstracto* and those which are concrete. SALMOND, *op. cit. supra* note 1, at 205. Thus the fact that *M*, a moneylender, deposited certain securities with the bank is necessarily unique, but the fact that banks ought to know that moneylenders have only a limited authority can be generalized. In the headnote to the Simmons case there is the statement that, "The decision of this House in Earl of Sheffield v. London Joint Stock Bank turned entirely upon the special facts of that case." The decision turned on the fact that *M* was a moneylender, the principle of the case being applicable to all similar cases in which moneylenders might be concerned.

[61] In the recent case of Hole v. Garnsey, 46 T. L. R. 312 (1930), Lord Buckmaster in the House of Lords, the Master of the Rolls, two Lords Justices in the Court of Appeal, and the judge who tried the case had no doubt that Biddulph v. Agricultural Wholesale Society, Ltd., [1927] A. C. 76, had been decided on certain facts and was therefore binding in the instant case, while the other four Law Lords were equally convinced that it had been decided on other facts and was not in point.

down too broad a principle. Thus in *Heaven v. Pender* [62] the
plaintiff, a workman employed to paint a ship, was injured
because of a defective staging supplied by the defendant dock
owner to the shipowner. Brett, M.R., held that the defendant
was liable on the ground that:

". . . whenever one person is by circumstances placed in such
a position with regard to another that every one of ordinary
sense who did think would at once recognise that if he did not
use ordinary care and skill in his own conduct with regard to
those circumstances he would cause danger of injury to the
person or property of the other, a duty arises to use ordinary
care and skill to avoid such danger." [63]

Cotton and Bowen, L.JJ., agreed with the Master of the Rolls
that the defendant was liable, but the material facts on which
they based their judgment were: (1) that the plaintiff was on
the staging for business in which the dock owner was interested,
and (2) he "must be considered as invited by the dock owner
to use the dock and all appliances provided by the dock owner
as incident to the use of the dock." [64] The principle of the
case cannot, therefore, be extended beyond the limitation of
these material facts.

(5) If the opinion does not distinguish between material and
immaterial facts then all the facts set forth in the opinion
must be considered material with the exception of those that
on their face are immaterial. There is a presumption against
wide principles of law, and the smaller the number of material
facts in a case the wider will the principle be. Thus if a case
like *Hambrook v. Stokes*,[65] in which a mother died owing to
shock at seeing a motor accident which threatened her child,
is decided on the fact that a bystander may recover for injury
due to shock, we have a broad principle of law.[66] If the additional fact that the bystander was a mother is held to be material we then get a narrow principle of law.[67] Therefore, unless
a fact is expressly or impliedly held to be immaterial, it must
be considered material.

(6) Thus far we have been discussing the method of determining the principle of a case in which there is only a single
opinion, or in which all the opinions are in agreement. How do
we determine the principle of a case in which there are several
opinions which agree as to the result but differ in the material
facts on which they are based? In such an event the principle

[62] 11 Q. B. D. 503 (1883).
[63] *Ibid.* 509.
[64] *Ibid.* 515.
[65] *Supra* note 29.
[66] See the judgment of Atkin, L.J., *ibid.* 152.
[67] See the judgment of Bankes, L.J., *ibid.* 146.

of the case is limited to the sum of all the facts held to be material by the various judges. A case involves facts A, B and C, and the defendant is held liable. The first judge finds that fact A is the only material fact; the second that B is material, the third that C is material. The principle of the case is, therefore, that on the material facts A, B and C the defendant is liable. If, however, two of the three judges had been in agreement that fact A was the only material one, and that the others were immaterial, then the case would be a precedent on this point, even though the third judge had held that facts B and C were the material ones. The method of determining the principle of a case in which there are several opinions is thus the same as that used when there is only one. Care must be taken by the student, however, to see that the material facts of each opinion are stated and analyzed accurately, for sometimes judges think that they are in agreement on the facts when they concur only in the result.[68]

Having established the material and the immaterial facts of the case as seen by the court, we can then proceed to state the principle of the case. It is to be found in the conclusion reached by the judge on the basis of the material facts and on the exclusion of the immaterial ones. In a certain case the court finds that facts A, B and C exist. It then excludes fact A as immaterial, and on facts B and C it reaches conclusion X. What is the *ratio decidendi* of this case? There are two principles: (1) In any future case in which the facts are A, B and C, the court must reach conclusion X, and (2) in any future case in which the facts are B and C the court must reach conclusion X. In the second case the absence of fact A does not affect the result, for fact A has been held to be immaterial. The court, therefore, creates a principle when it determines which are the material and which are the immaterial facts on which it bases its decision.

It follows that a conclusion based on a fact the existence of which has not been determined by the court, cannot establish a principle. We then have what is called a dictum. If, therefore, a judge in the course of his opinion suggests a hypothetical fact, and then states what conclusion he would reach if that fact existed, he is not creating a principle. The difficulty which is sometimes found in determining whether a statement is a dictum or not is due to uncertainty as to whether the judge is treating a fact as hypothetical or real. When a judge says, "In this case, as the facts are so and so, I reach conclusion X," this is not a dictum, even though the judge has been incorrect

---

[68] *Cf.* the various judgments in Great Western Ry. v. Owners of S. S. Mostyn, [1928] A. C. 57. See note (1928) 44 L. Q. Rev. 138 on this point.

in his statement of the facts. But if the judge says, "If the facts in this case were so and so then I would reach conclusion *X*," this is a dictum, even though the facts are as given. The second point frequently arises when a case involves two different sets of facts. Having determined the first set of facts and reached a conclusion on them, the judge may not desire to take up the time necessarily involved in determining the second set. Any views he may express as to the undetermined second set are accordingly dicta. If, however, the judge does determine both sets, as he is at liberty to do, and reaches a conclusion on both, then the case creates two principles and neither is a dictum. Thus the famous case of *National Sailors' and Firemen's Union v. Reed*,[69] in which Astbury, J., declared the General Strike of 1926 to be illegal, involved two sets of facts, and the learned judge reached a conclusion on each.[70] It is submitted that it is incorrect to say that either one of the conclusions involved a dictum because the one preceded the other or because the one was based on broad grounds and the other on narrow ones.[71] On the other hand, if in a case the judge holds that a certain fact prevents a cause of action from arising, then his further finding that there would have been a cause of action except for this fact is an obiter dictum. By excluding the preventive fact the situation becomes hypothetical, and the conclusion based on such hypothetical facts can only be a dictum.[72]

Having established the principle of a case, and excluded all dicta, the final step is to determine whether or not it is a binding precedent for some succeeding case in which the facts are prima facie similar. This involves a double analysis. We must first state the material facts in the precedent case and then attempt to find those which are material in the second one. If these are identical, then the first case is a binding precedent for the second, and the court must reach the same conclusion as it did in the first one. If the first case lacks any material fact or contains any additional ones not found in the second, then it is not a direct precedent.[73] Thus, in *Nichols v. Mars-*

---

[69] [1926] 1 Ch. 536.

[70] The first set of facts included the fact of the General Strike. The second set excluded the General Strike, but included the fact that the internal rules of the union were violated.

[71] For conflicting views on this point see note by Sir Frederick Pollock (1926) 42 L. Q. REV. 289, and note (1926) 42 L. Q. REV. 296.

[72] In Lynn v. Bamber, [1930] 2 K. B. 72, McCardie, J., held that unconcealed fraud was a good reply to a plea of the Statutes of Limitation. As, however, he found that there was no fraud in the case before him, it is submitted that his statement as to the Statutes of Limitation was a dictum. On this point see note (1930) 46 L. Q. REV. 261.

[73] It may, however, carry great weight as an analogy. Thus, if it has

land [74] the material facts were similar to those in *Rylands v. Fletcher* [75] except for the additional fact that the water escaped owing to a violent storm. If the court had found that this additional fact was not a material one, then the rule in *Rylands v. Fletcher* would have applied. But as it found that it was a material one, it was able to reach a different conclusion.

Before summarizing the rules suggested above, two possible criticisms must be considered. It may be said that a doctrine which finds the principle of a case in its material facts leaves us with hardly any general legal principles, for facts are infinitely various. It is true that facts are infinitely various, but the material facts which are usually found in a particular legal relationship are strictly limited. Thus the fact that there must be consideration in a simple contract is a single material fact although the kinds of consideration are unlimited. Again, if *A* builds a reservoir on Blackacre and *B* builds one on Whiteacre, the owners, builders, reservoirs and fields are different. But the material fact that a person has built a reservoir on his land is in each case the same. Of course a court can always avoid a precedent by finding that an additional fact is material, but if it does so without reason the result leads to confusion in the law. Such an argument assumes, moreover, that courts are disingenuous and arbitrary. Whatever may have been true in the past, it is clear that at the present day English courts do not attempt to circumvent the law in this way.

The second criticism may be stated as follows: If we are bound by the facts as seen by the judge, may not this enable him deliberately or by inadvertence to decide a case which was not before him by basing his decision upon facts stated by him as real and material but actually non-existent? Can his conclusion in such a case be anything more than a dictum? Can a judge, by making a mistake give himself authority to decide what is in effect a hypothetical case? The answer to this interesting question is that the whole doctrine of precedent is based on the theory that as a general rule judges do not make mistakes either of fact or of law. In an exceptional case a

---

been held in a case that a legatee who has murdered his testator cannot take under the will, this will be an analogy of some weight in a future case in which the legatee has committed manslaughter. It is important to note that when a case is used merely as an analogy, and not as a direct binding precedent, the reasoning by which the court reached its judgment carries greater weight than the conclusion itself. The second court, being free to reach its own conclusion, will only adopt the reasoning of the first court if it considers it to be correct and desirable. In such analogous precedents the *ratio decidendi* of the case can with some truth be described as the reason of the case.

[74] L. R. 10 Ex. 255 (1875).

[75] *Supra* note 52.

judge may in error base his conclusion on a non-existent fact, but it is better to suffer this mistake, which may prove of benefit to the law as a whole, however painful its results may have been to the individual litigant, than to throw doubt on every precedent on which our law is based.

Conclusion

The rules for finding the principle of a case can, therefore, be summarized as follows:

(1) The principle of a case is not found in the reasons given in the opinion.

(2) The principle is not found in the rule of law set forth in the opinion.

(3) The principle is not necessarily found by a consideration of all the ascertainable facts of the case and the judge's decision.

(4) The principle of the case is found by taking account (a) of the facts treated by the judge as material, and (b) his decision as based on them.

(5) In finding the principle it is also necessary to establish what facts were held to be immaterial by the judge, for the principle may depend as much on exclusion as it does on inclusion.

The rules for finding what facts are material and what facts are immaterial as seen by the judge are as follows.

(1) All facts of person, time, place, kind and amount are immaterial unless stated to be material.

(2) If there is no opinion, or the opinion gives no facts, then all other facts in the record must be treated as material.

(3) If there is an opinion, then the facts as stated in the opinion are conclusive and cannot be contradicted from the record.

(4) If the opinion omits a fact which appears in the record this may be due either to (a) oversight, or (b) an implied finding that the fact is immaterial. The second will be assumed to be the case in the absence of other evidence.

(5) All facts which the judge specifically states are immaterial must be considered immaterial.

(6) All facts which the judge impliedly treats as immaterial must be considered immaterial.

(7) All facts which the judge specifically states to be material must be considered material.

(8) If the opinion does not distinguish between material and immaterial facts then all the facts set forth must be considered material.

(9) If in a case there are several opinions which agree as to the result but differ as to the material facts, then the principle of the case is limited so as to fit the sum of all the facts held material by the various judges.

(10) A conclusion based on a hypothetical fact is a dictum. By hypothetical fact is meant any fact the existence of which has not been determined or accepted by the judge.

Meeting of the Aristotelian Society at 21, *Bedford Square, London, W.C.*1, *on May* 23rd, 1949, *at* 7.30 *p.m.*

THE ASCRIPTION OF RESPONSIBILITY
AND RIGHTS.

By H. L. A. HART.

THERE are in our ordinary language sentences whose primary function is not to describe things, events, or persons or anything else, nor to express or kindle feelings or emotions, but to do such things as claim rights (" This is mine "), recognise rights when claimed by others (" Very well this is yours "), ascribe rights whether claimed or not (" This is his "), transfer rights (" This is now yours "), and also to admit or ascribe or make accusations of responsibility (" I did it," " He did it," " You did it "). My main purpose in this article is to suggest that the philosophical analysis of the concept of a human action has been inadequate and confusing, at least in part because sentences of the form " He did it " have been traditionally regarded as primarily descriptive whereas their principal function is what I venture to call *ascriptive*, being quite literally to ascribe responsibility for actions much as the principal function of sentences of the form " This is his " is to ascribe rights in property. Now ascriptive sentences and the other kinds of sentence quoted above, though they may form only a small part of our ordinary language, resemble in some important respects the formal statements of claim, the indictments, the admissions, the judgments, and the verdicts which constitute so large and so important a part of the language of lawyers ; and the logical peculiarities which distinguish these kinds of sentences from descriptive sentences or rather from the theoretical model of descriptive

U

45

sentences with which philosophers often work can best be grasped by considering certain characteristics of legal concepts, as these appear in the practice and procedure of the law rather than in the theoretical discussions of legal concepts by jurists who are apt to be influenced by philosophical theories.   Accordingly, in the first part of this paper I attempt to bring out some of these characteristics of legal concepts ; in the second, I attempt to show how sentences ascribing rights function in our ordinary language and also why their distinctive function is overlooked ; and in the third part I attempt to make good my claim that sentences of the form " He did it " are fundamentally ascriptive and that some at any rate of the philosophical puzzles concerning " action " have resulted from inattention to this fact.

I.

As everyone knows, the decisive stage in the proceedings of an English law court is normally a *judgment* given by the court to the effect that certain facts (Smith put arsenic in his wife's coffee and as a result she died) are true and that certain legal consequences (Smith is guilty of murder) are attached to those facts.   Such a judgment is therefore a compound or blend of facts and law ; and, of course, the claims and the indictments upon which law courts adjudicate are also blends of facts and law, though claims, indictments, and judgments are different from each other. Now there are several characteristics of the legal element in these compounds or blends which conspire to make the way in which facts support or fail to support legal conclusions or refute or fail to refute them unlike certain standard models of how one kind of statement supports or refutes another upon which philosophers are apt to concentrate attention.   This is not apparent at once : for when the judge decides that on the facts which he has found there is a contract for sale between A and B, or that B, a publican, is guilty of the offence[1] of supplying liquor to a constable

---

[1] S. 16 of the Licensing Act, 1872.

on duty, or that B is liable for trespass because of what his horse has done on his neighbour's land, *it looks* from the terminology as if the law must consist of a set, if not a system, of legal concepts such as " contract," " the offence of supplying liquor to a constable on duty," " trespass," invented and defined by the legislature or some other " source," and as if the function of the judge was simply to say " Yes " or " No " to the question : " Do the facts come within the scope of the formula defining the necessary and sufficient conditions of ' contract,' ' trespass,' or ' the offence of supplying liquor to a constable on duty ' ?"

But this is for many reasons a disastrous over-simplification and indeed distortion, because there are characteristics of legal concepts which make it often absurd to use in connection with them the language of necessary and sufficient conditions. One important characteristic which I do not discuss in detail is no doubt vaguely familiar to most people. In England, the judge is not supplied with explicitly formulated general criteria defining " contract," or " trespass "; instead he has to decide by reference to past cases or precedents whether on the facts before him a contract has been made or a trespass committed, and in doing this he has a wide freedom in judging whether the present case is sufficiently near to a past precedent and also in determining what the past precedent in fact amounts to, or, as lawyers say, in identifying the *ratio decidendi* of past cases. This imports to legal concepts a vagueness of character very loosely controlled by judicial traditions of interpretation and it has the consequence that usually the request for a definition of a legal concept—" What is a trespass ? " " What is a contract ? "—cannot be answered by the provision of a verbal rule for the translation of a legal expression into other terms or one specifying a set of necessary and sufficient conditions. *Something* can be done in the way of providing an outline, in the form of a general statement of the effect of past cases, and that is how the student starts to learn the law. But beyond a point, answers to the questions " What is trespass ? " " What is contract ? " if they are not to mislead, must take the forms

U 2

of references to the leading cases on the subject, coupled with the use of the word " etcetera."

But there is another characteristic of legal concepts of more importance for my present purpose which makes the word " unless " as indispensable as the word " etcetera " in any explanation or definition of them and the necessity for this can be seen by examining the distinctive ways in which legal utterances can be challenged. For the accusations or claims upon which law courts adjudicate can usually be challenged or opposed in two ways. First, by a denial of the facts upon which they are based (technically called a traverse or joinder of issue) and secondly by something quite different, namely, a plea that although all the circumstances are present on which a claim could succeed, yet in the particular case, the claim or accusation should not succeed because other circumstances are present which brings the case under some recognised head of exception, the effect of which is either to defeat the claim or accusation altogether or to " reduce " it, so that only a weaker claim can be sustained. Thus a plea of " provocation " in murder cases, if successful, " reduces " what would otherwise be murder to manslaughter ; and so in a case of contract a defence that the defendant has been deceived by a material fraudulent misrepresentation made by the plaintiff entitles the defendant in certain cases to say that the contract is not valid as claimed nor " void " but " voidable " at his option. In consequence, it is usually not possible to define a legal concept such as " trespass " or " contract " by specifying the necessary and sufficient conditions for its application. For any set of conditions may be adequate in some cases but not in others and such concepts can only be explained with the aid of a list of exceptions or negative examples showing where the concept may not be applied or may only be applied in a weakened form.

This can be illustrated in detail from the law of contract. When the student has learnt that in English law there are positive conditions required for the existence of a valid contract, *i.e.*, at least two *parties*, an *offer* by one, *acceptance* by the other, a *memorandum* in writing in some cases and *consideration,* his understanding of the legal concept of a contract is still incomplete and remains so even if he has learnt the lawyers technique for the interpretation of the technical but still vague terms, " offer," " acceptance," " memorandum," " consideration." For these conditions, although necessary, are not always sufficient and he has still to learn what can *defeat* a claim that there is a valid contract, even though all these conditions are satisfied. That is the student has still to learn what can follow on the word " unless " which should accompany the statement of these conditions. This characteristic of legal concepts is one for which no word exists in ordinary English. The words " conditional " and " negative " have the wrong implications, but the law has a word which with some hesitation I borrow and extend : this is the word " *defeasible*" used of a legal interest in property which is subject to termination or " *defeat* " in a number of different contingencies but remains intact if no such contingencies mature. In this sense then, contract is a defeasible concept.

The list of defences with which an otherwise valid claim in contract can be met is worth a philosopher's inspection because it is here that reference to the factor that intrigues him—the mental factor—is mainly to be found. Thus the principal defences include the following :[2]

A. Defences which refer to the knowledge possessed by the defendant.
    i. Fraudulent misrepresentation.
    ii. Innocent misrepresentation.
    iii. Non-disclosure of material facts (in special cases, *e.g.,* contracts of insurance, only).

B. Defences which refer to what may be called the will of the defendant.
    i. Duress.
    ii. Undue influence.

---

[2] This list of course is only a summary reference to the more important defences sufficient to illustrate the point that the defeasible concept of contract cannot be defined by a set of necessary and always sufficient conditions. There are important omissions from this list, *e.g.,* the disputed topic known to lawyers as " Mistake." Adequate discussion and illustration of these and other defences will be found in legal textbooks on contract, *e.g.* Cheshire and Fifoot, " Law of Contract," Chap. IV.

C. Defences which may cover both knowledge and will.
    i. Lunacy.
    ii. Intoxication.
D. Defences which refer to the general policy of the law in discouraging certain types of contract, such as
    i. Contracts made for immoral purposes.
    ii. Contracts which restrain unreasonably the freedom of trade.
    iii. Contracts tending to pervert the course of justice.
E. The defence that the contract is rendered " impossible of performance " or " frustrated " by a fundamental and unexpected change of circumstance, *e.g.*, the outbreak of a war.
F. The defence that the claim is barred by lapse of time.

Most of these defences are of general application to all contracts. Some of them, *e.g.*, those made under (D), destroy altogether the claim that there is a contract so that it is void *ab initio* ; others, *e.g.*, those under (B) or (C), have a weaker effect rendering it merely " voidable " at the option of the party concerned and till this option is exercised the contract remains valid so that rights may be acquired by third parties under it ; while the lapse of time mentioned in (F) merely extinguishes the right to institute legal proceedings, but does not otherwise affect the existence of the contract. It is plain, therefore, that no adequate characterisation of the legal concept of a contract could be made without reference to these extremely heterogeneous defences and the manner in which they respectively serve to defeat or weaken claims in contract. The concept is irreducibly defeasible in character and to ignore this is to misrepresent it. But, of course, it is *possible* to obscure the character of such concepts by providing a general formula which seems to meet the demand often felt by the theorist for a definition in terms of a set of necessary and sufficient conditions and since philosophers have, I think, obscured in precisely this way the defeasible character of the concept of an action it is instructive to consider how such an obscuring general formula could be provided in the case of contract and to what it leads.

Thus the theorist bent on providing a general definition of contract could at any rate make a beginning by selecting the groups of defences (A), (B) and (C), which refer to the will and knowledge of the defendant and by then arguing that the fact that these defences are admitted or allowed shows that the definition of contract requires as necessary conditions that the minds of the parties should be " fully informed " and their wills " free."   And indeed legal theorists and also on occasion judges do attempt to state the " principles " of the law of contract much in this way. Thus Sir Frederick Pollock, writing[3] of the consent of the parties required for the constitution of a valid contract, says " but we still require other conditions in order to make the consent binding on him who gives it. . . . The consent must be true, full and free."   Now, of course, this method of exposition of the law may be innocuous and indeed helpful as a summary of various types of defences which usefully stresses their universal application to all contracts or emphasises the similarities between them and so suggests analogies for the further development of the law or what can be called " reasons " for that development. But unless most carefully qualified, such a general formula may be profoundly misleading ; for the positive looking doctrine " consent must be true, full and free " is only accurate as a statement of the law if treated as a compendious reference to the defences with which claims in contract may be weakened or met, whereas it suggests that there are certain psychological elements required by the law as necessary conditions of contract and that the defences are merely admitted as negative *evidence* of these.   But the defence, *e.g.*, that B entered into a contract with A as a result of the undue influence exerted upon him by A, is

---

[3] " Principles of the Law of Contract," 10th edn., p. 442. The words omitted are " though their absence in general is not to be assumed and the party seeking to enforce a contract is not expected to give affirmative proof that they have been satisfied."

not evidence of the absence of a factor called " true consent," but one of the multiple criteria for the use of the phrase " no true consent." To say that the law requires true consent is therefore, in fact, to say that defences are such as undue influence or coercion, and any others which should be grouped with them are admitted. And the practice of the law (in which general phrases such as " true consent " are of little importance) as distinct from the theoretical statement of it by jurists (in which general terms bulk largely) makes this clear ; for no party attempting to enforce a contract is required to give evidence that there was " true, full and free consent," though in special cases where some person in a fiduciary position seeks to enforce a bargain with the person in relation to whom he occupies that position, the onus lies upon him to prove that no influence was, in fact, exerted. But, of course, even here the proof consists simply in the exclusion of those facts which ordinarily constitute the defence of undue influence, though the onus in such cases is by exception cast on the plaintiff. Of course, the theorist could make his theory that there are psychological elements (" full and free consent ") required as necessary conditions of contract, irrefutable by ascribing the actual procedure of the courts to the practical difficulties of proving " mental facts "; and it is sometimes said that it is merely a matter of practical convenience that " objective tests " of these elements have been adopted and that the onus of proof is usually upon the defendant to prove the non-existence of these necessary elements. Such a doctrine is assisted by the ambiguity of the word " test " as between evidence and criteria. But to insist on this as the " real " explanation of the actual procedure of the courts in applying the defeasible concept of a contract would merely be to express obstinate loyalty to the persuasive but misleading logical ideal that all concepts must be capable of definition through a set of necessary and sufficient conditions. And, of course, even if this program were carried through for the defences involving the " mental " element it is difficult to see how it could be done for the other defences with which claims in contract can be met, and, accordingly, the defeasible character of the concept would still remain.

The principal field where jurists have I think created difficulties for themselves (in part under the influence of the traditional philosophical analysis of action) by ignoring the essentially defeasible character of the concepts they seek to clarify is the Criminal Law. There is a well-known maxim, " *actus non est reus nisi mens sit rea*," which has tempted jurists (and less often judges) to offer a general theory of " the mental element " in crime (*mens rea*) of a type which is logically inappropriate just because the concepts involved are defeasible and are distorted by this form of definition. For in the case of crime, as in contract, it is possible to compile a list of the defences or exceptions with which different criminal charges may be met with differing effect and to show that attempts to define in general terms " the mental conditions " of liability like the general theory of contract suggested in the last paragraph is only not misleading if its positive and general terms are treated merely as a restatement or summary of the fact that various heterogeneous defences or exceptions are admitted. It is true that in crime the position is more complicated than in contract since fewer defences apply to all crimes (there being notable differences between crimes created by statute and Common-law crimes) and for some crimes proof of a specific intention is required. Further, it is necessary in the case of crime to speak of defences *or exceptions* because in some cases, *e.g.*, murder, the onus of proof may be on the Prosecution to provide evidence that circumstances are not present which would if present defeat the accusation. Yet, none the less, what is meant by the mental element in criminal liability (*mens rea*) is only to be understood by considering certain defences or exceptions, such as Mistake of Fact, Accident, Coercion, Duress, Provocation, Insanity, Infancy,[4] most of which have come to be admitted in most crimes and in some cases exclude liability altogether, and in others merely " reduce " it. The fact that these are admitted as defences or exceptions constitute the cash value of the maxim " *actus non est reus*

---

[4] See for a detailed discussion of these and other defences or exceptions, Kenny : " Outlines of Criminal Law," Chap. IV.

nisi mens sit rea." But in pursuit of the will o' the wisp of a
general formula, legal theorists have sought to impose a
spurious unity (as judges occasionally protest) upon these
heterogeneous defences and exceptions, suggesting that they
are admitted as merely evidence of the absence of some
single element ("intention") or in more recent theory,
two elements ("foresight" and "voluntariness") universally required as necessary conditions of criminal responsibility. And this is misleading because what the theorist
misrepresents as evidence negativing the presence of necessary mental elements are, in fact, multiple criteria or
grounds defeating the allegation of responsibility. But it
is easy to succumb to the illusion that an accurate and
satisfying "definition" can be formulated with the aid of
notions like "voluntariness" because the logical character
of words like "voluntary" are anomalous and ill-under-
stood. They are treated in such definitions as words having
positive force, yet, as can be seen from Aristotle's discussion in
Book III of the Nicomachean Ethics, the word "voluntary"
in fact serves to exclude a heterogeneous range of cases
such as physical compulsion, coercion by threats, accidents,
mistakes, etc., and not to designate a mental element or
state ; nor does "involuntary" signify the absence of this
mental element or state.[5] And so in a murder case it is

---

[5] Thus Mr. J. W. C. Turner, in his well-known essay (in the Modern
Approach to Criminal Law. English Studies in Criminal Science, Vol. I,
p. 199) on the Mental Element in Crimes at Common Law lays down two
rules defining the mental element.
(First rule) : " It must be proved that the accused's conduct was voluntary."
(Second rule) : " It must be proved that . . . he must have foreseen
that certain consequences were likely to follow on his acts or omissions "
[p. 199]. Mr. Turner's view is indeed an improvement on previous attempts
to " define " the mental element in crime so far as it insists that there is not
a single condition named *mens rea* and also in his statement on page 199
that the extent to which " foresight of consequence " must have extended
differs in the case of each specific crime. But none the less this procedure is
one which really obscures the concepts it is meant to clarify for the words
" voluntary " and " involuntary " are used as if they refer to the presence
and absence respectively in the agent of some single condition. Thus on
page 204, Mr. Turner gives the same title of " involuntary conduct " to
cases of acts done under hypnotic suggestion, when sleepwalking, " pure "
accidents, and certain cases of insanity, drunkenness, and infancy, as well as
the case where B holds a weapon and A, against B's will, seizes his hand
and the weapon and therewith stabs C.

a defence that the accused pulled the trigger reasonably but mistakenly believing that the gun was unloaded, or that there was an accident because the bullet unexpectedly bounced off a tree ; or that the accused was insane (within the legal definition of insanity) or an infant ; and it is a partial defence " reducing " the charge from murder to manslaughter that the accused fired the shot in the heat of the moment when he discovered his wife in adultery with the victim. It is, of course, *possible* to represent the admission of these different defences or exceptions as showing that there is a single mental element (" voluntariness ") or two elements (" voluntariness " and " foresight ") required as necessary mental conditions (*mens rea*) of full criminal liability. But in order to determine what " foresight " and " voluntariness " are and how their presence and absence are established it is necessary to refer back to the various defences and then these general words assume merely the status of convenient but sometimes misleading summaries expressing the absence of all the various conditions referring to the agents knowledge or will which eliminate or reduce responsibility.

Consideration of the defeasible character of legal concepts helps to explain how statements of fact support or refute legal conclusions and thus to interpret the phrases used by lawyers for the connection between fact and law when they speak of " the legal effect or consequences of the facts " or " the conclusions of law drawn from the facts " or " consequences attached to the facts." In particular, it shows how wrong it would be to succumb to the temptation offered by modern theories of meaning to identify the meaning of a legal concept, say " contract," with the statement of the conditions in which contracts are held to exist since owing to the defeasible character of the concept such a statement though it would express the necessary and sometimes sufficient conditions for the application of " contract " could not express conditions which were always sufficient. But, of course, any such theory of the meaning of legal concepts would fail for far more fundamental reasons : for it could not convey the composite character of these concepts nor allow for the distinctive features due to the fact that the elements in the compound are of distinct logical types.

Two of these distinctive features are of special relevance to the analysis of action and arise out of the truism that what a Judge does is to judge ; for this has two important consequences. First, the Judge's function is, *e.g.*,[6] in a case of contract to say whether there is or is not a valid contract upon the claims and defences actually made and pleaded before him and the facts brought to his attention, and not on those which might have been made or pleaded. It is not his function to give an ideally correct legal interpretation of the facts, and if a party (who is *sui juris*) through bad advice or other causes fails to make a claim or plead a defence which he might have successfully made or pleaded, the judge in deciding in such a case, upon the claims and defences actually made, that a valid contract exists has given the right decision. The decision is not merely the best the Judge can do under the circumstances and it would be a misunderstanding of the judicial process to say of such a case that the parties were merely treated *as if* there were a contract. There *is* a contract in the timeless sense of " is " appropriate to judicial decisions. Secondly, since the judge is literally deciding that on the facts before him a contract does or does not exist, and to do this is neither to describe the facts nor to make inductive or deductive inferences from the statement of facts, what he does may be either a *right* or a *wrong* decision or a *good* or *bad* judgment and can be either *affirmed* or *reversed* and (where he has no jurisdiction to decide the question) may be *quashed* or *discharged*. What cannot be said of it is that it is either *true* or *false*, logically necessary or absurd.

There is perhaps not much to tempt anyone to treat a judicial decision as a descriptive statement, or the facts as related to legal conclusions as statements of fact may be related to some descriptive statement they justify, though I think the tendency, which I have already mentioned, to regard the exceptions or defences which can defeat claims

---

[6] Different considerations may apply in criminal cases.

or accusations merely as evidence of the absence of some necessary condition required by the law in the full definition of a legal concept is in fact an attempt to assimilate a judicial decision to a theoretical model of a descriptive statement ; for it is the expression of the feeling that cases where contracts are held not to exist " must " be cases where some necessary condition, required in the definition of contract, is absent. But sometimes the law is cited as an example of a deductive system at work. " Given the existing law " it will be said " the statement of facts found by the judge entail the legal conclusion." Of course, this could only be said in the simplest possible cases where no issue is raised at the trial except what commonsense would call one of fact, *i.e.*, where the parties are agreed that if the facts go one way the case falls within some legal rule and if they go another way it does not, and no question is raised about the meaning or interpretation of the legal rule. But even here it would be quite wrong to say that the judge was making a deductive inference ; for the timeless conclusion of law (Smith is guilty of murder) is not entailed by the statements of temporal fact (Smith put arsenic in his wife's coffee on May 1st, 1944) which support it ; and rules of law even when embodied in statutes are not linguistic or logical rules, but to a great extent rules for deciding.

II.

If we step outside the law courts we shall find that there are many utterances in ordinary language which are similar in important respects in spite of important differences, to the judicial blend of law and fact, but first, some cases must be distinguished which are not instances of this phenomenon but are important because they help to explain why it has been overlooked.

A. First, we, of course, very often make use of legal concepts in descriptive and other sentences and the sentences in which we so use them may be statements and hence (unlike the Judge's decision in which legal concepts are primarily used) they may be true or false. Examples of these are the obvious cases where we refer to persons or things by their known legal consequences, status or position. " Who is that woman ? " " She is Robinson's wife and the adopted daughter of Smith, who inherited all his property." " What is that in the wastepaper basket ? " " My contract with John Smith."

B. Secondly, we may refer to things, events and actions not by their known legal consequences, but by their intended or reputed legal consequence or position. " What did your father do yesterday ? " " He made his will." It should be noticed that this use may give rise to some curious difficulties if it is later found that the reputed or intended legal conclusion has not been established. What should we say of the sentence written in my diary that " My father made his will yesterday " if it turns out that since it was not witnessed and he was not domiciled in Scotland the courts refuse to recognise it as a will. Is the sentence in my diary false ? We should, I think, hesitate to say it is ; on the other hand, we would not repeat the sentence after the court's decision is made. It should be noticed also that we may make use of our own legal system and its concepts for the purpose of describing things or persons not subject to it as when we speak of the property of solitary persons who live on desert islands.

C. Thirdly, even outside the law courts we use the language of the law to make or reject claims. " My father made his will yesterday " may indeed be a claim and not a pure descriptive statement, though it will, of course, carry some information with it, because with the claim is blended reference to some justifying facts. As a claim it may be later upheld or dismissed by the courts, but it is not true or false.

But in all these instances, though such sentences are uttered in ordinary life, the technical vocabulary of the law is used in them and so we are alert to the possibility that they may not function as descriptive sentences though very often they do. But consider now sentences where the words used derive their meaning from legal or social institutions, for example, from the institution of property, but are simple non-technical words. Such are the simple indicative sentences in which the possessive terms " mine," " yours," " his " appear as grammatical predicates. " This is mine," " This is yours," " This is his " are primarily sentences for which lawyers have coined the expression " operative words " and Mr. J. L. Austin the word " performatory."[7] By the utterance of such sentences, especially in the present tense, we often do not describe but actually perform or effect a transaction; with them, we *claim* proprietary rights, *confer* or *transfer* such rights when they are claimed, *recognise* such rights or *ascribe* such rights whether claimed or not, and when these words are so used they are related to the facts that support them much in the same way as the judge's decision. But apart from this, these sentences, especially in past and future tenses, have a variety of other uses not altogether easy to disentangle from what I have called their primary use, and this may be shown by a sliding scale of increasing approximation to a pure descriptive use as follows :

(*a*) First, the operative or performatory use. " This is yours " said by a father handing over his gold watch to his son normally effects the transfer of the father's rights in the watch to the son ; that is, makes a gift of it. But said by the elder son at the end of a dispute with his brother over the family possessions, the utterance of such a sentence constitutes a recognition of the rights of the younger son and abandons the claims of the elder. Of course, difficulties can arise in various ways over such cases analogous to the problems that confront the Judge : we can ask whether the use of the words is a valid method of making gifts. If English law is the criterion, the answer is " yes " in the example given ; but it would be " no " if what the father had pointed to was not his watch but his house, though in this case it may be that we would consider the son morally entitled to the house and the

---

[7] See his discussion of some cases in " Other Minds." Proceedings of the Aristotelian Society, Suppl. Vol. XX, pp. 169 to 174.

father morally bound to make it over to him. This shows that the rules which are in the background of such utterances are not necessarily, legal rules. But the case to which I wish to draw attention is that where we use such sentences not to transfer or confer rights, but to ascribe or recognise them. For here, like a Judge, the individual decides *on* certain facts that somebody else has certain rights and his recognition is like a judgment, a blend of fact and rule if not of law.

(*b*) Secondly, sentences like " This is mine," " This is yours," " This is his " can be used simply as descriptive statements to describe things by reference to their owners. Taking visitors round my estate, I say, pointing to a field, " This is mine " or " I own this " purely by way of information.

(*c*) Thirdly, there are the more casual ascriptive use of these sentences in daily life which are difficult to classify. Suppose as we get up to go I see you have left a pen and give it to you, saying " This is yours " or suppose I am walking in the street and notice as the man in front takes out his handkerchief a watch falls from his pocket. I pick it up and hand it back to him with the words " This is yours." We might be tempted to say that we are using the sentence here simply as a descriptive statement equivalent to " You were carrying this and you dropped it or you left it " ; but that this is not at any rate clearly so can be seen from the following considerations. If after we have handed back the watch the police drive up in a car and arrest the man for theft, I shall not willingly repeat the sentence and say it was true, though if it were " descriptive " of the physical facts why should I not? On the other hand, I will not say of what I said that it was false. The position is, of course, that a very common good reason for recognising that a person has some rights to the possession of a thing is that he is observed physically in the possession of it ; and it is, of course, correct in such circumstances to ascribe such rights with the sentence " This is yours " in the absence of any claim or special circumstance which may defeat them. But as individuals we are not in the position of a Judge ; our decision is not final, and when we have notice of new circumstances or new claims we have to decide in the light of them again. But in other respects the function of sentences of this simple and non-technical sort resembles that of judicial decisions. The concepts involved are defeasible concepts like those of the law and similarly related to supporting facts. It would be possible to take the heroic course of saying that sentences like " This is his," " This is yours " have acquired, like the word " give," a purely descriptive sense to signify the normal physical facts on which it is customary to ascribe rights of possession ; but this would not account for the peculiarity of our usage and would commit the mistake of ignoring their defeasible character and identifying the meaning of an expression with which we make decisions or, ascriptions with the factual circumstances which, in the absence of other claims, are good reasons for them. With more plausibility it may be said that there is a sense of " mine," " yours," " his " which is descriptive—the sense in which my teeth (as distinct from my *false* teeth) are mine or my thought and feelings are mine. But, of course, with regard to these we do not make and challenge utterances like " This is mine," " This is yours," " This is his," and it is the logical character of these with which I am concerned.

III.

So much for the ascription and recognition of rights which we effect with the simple utterances " This is yours," " This is his " and the associated or derivative descriptive use of these sentences. I now wish to defend the similar but perhaps more controversial thesis that the concept of a human action is an ascriptive and a defeasible one, and that many philosophical difficulties come from ignoring this and searching for its necessary and sufficient conditions. The sentences " I did it," " you did it," " he did it " are, I suggest, primarily utterances with which we *confess* or *admit* liability, make accusations, or *ascribe* responsibility ;

x

and the sense in which our actions are ours is very much like that in which property is ours, though the connection is not necessarily a *vinculum juris,* a responsibility under positive law.   Of course, like the utterances already examined, connected with the non-descriptive concept of property, the verb " to do " and generally speaking the verbs of action, have an important descriptive use, especially in the present and future senses, their ascriptive use being mainly in the past tense, where the verb is often both timeless and genuinely refers to the past as distinguished from the present.   Indeed, the descriptive use of verbs of action is so important as to obscure even more in their case than in the case of " this is yours," " this is his," etc. the non-descriptive use, but the logical character of the verbs of action is, I think, betrayed by the many features which sentences containing these verbs, in the past tense, have in common with sentences in the present tense using the possessive pronouns (" this is his," etc.) and so with judicial decisions by which legal consequences are attached to facts.

I can best bring out my point by contrasting it with what I think is the mistaken, but traditional philosophical analysis of the concept of an action.   " What distinguishes the physical movement of a human body from a human action ? " is a famous question in philosophy.   The old-fashioned answer was that the distinction lies in the occurrence before or simultaneously with the physical movement of a mental event related (it was hoped) to the physical movement as its psychological cause, which event we call " having the intention " or " setting ourselves " or " willing" or " desiring " to do the act in question.   The modern answer is that to say that X performed an action is to assert a categorical proposition about the movement of his body, *and* a general hypothetical proposition or propositions to the effect that X would have responded in various ways to various stimuli, or that his body would not have moved as it did or some physical consequence would have been avoided, had he chosen differently, etc.   Both these answers seem to me to be wrong or at least inadequate in many different ways, but both make the common error of supposing that an adequate analysis can be given of the concept of a human action in any combination of the descriptive sentences, categorical or hypothetical, or any sentences concerned wholly with a single individual. To see this, compare with the traditional question about action the question " What is the difference between a piece of earth and a piece of property." Property is not a descriptive concept, and the difference between " this is a piece of earth " or " Smith is holding a piece of earth " on the one hand, and " this is someone's property " and " Smith owns a piece of property " on the other cannot be explained without reference to the non-descriptive utterances by means of which laws are promulgated and decisions made or at the very least without reference to those by which rights are recognised. Nor, I suggest, can the difference between " His body moved in violent contact with anothers " and " He did it " (*e.g.*, " He hit her ") be explained without reference to the non-descriptive use of sentences by which liabilities or responsibility are ascribed. What is fundamentally wrong in both the old and the new version of the traditional analysis of action as a combination of physical and psychological events or a combination of categorical and hypothetical descriptive sentences, is its mistake in identifying the meaning of a non-descriptive utterance ascribing responsibility in stronger or weaker form, with the factual circumstances which support or are good reasons for the ascription. In other words, though of course not all the rules in accordance with which, in our society, we ascribe responsibility are reflected in our legal code nor vice versa, yet our concept of an action, like our concept of property, is a social concept and logically dependent on accepted rules of conduct. It is fundamentally not descriptive, but ascriptive in character ; and it is a defeasible concept to be defined through exceptions and not by a set of necessary and sufficient conditions whether physical or psychological. This contention is supported by the following considerations :

First, when we say after observing the physical movements of a living person in conjunction with another today, " Smith hit her," or " Smith did it " in answer to the question " Who hit her ? " or " Who did it ? " we surely do not treat this answer as a combined assertion that a physical movement of Smith's body took place, and that some inferred mental event occurred in Smith's mind (he set himself or intended to hit her) ; for we would be adding something to this answer if we made any such reference to psychological occurrences. Nor do we treat this answer as a combination of categorical or hypothetical sentences descriptive of a physical movement and of Smith's disposition or what would have happened had he chosen differently. On the contrary, saying " He hit her " in these circumstances is, like saying " That is his," a blend. It is an ascription of liability justified by the facts ; for the observed physical movements of Smith's body are the circumstances which in the absence of some defence, support, or are good reasons for the ascriptive sentence " He did it." But, of course, " He did it " differs from " That is his " for we are ascribing responsibility not rights.

Secondly, the sentence " Smith hit her " can be challenged in the manner characteristic of defeasible legal utterances in two distinct ways. Smith or someone else can make a flat denial of the relevant statement of the physical facts, " No, it was Jones, not Smith." Alternatively (but since we are not in a law court, not also cumulatively), any of a vast array of defences can be pleaded by Smith or his friends which, though they do not destroy the charge altogether, soften it, or, as lawyers say, " reduce " it.

Thus it may be said " He did it " (" He hit her ")

1. " Accidentally " (she got in his way while he was hammering in a nail).

2. " Inadvertently " (in the course of hammering in a nail, not looking at what he was doing).

3. " By mistake for someone else " (he thought she was May, who had hit him).

4. " In self defence " (she was about to hit him with a hammer).
5. " Under great provocation " (she had just thrown the ink over him).
6. " But he was forced to by a bully " (Jones said he would thrash him).
7. " But he is mad, poor man."

Thirdly. It is, of course, possible to take the heroic line and say that all these defences are just so many signs of the absence in each case of a common psychological element, " intention," " voluntariness," " consciousness," required in a " full " definition of an action, *i.e.*, as one of its necessary and sufficient conditions, and that the concept is an ordinary descriptive concept after all. But to this, many objections can be made. These positive looking words "intention," etc. if put forward as necessary conditions of all action only succeed in posing as this if in fact they are a comprehensive and misleadingly positive-sounding reference to the absence of one or more of the defences, and are thus only understandable when interpreted in the light of the defences, and not vice versa. Again, when we are ascribing an action to a person, the question whether a psychological " event " occurred does not come up in this suggested positive form at all, but in the form of an inquiry as to whether any of these extenuating defences cover the case. Further, when a more specific description of the alleged common mental element is given, it usually turns out to be something quite special and characteristic only of a special kind of action, and by no means an essential element in all actions. This is plainly true of Professor H. A. Pritchards[8] " setting ourselves " which well describes some grim occurrences in our lives, but is surely not an essential ingredient in all cases where we recognise an action.

Fourthly. The older psychological criterion affords no explanation of the line we draw between what we still call an action though accidental and other cases. If I aim at a post and the wind carries my bullet so that it hits a

---

[8] See " Duty and Ignorance of Fact," p. 24 *et seq.*

man, I am said to have shot him accidentally, but if I aim at a post, hit it and the bullet then ricochets off and hits a man, this would not be said to be my action at all. But in neither case have I intended, set myself to do, or wished what occurred.

Fifthly. The modern formula according to which to say that an action is voluntary is to say that the agent could have avoided it if he had chosen differently either ignores the heterogeneous character of our criteria qualifying " He did it " when we use words like " accidentally," " by mistake " " under coercion," etc., or only avoids this by leaving the meaning of the protasis " If he had chosen differently " intolerably vague. Yet our actual criteria for qualifying " He did it," though multiple and heterogeneous, are capable of being stated with some precision. Thus, if the suggested general formula is used to explain our refusal to say " He did it " without qualification when a man's hand is forcibly moved by another, it is misleading to use the same formula in the very different cases of accident, mistake, coercion by threats or provocation. For in the first case the statement " the agent could not have acted differently if he had chosen " is true in the sense that he had no control over his body and his decision was or would have been ineffective ; whereas in, e.g., the case of accident the sense in which the statement is true (if at all) is that though having full control of his body the agent did not foresee the physical consequences of its movements. And, of course, our qualification of " He did it " in cases of coercion by threats or provocation (which have to be taken into account in any analysis of our usage of verbs of action) can only be comprehended under the suggested general formula if the protasis is used in still different senses so that its comfortable generality in the end evaporates ; for there will be as many different senses as there are different types of defences, or qualifications of " He did it." Some seek to avoid this conclusion by saying that in cases where we qualify " He did it," e.g., in a case of accident, there are, in fact, two elements of which one is *the genuine* action (firing the gun) and the other are its effects (the man being hit), and that our common usage whereby we say in such cases " He shot him accidentally " is inaccurate or loose.   " Strictly," it is urged, we should say " He fired the gun " (action in the strict sense) and " the bullet hit the man."   But this line of thought, as well as supposing that we can say what a " genuine " action is independently of our actual usage of verbs of action, breeds familiar but unwelcome paradoxes.   If cases of accident must be analysed into a genuine action *plus* unintended effects, then equally normal action must be analysed into a genuine action *plus* intended effects.   Firing the gun must be analysed on this view into pulling the trigger *plus* . . . and pulling the trigger into cocking the finger *plus* . . .. So that in the end the only " genuine actions " (if any) will be the minimal movements we can make with our body where nothing " can " go wrong.   These paradoxes are results of the insistence that " action " is a descriptive concept definable through a set of necessary and sufficient conditions.

Sixthly.   When we ascribe as private individuals rights or liabilities, we are not in the position of a judge whose decision is authoritative and final, but who is required only to deal with the claims and defences actually presented to him.   In private life, decisions are not final, and the individual is not relieved, as the judge often is, from the effort of inquiring what defences might be pleaded.   If, therefore, on the strength of merely the physical facts which we observe we judge " Smith hit her " and do not qualify our judgment, it can be wrong or defective in a way in which the judges decision cannot be.   For if, on investigating the facts, it appears that we should have said " Smith hit her accidentally," our first judgment has to be qualified.   But it is important to notice that it is not withdrawn as a false statement of fact or as a false inference that some essential mental event had occurred necessary for the truth of the sentence " He did it."   Our ascription of responsibility is no longer justified in the light of the new circumstances of which we have notice.   So we must judge again : *not describe again.*

67

Finally, I wish to say, out of what lawyers call abundant caution, that there are two theses I have not maintained. I have maintained no form of behaviourism for although it often is correct to say " He did it " on the strength only of the observed physical movements of another, " He did it " never, in my view, merely describes those movements. Secondly, I wish to distinguish from my own the thesis often now maintained as a solution or dissolution of the problem of free will that to say that an action is voluntary *means* merely that moral blame would tend to discourage the agent blamed from repeating it, and moral praise would encourage him to do so. This seems to me to confuse the question what we mean by saying that a man has done an action with the question why we bother to assign responsibility for actions to people in the way we do. Certainly, there is a connection between the two questions, that is between theories of punishment and reward and attempts to elucidate the criteria we do in fact employ in assigning responsibility for actions. No doubt we have come to employ the criteria we do employ because among other things in the long run, and on the whole not for the wretched individual in the dock but for " society," assigning responsibility in the way we do assign it, tends to check crime and encourage virtue ; and the social historian may be able to show that our criteria slowly alter with experience of the reformative or deterrent results obtained by applying them. But this is only one of the things which applying these criteria does for us. And this is only one of the factors which lead us to retain or modify them. Habit, or conservatism the need for certainty, and the need for some system of apportioning the loss arising from conduct, are other factors, and though, of course, it is open to us to regret the intrusion of " nonutilitarian " factors, it yet seems to me vital to distinguish the question of the history and the pragmatic value and, in one sense, the moraiity of the distinctions we draw, from the question what these distinctions are.

THE JUDGMENT INTUITIVE: THE FUNCTION OF THE "HUNCH"[1] IN JUDICIAL DECISION

Joseph C. Hutcheson, Jr.*

Many years ago, at the conclusion of a particularly difficult case both in point of law and of fact, tried to a court without a jury, the judge, a man of great learning and ability, announced from the Bench that since the narrow and prejudiced modern view of the obligations of a judge in the decision of causes prevented his resort to the judgment aleatory by the use of his "little, small dice" he would take the case under advisement, and, brooding over it, wait for his hunch.

To me, a young, indeed a very young lawyer, picked, while yet the dew was on me and I had just begun to sprout, from the classic gardens of a University, where I had been trained to regard the law as a system of rules and precedents, of categories and concepts, and the judge had been spoken of as an administrator, austere, remote, "his intellect a cold logic engine," who, in that rarified atmosphere in which he lived coldly and logically determined the relation of the facts of a particular case to some of these established precedents, it appeared that the judge was making a jest, and a very poor one, at that.

I had been trained to expect inexactitude from juries, but from the judge quite the reverse. I exalted in the law its tendency to formulize. I had a slot machine mind. I searched out categories and concepts and, having found them, worshiped them.

I paid homage to the law's supposed logical rigidity and exactitude. A logomachist, I believed in and practiced logomancy. I felt a sense of real pain when some legal concept in which I had put my faith as permanent, constructive and all-embracing opened like a broken net, allowing my fish to fall back into the legal sea. Paraphrasing Huxley, I believed that the great tragedy of the law was the slaying of a beautiful concept by an ugly fact. Always I looked for perfect formulas, fact proof, concepts so general, so flexible, that in their terms the jural relations of mankind could be stated, and I rejected most vigorously the suggestion that there was, or should be, anything fortuitous or by chance in the law. Like Jurgen I had been to the Master Philologist and with words he had conquered me.

I had studied the law in fragments and segments, in sections and compartments, and in my mind each compartment was nicely and logically arranged so that every case presented to me only the

---

*United States District Judge, Southern District of Texas.

[1] "A strong, intuitive impression that something is about to happen." WEBSTER, INTERNATIONAL DICTIONARY.

problem of arranging and re-arranging its facts until I could slip it into the compartment to which it belonged. The relation of landlord and tenant, of principal and agent, of bailor and bailee, of master and servant, these and a hundred others controlled my thinking and directed its processes.

Perceiving the law as a thing fullgrown, I believed that all of its processes were embraced in established categories, and I rejected most vigorously the suggestion that it still had life and growth, and if anyone had suggested that the judge had a right to feel, or hunch out a new category into which to place relations under his investigation, I should have repudiated the suggestion as unscientific and unsound, while as to the judge who dared to do it, I should have cried "Away with him! Away with him!"

I was too much influenced by the codifiers, by John Austin and Bentham, and by their passion for exactitude. I knew that in times past the law had grown through judicial action; that rights and processes had been invented by the judges, and that under their creative hand new remedies and new rights had flowered.

I knew that judges "are the depositories of the laws like the oracles, who must decide in all cases of doubt and are bound by an oath to decide according to the law of the land,"[2] but I believed that creation and evolution were at an end, that in modern law only deduction had place, and that the judges must decide "through being long personally accustomed to and acquainted with the judicial decisions of their predecessors."[3]

I recognized, of course, that in the preparation of the facts of a case there was room for intuition, for feeling; that there was a sixth sense which must be employed in searching out the evidence for clues, in order to assemble facts and more facts, but all of this before the evidence was in. I regarded the solution of the problem when the evidence was all in as a matter for determination by the judge by pure reason and reflection, and while I knew that juries might and did arrive at their verdicts by feeling, I repudiated as impossible the idea that good judges did the same.

I knew, of course, that some judges did follow "hunches,"— "guesses" I indignantly called them. I knew my Rabelais, and had laughed over without catching the true philosophy of old Judge Bridlegoose's trial, and roughly, in my youthful, scornful way, I recognized four kinds of judgments; first the cogitative, of and by reflection and logomancy; second, aleatory, of and by the dice;

---

[2] 1 BL. COMM. 169.   [3] *Ibid.*

third, intuitive, of and by feeling or "hunching;" and fourth, asinine, of and by an ass; and in that same youthful, scornful way I regarded the last three as only variants of each other, the results of processes all alien to good judges.

As I grew older, however, and knew and understood better the judge to whom I have in this opening referred; as I associated more with real lawyers, whose intuitive faculties were developed and made acute by the use of a trained and cultivated imagination; as I read more after and came more under the spell of those great lawyers and judges whose thesis is that "modification is the life of the law,"[4] I came to see that "as long as the matter to be considered is debated in artificial terms, there is danger of being led by a technical definition to apply a certain name and then to deduce consequences which have no relation to the grounds on which the name was applied;"[5] that "the process of inclusion and exclusion so often applied in developing a rule, cannot end with its first enunciation. The rule announced must be deemed tentative. For the many and varying facts to which it will be applied cannot be foreseen."[6]

I came to see that "every opinion tends to become a law."[7] That "regulations, the wisdom, necessity and validity of which as applied to, existing conditions, are so apparent that they are now uniformly sustained, a century ago, or even half a century ago, would probably have been rejected as arbitrary and oppressive, . . . and that in a changing world it is impossible that it should be otherwise."[8]

I came to see that "resort to first principles is, in the last analysis, the only safe way to a solution of litigated matters."[9]

I came to see that instinct in the very nature of law itself is change, adaptation, conformity, and that the instrument for all of this change, this adaptation, this conformity, for the making and the nurturing of the law as a thing of life, is the power of the brooding mind, which in its very brooding makes, creates and changes jural relations, establishes philosophy, and drawing away from the outworn past, here a little, there a little, line upon line, precept upon

---

[4]CARTER, LAW, ITS ORIGIN, GROWTH AND FUNCTION (1907). "Modification implies growth. It is the life of the law." Washington v. Dawson, 264 U. S. 219, 236, 44 Sup. Ct. 302 (1924), Brandeis, J., dissenting.

[5]Guy v. Donald, 203 U. S. 399, 406, 27 Sup. Ct. 63 (1926).

[6]Washington v. Dawson, *supra* note 4.

[7]Lochner v. New York, 198 U. S. 45, 76, 25 Sup. Ct. 539 (1905).

[8]Euclid Valley v. Ambler, 272 U. S. 365, 47 Sup. Ct. 114 (1926).

[9]Old Colony Trust Co. v. Sugarland Industries, 296 Fed. 129, 138 (S. D. Tex. 1924).

precept, safely and firmly, bridges for the judicial mind to pass the abysses between that past and the new future."[10]

So, long before I came to the Bench, and while I was still uncertain as to the function of the judge, his office seeming pale and cold to me, too much concerned with logomachy; too much ruled by logomancy, I loved jury trials, for there, without any body of precedent to guide them, any established judicial recognition of their right so to do, nay, in the face of its denial to them, I could see those twelve men bringing equity, "the correction of that wherein by reason of its universality the law is deficient," into the law.

There they would sit, and hearing sometimes the "still, sad music of humanity," sometimes "catching sight through the darkness of the fateful threads of woven fire which connect error with its retribution," wrestling in civil cases with that legal Robot, "the reasonably prudent man," in criminal cases with that legal paradox, "beyond a reasonable doubt," would hunch out just verdict after verdict by the use of that sixth sense, that feeling, which flooding the mind with light, gives the intuitional flash necessary for the just decision.

Later, when I became more familiar with the practices in admiralty and in equity, more especially when, a judge in such cases, I felt the restless, eager ranging of the mind to overcome the confusion and the perplexities of the evidence, or of constricting and outworn concepts, and so to find the hidden truth, I knew that not only was it the practice of good judges to "feel" their way to a decision of a close and difficult case, but that in such cases any other practice was unsound. "For it is no paradox to say that in our most theoretical moods we may be nearest to our most practical applications."

I knew that "general propositions do not decide concrete cases. The decision will depend on a judgment or intuition more subtle than any articulate major premise."[11]

And so, after eleven years on the Bench following eighteen at the Bar, I, being well advised by observation and experience of what I am about to set down, have thought it both wise and decorous to now boldly affirm that "having well and exactly seen, surveyed,

---

[10]"Judges do and must legislate, but they can do so only interstitially. They are confined from Molar to molecular motions. A common law judge could not say, I think the doctrine of consideration a bit of historical nonsense, and shall not enforce it in my court. No more could a judge exercising the limited jurisdiction of admiralty say I think well of the common law rules of master and servant, and propose to introduce them here *en bloc*." Southern Pacific v. Jensen, 244 U. S. 205, 221, 37 Sup. Ct. 524 (1917), Holmes, J., dissenting.   [11]*Ibid.*

overlooked, reviewed, recognized, read and read over again, turned and tossed about, seriously perused and examined the preparitories, productions, evidences, proofs, allegations, depositions, cross speeches, contradictions... and other such like confects and spiceries, both at the one and the other side, as a good judge ought to do, I posit on the end of the table in my closet all the pokes and bags of the defendants—that being done I thereafter lay down upon the other end of the same table the bags and satchels of the plaintiff."[12]

Thereafter I proceed "to understand and resolve the obscurities of these various and seeming contrary passages in the law, which are laid claim to by the suitors and pleading parties," even just as Judge Bridlegoose did, with one difference only. "That when the matter is more plain, clear and liquid, that is to say, when there are fewer bags," and he would have used his "other large, great dice, fair and goodly ones," I decide the case more or less off hand and by rule of thumb. While when the case is difficult or involved, and turns upon a hairsbreadth of law or of fact, that is to say, "when there are many bags on the one side and on the other" and Judge Bridlegoose would have used his "little small dice," I, after canvassing all the available material at my command, and duly cogitating upon it, give my imagination play, and brooding over the cause, wait for the feeling, the hunch—that intuitive flash of understanding which makes the jump-spark connection between question and decision, and at the point where the path is darkest for the judicial feet, sheds its light along the way.

And more, "lest I be stoned in the street" for this admission, let me hasten to say to my brothers of the Bench and of the Bar, "my practice is therein the same with that of your other worships."[13]

For let me premise here, that in feeling or "hunching" out his decisions, the judge acts not differently from, but precisely as the lawyers do in working on their cases, with only this exception; that the lawyer, having a predetermined destination in view,—to win his law suit for his client—looks for and regards only those hunches which keep him in the path that he has chosen, while the judge, being merely on his way with a roving commission to find the just solution, will follow his hunch wherever it leads him, and when, following it, he meets the right solution face to face, he can cease his labors and blithely say to his troubled mind—"Trip no farther, pretty sweeting, journeys end in lovers meeting, as every wise man's son doth know."

---

[12]RABELAIS, BOOK III, c. 39.   [13]*Ibid.*

Further, at the outset, I must premise that I speak now of the judgment or decision, the solution itself, as opposed to the apologia for that decision; the decree, as opposed to the logomachy, the effusion of the judge by which that decree is explained or excused. I speak of the judgment pronounced, as opposed to the rationalization by the judge on that pronouncement.

I speak, in short, of that act of definitive sentence of which Trinquamelle and Bridlegoose discoursed.

"But when you do these fine things" quoth Trinquamelle, "how do you, my fine friend, award your decrees and pronounce judgment?" "Even as your other worships," quoth Bridlegoose, "for I give out sentence in his favor unto whom hath befallen the best chance by the dice, judiciary, tribunian, pretorial, which comes first. So doth the law command."[14]

And not only do I set down boldly that I, "even as your other worships do," invoke and employ hunches in decisions, but I do affirm, and will presently show, that it is that tiptoe faculty of the mind which can feel and follow a hunch which makes not only the best gamblers, the best detectives, the best lawyers, the best judges, the materials of whose trades are the most chancey because most human, and the results of whose activities are for the same cause the most subject to uncertainty and the best attained by approximation, but it is that same faculty which has guided and will continue to guide the great scientists of the world,[15] and even those august dealers in certitude, the mathematicians themselves, to their most difficult solutions, which have opened and will continue to open hidden doors; which have widened and will ever widen man's horizon.

"For facts are sterile until there are minds capable of choosing between them and discerning those which conceal something, and recognizing that which is concealed. Minds which under the bare fact see the soul of the fact."[16]

I shall further affirm, and I think maintain, that the judge is, in the exercise of this faculty, popularly considered to be an attribute of only the gambler and the short story detective, in the most gallant of gallant companies; a philosopher among philosophers, and I shall not fear to stand, unrebuked and unashamed before my brothers of the Bench and Bar.

---

[14] *Ibid.*

[15] "The method of science indeed is the method of the Chancery Court—it involves the collection of all available evidence and the subjection of all such evidence to the most searching examination and cross examination." GREGORY, DISCOVERY, THE SPIRIT AND SERVICE OF SCIENCE 166, quoting H. E. Armstrong.

[16] *Ibid.*, at 170, quoting Henri Poincare.

I remember once, in the trial of a patent case, where it was contended with great vigor on the one side that the patent evidenced invention of the highest order, and with equal vigor on the other that the device in question was merely a mechanical advance, I announced, almost without any sense of incongruity, that I would take the case under advisement, and after "having well and exactly seen and surveyed, overlooked, reviewed, read and read over again" etc., all of the briefs, authorities and the record, would wait awhile before deciding to give my mind a chance to hunch it out, for if there was the flash of invention in the device my mind would give back an answering flash; while if there were none, my mind would, in a dully cogitative way, find only mechanical advance.

One of the lawyers, humself a "huncher," smiled and said— "Well, Your Honor, I am very grateful to you for having stated from the Bench what I have long believed, but have hesitated to avow, that next to the pure arbitrament of the dice in judicial decisions, the best chance for justice comes through the hunch." The other lawyer, with a different type of mind, only looked on as though impatient of such foolery.

But I, proceeding according to custom, got my hunch, found invention and infringement, and by the practice of logomachy so bewordled my opinion in support of my hunch that I found myself in the happy situation of having so satisfied the intuitive lawyer by the correctness of the hunch, and the logomachic lawyer by the spell of my logomancy, that both sides accepted the result and the cause was ended.

Now, what is this faculty? What are its springs, what its uses? Many men have spoken of it most beautifully. Some call it "intuition"—some, "imagination," this sensitiveness to new ideas, this power to range when the track is cold, this power to cast in ever widening circles to find a fresh scent, instead of standing baying where the track was lost.

"Imagination, that wondrous faculty, which properly controlled by experience and reflection, becomes the noblest attribute of man, the source of poetic genius, the instrument of discovery in science."[17]

"With accurate experiment and observation to work upon, imagination becomes the architect of physical theory. Newton's passage from a falling apple to a falling moon was an act of the prepared imagination without which the laws of Keppler could never have been traced to their foundations.

---

[17]Address to the Royal Society of England, November 3, 1859, Sir Benjamin Brodie, quoted from FRAGMENTS OF SCIENCE, 109.

"Out of the facts of chemistry the constructive imagination of Dalton formed the atomic theory. Scientific men fight shy of the word because of its ultra-scientific connotations, but the fact is that without the exercise of this power our knowledge of nature would be a mere tabulation of co-existences and sequences."[18]

Again—"There is in the human intellect a power of expansion, I might almost call it a power of creation, which is brought into play by the simple brooding upon facts. The legend of the spirit brooding over chaos may have originated in experience of this power."[19]

It is imagination which, from assembled facts, strikes out conclusions and establishes philosophies. "Science is analytical description. Philosophy is synthetic interpretation. The philosopher is not content to describe the fact; he wishes to ascertain its relation to experience in general, and thereby to get at its meaning and its worth. He combines things in interpretative synthesis. To observe processes and to construct means is science. To criticize and co-ordinate ends is philosophy. For a fact is nothing except in relation to desire; it is not complete except in relation to a purpose and a whole. Science, without philosophy, facts without perspective and valuation cannot save us from havoc and despair. Science gives us knowledge, but only philosophy can give us wisdom."[20] Cardozo expresses it most beautifully.

"Repeatedly, when one is hard beset, there are principles and precedents and analogies which may be pressed into the service of justice, if one has the perceiving eye to use them. It is not unlike the divinations of the scientist. His experiments must be made significant by the flash of a luminous hypothesis. For the creative process in law, and indeed in science generally, has a kinship to the creative process in art. Imagination, whether you call it scientific or artistic, is for each the faculty that creates."

"Learning is indeed necessary, but learning is the springboard by which imagination leaps to truth. The law has its piercing intuitions, its tense, apocalyptic moments. We gather together our principles and precedents and analogies, even at times our fictions, and summon them to yield the energy that will best attain the jural end. If our wand has the divining touch, it will seldom knock in vain. So it is that the conclusion, however deliberate and labored, has often the aspect of a lucky find."

---

[18]"Scientific Use of the Imagination" Address delivered before the British Association at Liverpool, Sept. 16, 1860 by Tyndall, quoted from FRAGMENTS OF SCIENCE, III.

[19]*Ibid.*, at 114.　　[20]DURANT, STORY OF PHILOSOPHY.

" 'When I once asked the best administrator whom I knew,' writes Mr. Wallas, 'how he formed his decisions, he laughed, and with the air of letting out for the first time a guilty secret, said: 'Oh, I always decide by feeling. So and so always decides by calculation, and that is no good.' When again I asked an American judge, who is widely admired both for his skill and for his impartiality, how he and his fellows formed their conclusions, he also laughed, and said that he would be stoned in the street if it were known that, after listening with full consciousness to all the evidence, and following as carefully as he could all the arguments, he waited until he "felt" one way or the other. He had elided the preparation and the brooding, or at least had come to think of them as processes of faint kinship with the state of mind that followed.' 'When the conclusion is there', says William James, 'we have already forgotten most of the steps preceding its attainment.' "[21]

Collision cases in admiralty furnish excellent illustrations of the difficulty of arriving at a sound fact conclusion by mere reasoning upon objective data. In these cases, as every trier knows, the adherents of the respective ships swear most lustily in true seagoing fashion for their side, and if a judge were compelled to decide the case by observing the demeanor of the witnesses alone, he would be in sad plight, for at the end of eleven years upon the Bench I am more convinced than ever that the shrewdest, smartest liars often make the most plausible and satisfactory witnesses, while the humblest and most honest fellows often, upon the witness stand, acquit themselves most badly.

Now, in such circumstances, deprived of the hunch which is the clue to judgment, "the intuition more subtle than any major premise," it would be better for the judge either to resort to the device of summoning the litigants "to personally compear before him a precise hundred years thereafter to answer to some interrogatories touching certain points which were not contained in the verbal defense"[22] or to use the "little small dice" in which Judge Bridlegoose placed so much confidence in tight cases, than to try to decide the case by rule of thumb upon the number of witnesses, or the strength of their asseverations.

Fortunately, however, in these cases the judge may, reconciling all the testimony reconcilable, and coming to the crux of the conflict, having a full and complete picture of the scene itself furnished by the actors, re-enact the drama and as the scene unfolds with the

---

[21]Cardozo, Paradoxes of Legal Science (1928) 59, 60.
[22]Rabelais, Book III, c. 44.

actors each in the place assigned by his own testimony, play the piece out, watching for the joints in the armor of proof, the crevices in the structure of the case or its defense. If the first run fails, the piece may be played over and over until finally, when it seems perhaps impossible to work any consistent truth out of it, the hunch comes, the scenes and the players are rearranged in accordance with it, and lo, it works successfully and in order.

If in other causes this faculty of "feeling" the correct decision is important to the successful trier of facts, it is doubly so in patent cases for "it is not easy to draw the line which separates the ordinary skill of a mechanic versed in his art, from the exercise of patentable invention, and the difficulty is especially great in the mechanic arts, where the successive steps in improvements are numerous, and where the changes and modifications are introduced by practical mechanics."[23]

Mr. Roberts, in his scholarly and exhaustive treatise on *Patentability and Patent Interpretation*, has this to say of the Krementz case:

"How the court could have arrived at the conclusion that this case furnished an instance of patentable invention is very difficult to understand in view of its attitude toward many other cases. . . . The explanation must be sought in the fact that no objective criteria has ever been recognized as decisive of the question of patentability, and that accordingly each case has had to be decided upon consideration of what the judicial mind could determine to be, on the whole, just and fair under the particular circumstances which happened to be present."[24]

Nevertheless, says Roberts, "There have frequently been unmistakable indications of perplexity on the part of the judges when endeavoring to assign reasons for their decision one way or another in cases where patentable invention was doubtful" and commenting further on the remarks of Mr. Justice Shiras in the Krementz case at page 559, parts of which are quoted herein, he concludes:—

"This was not a logical conclusion founded upon well established premises; it was only a confession of doubt, and a guess induced by special considerations which could not furnish a rule for the determination of any other question of a similar kind."[25]

To relieve this "perplexity" and to avoid these "confessions of doubt" and "guesses induced by special considerations" Mr. Roberts proposes to substitute for the subjective determination which breeds these undesirable conditions, decisions upon purely objective criteria,

---

[23]Krementz v. S. Cottle Co., 148 U. S. 559.
[24]ROBERTS, PATENTABILITY, AND PATENT INTERPRETATION 181.
[25]*Ibid.*, at 181.

wholly dependent upon objective evidence, and wholly free from the influence of subjective bias.

"In short," says Roberts, "it is utterly futile to attempt to settle questions of patentability by resorting to merely subjective tests. All changes effected in the industrial arts are the production of thought, but it is impossible to discover any certain gauge for their rank in the inventive scale by simply contemplating the mental processes which have accomplished their origination."[26]

Mr. Roberts' effort, while vigorous and sustained, and supported by a wealth of learning, leaves me, as to the proposition that questions of invention may in all cases be decided upon purely objective criteria, without "the intuition more subtle than any major premise," cold.

Judges who have tried many patent cases, who have heard the testimony of experts, the one affirming the matter to be merely an advance in mechanical steps, the other to be invention of the highest order; the one affirming prior use, the other denying it; the one affirming it to be the flight of genius into new fields, the other, the mere dull trudging of an artisan, know that for a just decision of such causes no objective criteria can be relied on. They well know that there must be in the trier something of the same imaginative response to an idea, something of that same flash of genius that there is in the inventor, which all great patent judges have had, that intuitive brilliance of the imagination, that luminous quality of the mind, that can give back, where there is invention, an answering flash for flash.

Time was when judges, lawyers, law writers and teachers of the law refused to recognize in the judge this right and power of intuitive decision. It is true that the trial judge was always supposed to have superior facilities for decision, but these were objectivized in formulas, such as—the trial judge has the best opportunity of observing the witnesses, their demeanor,—the trial judge can see the play and interplay of forces as they operate in the actual clash of the trial.

Under the influence of this kind of logomachy, this sticking in the "skin" of thought, the trial judge's superior opportunity was granted, but the real reason for that superior position, that the trial creates an atmosphere springing from but more than the facts themselves, in which and out of which the judge may get the feeling which takes him to the desired end, was deliberately suppressed.

Later writers, however, not only recognize but emphasize this faculty, nowhere more attractively than in Judge Cardozo's lectures

---

[26]*Ibid.*, at 247.

before the law schools of Yale University, in 1921[27] and Columbia University in 1927,[28] while Max Radin, in 1925, in a most sympathetic and charming way, takes the judge's works apart, and shows us how his wheels go round.[29]

He tells us, first, that the judge is a human being; that therefore he does not decide causes by the abstract application of rules of justice or of right, but having heard the cause and determined that the decision ought to go this way or that way, he then takes up his search for some category of the law into which the case will fit.

He tells us that the judge really feels or thinks that a certain result seems desirable, and he then tries to make his decision accomplish that result. "What makes certain results seem desirable to a judge?" he asks, and answers his question that that seems desirable to the judge which, according to his training, his experience, and his general point of view, strikes him as the jural consequence that ought to flow from the facts, and he advises us that what gives the judge the struggle in the case is the effort so to state the reasons for his judgment that they will pass muster.

Now what is he saying except that the judge really decides by feeling, and not by judgment; by "hunching" and not by ratiocination, and that the ratiocination appears only in the opinion?

Now what is he saying but that the vital, motivating impulse for the decision is an intuitive sense of what is right or wrong for that cause, and that the astute judge, having so decided, enlists his every faculty and belabors his laggard mind, not only to justify that intuition to himself, but to make it pass muster with his critics?

There is nothing unreal or untrue about this picture of the judge, nor is there anything in it from which a just judge should turn away. It is true, and right that it is true, that judges really do try to select categories or concepts into which to place a particular case so as to produce what the judge regards as a righteous result, or, to avoid any confusion in the matter of morals, I will say a "proper result."

This is true. I think we should go further, and say it ought to be true. No reasoning applied to practical matters is ever really effective unless motivated by some impulse.

"Occasionally and frequently, the exercise of the judgment ought to end in absolute reservation. We are not infallible, so we ought

---

[27]Cardozo, the Nature of the Judicial Process (1921).
[28]*Supra* note 21.
[29]Radin, *Theory of Judical Decision* (1925) 2 Am. B. A. J. 359.

to be cautious."[30]   "Sometimes," however, "if we would guide by the light of reason, we must let our minds be bold."[31]

The purely contemplative philosopher may project himself into an abstract field of contemplation where he reasons, but practical men, and in that judges must be included, must have impulses. The lawyer has them, and because he has them his work is tremendously important. If a lawyer merely reasoned abstractly and without motive he would do the judge no good. But the driving impulse to bring about his client's success not only makes him burrow industriously for precedents, and as industriously bring them forth, but also makes him belabor and cudgel the brains of the listening judge to bring him into agreement.

It is this factor in our jurisprudence, and only this, that clients have lawyers and that lawyers are advocates, which has made and will continue to make it safe for judges not only to state, but sometimes to make the law. "A thorough advocate in a just cause,—a penetrating mathematician facing the starry heavens, alike bear the semblance of divinity."

If the judge sat upon the Bench in a purely abstract relation to the cause, his opinion in difficult cases would be worth nothing. He must have some motive to fire his brains, to "let his mind be bold."

By the nature of his occupation he cannot have advocacy for either side of the case as such, so he becomes an advocate, an earnest one, for the—in a way—abstract solution. Having become such advocate, his mind reaches and strains and feels for that result. He says with Elihu, the son of Barachel, the Buzite, of the family of Ram—"There is a spirit in man, and the breath of the Almighty giveth him understanding. It is not the great that are wise, nor the aged that understand justice.———Hearken to me; I also will show mine opinion. For I am full of matter; the spirit within me constraineth me. Behold my belly is as wine which hath no vent. Like new wineskins it is ready to burst."[32]

And having travailed and reached his judgment, he struggles to bring up and pass in review before his eager mind all of the categories and concepts which he may find useful directly or by analogy, so as to select from them that which in his opinion will support his desired result.

---

[30]*Op. cit. supra* note 15, at 36, quoting Faraday.

[31]Burns v. Bryan, 264 U. S. 504, 520, 44 Sup. Ct. 412 (1923), Brandeis, J., dissenting.

[32]JOB, CHAPTER 32, verses 9, 10, 18, 19.

For while the judge may be, he cannot appear to be, arbitrary. He must at least appear reasonable, and unless he can find a category which will at least "semblably" support his view, he will feel uncomfortable.

Sometimes he must almost invent a category, but he can never do quite that thing, for as we have seen, the growth of the law is interstitial, and the new category cannot be new enough wholly to avoid contact and placement in the midst of prior related categories.

But whether or not the judge is able in his opinion to present reasons for his hunch which will pass jural muster, he does and should decide difficult and complicated cases only when he has the feeling of the decision, which accounts for the beauty and the fire of some, and the labored dullness of many dissenting opinions.

All of us have known judges who can make the soundest judgments and write the dullest opinions on them; whose decisions were hardly ever affirmed for the reasons which they gave. Their difficulty was that while they had the flash, the intuitive power of judgment, they could not show it forth. While they could by an intuitive flash leap to a conclusion, just as an inventor can leap to his invention, just as often as an inventor cannot explain the result or fully understand it, so cannot and do not they.

There is not one among us but knows that while too often cases must be decided without that "feeling" which is the triumphant precursor of the just judgment, that just as "sometimes a light surprises the Christian while he sings," so sometimes, after long travail and struggle of the mind, there does come to the dullest of us, flooding the brain with the vigorous blood of decision, the hunch that there is, or is not invention; that there is or is not, anticipation; that the plaintiff should be protected by a decree, or should be denied protection. This hunch, sweeping aside hesitancy and doubt, takes the judge vigorously on to his decision; and yet, the cause decided, the way thither, which was for the blinding moment a blazing trail, becomes wholly lost to view.

Sometimes again that same intuition or hunch, which warming his brain and lighting his feet produced the decision, abides with the decider "while working his judgment backward" as he blazes his trail "from a desirable conclusion back to one or another of a stock of logical premises."[33]

It is such judicial intuitions, and the opinions lighted and warmed by the feeling which produced them, that not only give justice in

---

[33]*Supra* note 29.

the cause, but like a great white way, make plain in the wilderness the way of the Lord for judicial feet to follow.

If these views are even partly sound, and if to great advocacy and great judging the imaginative, the intuitional faculty is essential, should there not be some change in the methods of the study and of the teaching of the law in our great law schools? Should there not go along with the plain and severely logical study of jural relations study and reflection upon, and an endeavor to discover and develop, those processes of the mind by which such decisions are reached, those processes and faculties which, lifting the mind above the mass of constricting matter whether of confused fact or precedent that stands in the way of just decision, enable it by a kind of apocalyptic vision to "trace the hidden equities of divine reward, and to catch sight through the darkness, of the fateful threads of woven fire which connect error with its retribution?"[34]

---

[34]Ruskin, Sesame and Lilies.

REMARKS ON THE THEORY OF APPELLATE DECISION AND THE RULES OR CANONS ABOUT HOW STATUTES ARE TO BE CONSTRUED

KARL N. LLEWELLYN *

I

One does not progress far into legal life without learning that there is no single right and accurate way of reading one case, or of reading a bunch of cases. For

(1) Impeccable and correct doctrine makes clear that a case "holds" with authority only so much of what the opinion says as is absolutely necessary to sustain the judgment. Anything else is unnecessary and "distinguishable" and noncontrolling for the future. Indeed, if the judgment rests on two, three or four rulings, any of them can be rightly and righteously knocked out, for the future, as being thus "unnecessary." Moreover, any distinction on the facts is rightly and righteously a reason for distinguishing and therefore disregarding the prior alleged holding. But

(2) Doctrine equally impeccable and correct makes clear that a case "holds" with authority the rule on which the court there chose to rest the judgment; more, that that rule covers, with full authority, cases which are plainly distinguishable on their facts and their issue, whenever the reason for the rule extends to cover them. Indeed, it is unnecessary for a rule or principle to have led to the decision in the prior case, or even to have been phrased therein, in order to be seen as controlling in the new case: (a) "We there said . . ." (b) "That case necessarily decided . . ."

These divergent and indeed conflicting correct ways of handling or reading a single prior case as one "determines" what it authoritatively holds, have their counterparts in regard to the authority of a series or body of cases. Thus

(1) It is correct to see that "That rule is too well settled in this jurisdiction to be disturbed"; and so to apply it to a wholly novel circumstance. But

(2) It is no less correct to see that "The rule has never been extended to a case like the present"; and so to refuse to apply it: "We here limit the rule." Again,

(3) It is no less correct to look over the prior "applications" of "the rule" and rework them into a wholly new formulation of "the true rule" or

---

* Betts Professor of Jurisprudence, Columbia University School of Law; author, numerous books and law review articles; draftsman, various uniform commercial acts; chief reporter, Uniform Commercial Code. The "Thrust and Parry" is in good part the work of Charles Driscoll.

"true principle" which knocks out some of the prior cases as simply "mis-applications" and then builds up the others.

In the work of a single opinion-day I have observed 26 different, describable ways in which one of our best state courts handled its own prior cases, repeatedly using three to six different ways within a single opinion.

What is important is that *all* 26 ways (plus a dozen others which happened not to be in use that day) are correct. They represent not "evasion," but sound use, application and development of precedent. They represent not "departure from," but sound continuation of, our system of precedent as it has come down to us. The major defect in that system is a mistaken idea which many lawyers have about it—to wit, the idea that the cases themselves and in themselves, plus the correct rules on how to handle cases, provide one single correct answer to a disputed issue of law. In fact the available correct answers are two, three, or ten. The question is: *Which* of the available correct answers will the court *select*—and *why?* For since there is always more than one available correct answer, the court always has to select.

True, the selection is frequently almost automatic. The type of distinction or expansion which is always *technically* available may be psychologically or sociologically unavailable. This may be because of (a) the current tradition of the court or because of (b) the current temper of the court or because of (c) the sense of the situation as the court sees that sense. (There are other possible reasons a-plenty, but these three are the most frequent and commonly the most weighty.)

The *current tradition* of the court is a matter of period-style in the craft of judging. In 1820-1850 our courts felt in general a freedom and duty to move in the manner typified in our thought by Mansfield and Marshall. "Precedent" guided, but "principle" controlled; and nothing was good "Principle" which did not look like wisdom-in-result for the welfare of All-of-us. In 1880-1910, on the other hand, our courts felt in general a prime duty to order within the law and a duty to resist any "outside" influence. "Precedent" was to control, not merely to guide; "Principle" was to be tested by whether it made for order in the law, not by whether it made wisdom-in-result. "Legal" Principle could not be subjected to "political" tests; even legislation was resisted as disturbing. Since 1920 the earlier style (the "Grand Style") has been working its way back into general use by our courts, though the language of the opinions moves still dominantly (though waningly) in the style (the "Formal Style") of the late 19th Century. In any particular court what needs study is how far along the process has gotten. The best material for study is the latest volume of reports, read in sequence from page 1 through to the end: the current mine-run of the work.

The *current temper* of the court is reflected in the same material, and represents the court's tradition as modified by its personnel. For it is plain that the two earlier period-styles represent also two eternal types of human being. There is the man who loves creativeness, who can without loss of sleep combine risk-taking with responsibility, who sees and feels institutions as things built and to be built to serve functions, and who sees the functions as vital and law as a tool to be eternally reoriented to justice and to general welfare. There is the other man who loves order, who finds risk uncomfortable and has seen so much irresponsible or unwise innovation that responsibility to him means caution, who sees and feels institutions as the tested, slow-built ways which for all their faults are man's sole safeguard against relapse into barbarism, and who regards reorientation of the law in our polity as essentially committed to the legislature. Commonly a man of such temper has also a craftsman's pride in clean craftsman's work, and commonly he does not view with too much sympathy any ill-done legislative job of attempted reorientation.[1] Judges, like other men, range up and down the scale between the extremes of either type of temper, and in this aspect (as in the aspect of intellectual power and acumen or of personal force or persuasiveness) the constellation of the personnel on a particular bench at a particular time plays its important part in urging the court toward a more literal or a more creative selection among the available accepted and correct "ways" of handling precedent.

More vital, if possible, than either of the above is *the sense of the situation as seen by the court*. Thus in the very heyday of the formal period our courts moved into tremendous creative expansion of precedent in regard to the labor injunction and the due process clause. What they saw as sense to be achieved, and desperately needed, there broke through all trammels of the current period-style. Whereas the most creative-minded court working in the most creative period-style will happily and literally apply a formula without discussion, and even with relief, if the formula makes sense and yields justice in the situation and the case.

So strongly does the felt sense of the situation and the case affect the court's choice of techniques for reading or interpreting and then applying the authorities that one may fairly lay down certain generalizations:

A. In some six appealed cases out of ten the court feels this sense so clearly that lining up the authorities comes close to being an automatic job. *In the very process of reading an authority* a distinction leaps to the eye, and that is "all" that that case holds; or the language of another authority (whether or not "really" in point) shines forth as "clearly stating the true rule." Trouble comes when the cases do not line up this clearly and semi-

---

1. Intellectually, this last attitude is at odds with the idea that reorientation is for the legislature. Emotionally, it is not. Apart from the rather general resistance to change which normally companions orderliness of mind, there is a legitimate feeling that within a team team-play is called for, that it is passing the buck to thrust onto a court the labor of making a legislative job make sense and become workable.

automatically, when they therefore call for intellectual labor, even at times for a conclusion that the law as given will not allow the sensible result to be reached. Or trouble comes when the sense of the situation is not clear.

B. Technical leeways correctly available when the sense of the situation and the case call for their use cease to be correctly available *unless used in furtherance of what the court sees as such sense.* There is here in our system of precedent an element of uprightness, or conscience, of judicial responsibility; and motive becomes a factor in determining what techniques are correct and right. Today, in contrast with 1890, it may be fairly stated that even the literal application of a thoroughly established rule is not correct in a case or situation in which that application does not make sense unless the court in honest conscience feels forced by its office to make the application.

C. Collateral to B, but deserving of separate statement, is the proposition that *the greater the felt need, because of felt sense, the wider is the leeway correctly and properly available in reshaping an authority or the authorities.* What is both proper and to be expected in an extreme case would become abuse and judicial usurpation if made daily practice in the mine-run of cases. All courts worthy of their office feel this in their bones, as being inherent in our system of precedent. They show the feeling in their work. Where differences appear is where they should appear: in divergent sizings up of what is sense, and of how great the need may be in any situation.

One last thing remains to be said about "sense."

There is a sense of *the type of situation* to be contrasted with the sense of *a particular controversy between particular litigants.* Which of these aspects of sense a court responds to more strongly makes a tremendous difference. Response primarily to the sense of the particular controversy is, in the first place, dangerous because a particular controversy may not be typical, and because it is hard to disentangle general sense from personalities and from "fireside" equities. Such response is dangerous in the second place because it leads readily to finding an out *for this case only*—and that leads to a complicating multiplicity of refinement and distinction, as also to repeated resort to analogies unthought through and unfortunate of extension. This is what the proverb seeks to say: "Hard cases make bad law."

If on the other hand the type of situation is in the forefront of attention, a solving rule comes in for much more thoughtful testing and study. Rules are thrust toward reasonable simplicity, and made with broader vision. Moreover, the idiosyncracies of the particular case and its possible emotional deflections are set for judgment against a broader picture which gives a fair chance that accidental sympathy is not mistaken for long-range justice for all. And one runs a better chance of skirting the incidence of the other proverb: "Bad law makes hard cases."

On the case-law side, I repeat, we ought all thus to be familiar with the fact that the right doctrine and going practice of our highest courts leave them a very real leeway within which (a) to narrow or avoid what seem today to have been unfortunate prior phrasings or even rulings; or (b), on the other hand, to pick up, develop, expand what seem today to have been fortunate prior rulings or even phrasings.

It is silly, I repeat, to think of use of this leeway as involving "twisting" of precedent. The very phrase presupposes the thing which is not and which has never been. The phrase presupposes that there was in the precedent under consideration some one and single meaning. The whole experience of our case-law shows that that assumption is false. It is, instead, the business of the courts to use the precedents constantly to make the law always a *little* better, to correct old mistakes, to recorrect mistaken or ill-advised attempts at correction—but always within limits severely set not only by the precedents, but equally by the traditions of right conduct in judicial office.

What we need to see now is that all of this is paralleled, in regard to statutes, because of (1) the power of the legislature both to choose policy and to select measures; and (2) the necessity that the legislature shall, in so doing, use language—language fixed in particular words; and (3) the continuing duty of the courts to make sense, under and within the law.

For just as prior courts can have been skillful or unskillful, clear or unclear, wise or unwise, so can legislatures. And just as prior courts have been looking at only a single piece of our whole law at a time, so have legislatures.

But a court must strive to make sense *as a whole* out of our law *as a whole*. It must, to use Frank's figure,[2] take the music of any statute as written by the legislature; it must take the text of the play as written by the legislature. But there are many ways to play that music, to play that play, and a court's duty is to play it well, and in harmony with the other music of the legal system.

Hence, in the field of statutory construction also, there are "correct," unchallengeable rules of "how to read" which lead in happily variant directions.

This must be so until courts recognize that here, as in case-law, the real guide is Sense-for-All-of-Us. It must be so, so long as we and the courts pretend that there has been only one single correct answer possible. Until we give up that foolish pretense there must be a set of mutually contradictory *correct* rules on How to Construe Statutes: either set available as duty and sense may require.

Until then, also, the problem will recur in statutory construction as in the handling of case-law: *Which* of the technically correct answers (a) *should* be given; (b) *will* be given—and Why?

And everything said above about the temper of the court, the temper

---

2. Frank, *Words and Music: Some Remarks on Statutory Interpretation,* 47 Col. L. Rev. 1259 (1947).

of the court's tradition, the sense of the situation and the case, applies here as well.

Thus in the period of the Grand Style of case-law statutes were construed "freely" to implement their purpose, the court commonly accepting the legislature's choice of policy and setting to work to implement it. (Criminal statutes and, to some extent, statutes on procedure, were exceptions.) Whereas in the Formal Period statutes tended to be limited or even eviscerated by wooden and literal reading, in a sort of long-drawn battle between a balky, stiff-necked, wrong-headed court and a legislature which had only words with which to drive that court. Today the courts have regained, in the main, a cheerful acceptance of legislative choice of policy, but they are still hampered to some extent in carrying such policies forward by the Formal Period's insistence on precise language.

II

One last thing is to be noted:

If a statute is to make sense, it must be read in the light of some assumed purpose. A statute merely declaring a rule, with no purpose or objective, is nonsense.

If a statute is to be merged into a going system of law, moreover, the court must do the merging, and must in so doing take account of the policy of the statute—or else substitute its own version of such policy. Creative reshaping of the net result is thus inevitable.

But the policy of a statute is of two wholly different kinds—each kind somewhat limited in effect by the statute's choice of measures, and by the statute's choice of fixed language. On the one hand there are the ideas consciously before the draftsmen, the committee, the legislature: a known evil to be cured, a known goal to be attained, a deliberate choice of one line of approach rather than another. Here talk of "intent" is reasonably realistic; committee reports, legislative debate, historical knowledge of contemporary thinking or campaigning which points up the evil or the goal can have significance.

But on the other hand—and increasingly as a statute gains in age—its language is called upon to deal with circumstances utterly uncontemplated at the time of its passage. Here the quest is not properly for the sense originally intended by the statute, for the sense sought originally to be *put into it,* but rather for the sense which *can be quarried out of it* in the light of the new situation. Broad purposes can indeed reach far beyond details known or knowable at the time of drafting. A "dangerous weapon" statute of 1840 can include tommy guns, tear gas or atomic bombs. "Vehicle," in a statute of 1840, can properly be read, when sense so suggests, to include an automobile, or a hydroplane that lacks wheels. But for all that, the sound quest does not run primarily in terms of historical intent. It runs in terms of what the words can be made to bear, in making sense in the light of the unforeseen.

III

When it comes to presenting a proposed construction in court, there is an accepted conventional vocabulary. As in argument over points of case-law, the accepted convention still, unhappily requires discussion as if only one single correct meaning could exist. Hence there are two opposing canons on almost every point. An arranged selection is appended. Every lawyer must be familiar with them all : they are still needed tools of argument. At least as early as Fortescue the general picture was clear, on this, to any eye which would see.

Plainly, to make any canon take hold in a particular instance, the construction contended for must be sold, essentially, by means other than the use of the canon : The good sense of the situation and a *simple* construction of the available language to achieve that sense, *by tenable means, out of the statutory language.*

CANONS OF CONSTRUCTION

Statutory interpretation still speaks a diplomatic tongue. Here is some of the technical framework for maneuver.

THRUST	BUT	PARRY
1. A statute cannot go beyond its text.[8]		1. To effect its purpose a statute may be implemented beyond its text.[4]
2. Statutes in derogation of the common law will not be extended by construction.[5]		2. Such acts will be liberally construed if their nature is remedial.[6]
3. Statutes are to be read in the light of the common law and a statute affirming a common law rule is to be construed in accordance with the common law.[7]		3. The common law gives way to a statute which is in consistent with it and when a statute is designed as a revision of a whole body of law applicable to a given subject it supersedes the common law.[8]

3. First National Bank v. DeBerriz, 87 W. Va. 477, 105 S.E. 900 (1921) ; SUTHERLAND, STATUTORY CONSTRUCTION § 388 (2d ed. 1904) ; 59 C.J., *Statutes,* § 575 (1932).
   4. Dooley v. Penn. R.R., 250 Fed. 142 (D. Minn. 1918) ; 59 C.J., *Statutes* § 575 (1932).
   5. Devers v. City of Scranton, 308 Pa. 13, 161 Atl. 540 (1932) ; BLACK, CONSTRUCTION AND INTERPRETATION OF LAWS § 113 (2d ed. 1911) ; SUTHERLAND, STATUTORY CONSTRUCTION § 573 (2d ed. 1904) ; 25 R.C.L., *Statutes* § 281 (1919).
   6. Becker v. Brown, 65 Neb. 264, 91 N.W. 178 (1902) ; BLACK, CONSTRUCTION AND INTERPRETATION OF LAWS § 113 (2d ed. 1911) ; SUTHERLAND, STATUTORY CONSTRUCTION §§ 573-75 (2d ed. 1904) ; 59 C.J., *Statutes* § 657 (1932).
   7. Bandfield v. Bandfield, 117 Mich. 80, 75 N.W. 287 (1898) ; 25 R.C.L., *Statutes* § 280 (1919).
   8. Hamilton v. Rathbone, 175 U.S. 414, 20 Sup. Ct. 155, 44 L. Ed. 219 (1899) ; State v. Lewis, 142 N.C. 626, 55 S.E. 600 (1906) ; 25 R.C.L., *Statutes* §§ 280, 289 (1919).

4. Where a foreign statute which has received construction has been adopted, previous construction is adopted too.[9]

4. It may be rejected where there is conflict with the obvious meaning of the statute or where the foreign decisions are unsatisfactory in reasoning or where the foreign interpretation is not in harmony with the spirit or policy of the laws of the adopting state.[10]

5. Where various states have already adopted the statute, the parent state is followed.[11]

5. Where interpretations of other states are inharmonious, there is no such restraint.[12]

6. Statutes *in pari materia* must be construed together.[13]

6. A statute is not *in pari materia* if its scope and aim are distinct or where a legislative design to depart from the general purpose or policy of previous enactments may be apparent.[14]

7. A statute imposing a new penalty or forfeiture, or a new liability or disability, or creating a new right of action will not be construed as having a retroactive effect.[15]

7. Remedial statutes are to be liberally construed and if a retroactive interpretation will promote the ends of justice, they should receive such construction.[16]

8. Where design has been distinctly stated no place is left for construction.[17]

8. Courts have the power to inquire into real—as distinct from ostensible—purpose.[18]

---

9. Freese v. Tripp, 70 Ill. 496 (1873) ; Black, Construction and Interpretation of Laws § 176 (2d ed. 1911) ; 59 C.J., *Statutes*, §§ 614, 627 (1932) ; 25 R.C.L., *Statutes* § 294 (1919).
10. Bowers v. Smith, 111 Mo. 45, 20 S.W. 101 (1892) ; Black, Construction and Interpretation of Laws § 176 (2d ed. 1911) ; Sutherland, Statutory Construction § 404 (2d ed. 1904) ; 59 C.J., *Statutes* § 628 (1932).
11. Burnside v. Wand, 170 Mo. 531, 71 S.W. 337 (1902).
12. State v. Campbell, 73 Kan. 688, 85 Pac. 784 (1906).
13. Milner v. Gibson, 249 Ky. 594, 61 S.W.2d 273 (1933) ; Black, Construction and Interpretation of Laws § 104 (2d ed. 1911) ; Sutherland, Statutory Construction §§ 443-48 (2d ed. 1904) ; 25 R.C.L., *Statutes* § 285 (1919).
14. Wheelock v. Myers, 64 Kan. 47, 67 Pac. 632 (1902) ; Black, Construction and Interpretation of Laws § 104 (2d ed. 1911) ; Sutherland, Statutory Construction § 449 (2d ed. 1904) ; 59 C.J., *Statutes* § 620 (1932).
15. Keeley v. Great Northern Ry., 139 Wis. 448, 121 N.W. 167 (1909) ; Black, Construction and Interpretation of Laws § 119 (2d ed. 1911).
16. Falls v. Key, 278 S.W. 893 (Tex. Civ. App. 1925) ; Black, Construction and Interpretation of Laws § 120 (2d ed. 1911).
17. Federoff v. Birks Bros., 75 Cal. App. 345, 242 Pac. 885 (1925) ; Sutherland, Statutory Construction § 358 (2d ed. 1904) ; 59 C.J., *Statutes* § 570 (1932).
18. Coulter v. Pool, 187 Cal. 181, 201 Pac. 120 (1921) ; 59 C.J., *Statutes* § 570 (1932).

9. Definitions and rules of construction contained in an interpretation clause are part of the law and binding.[19]

9. Definitions and rules of construction in a statute will not be extended beyond their necessary import nor allowed to defeat intention otherwise manifested.[20]

10. A statutory provision requiring liberal construction does not mean disregard of unequivocal requirements of the statute.[21]

10. Where a rule of construction is provided within the statute itself the rule should be applied.[22]

11. Titles do not control meaning; preambles do not expand scope; section headings do not change language.[23]

11. The title may be consulted as a guide when there is doubt or obscurity in the body; preambles may be consulted to determine rationale, and thus the true construction of terms; section headings may be looked upon as part of the statute itself.[24]

12. If language is plain and unambiguous it must be given effect.[25]

12. Not when literal interpretation would lead to absurd or mischievous consequences or thwart manifest purpose.[26]

13. Words and phrases which have received judicial construction before enactment are to be understood according to that construction.[27]

13. Not if the statute clearly requires them to have a different meaning.[28]

---

19. Smith v. State, 28 Ind. 321 (1867) ; BLACK, CONSTRUCTION AND INTERPRETATION OF LAWS § 89 (2d ed. 1911) ; 59 C.J., *Statutes* § 567 (1932).

20. *In re* Bissell, 245 App. Div. 395, 282 N.Y. Supp. 983 (4th Dep't 1935) ; BLACK, CONSTRUCTION AND INTERPRETATION OF LAWS § 89 (2d ed. 1911) ; 59 C.J., *Statutes* § 566 (1932).

21. Los Angeles County v. Payne, 82 Cal. App. 210, 255 Pac. 281 (1927) ; SUTHERLAND, STATUTORY CONSTRUCTION § 360 (2d ed. 1904) ; 59 C.J., *Statutes* § 567 (1932).

22. State *ex rel.* Triay v. Burr, 79 Fla. 290, 84 So. 61 (1920) ; SUTHERLAND, STATUTORY CONSTRUCTION § 360 (2d ed. 1904) ; 59 C.J., *Statutes* § 567 (1932).

23. Westbrook v. McDonald, 184 Ark. 740, 44 S.W. 2d 331 (1931) ; Huntworth v. Tanner, 87 Wash. 670, 152 Pac. 523 (1915) ; BLACK, CONSTRUCTION AND INTERPRETATION OF LAWS §§ 83-85 (2d ed. 1911) ; SUTHERLAND, STATUTORY CONSTRUCTION §§ 339-42 (2d ed. 1904) ; 59 C.J., *Statutes* § 599 (1932) ; 25 R.C.L., *Statutes* §§ 266-267 (1919).

24. Brown v. Robinson, 275 Mass. 55, 175 N.E. 269 (1931) ; Gulley v. Jackson, 165 Miss. 103, 145 So. 905 (1933) ; BLACK, CONSTRUCTION AND INTERPRETATION OF LAWS §§ 83-85 (2d ed. 1911) ; SUTHERLAND, STATUTORY CONSTRUCTION §§ 339-42 (2d ed. 1904) ; 59 C.J., *Statutes* §§ 598-99 (1932) ; 25 R.C.L., *Statutes* §§ 266, 267 (1919).

25. Newhall v. Sanger, 92 U.S. 761, 23 L. Ed. 769 (1875) ; BLACK, CONSTRUCTION AND INTERPRETATION OF LAWS § 51 (2d ed. 1911) ; 59 C.J., *Statutes* § 569 (1932) ; 25 R.C.L., *Statutes* §§ 213, 225 (1919).

26. Clark v. Murray, 141 Kan. 533, 41 P.2d 1042 (1935) ; SUTHERLAND, STATUTORY CONSTRUCTION § 363 (2d ed. 1904) ; 59 C.J., *Statutes* § 573 (1932) ; 25 R.C.L., *Statutes* §§ 214, 257 (1919).

27. Scholze v. Sholze, 2 Tenn. App. 80 (M.S. 1925) ; BLACK, CONSTRUCTION AND INTERPRETATION OF LAWS § 65 (2d ed. 1911) ; SUTHERLAND, STATUTORY CONSTRUCTION § 363 (2d ed. 1904).

28. Dixon v. Robbins, 246 N.Y. 169, 158 N.E. 63 (1927) ; BLACK, CONSTRUCTION AND INTERPRETATION OF LAWS § 65 (2d ed. 1911) ; SUTHERLAND, STATUTORY CONSTRUCTION § 363 (2d ed. 1904).

14. After enactment, judicial decision upon interpretation of particular terms and phrases controls.[29]

15. Words are to be taken in their ordinary meaning unless they are technical terms or words of art.[31]

16. Every word and clause must be given effect.[33]

17. The same language used repeatedly in the same connection is presumed to bear the same meaning throughout the statute.[35]

18. Words are to be interpreted according to the proper grammatical effect of their arrangement within the statute.[37]

19. Exceptions not made cannot be read.[39]

14. Practical construction by executive officers is strong evidence of true meaning.[30]

15. Popular words may bear a technical meaning and technical words may have a popular signification and they should be so construed as to agree with evident intention or to make the statute operative.[32]

16. If inadvertantly inserted or if repugnant to the rest of the statute, they may be rejected as surplusage.[34]

17. This presumption will be disregarded where it is necessary to assign different meanings to make the statute consistent.[36]

18. Rules of grammar will be disregarded where strict adherence would defeat purpose.[38]

19. The letter is only the "bark." Whatever is within the reason of the law is within the law itself.[40]

---

29. Eau Claire National Bank v. Benson, 106 Wis. 624, 82 N.W. 604 (1900) ; BLACK, CONSTRUCTION AND INTERPRETATION OF LAWS § 93 (2d ed. 1911).
30. State *ex rel.* Bashford v. Frear, 138 Wis. 536, 120 N.W. 216 (1909) ; BLACK, CONSTRUCTION AND INTERPRETATION OF LAWS § 94 (2d ed. 1911) ; 25 R.C.L., *Statutes* § 274 (1919).
31. Hawley Coal Co. v. Bruce, 252 Ky. 455, 67 S.W.2d 703 (1934) ; BLACK, CONSTRUCTION AND INTERPRETATION OF LAWS § 63 (2d ed. 1911) ; SUTHERLAND, STATUTORY CONSTRUCTION, §§ 390, 393 (2d ed. 1904) ; 59 C.J., *Statutes*, §§ 577, 578 (1932).
32. Robinson v. Varnell, 16 Tex. 382 (1856) ; BLACK, CONSTRUCTION AND INTERPRETATION OF LAWS § 63 (2d ed. 1911) ; SUTHERLAND, STATUTORY CONSTRUCTION § 395 (2d ed. 1904) ; 59 C.J., *Statutes* §§ 577, 578 (1932).
33. *In re* Terry's Estate, 218 N.Y. 218, 112 N.E. 931 (1916) ; BLACK, CONSTRUCTION AND INTERPRETATION OF LAWS § 60 (2d ed. 1911) ; SUTHERLAND, STATUTORY CONSTRUCTION § 380 (2d ed. 1904).
34. United States v. York, 131 Fed. 323 (C.C.S.D.N.Y. 1904) ; BLACK, CONSTRUCTION AND INTERPRETATION OF LAWS § 60 (2d ed. 1911) ; SUTHERLAND, STATUTORY CONSTRUCTION §§ 384 (2d ed. 1904).
35. Spring Canyon Coal Co. v. Industrial Comm'n, 74 Utah 103, 277 Pac. 206 (1929) ; BLACK, CONSTRUCTION AND INTERPRETATION OF LAWS § 53 (2d ed. 1911).
36. State v. Knowles, 90 Md. 646, 45 Atl. 877 (1900) ; BLACK, CONSTRUCTION AND INTERPRETATION OF LAWS § 53 (2d ed. 1911).
37. Harris v. Commonwealth, 142 Va. 620, 128 S.E. 578 (1925) ; BLACK, CONSTRUCTION AND INTERPRETATION OF LAWS § 55 (2d ed. 1911) ; SUTHERLAND, STATUTORY CONSTRUCTION § 408 (2d ed. 1904).
38. Fisher v. Connard, 100 Pa. 63 (1882) ; BLACK, CONSTRUCTION AND INTERPRETATION OF LAWS § 55 (2d ed. 1911) ; SUTHERLAND, STATUTORY CONSTRUCTION § 409 (2d ed. 1904).
39. Lima v. Cemetery Ass'n, 42 Ohio St. 128 (1884) ; 25 R.C.L., *Statutes* § 230 (1919).
40. Flynn v. Prudential Ins. Co., 207 N.Y. 315, 100 N.E. 794 (1913) ; 59 C.J., *Statutes* § 573 (1932).

20. Expression of one thing excludes another.[41]

20. The language may fairly comprehend many different cases where some only are expressly mentioned by way of example.[42]

21. General terms are to receive a general construction.[43]

21. They may be limited by specific terms with which they are associated or by the scope and purpose of the statute.[44]

22. It is a general rule of construction that where general words follow an enumeration they are to be held as applying only to persons and things of the same general kind or class specifically mentioned (*ejusdem generis*).[45]

22. General words must operate on something. Further, *ejusdem generis* is only an aid in getting the meaning and does not warrant confining the operations of a statute within narrower limits than were intended.[46]

23. Qualifying or limiting words or clauses are to be referred to the next preceding antecedent.[47]

23. Not when evident sense and meaning require a different construction.[48]

24. Punctuation will govern when a statute is open to two constructions.[49]

24. Punctuation marks will not control the plain and evident meaning of language.[50]

---

41. Detroit v. Redford Twp., 253 Mich. 453, 235 N.W. 217 (1931); BLACK, CONSTRUCTION AND INTERPRETATION OF LAWS § 72 (2d ed. 1911); SUTHERLAND, STATUTORY CONSTRUCTION §§ 491-94 (2d ed. 1904).

42. Springer v. Philippine Islands, 277 U.S. 189, 48 Sup. Ct. 480, 72 L. Ed. 845 (1928); BLACK, CONSTRUCTION AND INTERPRETATION OF LAWS § 72 (2d ed. 1911); SUTHERLAND, STATUTORY CONSTRUCTION § 495 (2d ed. 1904).

43. De Witt v. San Francisco, 2 Cal. 289 (1852); BLACK, CONSTRUCTION AND INTERPRETATION OF LAWS § 68 (2d ed. 1911); 59 C.J., *Statutes* § 580 (1932).

44. People *ex rel.* Krause v. Harrison, 191 Ill. 257, 61 N.E. 99 (1901); BLACK, CONSTRUCTION AND INTERPRETATION OF LAWS § 69 (1911); SUTHERLAND, STATUTORY CONSTRUCTION § 347 (2d ed. 1904).

45. Hull Hospital v. Wheeler, 216 Iowa 1394, 250 N.W. 637 (1933); BLACK, CONSTRUCTION AND INTERPRETATION OF LAWS § 71 (2d ed. 1911); SUTHERLAND, STATUTORY CONSTRUCTION §§ 422-34 (2d ed. 1904); 59 C.J., *Statutes* § 581 (1932); 25 R.C.L., *Statutes* § 240 (1919).

46. Texas v. United States, 292 U.S. 522, 54 Sup. Ct. 819, 78 L. Ed. 1402 (1934); Grosjean v. American Paint Works, 160 So. 449 (La. App. 1935); BLACK, CONSTRUCTION AND INTERPRETATION OF LAWS § 71 (2d ed. 1911); SUTHERLAND, STATUTORY CONSTRUCTION, §§ 437-41 (2d ed. 1904); 59 C.J., *Statutes* § 581 (1932); 25 R.C.L., *Statutes* § 240 (1919).

47. Dunn v. Bryan, 77 Utah 604, 299 Pac. 253 (1931); BLACK, CONSTRUCTION AND INTERPRETATION OF LAWS § 73 (2d ed. 1911); SUTHERLAND, STATUTORY CONSTRUCTION §§ 420, 421 (2d ed. 1904); 59 C.J., *Statutes* § 583 (1932).

48. Myer v. Ada County, 50 Idaho 39, 293 Pac. 322 (1930); BLACK, CONSTRUCTION AND INTERPRETATION OF LAWS § 73 (2d ed. 1911); SUTHERLAND, STATUTORY CONSTRUCTION §§ 420, 421 (2d ed. 1904); 59 C.J., *Statutes* § 583 (1932).

49. United States v. Marshall Field & Co., 18 C.C.P.A. 228 (1930); BLACK, CONSTRUCTION AND INTERPRETATION OF LAWS § 88 (2d ed. 1911); SUTHERLAND, STATUTORY CONSTRUCTION § 361 (2d ed. 1904); 59 C.J., *Statutes* § 590 (1932).

50. State v. Baird, 36 Ariz. 531, 288 Pac. 1 (1930); BLACK, CONSTRUCTION AND INTERPRETATION OF LAWS § 87 (2d ed. 1911); SUTHERLAND, STATUTORY CONSTRUCTION § 361 (2d ed. 1904); 59 C.J., *Statutes* § 590 (1932).

25. It must be assumed that language has been chosen with due regard to grammatical propriety and is not interchangeable on mere conjecture.[51]

25. "And" and "or" may be read interchangeably whenever the change is necessary to give the statute sense and effect.[52]

26. There is a distinction between words of permission and mandatory words.[53]

26. Words imparting permission may be read as mandatory and words imparting command may be read as permissive when such construction is made necessary by evident intention or by the rights of the public.[54]

27. A proviso qualifies the provision immediately preceding.[55]

27. It may clearly be intended to have a wider scope.[56]

28. When the enacting clause is general, a proviso is construed strictly.[57]

28. Not when it is necessary to extend the proviso to persons or cases which come within its equity.[58]

51. Hines v. Mills, 187 Ark. 465, 60 S.W.2d 181 (1933); BLACK, CONSTRUCTION AND INTERPRETATION OF LAWS § 75 (2d ed. 1911).
52. Fulghum v. Bleakley, 177 S.C. 286, 181 S.E. 30 (1935); SUTHERLAND, STATUTORY CONSTRUCTION § 397 (2d ed. 1904); 25 R.C.L., *Statutes* § 226 (1919).
53. Koch & Dryfus v. Bridges, 45 Miss. 247 (1871); BLACK, CONSTRUCTION AND INTERPRETATION OF LAWS § 150 (2d ed. 1911).
54. Jennings v. Suggs, 180 Ga. 141, 178 S.E. 282 (1935); Ewing v. Union Central Bank, 254 Ky. 623, 72 S.W.2d 4 (1934); BLACK, CONSTRUCTION AND INTERPRETATION OF LAWS § 151 (2d ed. 1911); 59 C.J., *Statutes* § 631 (1932).
55. State *ex rel.* Higgs v. Summers, 118 Neb. 189, 223 N.W. 957 (1929); BLACK, CONSTRUCTION AND INTERPRETATION OF LAWS § 130 (2d ed. 1911); SUTHERLAND, STATUTORY CONSTRUCTION § 352 (2d ed. 1904); 59 C.J., *Statutes* § 640 (1932).
56. Reuter v. San Mateo County, 220 Cal. 314, 30 P.2d 417 (1934); BLACK, CONSTRUCTION AND INTERPRETATION OF LAWS § 130 (2d ed. 1911).
57. Montgomery v. Martin, 294 Pa. 25, 143 Atl. 505 (1928); BLACK, CONSTRUCTION AND INTERPRETATION OF LAWS § 131 (2d ed. 1911); SUTHERLAND, STATUTORY CONSTRUCTION § 322 (2d ed. 1904).
58. Forscht v. Green, 53 Pa. 138 (1866); BLACK, CONSTRUCTION AND INTERPRETATION OF LAWS § 131 (2d ed. 1911).

PRAGMATICS AND THE MAXIMS OF INTERPRETATION

GEOFFREY P. MILLER*

Table of Contents

INTRODUCTION

How can one explain the puzzling persistence of maxims of statutory interpretation?[1] Their intellectual justification was long ago con-

*   Professor of Law, University of Chicago Law School. I would like to thank Cass R.
Sunstein, Richard A. Posner and Carol Rose for extremely insightful comments, as well as
John Goldsmith, Richard Helmholz, Zanvel Klein and Peter Stein for helpful suggestions.
     1. I use the term "maxims" in its conventional sense, as a brief, highly general
rule not embodied in legislation or other formal enactment by a law-making body.

sidered demolished by Karl Llewellyn's devastating critique, in which
he demonstrated—or appeared to demonstrate—that for every maxim
there is an equal and opposite counter-maxim, thus casting maxims
into a slough of indeterminacy.[2] Maxims, after Llewellyn's work, were
considered by most legal academics to be mere conclusory explanations
appended after the fact to justify results reached on other grounds. As
such, they were perhaps innocuous in the hands of judges who understood their proper use. When applied by the less sophisticated, however,
the maxims could be dangerous: they could mislead a decision-maker
into thinking that cases could actually be decided on the basis of maxims rather than on the sounder grounds of legislative intent or social
policy. Still, in the years following Llewellyn's work, it was conceivable
that the outdated reliance on maxims would soon give way to a more
enlightened approach to statutory interpretation.

    This optimism did not prove warranted. Judges have continued
to cite the maxims of statutory interpretation in deciding cases. Indeed,
they have continued to speak as if the maxims have real bite in determining outcomes. Consider the Supreme Court's recent decision in
Breininger v. Sheet Metal Workers International Association.[3] At issue
was a provision of the Labor-Management Reporting and Disclosure
Act, which forbids a union to "fine, suspend, or otherwise discipline"
a union member for exercising rights secured by the statute.[4] The union
had allegedly passed over a dissident member in making referrals
through its hiring hall. The Supreme Court held that the alleged discrimination did not fall within the phrase "otherwise discipline," since
the term "discipline" denotes only actions taken by a union to enforce
its own rules. However, the Court also observed that "the specifically
enumerated types of discipline—fine, expulsion, and suspension—imply
some sort of established disciplinary process rather than ad hoc retal-
iation by individual union officers."[5] As the Court acknowledged, this
was a reference to the hoary maxim of *ejusdem generis*—general terms
in a list should be interpreted with reference to the types of matters
contained in the specific items on the list.[6]

    There are many other cases like *Breininger* in which courts use
maxims of interpretation with apparent complacence. Thus, although
Llewellyn's critique has perhaps induced greater caution,[7] it has un-

---

    2. K. LLEWELLYN, THE COMMON LAW TRADITION: DECIDING APPEALS 521-35
(1966). *See also* Wald, *Some Observations on the Use of Legislative History in the 1981 Supreme
Court Term,* 68 IOWA L. REV. 195, 215 (1983).
    3. 110 S. Ct. 424 (1989).
    4. 29 U.S.C. § 411(a)(5) (1982).
    5. *Breininger,* 110 S. Ct. at 439.
    6. *Id. Ejusdem generis* means literally "of the same kind."
    7. Caution has been most marked with respect to the principle of *expressio unius
est exclusio alterius* (the expression of one thing implies the exclusion of other things not

questionably failed to extinguish the maxims as guides to interpretation.[8] Indeed, there is reason to believe that the maxims are making something of a comeback. Over the past decade, the Supreme Court has edged steadily away from reliance on legislative history in favor of plain meaning.[9] Moreover, the Court increasingly is willing to defer to statutory language even when the results appear misguided as a matter of social policy—thus undermining, although not entirely repudiating, the doctrine that a matter may be within the letter of a statute yet not be within its spirit.[10] All this enhanced attention to text creates a potentially fertile ground for a revival of the maxims.

The ferment in statutory interpretation in the courts has been more than matched by a revival of a long-moribund scholarly debate on the subject.[11] Here, too, we see at least the beginnings of a revival of interest

---

expressed). *See, e.g.,* Morris v. Gresette, 432 U.S. 491, 506 n.22 (1977) (maxim not to be regarded as conclusive when other factors counsel a different result); Wachovia Bank & Trust Co. v. National Student Mktg. Corp., 650 F.2d 342, 354-55 (D.C. Cir. 1980), *cert. denied,* 452 U.S. 954 (1981); National Petroleum Refiners Ass'n v. FTC, 482 F.2d 672, 676 (D.C. Cir. 1973), *cert. denied,* 415 U.S. 951 (1974) (maxim is "increasingly considered unreliable . . . for it stands on the faulty premise that all possible alternative or supplemental provisions were necessarily considered and rejected by the legislative draftsmen").

   8.   *See* Murphy, *Old Maxims Never Die: The "Plain-Meaning Rule" and Statutory Interpretation in the "Modern" Federal Courts,* 75 COLUM. L. REV. 1299 (1975).

   9.   *See, e.g.,* United States v. Ron Pair Enters., 109 S. Ct. 1026, 1030 (1989). Justice Scalia in particular has advanced this view. *See, e.g.,* Blanchard v. Bergeron, 109 S. Ct. 939, 97 (1989 (Scalia, J., dissenting) ("that the court should refer to . . . a document issued by a single committee of a single house as the action *of Congress* displays the level of unreality that our unrestrained use of legislative history has attained"); Pennsylvania v. Union Gas Co., 109 S. Ct. 2273, 2296 (1989) (Scalia, J., concurring in part and dissenting in part) ("it is our task, as I see it, not to enter the minds of Members of Congress—who need have nothing in mind in order for their votes to be both lawful and effective—but rather to give fair and reasonable meaning to the text of the United States Code"); Hirschey v. FERC, 777 F.2d 1, 7-8 (D.C. Cir. 1985) (Scalia, J., dissenting) ("I think it time for courts to become concerned about the fact that routine deference to the detail of committee reports, and the predictable expansion in that detail which routine deference has produced, are converting a system of judicial construction into a system of committee-staff prescription"). For a criticism of excessive reliance on legislative history, see OFFICE OF LEGAL POL'Y, USING AND MISUSING LEGISLATIVE HISTORY: A RE-EVALUATION OF THE STATUS OF LEGISLATIVE HISTORY IN STATUTORY INTERPRETATION, REP. TO THE ATT'Y GEN. (1989).

   10.   *See, e.g.,* Green v. Bock Laundry Mach. Co., 109 S. Ct. 1981 (1989); TVA v. Hill, 437 U.S. 153, 193-95 (1978). *But see* Public Citizen v. United States Dep't of Justice, 109 S. Ct. 2558 (1989) (Court declined to follow the plain meaning of a statute when doing so would have apparently run counter to the intent of Congress and raised a constitutional issue).

   11.   For a sampling of the important recent publications, see R. POSNER, THE FEDERAL COURTS: CRISIS AND REFORM 261-93 (1985); Aleinikoff, *Updating Statutory Interpretation,* 87 MICH. L. REV. 20 (1988); Easterbrook, *Statutes' Domains,* 50 U. CHI. L. REV. 537 (1982); Easterbrook, *The Role of Original Intent in Statutory Construction,* 11 HARV. J. L. & PUB. POL. 59 (1988); Eskridge, *Dynamic Statutory Interpretation,* 135 U. PA. L. REV. 1479 (1987); Eskridge, *The New Textualism,* 37 UCLA L. REV. 621 (1990); Eskridge & Frickey, *Statutory Interpretation and Practical Reasoning,* 42 STAN. L. REV. 321 (1990); Eskridge, *Spinning Legislative Supremacy,* 78 GEO. L. J. 281 (1989); Eskridge, *Public Values in Statutory Interpretation,* 4 U. PA. L. REV. 1007 (1989); Farber, *Statutory Interpretation and Legislative*

in the maxims. The leading figure in this enterprise is my colleague Cass Sunstein. In a recent article,[12] Sunstein claims that the Llewellyn critique of the maxims as indeterminate and mutually contradictory is greatly overstated—that in fact "some of the canons actually influenced judicial behavior insofar as they reflected background norms that helped to give meaning to statutory words or to resolve hard cases."[13] Sunstein's work is likely to stimulate greater attention to the maxims than they have received for years.[14]

This Article examines some of the more important maxims from the standpoint both of history and of contemporary linguistic philosophy. It demonstrates in Part I that certain interpretive principles seem to display a remarkable coherence over time. A variety of explanatory rules available in contemporary jurisprudence can also be observed in legal systems from very different times and places.

This is not to say that maxims of interpretation display perfect conservation of form across legal systems. There are many variants; maxims found in the current system are not observed in other traditions and maxims found in other systems are not reflected in contemporary jurisprudence. Nevertheless, sufficient continuity exists across systems to suggest that the maxims must reflect some relatively universal principles for interpreting legal rules.

In Part II, this Article turns to the work of a leading contemporary linguistic philosopher, the late Paul Grice. Grice proposed a system of maxims for interpreting language in conversational settings that appear remarkably similar in form to many of the leading maxims of statutory interpretation. This Article attempts to show that the maxims of statutory interpretation can be viewed as instances of Grice's general framework of interpretation. The Appendix summarizes the results of

---

Supremacy, 78 GEO. L. J. 281 (1989); Farina, *Statutory Interpretation and the Balance of Power in an Administrative State*, 89 COLUM. L. REV. 452 (1989); Hurd, *Sovereignty in Silence*, 99 YALE L. J. 947 (1990); Macey, *Promoting Public-Regarding Legislation Through Statutory Interpretation: An Interest-Group Method*, 86 COLUM. L. REV. 223 (1986); Popkin, *The Collaborative Model of Statutory Interpretation*, 61 S. CAL. L. REV. 541 (1988); Posner, *Legislation and Its Interpretation*, 68 NEB. L. REV. 431 (1989); Posner, *Legal Formalism, Legal Realism, and the Interpretation of Statutes and the Constitution*, 37 CASE W. RES. L. REV. 179 (1986); Posner, *Statutory Interpretation—In the Classroom and the Courtroom*, 50 U. CHI. L. REV. 800 (1983); Posner, *Economics, Politics, and the Reading of Statutes and the Constitution*, 49 U. CHI. L. REV. 263 (1982).

    12.   Sunstein, *Interpreting Statutes in the Regulatory State*, 103 HARV. L. REV. 405 (1989). *See also* C. SUNSTEIN, AFTER THE RIGHTS REVOLUTION: RECONCEIVING THE REGULATORY STATE 111-226 (1990).

    13.   *Id.* at 452. Sunstein goes on to provide an insightful and original catalogue of the canons by grouping them into four categories: orientation to meaning, interpretive instructions, institutional considerations for improvement of law-making and substantive purposes. *Id.* at 454-460.

    14.   For a promising use of maxims to resolve choice-of-law questions, see Kramer, *Rethinking Choice of Law*, 90 COLUM. L. REV. 277 (1990).

the analysis by incorporating the leading maxims within the Gricean framework.

The surprising similarity between Grice's philosophy of language and the maxims of statutory interpretation suggests that the maxims capture something important about the meaning of words. Again, however, it should be emphasized that this Article does not attempt to *prove* that the maxims are of value to judges in deciding cases. The goal is instead the more narrow one of showing that the traditional maxims of statutory interpretation are homologous in important respects to the work of a leading linguistic philosopher. One can infer from this relationship that the maxims state principles of interpretation that possess features of considerable generality, but the practical utility of the maxims and the validity of analogizing interpretation of legislation to the analysis of conversation, are issues beyond the scope of this Article.

I. The Maxims in History

The renewed attention to statutory language and to the canons of construction is a healthy development. Even a passing knowledge and respect for history would suggest that maxims are integral to the process of interpretation. Take an ancient example: the *Mimamsa* of Jaimini, dating from approximately 500 B.C., which systematized principles for interpreting sacred Hindu texts, including texts containing what we would now consider secular law.[15] Several of the *Mimamsa* principles display a striking similarity to modern maxims of statutory construction:

Mimansa *Principle*	*Maxim*
1. Every word should have a purposeful meaning.	A court is obliged to give effect if possible to every word Congress used.[16]
2. The same words should have the same meaning.	The same words used in the same statute should be taken to have the same meanings.[17]

---

15. *See* V. Sarathi, The Interpretation of Statutes 6 (1981).

16. Bowsher v. Merck & Co., 460 U.S. 824, 833 (1983); Fidelity Fed. Sav. & Loan Ass'n v. De La Cuesta, 458 U.S. 141, 163 (1982); American Textile Mfrs. Inst. v. Donovan, 452 U.S. 490, 514 (1981); Colautti v. Franklin, 439 U.S. 379, 392 (1979); Reiter v. Sonotone Corp., 442 U.S. 330, 339 (1979); Weinberger v. Hynson, Westcott & Dunning, Inc., 412 U.S. 609, 633 (1973).

17. Washington Metro. Transit Auth. v. Johnson, 467 U.S. 925, 935-36 (1984); BankAmerica Corp. v. United States, 462 U.S. 122, 129 (1983); Mohasco Corp. v. Silver, 447 U.S. 807, 826 (1980); Northcross v. Memphis Bd. of Educ., 412 U.S. 427, 428 (1973); Erlenbaugh v. United States, 409 U.S. 239, 243-44 (1972).

3.	All ideas should be reconciled with the principal one.	The meaning of a statute is to be looked for, not in any single section, but in all the parts together and in their relation to the end in view.[18]
4.	Contradiction should not be presumed and reconciliation should be attempted.	When two statutes are capable of coexistence, it is the duty of the courts, absent a clearly expressed congressional intention to the contrary, to regard each as effective.[19]
5.	An interpretation which makes a word or phrase meaningless should be avoided.	There is a strong presumption against interpreting a statute so as to render it ineffective.[20]

Maxims play important roles in Judeo-Christian systems of interpretation as well. Consider the following analogies with Christian interpretive principles:

	Principle	*Maxim*
1.	The meaning of an ambiguous word or passage should be understood as consistent with the preceding and following parts.[21]	The meaning of a statute is to be looked for, not in any single section, but in all the parts together.[22]

---

18. Richards v. United States, 369 U.S. 1, 11 (1962); Panama Ref. Co. v. Ryan, 293 U.S. 388, 433 (1935) (Cardozo, J., dissenting).

19. Rodriguez v. United States, 480 U.S. 522, 525 (1987); American Bank & Trust Co. v. Dallas County, 463 U.S. 855, 868 (1983); Kremer v. Chemical Constr. Corp., 456 U.S. 461, 468 (1982); Morton v. Mancari, 417 U.S. 535, 551 (1974).

20. Bird v. United States, 187 U.S. 118, 124 (1902); United States v. Blasius, 397 F.2d 203, 207 n.9 (2d Cir. 1968), cert. dismissed, 393 U.S. 1008 (1969).

21. See, e.g., St. Augustine, On Christian Doctrine, Book III, § 2 (D.W. Robertson ed. 1958): ("[I]t is necessary to examine the context of the preceeding and following parts surrounding the ambiguous place, so that we may determine which of the meanings among those which suggest themselves it would allow to be consistent"); J. Calvin, Institutes VI xvi 23 (1536) ("There are many statements in scripture the meaning of which depends upon their context").

22. Richards v. United States, 369 U.S. 1, 11 (1962); Panama Ref. Co. v. Ryan, 293 U.S. 388, 434 (1935 (Cardozo, J., dissenting).

2. The meaning of an ambiguous word or passage should be interpreted in light of the underlying purposes of the author.[23]

In all cases of statutory construction, our task is to interpret the words in light of the purposes Congress sought to serve.[24]

3. The meaning of an ambiguous word or passage should be interpreted in the manner in which it would be understood by the audience to which it is addressed.[25]

It is a fundamental canon of interpretation that unless otherwise defined, words be interpreted as taking their ordinary, contemporary common meaning.[26]

4. An ambiguous passage should be interpreted in light of other passages in the same text.[27]

A statute section should not be read in isolation from the context of the whole act; instead a court should look to the

---

23. *See, e.g.*, St. Augustine, *supra* note 21, at § 15 ("[s]cripture teaches nothing but charity, nor condemns anything except cupidity"); *id.* at § 23 ("what is read should be subjected to diligent scrutiny until an interpretation contributing to the reign of charity is produced"); St. Augustine, *The Harmony of the Gospels*, in 6 A Select Library of the Nicene and Post-Nicene Fathers of the Christian Church 135 (P. Schaff ed. 1886-89) [hereinafter Nicene and Post-Nicene Fathers] ("[i]n any man's words the thing which we ought narrowly to regard is only the writer's thought which was meant to be expressed, and to which the words ought to be subservient"); J. Calvin, Institutes II viii 8 (1536) ("[i]n each commandment we must investigate what it is concerned with; then we must seek out its purpose, until we find what the Lawgiver testifies there to be pleasing or displeasing to himself").

24. *See* Chapman v. Houston Welfare Rights Org., 441 U.S. 600, 608 (1979); Affiliated Ute Citizens v. United States, 406 U.S. 128, 151 (1972); Superintendent of Ins. v. Bankers Life & Casualty Co., 404 U.S. 6, 12 (1971); SEC v. National Sec., Inc., 393 U.S. 453, 467 (1969); Tcherepin v. Knight, 389 U.S. 332, 336 (1967).

25. St. Augustine, *supra* note 21, at § 25 ("[S]ome things are taught for everyone in general; others are directed toward particular classes of people").

26. Community for Creative Non-Violence v. Reid, 109 S. Ct. 2166, 2172 (1989); Kosak v. United States, 465 U.S. 848, 853 (1984); Bowsher v. Merck & Co., 460 U.S. 824, 862 (1983) (Blackmun, J., concurring and dissenting); Russello v. United States, 464 U.S. 16, 21 (1983); American Tobacco Corp. v. Patterson, 456 U.S. 63, 68 (1982); Diamond v. Chakrabarty, 447 U.S. 303, 308 (1980); Group Life & Health Ins. Co. v. Royal Drug Co., 440 U.S. 205, 211 (1979); Perrin v. United States, 444 U.S. 37, 42 (1979); Richards v. United States, 369 U.S. 1, 9 (1962).

27. St. Augustine, *supra* note 21, at § 38 ("[W]hen . . . from a single passage in the scripture not one but two or more meanings are elicited, even if what he who wrote the passage intended remains hidden, there is no danger if any of the meanings may be seen to be congruous with the truth taught in other passages of the holy scriptures"); T. Parker, Calvin's Old Testament Commentaries 80 (1986) (for Calvin, "the context is all important. Individual words or clauses are not allowed any eccentricity; they are controlled by the context. Conversely, the meaning of the context is understood by the interrelationship of the meanings of the individual parts").

4. *(continued)*   provisions of the whole law, and
                                      to its object and policy.[28]

5. A text should not be read   When two statutes are capable
   to be self-contradictory.[29]   of coexistence, it is the duty of
                                      the courts, absent a clearly
                                      expressed congressional
                                      intention to the contrary, to
                                      regard each as effective.[30]

6. A text should be read to   Interpretations which would
   avoid absurdity.[31]   produce absurd results are to be
                                      avoided if alternative
                                      interpretations consistent with
                                      the legislative purpose are
                                      available.[32]

---

28. Davis v. Michigan Dep't of Treasury, 109 S. Ct. 1500, 1504 (1989); Gomez v. United States, 109 S. Ct. 2237, 2241 (1989); Pilot Life Ins. Co. v. Dedeaux, 481 U.S. 41, 51 (1987); United States v. Morton, 467 U.S. 822, 828 (1984); Richards v. United States, 369 U.S. 1, 11 (1962); Helvering v. Gregory, 69 F.2d 809, 810-11 (2d Cir. 1934) (Hand, J.) ("The meaning of a sentence may be more than that of the separate words, as a melody is more than the notes, and no degree of particularity can ever obviate recourse to the setting in which all appear, and which all collectively create").

29. ST. AUGUSTINE, *supra* note 21, § 52-53 (interpreting apparently self-contradictory biblical passages as being internally consistent); St. Augustine, *Sermons on New Testament Lessons*, NICENE AND POST-NICENE FATHERS, *supra* note 23, at 360 ("holy scripture will in no part disagree with itself"); St. Augustine, *Reply to Faustus the Manichaean*, in 4 NICENE AND POST-NICENE FATHERS, *supra* note 23, at 180 ("[i]f we are perplexed by an apparent contradiction in scripture, it is not permissible to say, the author of this book is mistaken; instead, the manuscript is faulty, or the translation is wrong, or you have not understood . . ."); J. CALVIN, HARMONY OF THE FIRST FOUR BOOKS OF MOSES (1563); J. CALVIN, HARMONY OF THE SYNOPTIC GOSPELS (1555).

30. Morton v. Mancari, 417 U.S. 535, 551 (1974). *See also* American Bank & Trust Co. v. Dallas County, 463 U.S. 855, 868 (1983); Kremer v. Chemical Constr. Corp., 456 U.S. 461, 468 (1982).

31. Chrysostom, *Homily 17 on Genesis, cited in* J. ROGERS & D. McKIM, THE AUTHORITY AND INTERPRETATION OF THE BIBLE 19 (1979), explaining:
[W]e should not take these words [that God walked in the Garden of Eden] too lightly, but neither should we interpret them as they stand. We ought rather to reflect that such simple speech is used because of our weakness, and in order that our salvation be brought about in a manner worthy of God. For if we wish to take words just as they are, and not explain them in a way which befits God, will not the result be utter absurdity?

32. Public Citizen v. United States Dept. of Justice, 109 S. Ct. 2558, 2566-67 (1989); Brock v. Pierce County, 476 U.S. 253, 258-59 (1986); O'Connor v. United States, 479 U.S. 27, 31 (1986); Griffin v. Oceanic Contractors, 458 U.S. 564, 571 (1982).

7. A text in general should be interpreted according to its plain meaning.[33]

If the meaning of a statute is plain, that meaning is ordinarily conclusive.[34]

8. A purely literal interpretation is not favored if the context and evident intent of the author supports some other meaning.[35]

A particular interpretation may appear to be within the letter of the statute, yet not within the statute or the intention of its framers.[36]

In Jewish tradition maxims of interpretation also play an important role, although the correlation between Jewish maxims and those we recognize in contemporary American law is perhaps less exact than the instances discussed above.[37] The leading set of interpretive maxims in Jewish law is the thirteen rules of biblical interpretation set forth by Rabbi Ishmael ben Elisha, taken from the introduction to the *Sifra*, a Talmudic commentary to the Book of Leviticus. Among the thirteen rules are the following:

---

33. ROGERS & MCKIM, *supra* note 3, at 21 ("[t]he practice of importing into holy scripture alien ideas of one's own imagination instead of accepting what stands written in the text, in my opinion, carries great danger for those who have the hardihood to follow it"); J. WEIDENBACH, JOHN CALVIN AS BIBLICAL COMMENTATOR: AN INVESTIGATION INTO CALVIN'S USE OF JOHN CHRYSOSTOM AS AN EXEGETICAL TUTOR 30 (1974) ("not to turn aside even to the slightest degree from the genuine, simple sense of scripture and to allow . . . no liberties by twisting the plain meaning of the words").
34. Board of Governors v. Dimension Finan. Corp., 474 U.S. 361, 368 (1986); North Dakota v. United States, 460 U.S. 300, 312 (1983); Jefferson County Pharmaceutical Ass'n, Inc. v. Abbott Laboratories, Inc., 460 U.S. 150, 157 (1983); Griffin v. Oceanic Contractors, 458 U.S. 564, 570 (1982); Rodriguez v. Compass Shipping Co., 451 U.S. 596, 617 (1981); Rubin v. United States, 449 U.S. 424, 430 (1981); Consumer Product Safety Comm'n v. GTE Sylvania, Inc., 447 U.S. 102, 108 (1980); TVA v. Hill, 437 U.S. 153, 187 (1978); Caminetti v. United States, 242 U.S. 470, 485 (1917).
35. J. CALVIN, INSTITUTES II VIII 26 (1536) (rejecting literal interpretation of comments about swearing in the Sermon on the Mount, on the ground that "we will never attain the truth unless we fix our eyes on Christ's intention and give heed to what he is driving at in that passage").
36. United Steelworkers of America v. Weber, 443 U.S. 193, 201 (1979); Philbrook v. Glodgett, 421 U.S. 707, 713 (1975); Holy Trinity Church v. United States, 143 U.S. 457, 459 (1892).
37. It is doubtful, for example, that the Jewish (or Christian) tradition would endorse the maxim of contemporary American law that "shall" can sometimes mean "may." *See* United States v. Reeb, 433 F.2d 381, 383 (9th Cir. 1970), *cert. denied*, 402 U.S. 912 (1971).

Principle	*Maxim*
1. From the similarity of words or phrases occurring in two passages, it is inferred that what is expressed in the one applies also to the other.[38]	A particular word or phrase should have the same meaning when used in different parts of the same statute.[39]
2. A dubious word or passage is explained from its context or from a subsequent expression.[40]	A section of a statute should not be interpreted apart from the context of the whole act; instead a court should look to the provisions of the whole law, and to its object and policy.[41]
3. Whatever is first implied in a general law and afterwards specified to determine a new matter, the terms of the general law can no longer apply to it, unless Scripture expressly declares that they do apply.[42]	A more specific statute will be given precedence over the more general one, regardless of their temporal sequence.[43]

---

38. A. SCHREIBER, JEWISH LAW AND DECISION-MAKING: A STUDY THROUGH TIME 204 (1979) (citing explanation and translation in P. BIRNBAUM, DAILY PRAYER BOOK (1973)).

39. Washington Metropolitan Transit Auth. v. Johnson, 467 U.S. 925, 935-36 (1984); BankAmerica Corp. v. United States, 462 U.S. 122, 129 (1983); Mohasco Corp. v. Silver, 447 U.S. 807, 826 (1980); Northcross v. Board of Educ., 412 U.S. 427, 428 (1973); Erlenbaugh v. United States, 409 U.S. 239, 243-44 (1973).

40. A. SCHREIBER, *supra* note 38, at 204.

41. *See* Davis v. Michigan Dep't of Treasury, 109 S. Ct. 1500 (1989); Gomez v. United States, 109 S. Ct. 2237, 2241 (1989); Pilot Life Insurance Co. v. Dedeaux, 481 U.S. 41, 51 (1987); United States v. Morton, 467 U.S. 822, 828 (1984).

42. Jett v. Dallas Indep. School Dist., 109 S. Ct. 2702, 2722 (1989); Busic v. United States, 446 U.S. 398, 406 (1980); Presser v. Rodriguez, 411 U.S. 475, 489-90 (1973).

43. A. SCHREIBER, *supra* note 38, at 204.

4. Whatever is first implied in   See preceding passage.
   a general law and,
   afterwards, specified to add
   another provision which is
   not similar to the general
   law, is specified in order to
   alleviate, in some respects,
   and, in others, to increase
   the severity of that
   particular provision.[44]

Many of the thirteen hermeneutical rules of Judaism concern the various problems associated with interpreting words grouped in a list. Similarly, in contemporary American law one leading maxim is *ejusdem generis*: where general words follow an enumeration of specific items, the general words are read as applying only to these items akin to those specifically enumerated.[45] Jewish law contains a series of more elaborated maxims on this general subject, including the following: (1) when a generalization is followed by a specification, only what is specified applies; (2) when a specification is followed by a generalization, all that is implied in the generalization applies; (3) if a generalization is followed by a specification and this in turn by a generalization, one must be guided by what the specification implies; and (4) when clarity demands a generalization that requires specification, or when a specification requires a generalization, rules 1 and 2 above do not apply.[46] Although not entirely consistent with the common law maxim of *ejusdem generis*, the ancient Jewish maxims represent a similar approach to the same general problem area, and in this respect they are consistent in general spirit with the common law maxims.

Further consider Roman law, as summarized in the *Digest of Justinian*. The *Digest* contains a list of 211 maxims, most of which relate to matters of substantive law, but a few may be classified as interpretive maxims. Among them we find the following:

---

44. A. SCHREIBER, *supra* note 38, at 204.
45. *E.g.*, Breininger v. Sheet Metal Workers Int'l Assoc., 110 S. Ct. 424 (1989); Garcia v. United States, 469 U.S. 70, 74 (1984); Securities Indus. Assoc. v. Board of Governors, 468 U.S. 207, 218 (1984); Harrison v. PPG Indus., Inc., 446 U.S. 578, 588 (1980); Third Nat'l Bank v. Impac, Ltd., 432 U.S. 312, 322 & n.16 (1977); Jarecki v. G.D. Searle & Co., 367 U.S. 303, 307 (1961).
46. A. SCHREIBER, *supra* note 38, at 204.

1. Whenever there is doubt over liberty in an interpretation, a reply must be given in favor of liberty.[47]	In case of ambiguity, criminal statutes are interpreted in favor of the accused (the rule of lenity).[48]
2. Whenever the same expression contains two views, that one is most readily to be accepted which is more suitable to the conduct of the affair.[49]	Where several readings of a statute are equally plausible, the court's duty is to find the interpretation which can most fairly be said to serve the general purposes that Congress manifested.[50]
3. In the whole of law, species takes precedence over genus, and anything that relates to species is regarded as the most important.[51]	A precisely drawn statute prevails over a more general one.[52]
4. In ambiguous remarks one must most of all consider the intention of the man who made them.[53]	The key to the inquiry is the intent of the legislature.[54]

As the above discussion indicates, maxims are used in a number of interpretive systems. Further, many of the maxims we recognize today in our modern legal culture appear in one form or another in these other contexts. The apparent durability of the maxims suggests that they have some value for interpretation.

Accordingly, Llewellyn's critique of the maxims appears over-stated. Their very ability to endure, and, indeed, to proliferate suggests

---

47. IV THE DIGEST OF JUSTINIAN 958 (T. Mommsen & P. Kreuger eds. 1985). *See also id.* at 964 ("[d]efendants rather than prosecutors are regarded with greater favor").

48. Crandon v. United States, 110 S. Ct. 997, 1007 (1990); Dowling v. United States, 473 U.S. 207, 213 (1985); Dixson v. United States, 465 U.S. 482, 501 (1984) (O'Connor, J., dissenting); Williams v. United States, 458 U.S. 279, 290 (1982); Whalen v. United States, 445 U.S. 684, 695 n.10 (1980); Dunn v. United States, 442 U.S. 100, 112 (1979); United States v. Bass, 404 U.S. 336, 347 (1971); Rewis v. United States, 401 U.S. 808, 812 (1971); Bell v. United States, 349 U.S. 81, 83 (1955).

49. IV THE DIGEST OF JUSTINIAN, *supra* note 47, at 961.

50. Commissioner v. Engle, 464 U.S. 206, 217 (1984).

51. IV THE DIGEST OF JUSTINIAN, *supra* note 47, at 962.

52. Brown v. GSA, 425 U.S. 820, 834 (1976).

53. *See* IV THE DIGEST OF JUSTINIAN, *supra* note 47, at 962.

54. Merrill Lynch, Pierce, Fenner & Smith, Inc. v. Curran, 456 U.S. 353, 378 (1982); Middlesex County Sewerage Auth. v. National Sea Clammers Ass'n, 453 U.S. 1, 13 (1981).

that maxims do add something of value and importance. In the remainder of this Article, I argue that at least some maxims—mostly, although not wholly, those falling in the category Sunstein terms syntactic norms[55]—reflect common sense notions about meaning in conversation, notions recently recognized and formalized within the field of linguistic philosophy.

II. Pragmatics and Statutory Interpretation

A. Grice's Theory of Implicature

In statutes, as in ordinary conversation, words often take their meaning from context. Because we understand meaning as derived from context, we can make sense of statements such as, "Well, the milkman has come" as conveying more information than simply that the milkman has come, when uttered in response to the question, "Do you know what time it is?"[56] We all understand intuitively that the information about the milkman is not intended solely as a statement that the milkman has come; indeed, whether or not the milkman has come is not itself the subject of the conversation at all. The response, "Well, the milkman has come," used in this context, is understood to mean something such as: "I don't know what time it is exactly, but I do know that the milkman has come, and therefore it is probably no earlier than the time when the milkman usually comes, which we both know is 8:00 a.m." Despite the complete ease with which ordinary speakers of English interpret the statement that the milkman has come as used here, formalizing this understanding in terms of linguistic theory proves quite difficult.

In recent years a branch of linguistics—pragmatics—has developed to do just that: capture the meaning of statements used in conversational or other social settings.[57] Paul Grice, a philosopher, founded the field in 1967.[58] Grice's basic insight is that speech acts often take their

55. C. Sunstein, *supra* note 12, at 454-56.
56. The example is from S. Levinson, Pragmatics 97 (1983).
57. Scholars have quibbled over the best definition of pragmatics. The most succinct is that of Ralph Fasold: "[p]ragmatics, as a topic in linguistics, is the study of the use of context to make inferences about meaning." R. Fasold, Sociolinguistics of Language 119 (1990).
  It should go without saying that the usage of "pragmatics" in this Article has little to do—aside from an indirect grounding in the philosophical school of Pragmatism—with other, nonlinguistic usages, such as that found in Daniel Farber's theory of judicial review. *See* Farber, *Legal Pragmatism and the Constitution*, 72 Minn. L. Rev. 1331 (1988).
58. *See* P. Grice, Studies in the Way of Words 22-40 (1989). Grice originally proposed these ideas in his William James lectures at Harvard University in 1967, which were not published in full until 1989. Copies of Grice's paper circulated widely within the linguistics community prior to its publication in book form.

meaning from the social settings in which they occur. Such settings, according to Grice, are usually ones in which people try to get along with each other:

> [O]ur talk exchanges do not normally consist of a succession of disconnected remarks, and would not be rational if they did. They are characteristically, to some degree at least, co-operative efforts; and each participant recognizes in them, to some extent, a common purpose or set of purposes, or at least a mutually accepted direction.[59]

Grice does not deny that in some cases conversation is not a co-operative enterprise, that people sometimes deceive each other, become angry, and so on.[60] Rather, his point is that because people *usually* act cooperatively in conversational settings, most conversational speech acts can be interpreted as being cooperative in nature.

Grice formalizes this insight in a *cooperative principle*: "[m]ake your conversational contribution such as is required, at the stage at which it occurs, by the accepted purpose and direction of the talk exchange in which you are engaged."[61] The cooperative principle, in turn, generates a set of maxims that Grice classes under the rubrics *quantity*, *quality*, *relation* and *manner*. These maxims represent interpretive conventions that people use in understanding communications of others.

For the most part the maxims are not violated and operate almost invisibly. Because people usually cooperate in conversational settings and assume that others are cooperating, there is no reason for concern about the other party's meaning if the evidence does not suggest a lack of cooperation.

In certain unusual cases, however, a speech act may represent an apparent *flouting* of a maxim. This happens when a speaker utters something that appears, at least on its surface, to represent a lack of cooperation. In such cases the listener will ordinarily attempt, if possible, to interpret the statement in issue as actually being consistent with the maxim that was apparently flouted—as being cooperative after all. The principal device for reconciling the speech act with the maxim is a *conversational implicature*: a meaning attributed to the statement

---

An excellent recent account of pragmatic theory is found in S. LEVINSON, *supra* note 56. *See also* G. GAZDAR, PRAGMATICS (1979); A. AKMAJIAN, R. DEMERS & R. HARNISH, LINGUISTICS 390-420 (1984).

The discipline referred to here is that of Anglo-American pragmatics; there is also a broader continental usage. For an approach to statutory interpretation from the standpoint of continental pragmatic theory, see Dascal & Wro'blewski, *Transparancy and Doubt: Understanding and Interpretation in Pragmatics and in Law*, 7 LAW & PHIL. 203 (1988).

59. P. GRICE, *supra* note 58, at 26.
60. *Id.*
61. *Id.*

that is other than (broader, narrower or at variance with) its conventional or literal meaning.

Grice identifies four distinguishing features of conversational implicatures, two of which are relevant for present purposes. The first and perhaps most important feature is that implicatures are *defeasible* or *cancelable*. The statement "Jones has three puppies" implicates that Jones has three *and only three* puppies (otherwise the speaker would have said the actual number). But suppose the speaker adds, "Jones has three puppies, maybe more." Now the implicature that Jones has only three puppies is cancelled; the hearer understands that Jones may have more than three.

A typical way of canceling implicatures, not discussed by Grice, is through what I call "checking." Suppose that the hearer is unsure whether the speaker is talking about all of Jones' puppies, or only the puppies Jones has for sale. The hearer might then be inclined to check the implicature by requesting clarification: "Do you mean that there are only three in the *litter*, or that Jones is only *selling* three?" The speaker would then have the opportunity to cancel the implicature, by saying, "No, there were five in the litter; I mean he only has three for sale."

A second important feature of implicatures is that they are *nonconventional*. By this Grice simply means that the meaning of the implicature is not part of the conventional or logical meaning of the statement taken out of context. Suppose Able says, "I got arrested for running a red light," when in fact Able was stopped not only for running a red light, but also for smashing into the back of a police car. There is no logical inconsistency between Able's statement and the actual facts; as a logical matter, the statement "I got arrested for running a red light" does not entail "I didn't get arrested for anything else." But in many conversational contexts, the statement about the red light would implicate that no more serious offense occurred. Thus the implicature adds something to the conventional or logical meaning of the utterance.[62]

Grice's theories, including the theory of implicature summarized above, stimulated the development of pragmatics as an independent field of linguistics. Some of Grice's views have subsequently been questioned by Grice himself, among others,[63] and various revisions or

---

62. Grice also observes that implicatures are "non-detachable" (i.e., the implicature remains even if one changes the utterance by substituting synonyms) and "calculable" (i.e., it is possible to explain in some principled fashion why the implicature arises). P. GRICE, *supra* note 58, at 39-40.

63. *See, e.g.,* P. GRICE, *supra* note 58, at 371-72; R. KEMPSON, RESUPPOSITION AND THE DELIMITATION OF SEMANTICS 146-56 (1975).

amendments to his basic scheme have been proposed.[64] Perhaps the leading criticism—one that should sound familiar to those schooled in the debate over the maxims of statutory interpretation—is that the Gricean maxims are "so vague and general that they allow the prediction of any implication whatever."[65] Yet for the most part, Grice's theory has stood up well over time and continues to enjoy widespread acceptance among scholars working in the area.[66]

In the following pages I argue that maxims of statutory interpretation can often be understood within the conceptual framework of pragmatics theory as set forth in Grice's path-breaking study.[67]

B. The Maxims of Quantity

1. CONVERSATIONAL SETTINGS

The "quantity" category, according to Grice, contains two principal maxims. First, "[m]ake your contribution as informative as is required (for the current purposes of the exchange)."[68] If Smith, when negotiating to buy a used car, asks Jones, the owner, what kind of shape

---

64. See D. SPERBER & D. WILSON, RELEVANCE (1986) (attempting to collapse all pragmatics inferences under a single criterion of relevance). Theorists have also formulated maxims of politeness analogous to Grice's maxims of meaning. See, e.g., P. BROWN & S. LEVINSON, POLITENESS (1989).

For an attempt to develop a set of pragmatics maxims to govern substantive (as opposed to interpretive) legal decision-making, see J.W. FORRESTER, WHY YOU SHOULD: THE PRAGMATICS OF DEONTIC SPEECH (1989).

65. R. KEMPSON, supra note 63, at 146. Kempson here states the criticism in the strongest possible form; her own views on the value of Grice's system of maxims are much more favorable. See id. at 157-205.

66. See S. LEVINSON, supra note 56, at 118-66.

67. As far as I am aware, the only prior application of Grice's maxims to statutory construction problems is in Sinclair, Law And Language: The Role of Pragmatics in Statutory Interpretation, 46 U. PITT. L. REV. 373 (1985). Unlike the present Article, however, Sinclair does not give a full account of the maxims of statutory interpretation, treating in detail only expressio unius est exclusio alterius and ejusdem generis. The present Article extends the Gricean analysis to most of the important contemporary maxims. The present Article differs from Sinclair's pioneering work in a number of other respects as well. Some of the most important of these are as follows: its identification of the three standard strategies for dealing with apparent floutings of the maxims of quality; its discussion of presupposition in statutory language; its treatment of problems of meaninglessness and contradiction; and its analysis of the recurring situations in which maxims collide.

The potential applicability of the pragmatic maxims to statutory interpretation has also been noted by a few prior authors. See F. BOWERS, LINGUISTIC ASPECTS OF LEGISLATIVE EXPRESSION 24-27 (1989); Berk-Seligson, The Importance of Linguistics in Court Interpreting, 2 LA RAZA L.J. 14, 25-30 (1988).

For an interesting critique of the view of statutes as communication which takes account of some aspects of Grice's philosophy, although not his theory of implicature, see Hurd, Sovereignty in Silence, 99 YALE L. J. 945, 953-67 (1990).

68. P. GRICE, supra note 58, at 26.

the car is in, and Jones responds, "Well, it hasn't died yet," we sense at once an apparent flouting of this maxim: Smith wants information about the condition of the car, and Jones responds with only minimal information even though Jones, as the owner, surely knows more than she is saying. But if we assume that Smith and Jones are cooperating—that Jones is not trying to deceive or defraud Smith about the condition of the car—then an implicature arises from the application of the cooperative principle. Jones' reply, reformulated as consistent with the first maxim of quantity, might be taken as meaning "for the price I'm asking you're not going to get a car in good shape; this car isn't in good shape, but it does run, at least for now, even though it might need a lot of work." So understood, Jones' reply is consistent with the first maxim of quantity: it provides information that Smith needs and has requested in evaluating whether to purchase the car.

Grice's second maxim of quantity is "do not make your contribution more informative than is required."[69] So, if in a journal reference report, Jones says, "Smith's paper in general does a good job at answering criticisms of his position," but goes on to list many criticisms to which Smith has *not* responded, the reader might infer that Jones is really not so confident that Smith has done a good job at answering criticisms and that Jones has merely made a positive statement to satisfy standards of politeness in the profession. Otherwise, the second maxim of quantity would be flouted: Jones has provided more information than required under the circumstances (assuming that the generalization about Smith's work would satisfy the interest of the journal, the elaboration would be excessive unless intended to convey a modification of the general statement).

2. STATUTORY INTERPRETATION

It is not difficult to conceptualize some of the maxims of statutory interpretation as reflecting the Gricean maxims of quantity. Consider the maxim *expressio unius est exclusio alterius*: the expression of one thing signifies the exclusion of others.[70] Imagine a statute providing

---

69. *Id.*
70. This venerable maxim continues to be used with qualified approval in federal courts. *See, e.g.,* Lukhard v. Reed, 481 U.S. 368, 376 (1987); Omni Capital Int'l v. Rudolf Wolff & Co., Ltd., 484 U.S. 97, 106 (1987); Rodriguez v. United States, 480 U.S. 522, 525 (1987); United States v. Russello, 464 U.S. 16, 23 (1983); Andrus v. Glover Constr. Co., 446 U.S. 608, 616-17 (1980); FTC v. Sun Oil Co., 371 U.S. 505, 514-15 (1963); SEC v. Ralston Purina Co., 346 U.S. 119 (1953); Continental Casualty Co. v. United States, 314 U.S. 527, 533 (1951); Marshall v. Gibson's Prod., Inc. of Plano, 584 F.2d 668, 675-76 (5th Cir. 1978). Arguments based on the principle of *expressio unius* have proved important in the implied right of action context. *See, e.g.,* Herman & McLean v. Huddleston, 459 U.S. 375, 383 (1983); Middlesex City Sewerage Auth. v. National Sea Clammers Ass'n, 453 U.S. 1, 14-15 (1981); Touche Ross & Co. v. Redington, 442 U.S. 560, 571-74 (1979).

that no one under eighteen may operate a motor vehicle on a public street. A question arises as to whether someone under eighteen may drive a tractor in a farmer's field. The *expressio unius* principle suggests a positive answer, on the theory that by expressly limiting its prohibition to public streets the legislature intended to permit persons under eighteen to operate motor vehicles in places other than public streets.

This familiar principle of construction is an application of Grice's first maxim of quantity.[71] When a legislature expressly provides a particular bit of information, it creates a "conversational" setting between the legislature and its audience—courts and citizens—in which other information of the same type is expected to be conveyed. By virtue of banning drivers under eighteen from the public streets, the legislature has made a statement about the locations where the statute applies. Since the legislature is obviously capable of stating other areas in which the statute applies, the fact that it did not do so gives rise to the implicature that it did not intend the statute to apply in settings other than in those expressly mentioned. This is the maxim of *expressio unius*.[72]

Consider also the closely related (perhaps identical) principle of the negative pregnant. If a reporter were to file a news report that "Imelda Marcos owns twenty-five pairs of shoes," this would not be inconsistent, as a logical matter, with the proposition that Imelda Marcos owns two thousand pairs of shoes. But aside from the fact that the report is not news (lots of people own twenty-five pairs of shoes), the statement represents a flouting of the first maxim of quantity because it provides less information than would be expected by readers of the report (we expect to be told the total number of shoes, not just a partial count). Similarly, regarding legislation, if a statute says, "All cats born on or after January 1, 1989, shall be vaccinated for feline leukemia," this is not inconsistent logically with the proposition that cats born *before* January 1, 1989, shall be vaccinated; yet any reader would understand intuitively that construing the statute to cover this second class of cats would flout a standard convention of interpretation. If your cat is born before January 1, 1989, and you do not vaccinate, you are in the clear as far as the law is concerned (but must answer to your conscience).

Consider the maxim that statutes in derogation of the common law should be strictly construed.[73] This maxim has come under heavy

---

71. For prior analysis of *expressio unius* as an application of Grice's maxims of quantity, see Sinclair, *supra* note 67, at 414-20.

72. Grice uses the example of a recommendation letter for a candidate seeking a philosophy teaching job, which states, "Dear Sir, Mr. X's command of English is excellent, and his attendance at tutorials has been regular. Yours, etc." Since the writer knows her pupil's philosophy ability and is not opting out by failing to write, there would appear to be an obvious flouting of the first maxim of quantity unless we understand the writer to make an implicature that Mr. X is not good at philosophy. P. GRICE, *supra* note 58, at 33.

73. *See* Independent Fed'n of Flight Attendants v. Zipes, 109 S. Ct. 2732 (1989);

fire from academics who see it as device by which courts may frustrate beneficial legislative reforms.[74] Used appropriately, however, the maxim represents a straightforward application of pragmatics theory. If the legislature intends to change traditional ways of organizing human affairs, it would be reasonable for the audience to expect that fact to be announced in clear terms. It is only "news" when things change, not when they remain the same (at least not unless the public has developed a strong expectation that things indeed will change). Thus, interpreting an ambiguous statute to preempt the common law would represent an apparent flouting of the first maxim of quantity, in that the legislature would then be providing less information than would be required under the circumstances. The resulting implicature calls for the interpretation of the statute, if possible, as consistent with the common law background.

This is not to say, of course, that the maxim cannot be misused. If a statute clearly preempts the common law, the implicature would not arise (or if it arises, would be cancelled). Similarly, if the common law background has been eroded by statutory change already, the audience would no longer expect a clear announcement that the common law has been displaced, and no flouting of the first maxim of quantity would occur. If the statute at issue is so comprehensive in scope as to suggest that the legislature must have intended the common law background to be displaced, the implicature is again cancelled. The same follows if the evident legislative purposes cannot be accomplished consistently with the common law. In all of these cases, however, the objection to the maxim of strict construction does not go to the validity of the basic inference, but only to the possibility that it will be misused or given greater force than is warranted under the circumstances.

From the standpoint of pragmatic theory, strict construction of statutes in derogation of the common law appears quite similar to the principle that repeals by implication are not favored.[75] The analytical structure is precisely the same: if the legislature intended to change existing law—in this case statutory law—it would be expected to say so explicitly. Statutory language suggesting an implied repeal of previous

---

Wards Cove Packing Co. v. Atonio, 109 S. Ct. 2732 (1989); Washington Metro. Area Transit Auth. v. Johnson, 467 U.S. 925, 946 (1984) (Rehnquist, J., dissenting); Norfolk Redev. & Hous. Auth. v. Chesapeake & Potomac Tel. Co., 464 U.S. 30, 35 (1983); Pierson v. Ray, 386 U.S. 547, 554-55 (1967). *But cf.* United States v. Fausto, 484 U.S. 439 (1988) (declining to endorse a rule "akin" to the maxim against statutes in derogation of the common law).

74. For the most recent attack from this perspective, see Sunstein, *supra* note 12.

75. *See, e.g.,* Pittsburgh & Lake Erie R.R. Co. v. Labor Executives Ass'n, 109 S. Ct. 2584 (1989); Kremer v. Chemical Constr. Co., 456 U.S. 461, 468 (1982); American Bank & Trust Co. v. Dallas County, 463 U.S. 855, 868 (1983); National Gerimedical Hosp. & Gerontology Cent. v. Blue Cross of Kansas City, 452 U.S. 378, 389 (1981); St. Martin Evangelical Lutheran Church v. South Dakota, 451 U.S. 772, 787-88 (1981); Watt v. Alaska, 451 U.S. 259, 267 (1981); Morton v. Mancari, 417 U.S. 535, 549 (1974).

legislation therefore constitutes a flouting of the first maxim of quantity, since the legislature would then be seen as providing less information than would be called for under the circumstances. The resulting implicature overcomes the flouting by reconciling the later statute with the earlier one. As in the case of the maxim against statutes in derogation of the common law, the maxim against implied repeals can be misused. If a later statute cannot be applied in a sensible fashion without displacing an earlier one, then the implicature should be considered cancelled, and the court should apply the later rather than the earlier statute.[76] Again, the fact that the maxim can be misused is no argument against the validity of the inference embodied in the maxim, but merely an objection to the force attributed to the inference in a particular case.

A variety of other maxims are designed to preserve the existing framework of legal rules and private expectations as to the meaning of those rules against unwarranted alteration through interpretation. The maxim instructing courts to defer to longstanding administrative interpretations is one example,[77] as is the maxim that congressional reenactment of a statute ordinarily will be interpreted as incorporating administrative interpretations of the statute being superseded.[78] A similar rule applies to reenactments of statutes that have received consistent judicial interpretations.[79] Consider also the maxim requiring a clear statement if Congress is to regulate matters traditionally governed by state law.[80] All of these rules appear based, at least in part, on a judicial concern to avoid undue interference with the existing legal framework and private expectations—a concern that can be conceptualized as reflecting a practical application of the first maxim of quantity.

76. *See* Erlenbaugh v. United States, 409 U.S. 239, 244 (1972).

77. *See, e.g.*, United States v. Riverside Bayview Homes, Inc., 474 U.S. 121, 131 (1985); Chevron, U.S.A., Inc. v. National Resources Defense Council, Inc. 467 U.S. 837, 842-45 (1984); United States v. Morton, 467 U.S. 822, 834 (1984); Haig v. Agee, 453 U.S. 280, 291 (1981); CBS, Inc. v. FCC, 453 U.S. 367, 382 (1981).

78. *See, e.g.*, *Haig*, 453 U.S. at 292-306; Federal Reserve Bd. v. First Lincolnwood Corp., 439 U.S. 234, 248 (1978); Saxbe v. Bustos, 419 U.S. 65, 74 (1974).

79. *See, e.g.*, Merrill, Lynch, Pierce, Fenner & Smith, Inc. v. Curran, 456 U.S. 353, 378-79 (1982); Lorillard v. Pons, 434 U.S. 575, 580-81 (1978). On the other hand, the deference accorded prior judicial decisions or administrative interpretations is less if the prior rules are vacillating or inconsistent. *See, e.g.*, Secretary of the Interior v. California, 464 U.S. 312, 320 n.6 (1984) (no deference is due when the administrator has "walked a path of . . . tortured vacillation and indecision").

80. *See, e.g.*, Southland Corp. v. Keating, 465 U.S. 1, 18 (1984) (Stevens, J., concurring in part and dissenting in part) ("the exercise of state authority in a field traditionally occupied by state law will not be deemed preempted by a federal statute unless that was the clear and manifest purpose of Congress"); Kremer v. Chemical Constr. Corp., 456 U.S. 461, 476 (1982) (clear statement required if statute is to be construed as interfering with principles of comity and federalism); Chicago & Northwest Transp. Co. v. Kalo Brick & Tile Co., 450 U.S. 311, 317 (1981) (federal preemption not favored absent clear statement); Pennhurst State Hosp. v. Halderman, 465 U.S. 89, 99-100 (1981) (Court will not quickly attribute to Congress an intent to impose federal policy on states and intrude on traditional state authority).

Maxims bearing on the scope of powers to interpret statutes provide yet another example. One such maxim is that an administrative agency has greater discretion in interpreting statutes framed in broad and general terms than it does in interpreting statutes framed in specific and narrow terms.[81] This maxim appears to be simply a legislative application of an interpretive principle that everyone would recognize from standard conversational settings. If A says to her employee, B, "Please take care of things at the store for me today," the normal implication is that B is to exercise a considerably greater degree of discretion than if A had said, for example, "Please do all one hundred tasks I have written out on this list." By the same token, broad legislative language implicates greater scope of discretion for an agency than does narrow legislative language. Arguably, the first maxim of quantity would be flouted if general language were read to accord no more scope to an agency's discretion than narrow language. In this case, Congress could provide more and better information with the more specific language and, accordingly, would not be communicating a sufficient amount of information given the nature and purposes of the exchange. The apparent flouting of the first maxim of quantity in the case of highly general statutory commands is resolved through the implicature that the agency enjoys a large measure of interpretive discretion.

Consider also the maxims by which a court evaluates the degree of its *own* discretion to interpret legislation. Most relevant here is the plain meaning rule, discussed at some length below.[82] Viewed from the standpoint of pragmatics theory, the plain meaning rule serves purposes analogous to the maxim that agencies have greater discretion to interpret broad statutory language than narrow language. The plain meaning rule expresses the principle that where the statute is narrowly and tightly drawn, the courts have considerably less interpretive flexibility than when the statute is phrased in vague or general terms. In this respect the plain meaning rule can be said to derive in part from the intuitions underlying the first Gricean maxim of quantity.

Turn now to the maxim *ejusdem generis* (general terms in a list take their meaning from the specific terms). On analysis, this appears

81. *See, e.g.*, Securities Indus. Ass'n v. Board of Governors, 468 U.S. 207, 214 (1984); Federal Election Comm'n v. Democratic Senatorial Campaign Comm., 454 U.S. 27, 37 (1981); National Muffler Dealers Ass'n, Inc. v. United States, 440 U.S. 472, 476 (1979); Chisolm v. FCC, 538 F.2d 349, 357 (D.C. Cir. 1976), *cert. denied*, 429 U.S. 890 (1977). This maxim is often expressed negatively—e.g., that an agency does *not* have broad discretion to interpret a statute when the terms of the statute are specific and clear. *See, e.g.*, Commissioner v. Engle, 464 U.S. 206, 224-25 (1984); Bureau of Alcohol, Tobacco, & Firearms v. FLRA, 464 U.S. 89, 97 (1984); United States v. Vogel Fertilizer Co., 455 U.S. 16, 24 (1982); International Brotherhood of Teamsters v. Daniel, 439 U.S. 551, 565-66 n.20 (1979); SEC v. Sloan, 436 U.S. 103, 117 (1978).
82. *See infra* notes 133-41 and accompanying text.

to be an application of Grice's second maxim of quantity (don't provide more information than is called for in the conversational setting).[83] For example, say a city council bars from a public park all "cats, dogs and other animals." The question arises as to whether a mounted policeman may enter the park. The policeman's horse is clearly an animal (as is the policeman, for that matter). So the plain meaning of the term would bar the policeman from the park. But such a reading would represent a flouting of the second maxim of quantity, since if the term "animal" covered all fauna, the reference to cats and dogs would provide more information than is needed in the setting. Compliance with the maxim can be reestablished, however, if we gloss the reference to cats and dogs as *modifying* the term "animals"—limiting its application to animals which are *like* cats and dogs for some reason, such as that they have the attribute of being pets.[84] Thus, we arrive at the principle of *ejusdem generis*: the preceding specific references are understood to modify general term "animal."

The implicatures rising from the maxims of quantity can be quite subtle in both statutory interpretation and ordinary speech. Conflicting implicatures often arise, and we must determine which implicature has the most weight—which one most likely reflects the speaker's intention. Consider the example given above of a statute banning "cats, dogs and other animals" from a public park. The interpretation of "other animals" as meaning "pets," which we draw from the second maxim of quantity, creates a potential flouting of the first maxim of quantity. The statutory language creates a conversational setting in which the city council would be expected to communicate as much information as is reasonably available about the types of creatures which are barred from the park. If only "pets" were intended, then the use of the general term "other animals" appears to flout the first maxim because the general term provides less information than the more specific term. If the city council had *meant* pets, why did it not say pets? Thus, we have conflicting implicatures. The question becomes which implicature is stronger.

There are several common defenses of *ejusdem generis* against this sort of criticism. First, one can imagine that the legislature intentionally used the term "other animals," even when it meant "pets," because it

---

83. Sinclair views *ejusdem generis* as based on both of the maxims of quantity as well as the postulate that language should be used "maximally." *See* Sinclair, *supra* note 67, at 410-14. I believe that the maxim can be justified more parsimoniously with reference only to the second maxim of quantity.

84. Presumably the reference to cats and dogs would not flout the second maxim of quantity as being repetitive, since the inclusion of both types of animals would imply the inclusion of features peculiar to one and not the other; for example if dogs alone were referenced, one could argue that only animals that made loud noises were barred and, therefore, cats were permitted.

was concerned about the possibility of loopholes. Suppose somebody maintains a thoroughbred Great Dane for breeding purposes. If the city council had used the term "pets," instead of "other animals," the Great Dane's owner might argue that *he* can walk his dog in the park because the animal is a business investment, not a pet. The city council can minimize the possiblity that opportunistic dog breeders would assert such arguments by adopting the more general term.

The more general interpretation, of course, creates a danger of over-inclusiveness. Suppose a blind person wanted to walk in the park with a Seeing Eye dog. Would she violate the ordinance if she did walk in the park, on the theory that a Seeing Eye dog is an "animal"? The city council is protected against over-inclusive interpretations because its ordinance will likely have been drafted by a decision-maker capable of applying the *ejusdem generis* principle sensitively in order to effectuate the city council's most probable intentions. If the city code contains many other exceptions for Seeing Eye dogs (they are permitted on busses and in public buildings, for example), it would be reasonable to assume that a similar exception would be appropriate for Seeing Eye dogs in the park.

Another standard defense of *ejusdem generis* is to contend that the costs of greater specificity outweigh the benefits. This is essentially a gloss on the Gricean notion of what is required for the current purposes of the exchange. The cooperative principle implies, presumably, that both parties to the conversation benefit in some fashion from the exchange. I use the notion of benefit here in a broad sense, meaning not only direct pecuniary benefit (as in the case of parties conversing while negotiating a contract), but also indirect benefit of any sort (I will gladly tell my neighbor what time it is because I thereby cement a relationship in which I will feel free to call on my neighbor for a favor in the future), as well as selfless or altruistic actions (I will tell a stranger what time it is because I believe the benefit to her outweighs the cost to me of providing the information). What is excluded by the notion of benefit are cases where both parties lose, or where one party loses more than the other party gains. These are negative sum games which could not reasonably represent cooperative behavior.

Among the costs of providing information are the cost of obtaining and relating it, as well as the cost of interpreting the information once provided. In many situations we would not expect the speaker to use the most exacting language simply because doing so would be excessively costly in terms of the benefits conferred. It may be, for example, that a more specialized term is not readily available, so that a general term can be expressly qualified only by use of an explicit definition, which will add length and complexity to a statute intended to be readily understood by ordinary citizens.[85] Even if a more specific term is available—"pet" for instance—we have seen that such a term may itself require qualification (breed dogs are included, but Seeing Eye dogs are not). Moreover, there are costs to the lawgiver: greater specificity tends to strengthen the *expressio unius* implicature. For example, if breed dogs are specifically included within the definition of "pets," would a canine model used to film a dog food commercial be outside the definition because models are not specifically mentioned? Thus, the benefits of greater specificity must be weighed against the costs; in many cases the cooperative purposes of the communication would be best served by a more general term even if it is slightly less precise. Hence, the *ejusdem generis* implicature may prevail in many cases against countervailing implicatures arising under the maxims of quantity.[86]

It is important to keep in mind, however, that the analysis involves a balancing of the weight of competing implicatures. Because competing implicatures are involved, the maxims in many cases will not yield a single unambiguous result; indeed, the maxims can be characterized as contradictory, as Llewellyn did with such rhetorical panache in 1966. But the fact that the maxims may work against each other—that *expressio unius* may stand in tension with *ejusdem generis*—does not establish the hopeless confusion posited by Llewellyn's model. It is simply a matter of competing inferences drawn from the evidence; the fact that the evidence may be ambiguous does not mean that the inferences themselves are useless.

C. The Maxims of Quality

Grice's second broad category of maxims is that of quality, which he associates with a general injunction to "try to make your contribution one that is true."[87] Grice proposes two maxims here: first, do not say what you believe to be false, and second, do not say that for which you lack adequate evidence.[88] Two other maxims not identified by Grice also appear appropriate under the general heading of quality:

---

85. *See* United States Civil Serv. Comm'n v. Letter Carriers, 413 U.S. 548, 578-79 (1973) ("there are limitations in the English language with respect to being both specific and manageably brief").

86. This "economic" interpretation of the cooperative principle—that the expected precision of legislative language is, in part, a function of the costs and benefits of greater or lesser precision—is lacking in Sinclair's otherwise insightful account of *expressio unius* and *ejusdem generis. See* Sinclair, *supra* note 67, at 416. Sinclair proposes that the legislature should be seen as using language "maximally," which in the context of these maxims implies that the legislature "aways cover[s] all but only the persons and actions it intends to" and "always say[s] as much as, but not more than it can . . . ." *Id.*

87. P. GRICE, *supra* note 58, at 27.

88. *Id.*

do not say anything you know to be meaningless, and do not say anything you know to be self-contradictory.[89]

The quality maxims are explicitly based on the truth value of an utterance. They might appear, therefore, to have no application to utterances couched in forms that lack truth value, such as questions or commands. However, implicatures do arise from floutings of the maxims of quality in nondeclarative speech acts.

The occurrence of implications in nondeclarative speech acts can usefully be understood with reference to the pragmatics concept of *presupposition.*[90] For present purposes, we can define a presupposition as a factual assertion that is implicit or apparently implicit in an utterance. If I ask A, "When did you stop drinking?", I am assuming—presupposing—that A did at one time drink, probably heavily. If I tell A, "I want you to give up drinking for Lent," I am presupposing that A has indeed been drinking, probably heavily, and that she will probably continue to drink unless she makes some kind of commitment to interrupt the habit. Thus, in many cases, questions and commands can be unpacked and seen to contain implicit declarative statements of fact in the form of presuppositions.

Implicatures arise when the factual presuppositions in nondeclarative utterances appear to flout the maxims of quality. Suppose A says to B, "As long as you're up, would you please get me a gin and vodka?" (assume B interprets this as a command). A's remark flouts the first maxim of quality because of the discrepancy between what B knows (people don't like gin mixed with vodka) and what A has presupposed (she would like gin mixed with vodka). The flouting therefore gives rise to implicatures: interpretations of A's statement as meaning something other than it appears to mean on the literal or conventional level. B would probably surmise that A had simply misspoken and that she really wanted a gin and *tonic.* But the implicature is not overwhelmingly strong; B might have the impulse to check ("Did you really mean gin and *vodka?*") in order to allow A to correct herself and thus confirm the implicature.

The standard pragmatics approach to the quality maxims can use-

---

89.   Grice would probably acknowledge these two additional maxims as falling under the rubric of quality. In analogizing speech with other forms of activity and suggesting that the maxims may apply to certain forms of human activity outside the speech context, Grice glosses the maxim of quality as meaning:

> I expect your contributions to be genuine and not spurious. If I need sugar as an ingredient in the cake you are assisting me to make, I do not expect you to hand me salt; if I need a spoon, I do not expect a trick spoon made of rubber.

P. GRICE, *supra* note 58, at 28. Statements which are known by the speaker to be meaningless or self-contradictory can easily be said to be spurious rather than genuine.

90.   *See generally* R. KEMPSON, *supra* note 63. Grice's work on presupposition is found in P. GRICE, *supra* note 58, at 269-282.

fully be supplemented by distinguishing three strategies for coping with
apparent floutings of these maxims: attributing implicatures, adjusting
beliefs about the facts and adjusting beliefs about the cooperative nature
of the interchange. These three strategies appear useful both in conversational settings and in the context of statutory interpretation.

1. CONVERSATIONAL SETTINGS

a. Implicatures

Consider situations in which the first maxim of quality (don't say
anything untrue) is apparently flouted. For the most part these situations involve figures of speech or rhetorical forms such as irony, metaphor, understatement or hyperbole.[91] If, for example, someone refers
to the movie *Bambi* as a "hard-hitting docudrama," the statement raises
an implicature because it is patently contradicted by the evidence. The
audience would ordinarily interpret the statement as an ironic reversal
of the speaker's true opinion.

As to the second maxim of quality (don't say anything for which
you lack adequate evidence), an example might be someone saying of
her new automobile, "It's sure to fall apart in two years; it's made in
Detroit." The audience, we may assume, knows full well, as does the
speaker, that most cars made in Detroit last longer than two years. The
statement is made without sufficient evidence, thus apparently flouting
the second maxim. Most listeners, however, would not take the statement at face value, but rather would interpret it as implicating something like this: "I feel I'm taking a risk buying an American car because
I believe foreign cars are more reliable." This statement would be consistent with the second maxim of quality because there is sufficient
evidence of the reliability of foreign cars to warrant a belief that an
American-made car may be at greater risk of breaking down.[92]

Applications of the third maxim of quality (don't say anything
meaningless) should also be familiar from ordinary conversational settings.[93] The cooperative principle suggests that parties involved in a

---

91. P. GRICE, *supra* note 58, at 34.

92. Note that the speaker may be implicating other propositions as well. She might
be saying that she has mixed feelings about buying the car (otherwise, if she believed it such
a bad risk, why did she buy it at all?). She might also be communicating certain attitudes
about herself: "I don't want to be disappointed with this car, so I'm going to assume the
worst in order to be pleasantly surprised by how well the car actually performs."

93. This maxim of meaningfulness could also be seen as deriving from either of the
maxims of quantity. A meaningless statement, in a situation where the conversational setting
calls for meaning, provides less information than is required by the context and thus violates
the first maxim of quantity. At the same time, a meaningless statement provides more information—or more accurately, more words for the listener to attempt to interpret—than
would be demanded by the context and therefore violates a generalized statement of the
second maxim of quantity: because the context does not call for meaningless words, any
meaningless words exceed what is appropriate in the setting.

communicative endeavor will not waste each other's time with words that contain no meaning, and that they especially will not engage in speech that appears to contain meaning but in fact does not. If the implicit ground rules of the communication are that information is to be communicated (i.e., the conversation is not some sort of performance or other agreed-upon transaction in which the parties understand that meaningless words will be exchanged), then no one will benefit if one party utters words which appear meaningful but in fact are not. So if A says to B, "Can you tell me the fastest way to a gas station?" and B responds, "Fritos and bean dip," A would attempt to make sense of the communication rather than assume a flouting of the maxim of meaningfulness. Perhaps B is speaking with an unusual accent or has a speech defect, so that what she is really saying is "three streets down and to the left." Or maybe B is attempting to say that she "speaks no English." Perhaps B has misunderstood the question as requesting information on what foods give you gas the fastest. Maybe B is using some obscure local jargon to indicate directions. Probably A would check with some standard device such as "Come again?" or "What did you say?" rather than assume that one or another of these implicatures was correct. In any event, A will feel a powerful impulse to interpret the comment as meaningful and not gibberish.

Consider the use of the fourth quality maxim (don't contradict yourself) in standard conversational settings. A says to B, "I want to do it and I don't want to do it!" Ordinarily such a statement is not taken as a contradiction, despite its logical form. Understood as contradictory, the statement would represent an obvious violation of the cooperative principle, since inconsistent and contradictory statements communicate little (if anything) of value to the other party. Most people would resolve the apparent violation of the cooperative principle by resort to an implicature, interpreting the statement as meaning, "I have strong mixed feelings about this matter." Implicatures generated by apparent floutings of this fourth maxim of quality are often found in literature: "It was the best of times; it was the worst of times," "Love's not love that alters when it alteration finds," and so on. The arresting quality of these figures of speech comes from their apparently contradictory nature; the reader wants to see how the contradiction is resolved, and the author usually goes on to explain why the statements are not in fact contradictory even though they appear so at first.

b. Changes in belief about facts

We have observed that implicatures are a standard strategy for overcoming apparent floutings of the maxims of quality. It is possible, however, to resolve such apparent floutings without recourse to implicatures. The alternative approach is to change beliefs about the underlying facts.

Suppose A tells you, "B cooked dinner for me last night; it was spectacular!" You happen to know or believe that B is a terrible chef, having eaten undercooked chicken and overcooked zuccini at B's house three times in the last year. From your perspective, the statement represents a flouting of the first two maxims of quality: A must be intentionally stating a falsehood or lack sufficient evidence to judge B's cooking. You might attempt to resolve the flouting through an implicature: A is being ironic and is attempting to share with you a common experience of disappointment. But irony is usually accompanied by an exaggerated or overemphatic tone of voice. What if A seems genuinely enthusiastic about B's cooking? You might respond at this point with a common conversational gambit, such as, "Seriously?" or "You've got to be kidding!", which invites A to cancel (or confirm) the implicature. The response might be "Oh, I know he used to be a rotten cook, but he just spent three weeks at a culinary institute and the improvement is amazing." Now you might decide that rather than resolving the flouting through an implicature, you can do so better or more efficiently by adjusting your beliefs about the underlying facts. If you conclude that B has indeed become a good cook, there is no flouting of the maxims of quality in A's statement and no objection to taking his comment at face value.

Changes in beliefs about the facts work with many apparent floutings of the maxims of quality. Consider a case of contradiction. During the course of a history lecture A says: "St. Augustine's principal accomplishment was founding the Christian Church in England" and a few minutes later says, "St. Augustine spent his adult life as Bishop of Hippo in North Africa." B, a student, is confused because the statements appear contradictory. B might attempt to resolve the confusion by searching for some kind of implicature to resolve the apparent flouting of the quality maxims (was A joking or being ironic?). Or, after the lecture, B might seek clarification. B might then discover that A was referring to two *different* St. Augustines, one the founder of the Christian Church in Britain, the other the Bishop of Hippo in North Africa. B would then likely abandon her previously-held belief that there was only one St. Augustine, thus resolving the contradiction.

c. Changes in beliefs about the cooperative nature of the interchange

What if your interlocutor insists on asserting the truth of a proposition that you know or believe to be false and that you know the speaker knows or believes to be false? He says, "I never borrowed your chain saw," when first, you know very well that he did borrow the chain saw, and second, you believe that he broke or lost the chain saw (or worse, is keeping it somewhere) and that he is dissimulating in order to evade responsibility for returning it. At this point you would have to conclude that the first maxim of quality has been deliberately flouted and that the flouting cannot be resolved by means either of an implicature or a change in your factual beliefs. You would then have no choice but to conclude—presumably reluctantly—that the rules of the language game are different than you had assumed them to be, that it is not a cooperative game but a noncooperative game, and that you cannot rely on your interlocutor to be helpful or provide you with accurate and dependable information.

d. Choice of strategies

We have seen that a listener confronted with a flouting of the maxims of quality has a choice of three principal strategies: interpret the statement as conveying an implicature, change beliefs about the underlying facts or conclude that the speaker is not being cooperative after all. How is that choice to be made? What principles determine how the listener should respond? Grice does not speak to this question in any detail. It is possible, however, to make some tentative observations on the subject.

Consider the choice between accepting an implicature or changing one's factual beliefs. That choice appears to turn on a weighing of two principal variables. One is our degree of confidence about the facts. In the case discussed above, where A says, "B cooked a delicious dinner for me last night," our willingness to accept an implicature (A is being ironic) is determined largely by our degree of confidence that B is in fact a terrible cook. If B has cooked many dinners for us, all of them terrible, we might hold the belief with a fair degree of confidence that B is a bad cook. If, on the other hand, we had only one bad meal at B's house, and that several years ago, we might have only slight confidence in our opinion that B is a bad cook and therefore be more inclined to change our factual beliefs than to assume that A is making an implicature.

The other variable is the strength of the implicature itself. The statement "B cooked a delicious dinner for me last night" is more likely to be interpreted as ironically intended if spoken with exaggerated emphasis on one or more words, or if accompanied by winks, pokes in the ribs or other gestures indicating a nonliteral meaning. On the other hand, if the statement is made in a deadpan or flat manner, we would tend to discount the possibility that an implicature is intended. The strength of the implicature also depends on facts known to the speaker and the listener, as well as their knowledge about each other's knowledge. If A informed us in the past of how terrible B's cooking is, we are more likely to interpret the utterance as conveying an ironic meaning than if A doesn't know that we think B's cooking is for the birds. A's knowledge of our feelings for B is also relevant: if A knows that we are a loyal friend of B, she might be less inclined to criticize B's cooking than otherwise. Similarly, if our relationship with A is such that we often engage in irony or double entendre, or if we know A to be a person prone to such habits of speech, we are more likely to assume that an implicature is intended. More generally, the likelihood that an implicature is intended would appear to increase with the degree of intimacy existing between the parties. If we are on close terms with A, the possibility of irony would appear to be increased over a situation where we are merely nodding acquaintances.

Consider now the choice between a belief that the cooperative principle is respected (A's comment is intended to be cooperative in some sense with the overall aims and direction of our conversation) and a belief that the cooperative principle is violated (A's comment is not intended to cooperate with the overall aims of the exchange). The most important observation here is that, as Grice notes, the cooperative principle represents a powerful social force. People will go far to avoid concluding that their conversational relationship with others is not in fact cooperative. Recognizing a breakdown in the cooperative principle entails that our interlocutor is lying to us or attempting to trick or manipulate us. Not only is such behavior insulting and demeaning, but it is also likely to trigger anger, hard feelings and a possible rupture of social relationships. Thus, breakdowns in the cooperative principle are dangerous and costly; for this reason people in normal social intercourse preserve the principle if at all possible.

However, there is obviously a threshold beyond which the inference is inescapable that the party with whom we are speaking is not cooperating. The variables that would support an inference that the cooperative principle has broken down are, first, the ones noted above as relevant to the choice between implicatures and changes in factual beliefs. If the available implicatures are weak or have been cancelled, and if we are very confident of the truth of our own factual understanding, then we may be driven, even if unwillingly, to the conclusion that the other party is not cooperating. But we would tend to maintain the assumption of cooperation if implicatures are available and not cancelled, or if we hold less firm beliefs about the underlying facts. Second, we might infer that the cooperative principle has broken down based on other facts that we know about our interlocutor. We are more likely to assume a breakdown of cooperation if we know the other person to be angry, disappointed, frustrated, envious or deceitful. We are less likely to assume a breakdown of the cooperative principle the more we are attached to a person by bonds of friendship or family. We simply have more to lose from recognizing a breakdown of cooperation with a family member or close friend than we do in recognizing that a stranger is not behaving cooperatively.

2. STATUTORY INTERPRETATION

Let us now apply these principles to statutory interpretation. We have noted already that in conversational settings the maxims of quality can be flouted even when the utterance in question is stated in the imperative. The same is true for legislation; although typically phrased as commands, statutes are subject to the quality maxims.

The analytic process in statutory settings is roughly this. First, identify the goals which the legislature sought to advance in the statute under review. Second, identify the legislature's presuppositions by relating the apparent legislative commands to the goals which the legislature attempted to advance. Legislative presuppositions, in other words, are statements of the form "implementing the statutory command 'do X' will, as a factual matter, advance legislative goal Y." Third, check whether the legislative presuppositions so identified are consistent with the interpreter's understanding of the factual background.

This third step determines whether or not the quality maxims are flouted. If the interpreter believes that as a factual matter doing X will, indeed, advance legislative goal Y, then there is no flouting, and the conventional meaning of the statute is perfectly acceptable. But suppose that the apparent legislative presupposition is at variance with the interpreter's understanding of the facts. The interpreter is firmly of the view that doing X will not, as a factual matter, advance legislative goal Y; indeed, doing X will *disserve* some goal, either Y itself or another goal Z which the interpreter attributes to the legislature. At this point there arises an apparent flouting of the maxims of quality. If, indeed, the legislature has engaged in the presupposition at issue, then the interpreter might infer that the legislature has either implied a falsehood or at least implied a statement lacking adequate factual support.

If a given statute does indeed represent an apparent flouting of the quality maxims, the interpreter—we will assume a court—has available the same three strategies that we noted are available in ordinary conversation: conclude that an implicature is intended, change beliefs about the underlying facts or conclude that the cooperative principle has been violated.

a. Implicatures

As we have seen, the first standard conversational approach is to resolve apparent floutings of the quality maxims by use of implicatures.

In the case of statutory interpretation, the relevant implicatures are meanings attributed to the legislative language which differ from the purely conventional or literal meaning and which generate presuppositions consistent with the interpreter's view of the underlying facts. In other words, the statute as conventionally interpreted may contain the presupposition "doing X will advance legislative goal Y," when court knows or believes that doing X will not in fact advance legislative goal Y and will in fact disserve some legislative goal. But another interpretation—an implicature—may be available which contains a different presupposition that is compatible with the court's view of the underlying facts. Other things being equal, pragmatics theory suggests that the implicature should be preferred in order to avoid a violation of the quality maxims.

Something very like this approach is in fact present in our statutory jurisprudence, in the traditional maxim that a court should not interpret a statute to yield an absurd result.[94] In pragmatic terms, this maxim embodies the proposition that a court may search for implicatures when confronted with an apparent legislative violation of the maxims of quality—and may do so even when the implicatures are not otherwise particularly compelling because the statutory language, taken literally, calls for a different result.

Consider the United States Supreme Court's most recent encounter with this rule in *Public Citizen v. United States Department of Justice*.[95] At issue was whether the American Bar Association's Committee on the Federal Judiciary was an "advisory committee" under the Federal Advisory Committee Act. The relevant statute defined an advisory committee as any group "established or utilized" by the president or an agency to give advice on public questions. The Supreme Court recognized that the ABA committee did advise the justice department on judicial candidates, and it therefore fell within the literal terms of the statute.[96] But such a result would be "odd"[97] because it would not appear to serve the statutory purposes of conserving public funds and reducing the danger of biased proposals.[98] The Court concluded that because the result was odd, it was permissible to look beyond the plain language and to evaluate other evidence of legislative intent. Not unexpectedly, given this framing of the problem, the Court then construed the statute as not covering the ABA Committee.[99]

---

94. *E.g.*, Public Citizen v. United States Dep't of Justice, 109 S. Ct. 2558, 2566-67 (1989); O'Connor v. United States, 479 U.S. 27, 31 (1986); Brock v. Pierce County, 476 U.S. 253, 258-59 (1986); Griffin v. Oceanic Contractors, 458 U.S. 564, 575 (1983).
95. 109 S. Ct. 2558.
96. *Id.* at 2565.
97. *Id.* at 2566 (quoting Green v. Bock Laundry Machine Co., 109 S. Ct. 1981, 1984 (1989)).
98. *Id.* at 2565.
99. *Id.* at 2572.

Rephrased in pragmatic terms, the Court's inquiry was as follows. First, it identified the relevant statutory goals (conserving public funds and reducing the danger of biased proposals). Then it compared the statutory text with these goals to identify the presupposition (that designating the ABA Committee an advisory committee would further the policies underlying the statute). The Court then checked this presupposition against its own view of the facts, and found conflict (the Court believed that the congressional goals would not be served if the ABA Committee were treated as an advisory committee). Thus, there was an apparent flouting of the maxims of quality (interpreting the statute according to its conventional meaning would entail that Congress was either deceptive or lacked sufficient evidence for the presupposition). To overcome the flouting the Court endorsed an implicature (the words "advisory committee" did not apply to the ABA Committee even though on their face they appeared to do so).

Consider the maxim that a court is obliged to give effect, if possible, to every word the legislature used.[100] Suppose a city council passes an ordinance stating "Anyone bringing a dog into the park shall pay a fine of fifty dollars." It then passes another ordinance stating "All dogs in the park shall be licensed and leashed." If we read the first provision to exclude all dogs from the park, then the second ordinance requiring that dogs in the park be licensed and leashed becomes meaningless. The maxim of giving effect to every word of the lawgiver would call for some interpretation in which the two rules would each have meaning.

This is an application of the third maxim of quality identified above: avoid making statements that are meaningless. A court would naturally prefer an interpretation that does not nullify the meaning of statutory words or provisions. If we read the rule against bringing dogs into the park for all it may be worth, the consequence would be an apparent flouting of the maxim of meaningfulness because the provision about leashes and licenses would have no force. This apparent flouting of the maxim gives rise to a number of possible implicatures. For example, the ban on bringing dogs into the park might be construed as setting forth the penalty payable by any person who violates the prohibition against dogs in the park that are not leashed and licensed. The two statutes are thereby harmonized in such a way that both are given meaning and each has a meaning independent of the other.

Similar analysis can easily be applied to the maxim that, where two statutes are capable of coexistence, it is the duty of the courts to

---

100. *See, e.g.*, Bowsher v. Merck & Co., 460 U.S. 824, 833 (1983); Fidelity Fed. Sav. & Loan Ass'n v. De La Cuesta, 458 U.S. 141, 163 (1982); American Textile Mfrs. Inst., Inc. v. Donovan, 452 U.S. 490, 513 (1981).

reconcile them if possible.[101] Here we have an apparent flouting of the maxim that the speaker should avoid contradiction. It would be odd indeed if the legislature intended to impose directly conflicting obligations on citizens, or to prohibit an activity in one part of a code while permitting it in another. Accordingly, courts faced with apparently conflicting statutes will search diligently for implicatures that resolve the apparent contradictions.

Another important application of the quality maxims might be found in various maxims designed to provide information regarding the scope of power granted by the legislature to the executive or judicial branches in a given statute. It is commonly said, for example, that when a statute imposes a duty it authorizes by implication all reasonable and necessary means to effectuate such a duty.[102] The pragmatic analysis of this maxim is as follows. When the legislature charges an administrative agency with a duty, the statutory language creating the duty and vesting it in the agency carries the presupposition that the agency is capable of performing the duty. The presupposition is of the form "given statutory powers A, B and C, the agency is capable of effectuating duty X." The interpreter must then compare this presupposition with the interpreter's own view of the facts. If the interpreter believes that the agent can satisfactorily effectuate duty X through the use of powers A, B and C, then no flouting of a maxim arises and the statute can be interpreted as written. But if the interpreter believes that powers A, B and C are not sufficient to effectuate duty X, there is an apparent flouting of quality maxims, since the legislature's presupposition is then seen as either being false or based on insufficient evidence. The apparent flouting can be resolved by an implicature, namely that in addition to express powers A, B and C, the agency has implicit power D, which the interpreter believes is sufficient, when added to the express powers, to effectuate the statutory duty X.

b. Changes in belief about facts

Courts do not always resolve apparent floutings of the quality maxims through the use of implicatures, however. They may also adopt

---

101. *See, e.g.*, Kremer v. Chemical Constr. Co., 456 U.S. 461, 468 (1983); American Bank & Trust Co. v. Dallas County, 463 U.S. 855, 868 (1982); Morton v. Mancari, 417 U.S. 535, 551 (1974).

102. *See, e.g.*, United States v. Stewart, 311 U.S. 60 (1940); 3 C. SANDS, SUTHERLAND STATUTORY CONSTRUCTION 164 (1974) ("The grant of an express power carries with it the authority to exercise all other activities reasonably necesary to carry it into effect"). *Compare* Gomez v. United States, 109 S. Ct. 2237, 2241 (1989) ("When a statute creates an office to which it assigns specific duties, those duties outline the attributes of the office. Any additional duties performed pursuant to a general authorization in the statute reasonably should bear some relation to the specified duties").

the jurisprudential analog of the second conversational strategy discussed above: they may change their views about the facts.

In American jurisprudence, this strategy is often articulated in terms of constitutional law. If a court faced with an apparent flouting of the maxims of quality concludes that an implicature is simply not available—if, for example, the legislature has expressed beyond doubt that it intends a particular interpretation and no other—that ordinarily is the end of the matter; the court must swallow hard and apply the statute as written. If the flouting of the maxims is especially severe, however, the court has the option of declaring the statute unconstitutional as lacking any rational basis. Thus, challenges to the factual bases of legislative presuppositions are typically framed as questions of constitutional law.

Take the *Carolene Products* case,[103] a classic example of rational basis scrutiny. At issue was the constitutionality of a federal statute which prohibited interstate commerce in "filled milk" (evaporated skimmed milk laced with vegetable oil). A manufacturer of filled milk claimed that the statute was irrational because there was no evidence of any health risks or of any consumer fraud associated with the product. The Supreme Court upheld the statute, however, on the ground that Congress could reasonably have concluded not only that filled milk posed a threat to health (because it lacked vitamins), but also that its sale encouraged consumer fraud (because it might be confused with evaporated whole milk).[104]

In pragmatic terms, the analytical process that a reasonable law interpreter would follow in order to reach the result in *Carolene Products* can be described as follows. First, a reasonable interpreter would look at the statute in question to identify the relevant legislative presuppositions. Here, the presuppositions were that filled milk poses a danger to health and to consumer welfare. A reasonable interpreter would then compare these presuppositions to her own view of the facts. Again the interpreter would find conflict. There was little, if any, credible evidence of record in the *Carolene Products* case to indicate any threat to health from the sale of filled milk.[105] Nor was there evidence that consumers had been misled or were likely to be misled by the product.

Faced with this apparent violation of the cooperative principle, a reasonable intepreter might look for an implicature as a means of restoring the assumption of cooperation. Perhaps Congress intended the words "filled milk" to denote only adulterated products which in fact did pose a risk to health or consumer welfare. But in the *Carolene*

---

103. United States v. Carolene Products Co., 304 U.S. 144 (1938).
104. *See* Miller, *The True Story of Carolene Products*, 1987 SUP. CT. REV. 397, 412.
105. *See id.* at 420-21.

Products case, no implicature was available. It was evident beyond doubt that Congress had indeed intended to outlaw this particular product from interstate commerce, even though the product would appear to most reasonable observers to be perfectly safe and not subject to any particular dangers of fraud.

In the absence of an available implicature, a reasonable interpreter might instead reconsider its own view of the facts. The cooperative principle would be preserved if the interpreter abandoned the premise that the apparent legislative presuppositions were false. Perhaps filled milk *does* pose a risk to health or consumer welfare; perhaps Congress got the facts right after all. If so, there is no flouting of the maxims of quality, and the statute may be enforced as written.[106]

Arguably, a reasoning process of this sort underlies cases such as *Carolene Products*. The Court in that case deferred to congressional "findings" that commerce in filled milk threatened the public interest. The principle of deference found in *Carolene Products* is, in pragmatic terms, nothing other than an institutionalized attitude of willingness to accept legislative presuppositions even when those presuppositions differ markedly from the factual analyses that the justices on the Court might make if they were examining the matter *de novo*. By mandating judicial deference to congressional fact-finding—and even to congressional presuppositions in the absence of explicit fact-finding[107]—the Supreme Court in cases such as *Carolene Products* insists that the cooperative principle be maintained if at all possible, even in the face of apparent congressional floutings of the maxims of quality.

c. Changes in belief about the cooperative nature of the interchange

Courts do not always resolve apparent floutings of the maxims of quality by the use of implicatures or by accepting legislative presuppositions. In some contexts, courts will conclude that the connection between legislative means and ends is without a sufficient factual basis and will accordingly strike down the legislation as unconstitutional. In pragmatic terms, the conclusion that there is an insufficient connection between legislative means and ends represents a determination that the maxims of quality have been flouted. In such cases, the legislative presuppositions will either be found to be untrue (a violation of the first maxim of quality), to be based on insufficient evidence (a violation of the second maxim of quality) or to be meaningless or incoherent (a violation of the third maxim of quality).

---

106. *See* Williamson v. Lee Optical of Oklahoma, 348 U.S. 483 (1955) (supplying factual premises to justify a statute even though those premises had not been identified by the legislature).

107. *See id.*

If the court does not resolve the flouting either by implicatures or by accepting the legislature's factual predicates, the court may conclude that the legislature was not, in fact, observing the cooperative principle when it enacted the statute in question. A violation of the cooperative principle can be equated, at least roughly, with a judicial finding that the statute in question is unconstitutional.

As noted, courts today almost never strike down economic regulation on constitutional grounds.[108] They are, however, much more inclined to invalidate statutes that limit fundamental rights or that involve suspect classifications. Here the courts insist on a high degree of fit between legislative means and ends. Put another way, they are much less likely to adjust their beliefs about the facts by deferring to the legislature's presuppositions. Take the case of *Craig v. Boren*,[109] involving a statute prohibiting the sale of 3.2 percent beer to males under age twenty-one and females under age eighteen. The Court identified the legislative goal as "enhancement of traffic safety,"[110] and proceeded to analyze the state's argument that the statute in question adequately served that goal insofar as it distinguished between men and women. The Court held that the discrimination between men and women was not warranted by the evidence, despite the fact that at trial the state had introduced surveys showing that two percent of males in the eighteen-to-twenty age group were arrested for driving under the influence while only .18 percent of the females in the age group encountered the same fate.[111] Accordingly, the Court held the statute unconstitutional as a violation of the equal protection clause.

In pragmatic terms, the reasoning in *Craig v. Boren* was as follows. First, the Court identified the legislative purpose as being that of enhancing traffic safety. It then identified the relevant presupposition, namely that the goal of enhancing traffic safety would be served if males between eighteen and twenty-one were prohibited from drinking 3.2 percent beer, but would not be served if females in the same age group were prohibited from drinking 3.2 percent beer. The Court then compared this presupposition with its own view of the facts, which included a strong presumption of sexual equality. Because the Court found the evidence of record insufficient to overcome its own view of the facts, and because no implicature was available to overcome the apparent flouting of the maxims of quality (the statutory language was clear and could not reasonably be interpreted to treat men and women the same),

108. *See, e.g.*, Gunther, *Foreword: In Search of Evolving Doctrine on a Changing Court: a Model for a Newer Equal Protection*, 86 Harv. L. Rev. 1, 21 (1972).
109. 429 U.S. 190 (1976).
110. *Id.* at 199.
111. *Id.* at 223 (Rehnquist, J., dissenting).

the Court concluded that the cooperative principle had broken down and that the statute was therefore unconstitutional.

d. Choice of strategies

How does a court decide which of the three strategies to adopt when faced with an apparent flouting of a quality maxim?

First, consider the choice between recognizing an implicature and changing beliefs about the facts. As in ordinary conversation, the preferred strategy here would appear to depend on several variables. One is the clarity of the statutory language. If the statute is phrased in general, vague, or ambiguous terms, there is considerably more room for implicature than if the statute is stated in clear terms.[112] The other important variable is the degree of confidence with which the court holds its own view of the underlying facts. The significance of that variable depends in part on the judge's general knowledge of the world, in part on the facts presented in evidence (if proof on the matter is allowed),[113] and in part on the strength of presumptions based on substantive social policy (such as the presumption that there is no factual basis for certain legislative classifications). If the language is clear, but the court holds its factual beliefs with only a slight degree of confidence, it is likely to defer to the legislature's factual presuppositions and uphold the statute on that ground (as in *Carolene Products*). If, conversely, the court holds its factual beliefs with a high degree of confidence, but the statutory language is reasonably susceptible to differing interpretations, the court will be inclined to resolve apparent floutings of quality maxims by resort to implicatures which generate presuppositions consistent with the court's view of the facts (as in cases applying the maxim that a statute will be interpreted to avoid absurd results).

Harder questions arise when the statute appears relatively clear and the court has a relatively high degree of confidence in its factual beliefs. Here the court must consider the possibility that the cooperative principle has broken down—that the legislation in question must be invalidated as unconstitutional. But just as a breakdown of the cooperative principle in ordinary conversation is a serious and difficult matter, so is a ruling that a statute is unconstitutional. When a court invalidates a statute, it upsets the conscious directive that represents much labor and thought by the legislature and the affected interest

---

112. The force of conventional meaning is explicable in pragmatics terms. *See infra* notes 131-43 and accompanying text.

113. In some interpretive contexts the legislative presuppositions may be conclusively presumed to be factually accurate, thus precluding proof on the question. *See* Minnesota v. Clover Leaf Creamery, 449 U.S. 456 (1981) (where there was evidence before the legislature reasonably supporting a classification, the party challenging the statute was not permitted to tender evidence in court that the legislature was mistaken).

groups. The court in such cases effectively insults a coordinate branch of government, thus disturbing the tranquility of the constitutional balance and placing the court's own institutional capital on the line for possible attack. Further, when a state statute is at issue, concerns about federal-state relations enter the picture as well.

For all these reasons courts tend to shy away from invalidating statutes on constitutional grounds. A powerful set of maxims expresses this concern by instructing a court to seek, if possible, resolution of cases by means of implicatures rather than by constitutional invalidation. The Supreme Court has repeatedly announced that if a case can be decided on either constitutional or legislative grounds, a court should opt for the legislative approach.[114] Often the admonition to avoid constitutional issues is phrased in stronger terms: courts may "strain" to avoid the constitutional issue,[115] should construe the statute as valid where "fairly possible,"[116] and so on.[117] The message is to seek an implicature that would remedy the potential constitutional defect. But the Court also warns that the statute cannot be rewritten; if no saving construction is possible then the constitutional issue must be faced.[118]

A separate set of principles informs the court as to the choice between adopting an implicature or changing its view of the facts, on the one hand, or invalidating the statute on constitutional grounds, on the other. The key variables here are the clarity of the statutory language, the degree of confidence the court has in its own factual judgments and the strength of the evidentiary basis supporting the legislature's presuppositions. Other things being equal, the court will be more inclined to resolve an interpretive problem through the use of an implicature if the statute is vague and uncertain than if it is tightly and narrowly drawn. Similarly, a court will be more likely to defer to the legislature's factual presuppositions when the court has only slight confidence in its own factual views or the legislature has compiled a convincing factual record (for example, by holding extensive hearings at which experts testify, and so on). On the other hand, the court will be

---

114. *See, e.g.,* Communications Workers of America v. Beck, 487 U.S. 735, 762 (1988); Rescue Army v. Municipal Court, 331 U.S. 549, 568-69 (1947); Alma Motor Co. v. Timken Co., 329 U.S. 129, 136 (1946); Ashwander v. TVA, 297 U.S. 288, 347 (1936).

115. Apthecker v. Secretary of State, 378 U.S. 500, 515 (1964).

116. *E.g.,* St. Martin Lutheran Church v. South Dakota, 451 U.S. 772, 780 (1981); Graham v. Richardson, 403 U.S. 365, 382-83 (1971); Crowell v. Benson, 285 U.S. 22, 62 (1932).

117. *See* Public Citizen v. United States Dep't of Justice, 109 S. Ct. 2558 (1989) (construe statutes to avoid serious constitutional problems unless such a construction is "plainly contrary" to intent of Congress); DeBartolo Corp. v. Florida Gulf Coast Building & Constr. Trades Council, 485 U.S. 568, 575 (1988) (same).

118. *E.g.,* Heckler v. Mathews, 465 U.S. 728, 741-42 (1984); Swain v. Pressley, 430 U.S. 372, 378 n.11 (1977).

less inclined to defer to the legislature when the court holds a high degree of confidence in its own factual views. The factors contributing to the court's confidence level are matters of general knowledge to which the court can take judicial notice, matters proved at trial if proof on the legislative presuppositions is allowed, and the strength of the presumptions that the court holds a priori as a matter of social policy (such as presumptions of sexual and racial equality).

D. Relation

In addition to maxims of quantity and quality, Grice proposes a general category of "relation," which encompasses only one maxim: "be relevant."[119] By this Grice apparently means that one should not engage in non sequiturs. There is a general understanding in cooperative conversational settings that A's comment relates to what B has just said and in general relates to the overall goals and tenor of the conversation.

The urge to interpret statements in conversational settings as relevant to what has gone before is extraordinarily strong. It is this urge, I believe, that makes sudden changes of subject so unsettling in social contexts. Good conversational manners demand an appropriate segue if one desires to change the subject. Standard conventions here are remarks such as "that reminds me of Y," "as long as we're talking about X, what about Y?" and so on. Complete changes of subject require express acknowledgement, often accompanied by an implicit apology: "Apropos of nothing, what about Y?", "This isn't what we've been talking about, but what about Y?" and so on.

The maxim of relevance creates the potential for implicatures when the maxim appears to be flouted. Return to an earlier example: A says, "Do you know what time it is?" and B responds, "Well, the milkman has come." B's response appears to be irrelevant to A's question. Perhaps B has not heard the question, or is acting like an insensitive cad by ignoring it. But ordinarily, as we have seen, B's comment will be interpreted as responsive to the question and as providing some sort of relevant information.

The maxim of relevance has obvious force in statutory contexts. First, there appears to be a powerful presumption that individual statutes deal with discrete issues, or at least with issues that are related to each other in important respects. This presumption is acknowledged in legislatures; it is usually out of order, in the legislative process, to propose amendments to a statute that have no bearing on the general subject of the statute itself. Courts likewise presume that statutes deal with one or at most a few related subject areas.

---

119. P. Grice, *supra* note 58, at 27.

Consider further the maxim of *in pari materia*—a word found in different places in a single statute will be interpreted in the same way throughout.[120] The Gricean principle of relevance suggests that all parts of a single statute are relevant to each other; a statute represents a "conversation" in which the various utterances will ordinarily be considered as bearing on the same topic, and therefore as using terms with consistent definitions.

Also of interest here is the rule that appropriations measures will not be ordinarily interpreted to amend or repeal other statutes.[121] This rule is based on the observation (perhaps more valid in the past than today) that appropriations measures are concerned with spending, not regulating, and therefore that language in appropriations measures will be interpreted as limited to the spending function when a regulatory interpretation would supersede other statutes. All these interpretive rules can be seen as grounded in the Gricean maxim of relevance.

More generally, something like a relevance principle appears to undergird the basic principle of statutory construction that the words of a statute are to be interpreted in light of the overall context and the purposes which the legislature evidently sought to achieve.[122] The relevance principle suggests that words in a statute should pertain to the overall purposes of the legislation. Thus, where the statutory language can be interpreted as inconsistent with or not serving the statutory purposes, an implicature arises under the maxim of relevance that the language should be reinterpreted actually to serve the purposes in question. Like all implicatures, however, those relating language to the legislature's apparent purposes are not ineluctable; they can be avoided— or better, do not arise at all—if the language is so clear that it cannot reasonably be construed in accordance with the apparent legislative purposes. Thus, mere generalized references to remedial purposes will not support an interpretation at odds with the statutory language and scheme.[123] Similarly, if the conventional meaning of a statute is clear,

---

120. *See, e.g.,* Washington Metro. Area Transit Auth. v. Johnson, 467 U.S. 925, 935-36 (1984); BankAmerica Corp. v. United States, 462 U.S. 122, 129 (1983); Mohasco Corp. v. Silver, 447 U.S. 807, 826 (1980); Northcross v. Board of Educ., 412 U.S. 427, 428 (1973); Erlenbaugh v. United States, 409 U.S. 239, 243-44 (1972). The converse of the *in pari materia* rule is the principle that the same or similar words do not necessarily have the same meaning when found in different statutes. *See, e.g.,* Russello v. United States, 464 U.S. 16, 25 (1983) ("[l]anguage from one statute usually sheds little light upon the meaning of different language in another statute, even when the two are enacted at or about the same time").

121. TVA v. Hill, 437 U.S. 153, 190-91 (1978).

122. *E.g.,* Commissioner v. Engle, 464 U.S. 206, 217 (1984 (where several readings of a statute are equally plausible, the court's duty is to "find that interpretation which can most fairly be said to be imbedded in the statute, in the sense of being most harmonious with its scheme and with the general purposes that Congress manifested"); Dickerson v. New Banner Inst., Inc., 460 U.S. 103, 118 (1983); Chapman v. Houston Welfare Rights Org., 441 U.S. 600, 608 (1979).

123. *E.g.,* Touche, Ross & Co. v. Redington, 442 U.S. 560, 578 (1979); SEC v. Sloan, 436 U.S. 103, 116 (1978).

courts are wary of supplying implicatures that rectify apparent an-omolies,[124] at least not unless the purposes of the statute would clearly be frustrated by a literal intepretation.[125] The fact that these maxims may appear to work against each other in particular cases does not, contrary to what Llewellyn suggested,[126] demonstrate their incoherence; it merely suggests that the analysis is subtle and requires, in legislation as in all communicative contexts, a careful weighing of the strengths of competing implicatures.

E. Manner

Grice's final class of maxims concerns those arising under the principle of "manner." The overall directive here—"be perspicuous"— is implemented by four sub-maxims: avoid obscurity, avoid ambiguity, be brief and be orderly.[127]

1. CONVERSATIONAL SETTINGS

Most of these maxims can readily be recognized in conventional conversational settings. Suppose that on a crowded elevator, attorney A says to her partner B, "Has that matter we were talking about a few days ago turned out as we hoped?" This utterance appears to violate the injunction to avoid obscurity, since it would have been much clearer if A had said, "Has Smith been forced off the board of directors of the Jones Company yet?" The apparent flouting of the obscurity maxim is easily resolved, however, under the assumption that the matter in ques-tion involves attorney-client confidences or is otherwise a subject of some sensitivity. The cooperative principle is preserved with the in-ference that A's obscurity is intended to convey to B the message, "I want to ask you a question in a code that others on this elevator will not understand."

Suppose instead that A says to B, "I got plastered last night." Almost everyone would interpret this statement as meaning that A had too much to drink. But the sentence isn't perfectly unambiguous: A *might* mean that he went to an artist's studio and had a plaster cast made of his face, or something of this sort. The latter interpretation, however, would flout the ambiguity maxim. If A had intended to say that he had a plaster cast made, he would ordinarily say so in some

---

124. *See, e.g.,* Green v. Bock Laundry Mach. Co., 109 S. Ct. 1981 (1989); *Hill,* 437 U.S. at 153; Union Elec. Co. v. EPA, 427 U.S. 246 (1976).

125. *See, e.g.,* United Steelworkers of America v. Weber, 443 U.S. 193, 201 (1979); Holy Trinity Church v. United States, 143 U.S. 457, 459 (1892).

126. K. LLEWELLYN, *supra* note 2, at 521-35.

127. P. GRICE, *supra* note 58, at 27. In an apparent self-referential joke, Grice glosses the maxim "be brief" with the comment "avoid unnecessary prolixity." *Id.*

other way not susceptible to a conventional interpretation at variance with the facts. The ambiguity maxim suggests that if a statement is ambiguous in any respect, the speaker will ordinarily be understood to intend the more common meaning. But the ambiguity maxim is, again, not ineluctable. Suppose B has good reason to think that A could *not* have had too much to drink, or that it would be very odd if he did (A, for instance, might possess deep religious scruples against consuming alcohol). Now B is likely to search A's statement for some way of reconciling it with the cooperative principle. One possibility B might entertain is that A is making a joke of some sort by playing on an ambiguity in the term "plastered."[128]

As to the maxim "be brief," consider the following example from Grice: a performance review states that "Miss X produced a series of sounds that corresponded closely with the score of 'Home Sweet Home.' "[129] Grice observes that this sentence is much more verbose than the alternative, "Miss X sang 'Home Sweet Home,' " and that the apparent flouting of the brevity maxim raises the implicature that Miss X's performance in fact suffered from some hideous defect.[130]

2. STATUTORY INTERPRETATION

Now let us apply these principles to statutory interpretation. Consider first the maxims according priority to certain conventional over unconventional interpretations. There are two principal maxims of statutory interpretation here. First, courts assume that legislatures use words in their ordinary, common senses unless the legislature expressly states otherwise.[131] Second, technical language is usually interpreted according to the usages of the trade within which the language is used—at least if the persons regulated or affected by the statute can be expected

---

128. Although linguists working in pragmatics theory do not discuss jokes at length, it appears that many forms of humor can be understood in pragmatic terms as representing apparent floutings of the cooperative principle.

129. P. GRICE, *supra* note 58, at 37.

130. Grice does not provide any examples of the maxim "be orderly" in ordinary conversation, and it is somewhat difficult to imagine any cases in which the orderliness maxim would have meaning apart from the maxim of relevance (the assumption that the speaker's utterances are relevant implies that the utterances have some sort of coherence and order). Possibly an example would be that of a speaker whose apparently disjointed remarks are intended to illustrate the disorderliness of the matter under discussion.

131. *See, e.g.,* H.J., Inc. v. Northwestern Bell Tel. Co., 109 S. Ct. 2893, 2900 (1989); Community for Creative Non-Violence v. Reid, 109 S. Ct. 2166, 2172 (1989); Mississippi Band of Choctaw Indians v. Holyfield, 109 S. Ct. 1597, 1607-08 (1989); Kosak v. United States, 465 U.S. 848, 853 (1984); Russello v. United States, 464 U.S. 16, 21 (1983); American Tobacco Co. v. Patterson, 456 U.S. 63, 68 (1982); Diamond v. Chakrabarty, 447 U.S. 303, 308 (1980); Group Life & Health Ins. Co. v. Royal Drug Co., 440 U.S. 205, 211 (1979); Perrin v. United States, 444 U.S. 37, 42 (1979); Ernst & Ernst v. Hochfelder, 425 U.S. 185, 199 n.19 (1976); Richards v. United States, 369 U.S. 1, 9 (1962).

to be familiar with the usages. The most prominent application of this latter principle is as follows: when a legislature uses terms that have accumulated settled meanings under either equity or common law, a court infers, unless the statute otherwise dictates, that the legislature means to incorporate the established meaning of these terms.[132]

Analyzed in pragmatic terms, these rules appear to represent applications of the Gricean maxim "avoid obscurity." A legislature is engaged in a process of communication when it enacts a statute. Other things being equal, a court would ordinarily assume that the legislature intended its communication to be as effective as possible. This implies that language found in statutes should be given the application that is most conventional within the audience to which the statute is addressed. Otherwise, Congress could be accused of being deliberately obscure and thus flouting the first maxim of manner.

For the most part the maxim that words in a statute should be interpreted according to their ordinary usages does not give rise to implicatures, simply because the maxim is not flouted. It is possible to imagine situations, however, where an implicature could arise. Say a legislature enacts a statute in which a word has both a conventional meaning in ordinary speech and a specialized meaning in a trade (for example, "dozen" used in popular speech and among bakers). The first maxim of manner suggests that the popular usage would be preferred. But suppose further that other evidence in the statute makes clear that the technical meaning is more consistent with the scheme of the statute or its legislative history. Thus, there is an apparent flouting of the maxim, which might be overcome by resort to an implicature that the statute is intended to apply only within a specialized industry and not to the public at large.

Also relevant here is the "plain meaning" maxim, which expresses a strong preference for literal or conventional interpretations.[133] The plain meaning rule has several variants, ranging from a virtually conclusive presumption that the plain language governs,[134] to milder formulations under which the plain meaning governs except in "rare" or "exceptional" circumstances,[135] or under which the plain meaning "or-

---

132. *See, e.g., Community for Creative Non-Violence,* 109 S. Ct. at 2173; NLRB v. Amax Coal Co., 453 U.S. 322, 329 (1981).

133. *See generally* Epstein, *The Pitfalls of Interpretation,* 7 HARV. J. L. & PUB. POL. 101 (1984).

134. *See, e.g.,* United States v. Ron Pair Enter., 109 S. Ct. 1026, 1030 (1989) (where meaning of a statute is plain "the sole function of the courts is to enforce it according to its terms"); Board of Governors v. Dimension Fin. Corp., 474 U.S. 361, 368 (1985) (if the statute is clear and unambiguous, "that is the end of the matter").

135. *See, e.g.,* Amoco Production Co. v. Village of Gambell, 480 U.S. 531, 548 (1987); Howe v. Smith, 452 U.S. 473, 483 (1981); Rubin v. United States, 449 U.S. 424, 430 (1981).

dinarily" controls.[136] The Court also often says that the statutory language is the "starting place" for interpretation,[137] an ambiguous formulation that could refer either to the temporal order of analysis (start with the language and then go on to other evidence) or to some substantive priority for linguistic analysis over analysis based on other sources of evidence, such as legislative history. The latter interpretation could be taken to represent a diluted version of the plain meaning rule—i.e., that the conventional or literal meaning of the words is the most important, but by no means the only, factor for a court to consider in construing a statute.[138]

The pragmatic force underlying these variants of the plain meaning rule appears to be the maxim that a speaker should avoid ambiguity. A statute will ordinarily be interpreted according to its conventional or literal meaning if that meaning is sufficiently clear. Given a clear conventional meaning, courts will not search the language to detect hidden or latent ambiguities that might be exploited by drawing on extrinsic aids to interpretation such as legislative history. Thus, unless sufficiently strong implicatures can be derived elsewhere, the plain language of a statute governs and controls interpretation. But if a sufficiently compelling implicature can be derived elsewhere—for example, if it can be shown that applying the plain meaning will lead to absurd results, thus flouting maxims of quality—[139] then the plain meaning might give way to an alternative reading in a given case.

Conceptualizing the plain meaning rule in this light undermines one of the classic objections to the rule. The objection is this: the plain meaning rule applies only when the meaning is "plain." Such a determination, however, fails to recognize the fact that whether the meaning is plain is itself often unclear. A statute may appear plain to one observer and ambiguous to another. An example is *United States v. Yermian*,[140] in which the majority opinion concluded that the statute was unambiguous and the dissenting opinion, following the majority opin-

---

136. *See, e.g.*, Kaiser Aluminum & Chemical Corp. v. Bonjorno, 110 S. Ct. 1570 (1990); Russello v. United States, 464 U.S. 16, 20 (1984); Consumer Prod. Safety Comm'n v. GTE Sylvania, 447 U.S. 102, 108 (1980); Rodriguez v. Compass Shipping Co., 451 U.S. 596, 617 (1981); TVA v. Hill, 437 U.S. 153, 187 n.33 (1978).

137. *See, e.g.*, Bowsher v. Merck & Co., 460 U.S. 824, 830 (1983); North Dakota v. United States, 460 U.S. 300, 312 (1983); Rubin v. United States, 449 U.S. 424, 429 (1981); Watt v. Alaska, 451 U.S. 259, 265 (1981); American Textile Manuf. Ass'n v. Donovan, 452 U.S. 490, 508 (1981); Steadman v. SEC, 450 U.S. 91, 97 (1981); Diamond v. Chakrabarty, 447 U.S. 303, 308 (1980); Group Life & Health Ins. Co. v. Royal Drug Co., 440 U.S. 205, 210 (1979); Teamsters v. Daniel, 439 U.S. 551, 558 (1979).

138. These different formulations of the plain meaning principle should not be taken to substantiate Llewellyn's claim that the maxims are incoherent and self-contradictory; rather, they appear to express the inherent inexactitude—the "cancelability"—of conversational implicatures in the statutory setting.

139. *See supra* notes 87-118 and accompanying text.

140. 468 U.S. 63 (1984).

ion in the appeals court, concluded that the statute was ambiguous. The dissent chastized the majority for "simply pointing to the ambiguous phrases and proclaiming them clear."[141] The fact that ambiguity may be in the eyes of the beholder apparently drains the plain meaning rule of much of its claim to certainty and consistency of application.

But the plain meaning rule should not be understood as based on a claim of certainty of application. Instead, the rule refers, albeit inexactly, to a pragmatic process of weighing competing considerations: the clarity of the statutory language, its consistency with the underlying legislative purposes and whether the costs of resort to extrinsic aids to interpretation (such as legislative history) are likely to outweigh whatever benefits might be realized from such an enterprise. Seen in this light, the plain meaning rule states a sensible approach to statutory construction that accords well with the interpretive techniques used in the analysis of ordinary conversational settings.

Finally let us consider the Gricean maxim, "be brief." Here we can revert to some principles of statutory interpretation already discussed. For example, the maxim that a court is obliged to give effect, if possible, to every word used by the legislature[142] can be understood as reflecting, not only the maxims of quantity,[143] but also the injunction of brevity. A legislature ordinarily should not express itself in unduly verbose terms unless it has a reason to do so. Thus an elaborate and long-winded statutory formulation would appear to flout the Gricean maxim of brevity if a shorter phrase would accomplish the same result. The implicature is that all words used in legislation should be given effect if possible. A similar analysis can be applied to the maxim *expressio unius est exclusio alterius*. Where terms are grouped in a list followed by a general phrase or term, the legislature would flout the brevity maxim if it intended the general term to be understood in its broadest sense (because then the other words in the list would be superfluous). But the apparent flouting of the brevity maxim can be overcome if we accept the implicature that the general term is qualified by the preceding specific terms, and thus takes its meaning from the other words in the list (because a list followed by a general term may be the most succinct way of expressing the legislature's intent).

CONCLUSION

The foregoing discussion has attempted to adduce evidence suggesting that many traditional maxims of statutory interpretation embody legitimate and valid inferences of legislative intent. I have at-

141. *Id.* at 77 (Rehnquist, J., dissenting).
142. *See supra* note 93.
143. *See supra* text accompanying notes 70-86.

tempted to show that some of these maxims have endured across a wide variety of legal systems, and that the insights captured by the maxims reflect common sense methods of interpreting utterances in ordinary conversation, as formalized by Grice's theory of implicatures. The general goal here is to rehabilitate the maxims against Llewellyn's claim that they are mutually contradictory and incoherent. I suggest that the maxims often do reflect reasonable inferences about legislative meaning, and that their apparent inconsistency and indeterminancy stems from the fact that the implicatures arising from the maxims are always cancelable and often have to be weighed against one another to determine which implicature is the strongest in a given case. Despite Llewellyn's apparent coup de grâce, the maxims survive. This Article has suggested some possible explanations for the puzzling persistence of the maxims of interpretation.

LEGAL FORMALISM, LEGAL REALISM, AND THE INTERPRETATION OF STATUTES AND THE CONSTITUTION

Richard A. Posner*

A current focus of legal debate is the proper role of the courts in the interpretation of statutes and the Constitution. Are judges to look solely to the naked language of an enactment, then logically deduce its application in simple syllogistic fashion, as legal formalists had purported to do? Or may the inquiry into meaning be informed by perhaps unbridled and unaccountable judicial notions of public policy, using legal realism to best promote the general welfare?

Judge Posner considers the concepts of formalism and realism to be meaningful and useful in common law reasoning, but in interpretation to be useless and, worse, forbidden. He analogizes unclear "orders" from a legislature to garbled battlefield communications, and argues that the duty of the recipient of those orders (the judge) is to advance as best he can the enterprise set on foot by the superiors. Case studies elaborate this thesis. Judicial decisions interpreting fixed texts, Judge Posner concludes, can be neither logically correct or incorrect, philosophically sound or unsound, until the ultimate jurist, time, has adjudged their results.

INTRODUCTION

SEVERAL YEARS AGO I wrote a paper that tried to give "judicial self-restraint" and its opposite, "judicial activism," precise meanings, so that "restraint" would no longer be just an all-purpose

* Judge, United States Court of Appeals for the Seventh Circuit; Senior Lecturer, University of Chicago Law School. This is the revised text of the Sumner Canary Lecture given at Case Western Reserve University School of Law on October 15, 1986. I thank Paul Bator, Frank Easterbrook, William Eskridge, Dennis Hutchinson, Richard Porter, Andrew Rosenfield, David Strauss, Cass Sunstein, and participants in the Harvard Law School Faculty Discussion Group for many extremely helpful comments on a previous draft, and Paul Eberhardt for his valuable research assistance.

term of approbation and "activism" just an all-purpose term of disapprobation.[1] The first purpose of the present Article is to perform
a similar task of redefinition on an equally popular pair of highly
charged terms in legal debate, "legal formalism" and "legal realism." I argue that when these terms are given a useful definition, it
becomes apparent that they have no fruitful application to statutory
(or constitutional) interpretation. The task of interpretation is fundamentally different from the tasks performed in formalist and realist analysis. Formalism and realism are useful concepts, but only
for the analysis of common law cases and doctrines. For interpretation we need different intellectual tools. The second purpose of this
Article is to suggest what they might be. I propose an analogy between the judicial interpretation of legislation and the interpretation
of military orders in battlefield conditions where communications
break down, and I defend the analogy with a series of case studies.
The two divisions of the Article are linked by the idea of interpretation as a mental activity distinct from both logical reasoning and
policy analysis.

Although I touch on constitutional issues, this is not an essay on
constitutional law. I assume, rather than argue, what is no longer
the universal view: that the function of judge-made constitutional
law is to interpret the written Constitution.

I.   FORMALISM AND REALISM DEFINED

The terms "legal formalism" and "legal realism" have a long
history in legal thought.[2] Over the years they have accreted so
many meanings and valences that each has become an all-purpose
term both of approbation and of disapprobation, surpassing in this
respect even "judicial self-restraint" and "judicial activism."[3] "Formalist" can mean narrow, conservative, hypocritical, resistant to
change, casuistic, descriptively inaccurate (that is, "unrealistic" in

---

1. Posner, *The Meaning of Judicial Self-Restraint*, 59 IND. L.J. 1 (1983), *revised and
reprinted in* R. POSNER, THE FEDERAL COURTS: CRISIS AND REFORM 198 (1985).

2. The extensive literature on legal realism and legal formalism is well summarized in
Comment, *Formalist and Instrumentalist Legal Reasoning and Legal Theory*, 73 CALIF. L.
REV. 119 (1985). On formalism, Grey, *Langdell's Orthodoxy*, 45 U. PITT. L. REV. 1 (1983),
is particularly good. On realism, see the authoritative collection of readings in Dennis J.
Hutchinson, History of American Legal Thought II: The American "Legal Realists" (Uni-
versity of Chicago Law School, mimeo., 1984), and the excellent brief summary in Altman,
Legal Realism, Critical Legal Studies, and Dworkin, 15 PHIL. & PUB. AFF. 205-14 (1986).
For an effort, somewhat parallel to my own, to relate formalism, realism, and interpretation
see Moore, *The Semantics of Judging*, 54 S. CAL. L. REV. 151 (1981).

3. I plead guilty to vague use of "formalism" and "realism" throughout THE FEDERAL
COURTS, *supra* note 1.

the ordinary-language sense of the word), ivory-towered, fallacious, callow, authoritarian—but also rigorous, modest, reasoned, faithful, self-denying, restrained. "Realist" can mean cynical, reductionist, manipulative, hostile to law, political, left-wing, epistemologically naive—but also progressive, humane, candid, mature, clear-eyed. These usages reflect the polemical character of so much writing about law. Legal realism is also used to refer to the work of particular academic lawyers, mainly on the Yale and Columbia faculties during the 1920's and 1930's, and to specific (and diverse) ideas held by those men. Legal formalism refers to the work of judges and academic lawyers whom the legal realists attacked and who attacked the realists in turn.

I want to give formalism a precise sense that is related but not identical to the "formalism" of Langdell[4] and the other nineteenth-century American legal formalists. I want it to mean the use of deductive logic to derive the outcome of a case from premises accepted as authoritative. Formalism enables a commentator to pronounce the outcome of the case as being correct or incorrect, in approximately the same way that the solution to a mathematical problem can be pronounced correct or incorrect. By "realism" I mean deciding a case so that its outcome best promotes public welfare in nonlegalistic terms; it is policy analysis. A "realist" decision is more likely to be judged sound or unsound than correct or incorrect—the latter pair suggests a more demonstrable, verifiable mode of analysis than will usually be possible in weighing considerations of policy. Such equity maxims as "no person shall profit from his own wrongdoing," which Professor Ronald Dworkin calls "principles,"[5] are in my analysis "policy considerations." My definitions of formalism and realism enable these terms to be used descriptively rather than evaluatively, and precisely rather than vaguely. One can speak of good and bad formalism, and good and bad realism. A more important point is that one can use formalism and realism, as I have defined them, only in discussing common law. The common law has a logical structure, and its premises are determined by notions of public policy. Statutes and constitutions are fundamentally different. They are communications, and neither logic nor policy is the key to decoding them (unless, of course, the communication, when decoded, is discovered to be saying to the courts, "make com-

---

4. Christopher Columbus Langdell, Dean of the Faculty of Law at Harvard University from 1870 until 1895.

5. *See* Dworkin, *The Model of Rules*, 35 U. CHI. L. REV. 14, 23-24 (1967).

mon law"). This distinction, which is central to this Article, has now to be explained.

II. FORMALISM, REALISM, AND THE COMMON LAW

The common law (which I use broadly to mean all legitimately judge-made law) is a collection of concepts, such as negligence, consideration, possession, good faith, conspiracy, impossibility, and laches. These concepts furnish major premises for the decision of cases. The minor premises are the facts of the case. The model is: "All men are mortal; Socrates is a man; therefore Socrates is mortal." The major premise is a concept or definition, the minor premise a factual statement. So if an enforceable contract is a promise supported by consideration, and A's promise to B was supported by consideration, the promise is a contract. Of course, the syllogistic structure of a real case is more complicated (because of defenses, exceptions, etc.), but that no more affects my analysis than does the fact that some mathematical problems are harder than others. Obviously the choice of premises is critical, and that is where public policy comes in. Why enforce only promises supported by consideration, or only promises that are consciously accepted? The reason, if it is a good reason, has to be traceable to some notion of policy rather than just be the result of arbitrary personal preferences or antipathies, or class bias, or some other thoroughly discredited ground of judicial action. It cannot be logic. Logic is used to go from the premises to the conclusion, not to obtain the premises. Of course, a premise may be the result of deduction from some more basic premise, but eventually one is forced back to a premise that cannot be obtained or proved by deduction. The nineteenth-century formalists sometimes overlooked (or perhaps deliberately concealed) this point. Since the correct choice of premises on grounds of policy is more uncertain than the correct deduction of a conclusion from its premises, the formalists preferred to focus on the process of deduction rather than on the choice of premises. They liked to give the impression that the premises were self-evident—meanwhile packing as much into the major premises as possible, to shorten the chain of deductions. The result is Platonism: the idea that concepts exist "out there," like trees or rocks, rather than are created.

Thus, Langdell said that a person who returns a lost article for which the owner has offered a reward has no contractual right to the reward if he did not know about the offer, because then the act of return could not have been a conscious acceptance of the offer, and without such acceptance, there can be no contract.[6] But in so reasoning, Langdell was treating the concept of contract as if it were a thing which couldn't be altered without becoming something different. If you take the legs off of a table (permanently—not just for storage or moving), it is no longer a table. But it doesn't follow that if you don't have an acceptance you don't have a contract. A contract is just a promise that courts will enforce, and if there is a good policy reason for doing so they can decide to enforce a promise even though it was not consciously accepted. Nor is it a good reply that a contract without acceptance is like a table missing only one leg; that no essential, defining characteristic of the concept of contract is missing, as would be the case if there were neither offer nor acceptance. What should count as the essential, defining characteristics of contract is not a semantic question; it is a policy question. We may enforce any promise we want, and call it a contract, just as we can punish a drug dealer for his agent's possession of illegal drugs by saying that the dealer has "constructive" possession. In the reward case, the question for the court should be (putting aside the issue of adherence to precedent): ought the unconscious acceptance be deemed to create a contract? I would think the answer should depend on whether, if it is, more lost articles will be returned, at an acceptable cost to the legal system. This happens to be a difficult question.[7]

The problem was not that Langdell was a bad formalist, in the sense of making errors of logic, but that he was uncritical about his premises. Another example from his time was the generalizing of the rule of capture for wild animals—the rule that a wild animal, such as a rabbit, is not owned until you catch it—into the concept that ownership of natural resources without a fixed locus is governed by the rule of capture, and then the deducing from that concept that rights in fish, valuable fur-bearing animals, and oil and gas ought to be governed by the rule too.[8] The conclusion, in syllogistic form but only because too much has been packed into the major

6. *See* C. LANGDELL, A SUMMARY OF THE LAW OF CONTRACTS 1-3 (2d ed. 1880).

7. *See* R. POSNER, ECONOMIC ANALYSIS OF LAW 89-90 (3d ed. 1986). In fairness to Langdell, I must point out that, considering when it was written, Langdell's treatise on contract law is a splendid piece of legal analysis, unjustly maligned by Oliver Wendell Holmes in an anonymous review, *see* 14 AM. L. REV. 233, 234 (1880) (Langdell is "the greatest living legal theologian") and more recently and less elegantly by Grant Gilmore, G. GILMORE, THE DEATH OF CONTRACT 13 (1974) ("To judge by the casebook and the Summary, Langdell was an industrious researcher of no distinction whatever either of mind or . . . of style.").

8. *See, e.g.,* 1 H. WILLIAMS & C. MEYERS, OIL AND GAS LAW § 203, at 26-28 (1985) (discussing the application of the rule of capture to oil and gas).

premise, can lead to inefficient exploitation of these natural resources even though the rule is efficient when applied to rabbits, ducks, and other wild animals of no great value. A rule of capture creates no incentive to defer exploiting a natural resource, since there is no way of obtaining a property right to future use. This is all right if the resource is not scarce, which is to say not valuable in an economic sense, but it is inefficient if the resource is scarce and we therefore want to conserve some of it for future use, or to make investments in expanding the supply of the resource that will bear fruit only in the future.[9] This distinction, which is crucial in choosing the premise for decision (that is, in determining the scope of the rule of capture), tends to be ignored if the rule is stated in its broadest, most "conceptual" form, and then is treated as a given rather than as an object of choice, and is not open to modification or qualification on the basis of experience. As this example shows, reasoning by analogy (e.g., from fish to gas) is often a form of logical reasoning, in which the first step is elevating the first thing compared to a general principle (any "fugitive" resource is governed by the rule of capture). But whether to elevate it or not is or should be a policy question; logic won't do the trick.

The fallacy in legal reasoning of smuggling the conclusion into the premise (as in this too simple argument against the legality of affirmative action: racial discrimination is illegal; affirmative action discriminates against whites; therefore affirmative action is illegal) is common enough to deserve a name, and let us call it "Langdellism." Let us also purge "formalism" of its pejorative connotations by using it simply to mean decision by deductive logic.

Holmes mounted a series of fierce realist attacks on Langdellism, insisting that the law was not a set of preexisting concepts of fixed scope but a tool of government which would and should be reshaped as the desires of the community or (more realistically) of its politically dominant groups changed. He made the point in his most memorable nonjudicial aphorism ("The life of the law has not been logic: it has been experience"[10]) and in his famous definition of law as a prophecy of what the judges would do when confronted with a given set of facts.[11] The definition is incomplete. It cannot be used by the judges of the highest court in the jurisdiction, or even by the judges of the lower courts in the absence of clear precedent on the question at issue or personal knowledge of their judicial

---

9. *See* R. POSNER, *supra* note 7, at 34, 58.
10. O.W. HOLMES, THE COMMON LAW 1 (1881).
11. Holmes, *The Path of the Law*, 10 HARV. L. REV. 457, 461 (1897).

superiors' views on it. Nevertheless, it is significant in pointing us away from concepts as the defining characteristic of law.

Despite much derision by Holmes of formal logic (the syllogism cannot wag its tail,[12] and so forth), there is no inconsistency between realism in Holmes' sense and formalism in the sense of deductive reasoning. Once the basic premises are chosen on realist grounds (e.g., once the rule of capture is given a scope coterminous with its economic rationale), deduction can proceed without violating realist norms. Holmes himself deduced some highly formal legal concepts, notably a concept of contract not far removed from that of Langdell.[13] Holmes was more likely, however, to deduce legal concepts from ideas of what was good for society or what its dominant classes wanted than merely to posit them as axioms for decision. He thought he was attacking logic; that is, formalist reasoning. He really was attacking what I am calling Langdellism.

The modern exemplar of formalism in common law is the positive economic analysis of that law which Professor Landes and I and others have expounded.[14] Taking as our premise the claim that the common law seeks to promote efficiency in the sense of wealth maximization (that is, abstracting from distributive considerations), and adding some data and assumptions about technology and human behavior, we deduce a set of optimal common law doctrines and institutions and then compare them with the actual common law. I use "deduction" in a literal sense. Microeconomic theory is a logical system like calculus or geometry (hence economic theory can be and often is expressed mathematically); more precisely a family of such systems. If the positive economic theory of the common law is right, the common law is a logical system, and deductive logic—formal reasoning—can be used (by the judge) to reach demonstrably correct results in particular cases or (by the scholar) to demonstrate the correctness of results in particular cases—provided, of course, that our major premise (that of wealth maximization), along with a slew of minor premises, is accepted. Whether it

12. Letter to John C.H. Wu, in THE MIND AND FAITH OF JUSTICE HOLMES: HIS SPEECHES, ESSAYS, LETTERS AND JUDICIAL OPINIONS 419 (M. Lerner ed. 1943).

13. For example, Holmes agreed with Langdell that someone who returned a lost article without knowledge of the reward was not entitled to claim the reward, because the offer of the reward had not induced the return. *See* O.W. HOLMES, *supra* note 10, at 294. *See also* G. GILMORE, *supra* note 7, at 19-21. The notion that Holmes, by using formalist reasoning, showed he was not really a realist, reveals the potential for confusion in the use of these terms.

14. *See, e.g.*, W. LANDES & R. POSNER, THE ECONOMIC STRUCTURE OF TORT LAW (forthcoming, Harvard University Press, 1987); R. POSNER, *supra* note 7, 3-55.

is or is not belongs to the realm of policy analysis; that is the realist component of the economic theory of the common law. It is realist because the concepts which provide the major premises for common law reasoning (whether an overarching premise such as wealth maximization, or particular legal concepts such as negligence that can be deduced from it) could be, and no doubt would be (and to some extent have been), altered by the judges in response to changing perceptions of public policy. The pace of change is affected by the need to preserve a reasonable degree of stability in law but that is just another policy consideration.

The essence of common law is that the law itself is made by the judges. They are the legislators. They create and modify the doctrines of the common law, from which further doctrines are deduced. The entire doctrinal structure then supplies major premises and the trial process supplies the minor ones (the facts), thus enabling case outcomes to be produced by a deductive method. The actuality is far messier, in part because a number of minor premises involving motivation, information, and so forth are contested, but the nature and direction of the process are clear enough to suggest the utility of the terms legal formalism and legal realism, as I have defined them, in analyzing common law decisionmaking.

III. THE NATURE OF TEXTUAL INTERPRETATION: DECODING COMMUNICATIONS

The major premise of a syllogism is a definition (like "All men are mortal"), or, what is the same thing, a rule (e.g., the perfect-tender rule), or, what is again the same thing, a concept (e.g., negligence, which stated as a rule or definition is "All persons are prima facie liable for accidents resulting from their failure to take due care, i.e., the cost-justified level of care"). The common law, like the system of real numbers, is a conceptual system—not a textual one. The concepts of negligence, of consideration, of reliance, are not tied to a particular verbal formulation, but can be restated in whatever words seem clearest in light of current linguistic conventions. Common law is thus unwritten law in a profound sense. There are more or less influential statements of every doctrine but none is authoritative in the sense that the decision of a new case must be tied to the statement, rather than to the concept of which the statement is one of an indefinite number of possible formulations.

Considering the importance that the common law attaches to decision in accordance with precedent, it may seem odd to divorce common law from the verbal formulas in the judicial opinions that create it. A common law doctrine, however, is no more textual than Newton's universal law of gravitation. The doctrine is inferred from a judicial opinion, or more commonly a series of judicial opinions, but it is not those opinions, just as Newton's law is learned from a text but is not the text itself. Decision according to precedent means decision according to the doctrines of the common law, not according to specific verbal expressions of those doctrines.

Statutory and constitutional law differs fundamentally from common law in that every statutory and constitutional text—the starting point for decision, and in that respect (but that respect only) corresponding to judicial opinions in common law decision-making—is in some important sense not to be revised by the judges. They cannot treat the statute as a stab at formulating a concept which they are free to rewrite in their own words.[15] This might seem to entail just that formalist reasoning in statutory or constitutional law would be deduction from a text and therefore would be possible as long as the text was as precise as a common law concept. But there is no such thing as deduction from a text. No matter how clear the text seems, it must be interpreted (or decoded) like any other communication, and interpretation is neither logical deduction nor policy analysis. The terms formalism and realism as I have defined them thus have no application to statutory or constitutional law, except, as I have said, when the framers' command is simply that the judges go out and make common law.

A conclusion obtained by deduction is already contained in the premises in the sense that the only materials used to obtain the conclusion are the premises themselves and the rules of logic. But meaning cannot be extracted from a text merely by taking the language of the text and applying the rules of logic to it. All sorts of linguistic and cultural tools must be brought to bear on even the simplest text to get meaning out of it. This is not to suggest that all texts are ambiguous. A text is clear if all or most persons, having the linguistic and cultural competence assumed by the authors of the text, would agree on its meaning. Most texts are clear in this sense, which is the only sense that captures the meaning of the word "clear" as applied to texts.

I shall illustrate the distinction between logic and interpretation

---

15. *See, e.g.,* E. LEVI, AN INTRODUCTION TO LEGAL REASONING 6-7, 28-30 (1949); Simpson, *The* Ratio Decidendi *of a Case and the Doctrine of Binding Precedent,* in OXFORD ESSAYS IN JURISPRUDENCE 148, 165-67 (A.G. Guest ed. 1961). Hart and Sacks imply a contrary view, which I consider later. *See infra* text accompanying note 19.

by reference to the clearest of constitutional provisions—the provision that fixes thirty-five years as the age of eligibility for the Presidency.[16] It might seem that if the question were whether X, who is thirty-two years old, is eligible to be President, the answer would involve an application of formalist reasoning: one must be at least thirty-five to be eligible, X is not thirty-five, therefore X is not eligible. But the answer is open to attack along the following lines: the framers may not have intended to set a rigid limitation; they may have meant that the candidate must either be thirty-five years old or be at least as mature as the average thirty-five year old; they might have countenanced a change if life expectancy changed.[17] The attack is, as we shall see, very weak, but the only point I want to make here is that it cannot be repelled by formal logic. The legal task in this case is not to make deductions from a definition—it is not to apply a rule—it is to do something prior, to interpret a text. The proper riposte to the attempted "deconstruction" of the age thirty-five provision is not that the attempt is illogical or is bad public policy but that the meaning of the text is clear. We do not decide the clarity of texts, or decode communications generally, by syllogistic reasoning or appeals to policy (though logic and policy may enter indirectly, as we shall see). If a message is unclear we ask the sender to repeat or amplify it until we no longer doubt what he meant to say. We do not use that approach to solve a mathematical problem or to decide what course of action will best promote the public welfare.

Consulting post-enactment legislative history, and even hearing testimony by legislators in cases in which the meaning of legislation is contested, are methods by which courts sometimes try to get legislatures, in effect, to repeat unclear messages. These methods have plenty of problems, and I don't mean by mentioning them to endorse them, but they do serve to show that the enactment of legislation is a method of communication with judges, in a way that the statement of a common law doctrine is not. If we are puzzled about the formulation of the doctrine of consideration in some opinion, we are not likely to feel an urge to ask the author of the opinion what he meant. This is because we are always free to reformulate the

---

16. "[N]either shall any Person be eligible to that Office who shall not have attained to the age of thirty five Years . . . ." U.S. CONST. art. II, § 1, cl. 5.

17. *See* Peller, *The Metaphysics of American Law*, 73 CALIF. L. REV. 1151, 1174 (1985); Tushnet, *A Note on the Revival of Textualism in Constitutional Theory*, 58 S. CAL. L. REV. 683, 686-88 (1985).

doctrine in a way that will describe the underlying concept more accurately.

The idea of legislation as communication may seem to have no utility beyond showing the fatuity and confusion of applying the terms legal formalism and legal realism to the interpretation of legislation. For most of the time it is impossible to ask the legislature to repeat an unclear message. But by considering what the possible responses are to an unclear message when the sender cannot be queried about his intended meaning, we shall see that the notion of legislation as communication has considerable utility. One possible response of the receiver is to ignore the message, and this might seem the appropriate posture for a court faced with an enactment whose meaning, with respect to the case at hand, cannot be deciphered. Yet that kind of response can be profoundly unresponsive. Suppose the commander of the lead platoon in an attack finds his way blocked by an unexpected enemy pillbox. He has two choices: go straight ahead at the pillbox, or try to bypass it to the left. He radios the company commander for instructions. The commander replies, "Go—"; but the rest of the message is garbled. When the platoon commander radios back for clarification, he is unable to get through. If the platoon commander decides that, not being able to receive an intelligible command, he should do nothing until communications can be restored, his decision will be wrong. For it is plain from the part of the message that was received that the company commander wanted him to get by the enemy pillbox, either by frontal attack or by bypassing it. And surely the company commander would have preferred the platoon commander to decide by himself which course to follow rather than to do nothing and let the attack fail. For the platoon commander to take the position that he may do nothing, just because the communication was garbled, would be an irresponsible "interpretation."

The situation with regard to legislative interpretation is analogous. In our system of government the framers of statutes and constitutions are the superiors of the judges. The framers communicate orders to the judges through legislative texts (including, of course, the Constitution). If the orders are clear, the judges must obey them. Often, however, because of passage of time and change of circumstance the orders are unclear and normally the judges cannot query the framers to find out what the order means. The judges are thus like the platoon commander in my example. It is irresponsible for them to adopt the attitude that if the order is unclear they will refuse to act. They are part of an organization, an enterprise—the enterprise of governing the United States—and when the orders of their superiors are unclear, this does not absolve them from responsibility for helping to make the enterprise succeed. The platoon commander will ask himself, if he is a responsible officer: what would the company commander have wanted me to do if communications failed? Judges should ask themselves the same type of question when the "orders" they receive from the framers of statutes and constitutions are unclear: what would the framers have wanted us to do in this case of failed communication? The question is often difficult to answer, but it is the right question to frame the interpretive issue in cases where the enactment is unclear. There are objections to this way of looking at the problem of statutory interpretation and to my military analogy but I defer them for the moment.

My analysis of common law and statutes casts doubt on the traditional view that common law reasoning resembles induction and statutory interpretation, deduction.[18] It is true that the common law concept must be extracted from a line of cases and that the facts of a new case may cause the judges to modify the concept (an example of the role of policy analysis in judicial decisionmaking), but from there on the analysis is conceptual, deductive. It is also true that judges interpreting a statute may extract from it a concept (such as the economic concept of monopoly, in the case of the antitrust statutes, discussed later), which then goes on to lead a life of its own, in common law fashion; but the essential step is interpretation, and it is not a deductive process. Elements of formalism, realism, and interpretation are differently mixed in common law reasoning and statutory application, and it is unhelpful and misleading to distinguish these two basic forms of legal reasoning by calling the first inductive and the second deductive.

IV. CLEAR VERSUS UNCLEAR CASES

I am naturally more interested in the unclear cases of interpretation than the clear ones. But it is important to insist that there are clear cases, though they are underrepresented both in appellate opinions and in academic debate. The age thirty-five case is easy, despite Peller's and Tushnet's efforts to make it seem hard. They are quite right, though, that no text is really "clear on its face." The provision is profoundly unclear to a person who does not know English; and if it is still in force in a thousand years, it may be as

---

18. For a carefully qualified statement of this view see E. LEVI, *supra* note 15, at 19-20.

unclear as Anglo-Saxon or Old English is to us. In India, where the official language is English but age is measured from conception rather than birth, it would mean something different from what it means to us. It would mean something different in a society that did not record the date of birth. A text is clear only by virtue of linguistic and cultural competence. What makes the age thirty-five provision clear is that American lawyers recognize it as part of a family of rules that establish arbitrary eligibility dates in preference to making eligibility turn on uncertain qualitative judgments. Legislatures set eighteen or twenty-one years as the age of majority rather than provide that one is legally an adult when one is mature. They also refuse to allow precocious twelve-year-olds to take the driving test. If eligibility for the Presidency were not fixed at a definite age, there would be great difficulty in determining in advance of the election who is eligible; after the election it's too late. When all these considerations are taken into account, as can be done only by people living in a certain kind of society (e.g., one where the date of birth is recorded and age is measured in years from that date), the age thirty-five provision becomes clear.

We shall see later that provisions that seem equally clear "on their face" may become unclear when the various contextual considerations that we use in decoding messages are taken into account. But the present point is that the rejection of formalism as a method of statutory interpretation doesn't condemn us to universal skepticism about the possibility of interpretation. Interpretation is no less a valid method of acquiring knowledge because it necessarily ranges beyond the text. No text is clear except in terms of a linguistic and cultural environment, but it doesn't follow that no text is clear. The relevant environment, and its bearing on the specific interpretive question, may be clear.

Nevertheless, it is true that many statutory and constitutional texts, including the most illustrious and also many that seem clear "on their face" (a pernicious usage), are unclear in the sense of my hypothetical company commander's order. But the lack of clarity does not entitle the court to say that it will not apply the text until the authors rewrite it. The court still has the duty to interpret, which requires, as I have suggested, figuring out what outcome will best advance the program or enterprise set on foot by the enactment. This conclusion is entailed by my assumption that the best way to look at the relationship between legislatures (or the adopters of the Constitution and its amendments) and courts is as superior and subordinate officers, with the former often being unable to communicate clearly with the latter.

V. Some Other Approaches to the Interpretation of Legislation

Before defending and then illustrating my approach, let me contrast it briefly with some others. One that is particularly interesting in light of my desire to banish talk of formalism and realism from the interpretive domain is that of Hart and Sacks, which is broadly similar to my approach but differs crucially in requiring that courts deem the enacting legislators reasonable persons intending reasonable results in the public interest.[19] If this is a permissible assumption, and if there is broad agreement on what is reasonable and public-interested, the interpretive problem disappears; interpretation disappears. All statutes become pellucid and unequivocal directives to courts to achieve sound results. A court complies with these directives by creating concepts (like "concerted activities" under the National Labor Relations Act[20] or "public convenience and necessity" under common carrier and public utility statutes[21]) which the court then proceeds to apply formalistically, maybe after deducing subconcepts from them, to particular cases. Suppose—though this was not Hart and Sacks' view, nor is it mine—that all legislators are reasonable in the special sense of wanting to maximize society's wealth. Then they would want the court to "interpret" their every statute to make it conduce to this end. The same formal analysis used to explain, and for those accepting its substantive premises to justify, common law decisions could be used to explain and justify statutory decisions. In effect, the statutes would be precedents:[22] that is, tentative formulations of legal concepts. The courts would be free to revise the formulations.

Unfortunately, neither the specific assumption that legislators seek to maximize society's wealth nor the general assumption that they seek to achieve reasonable results in some consensus sense of reasonableness (for example, one that combined efficiency with the most widely accepted distributive norms, such as that condemning

---

19. *See* 2 H. Hart & A. Sacks, The Legal Process: Basic Problems in the Making and Application of Law 1410-17 (tent. ed. 1958).

20. 29 U.S.C. § 151 (1982).

21. *See, e.g.*, 47 U.S.C. § 214 (1982).

22. This position was urged by one of Hart and Sacks' predecessors in the school of "progressive formalism." *See* Landis, *Statutes and the Sources of Law*, in Harvard Legal Essays 213 (R. Pound ed. 1934).

racial discrimination) is tenable in light of intellectual and political developments since Hart and Sacks wrote in the middle 1950's. And if the second assumption were tenable, it would not be usable as a guide to applying statutes.

First, the spectrum of respectable opinion on political and social questions has widened so enormously that even if we could assume that legislators intended to bring about reasonable results in all cases, the assumption would not generate specific legal concepts. To learn what sense of reasonableness the legislators meant the courts to use would require interpretation of the legislative text. We cannot escape interpretation.

Second, recent studies of the legislative process stress the importance of interest groups, pursuing private goals rather than the public interest, in shaping legislation.[23] There is nothing new in the recognition that interest groups are important in the legislative process, but at the time Hart and Sacks wrote it was thought that the competition of interest groups would achieve a social optimum. The fact that differential ability to organize an effective interest group could well result in serious departures from optimality was not widely recognized, as it is today. The recognition of this danger has made it more difficult to regard statutory texts as the equivalent of precedents, reflecting the same values and goals as the judges hold; many statutes appear to reflect compromises between contending groups pursuing (but not avowing) selfish ends.

I have exaggerated Hart and Sacks' position in order to make its contrast with mine clearer. Far from thinking interpretation irrelevant, they devote most of their discussion of statutory interpretation to techniques for "decoding" the statutory communication. It is only when all else fails that a court is to assume that the legislators were trying to do the same thing that courts do; it is only the most difficult, the indeterminate, issues of statutory interpretation that are to be subjected to common law formalist-realist reasoning. The fact that the court is to decode first, and reason in common law fashion only if the effort to decode fails, suggests that Hart and Sacks were well aware that not all legislation is reasonable in a common law sense. Nevertheless their discussion implies a more com-

---

23. For recent and comprehensive reviews of this literature see Farber & Frickey, *The Jurisprudence of Public Choice: Empiricism, Cynicism, and Formal Models in Public Law Theory*, forthcoming in Texas Law Review, and Macey, *Promoting Public-Regarding Legislation Through Statutory Interpretation: An Interest Group Model*, 86 COLUM. L. REV. 223 (1986). For a briefer treatment, see R. POSNER, *supra* note 7, at 496-98.

fortable and confident view of "interpretation" (broadly conceived) than is likely to gain many adherents today.

Not only can few today accept the assumption that the legislative intent typically is to maximize the general welfare, but there is also greater awareness of the inherent uncertainties of interpretation.[24] The reason for this greater awareness may simply be that interpretation presupposes shared cultural values, and the United States—including its legal community—is politically, socially, and culturally more diverse than it was thirty years ago. But, whatever the reason, the grounds for skepticism about the feasibility of definitive interpretation in difficult cases are better understood today than they were then. There is, for example, greater awareness of the problem of intention about intention. Supposing that we knew for certain that the legislators whose votes were necessary for the enactment of the fourteenth amendment did not want it to prevent the southern states from operating a segregated public school system, we would still have to decide whether they intended the application of the amendment to be bounded by their knowledge and preferences, or instead wanted it to be informed by the knowledge and preferences of future generations—of judges.[25] Who knows? Probably they didn't think about the distant future. Can the gap sensibly be filled simply by assuming the framers of the fourteenth amendment were reasonable men seeking reasonable results? Or consider the key term of the Mann Act: "immoral practice."[26] In a case decided today, should this term be taken to refer to the moral ideas of 1910, when the Mann Act was passed, or to the moral ideas prevailing in 1987? An argument for the latter position is that the main purpose of the Mann Act is to back up state regulation of the family and sex; as that regulation changes in conformity with changes in the moral climate, so should the prohibitions of the Mann Act. But it is only an argument, for we have no good information on what the framers of the Act would have wanted courts to do with respect to future changes in sexual mores.[27]

---

24. Of course, there is nothing new about interpretive skepticism. See the precocious work by F. LIEBER, LEGAL AND POLITICAL HERMENEUTICS (enlarged ed. 1839), especially chapter 5.

25. For inconclusive speculation on this specific question see Bickel, *The Original Understanding and the Segregation Decision*, 69 HARV. L. REV. 1, 63-64 (1955). I return to this issue in the last part of this Article. *See infra* notes 70-77 and accompanying text.

26. White-Slave Traffic (Mann) Act, ch. 395, 36 Stat. 825 (1910) (codified as amended at 18 U.S.C. §§ 2421-2424 (1982)).

27. On the legislative history and judicial interpretation of the Mann Act see E. LEVI, *supra* note 15, at 33-46.

A famous example of the problem of intention about intention concerns state statutes that provide that jurors are to be selected from a list of persons eligible to vote. When these statutes were passed, women were not eligible to vote. Later they became eligible. Does this mean they could now be jurors?[28] We know that the legislators did not intend that women be jurors. But did they intend this intention to govern the indefinite future? I should think not. It would have been easy enough to provide that only men were eligible. Probably the legislators didn't care, or at least didn't care much, about the sex of jurors—they just wanted to tie juror eligibility to voter eligibility, figuring that anyone qualified to vote was qualified to serve on a jury. If so, there is no reason to exclude women. But the argument is no more than plausible.

Another general problem of interpretation is that no one knows for sure whether the framers of the Constitution intended federal courts merely to translate (so far as they were able) the specific commands of Congress into particular case outcomes, or instead, as suggested by Alexander Hamilton, to exercise a civilizing influence—to act as a buffer between the legislators and the citizenry even when no constitutional issue was raised.[29] The role of the judge in "civilizing" statutes was not problematic for Hart and Sacks because they were willing to assume in all doubtful cases that the statute was intended to achieve the civilized result. On such an assumption there is no difference between being a translator and being a buffer, so Hamilton could be left in peace.

Then there is the growing skepticism about the traditional props of statutory interpretation, such as reference to purpose, to legislative history, and to rules of interpretation. Public-choice theory makes the attribution of unified purpose to a collective body increasingly difficult to accept—though I think it is possible to overdo

---

28. The courts divided on the question. *Compare* Commonwealth v. Maxwell, 271 Pa. 378, 114 A. 825 (1921) (women became eligible), *with* People *ex rel.* Fyfe v. Barnett, 319 Ill. 403, 150 N.E. 290 (1926) (women remain ineligible) *and* Commonwealth v. Welosky, 276 Mass. 398, 177 N.E. 656 (1931) (same).

29. [I]t is not with a view to infractions of the Constitution only, that the independence of the judges may be an essential safeguard against the effects of occasional ill humors in the society. These sometimes extend no farther than to the injury of the private rights of particular classes of citizens, by unjust and partial laws. Here also the firmness of the judicial magistracy is of vast importance in mitigating the severity and confining the operation of such laws. It not only serves to moderate the immediate mischiefs of those which may have been passed, but it operates as a check upon the legislative body in passing them; who, perceiving that obstacles to the success of iniquitous intention are to be expected from the scruples of the courts, are in a manner compelled, by the very motives of the injustice they meditate, to qualify their attempts.

THE FEDERALIST No. 78, at 227, 231-32 (A. Hamilton) (R. Fairfield ed. 1981).

one's skepticism in this regard. Institutions act purposively, therefore they have purposes. A document can manifest a single purpose even though those who drafted and approved it had a variety of private motives and expectations.

In addition, however, the canons of statutory construction, which purport to resolve specific issues of statutory interpretation, are (most of them, anyway) increasingly criticized as contradictory, fatuous, and unclear. And there is growing realization that legislative history is frequently unknown to the majority of the legislators who vote to enact the legislation in question.[30] The more we learn about legislation, the harder it becomes to extract definite meanings from particular statutes with any confidence. The new learning seems overwhelmingly negative.[31]

One possible inference from the skeptical literature about statutory interpretation is that courts should pull in their horns and stop trying to apply statutes to problems not specifically foreseen and resolved by the legislature. An equally plausible inference, however, is the opposite one—that the courts must do more to help the legislature, and in the process must free themselves from dependence on the incoherent guides to meaning on which courts traditionally rely. So it is possible to argue from the same data that statutory interpretation should be narrower than it once was and that it should be broader. One cannot choose between these positions by invoking bromides about democracy, because the issue is not whether the courts should exceed the limits of their role in the constitutional scheme but how they can best play that role given current knowledge of, or rather uncertainty about, the interpretive process.

I shall illustrate these points by reference to the contrasting positions taken by Guido Calabresi and Frank Easterbrook.[32] Writing

---

30. *See* Judge (now Justice) Scalia's concurring opinion in Hirschey v. Federal Energy Regulatory Comm'n, 777 F.2d 1, 7-8 (D.C. Cir. 1985). Judge Scalia "frankly doubt[ed] that it is ever reasonable to assume that the details, as opposed to the broad outlines of purpose, set forth in a committee report come to the attention of, much less are approved by, the house which enacts the committee's bill" and expressed concern over "the fact that routine deference to the detail of committee reports . . . [is] converting a system of judicial construction into a system of committee-staff prescription." *Id.*

31. *See, e.g.*, Easterbrook, *Statutes' Domains*, 50 U. CHI. L. REV. 533 (1983); R. POS-NER, *supra* note 1, at 223. For notable recent contributions to the growing debate over statutory interpretation see W. Eskridge, Jr., Dynamic Statutory Interpretation in Light of Changed Circumstances (University of Virginia Law School, mimeo., 1986); Farber & Frickey, *supra* note 23.

32. *See* G. CALABRESI, A COMMON LAW FOR THE AGE OF STATUTES (1982); Easterbrook, *supra* note 31.

from a liberal political standpoint, Calabresi urges that courts be empowered to declare constitutional statutes invalid by reason of obsolescence. At first I thought this was an "anti-legislation" position, surprising in a liberal, because it would expand the power of the courts to invalidate legislation that does not trench on constitutional rights, and liberals tend to support such legislation. I no longer think this evaluation correct. First, if you think the future belongs to liberalism (which many liberals believe, though with less confidence than in the 1960's and 1970's), then the systematic discarding of old legislation will make public policy more and more liberal. Second, the concept of statutory "obsolescence" is so vague that a liberal judge could easily believe, in good faith, that only illiberal statutes obsolesce. Third, Calabresi's proposal if adopted might actually make the enacting of legislation easier. Legislatures would not have to waste time repealing obsolete enactments and they could use the time thus saved for new legislative initiatives. They also would not be deterred from passing legislation by fear that it might become obsolete, and they would not have to worry about adding a "sunset" provision, either, which might make the statute lapse prematurely. But, supposing the dominant effect of Calabresi's proposal would indeed be more legislation, there is still the problem of justifying an expansion in the effective power of legislatures. The framers of the Constitution were suspicious of legislatures and hedged about the legislative power with many restrictions. If Congress passed the sort of law that Calabresi advocates, delegating to the courts the power to declare statutes obsolete, could one not argue that Congress was circumventing limitations on the legislative power that had been deliberately built into the constitutional structure?

Concern with preserving these limitations animates Easterbrook's quite different approach. He divides statutes into two categories. One, which includes the Sherman Act,[33] he treats as telling the courts to create common law doctrine—in the case of the Sherman Act, a common law of antitrust. The other category consists of statutes that, perhaps because worded very specifically, do not seem intended to authorize the courts to fashion common law. These statutes are to be strictly construed against the party to a lawsuit who seeks an advantage from them. Easterbrook thus proposes "[d]eclaring legislation inapplicable unless it either expressly addresses the matter or commits the matter to the common law."[34]

---

33. 15 U.S.C. §§ 1-7 (1982). *See infra* text accompanying note 61.
34. Easterbrook, *supra* note 31, at 552.

If adopted, this proposal might well reduce the effective power of the legislative branch. In the class of statutes that judges classified as authorizing common law, the legislature would have little or no effect on policy; policy would be made by the courts. In the residual class the legislature would have little power also, for its statutes would be given no effect beyond the applications "expressly addressed" by the legislators. Ordinarily, this would mean just the applications that the legislators, having actually foreseen, made express provision for; so the statute's application would be circumscribed by the vision of its enactors. Even in the best of circumstances, however, people find it very difficult to rule the future, and legislators do not work under the best conditions.[35] They are not chosen or rewarded for their foresight, they work under severe time pressures, and they are pulled hither and yon by special interest groups. If courts do not conceive their interpretive role as a helping one, much legislation will become obsolete within a few years of enactment. Easterbrook defends his approach to statutory interpretation by reference to the constitutionally in-built limitations of the legislative process, which he thinks are circumvented if judges allow themselves to interpret the spirit (when it has a spirit) as well as the letter of legislation.[36] And yet he would allow circumvention of those limitations through delegation, explicit and implicit, to the courts of the power to make common law. Although the framers of the Constitution were concerned with legislative excesses, they did not seek to curb them by making legislation expire with the enacting Congress. Easterbrook also defends his position by reference to the political principle of limited government. "There is still at least a presumption that people's arrangements prevail unless expressly displaced by legal doctrine."[37] But in the words "still at least" I sense an acknowledgment that the presumption is controversial. It is, in fact, ideological.

In some cases Easterbrook's position, which is textualist rather than intentionalist, may result in expanding a statute in unforeseen ways. For, to take an old chestnut, if the legislature declares it a crime to bring a vehicle into the park, might not the veterans' or-

---

35. *See* Sorenson v. Secretary of the Treasury, 106 S. Ct. 1600, 1610 (1986) (Stevens, J., dissenting). Justice Stevens cites an amusing New York Times report of the enactment of a bill, " 'with parts of it photocopied from memorandums, other parts handwritten at the last minute . . . some final sections hastily crossed out in whorls of pencil marks [and] such cryptic and acccidental entries in the bill as a name and phone number—"Ruth Seymour, 225-4844"—standing alone as if it were a special appropriation item.' " *Id.* n.2.

36. *See* Easterbrook, *supra* note 31, at 548-49.

37. *Id.* at 549.

ganization that placed a tank (in working order) there as a war memorial, be guilty, under Easterbrook's approach, of a crime? But probably he would regard this as a case where the statute was not really clear, so that the prosecution would fail. His basic position, as I understand it, is that if the command of the legislature is unclear, the court should ignore it by resolving the case against the party relying on the statute; and a superficially clear text may become unclear when context is considered. In any event his basic position does not, for me, solve the problem of unclear (and unclarifiable) "orders" within an organization, as I conceive the triple-branched government of the United States to be, having a common purpose. The task of interpretation is made neither irrelevant nor impossible by a failure of clear communication. The recipient must determine what his superiors would have wanted him to do to advance the common enterprise under conditions of broken communication.

VI. Objections to the Military Analogy

Before proceeding to illustrate my suggested approach, I take up some likely objections to it.

There is first the problem that the organization in question (i.e., the government) lacks the clear hierarchical command structure of a military organization or a business firm. But as we know from the literature on organizations and "agency costs," nominally hierarchical organizations are not monoliths either. The inevitable breakdown of communications in combat, which provides the model for my conception of statutory interpretation, is at least as serious as that which attends a legislature's trying to communicate its decisions to judges.

Nor (a related point) am I troubled by the fact that legislators and judges may not share the same values. A given piece of legislation may reflect nothing more exalted than the political muscle of an interest group able to obtain a legislative redistribution of wealth from a less well-organized group (though it would be incorrect to think that all legislation is exclusively of this character). The common enterprise that judges are pledged to advance is not a set of shared substantive values but the peaceable and orderly governance of the United States. One element of such governance is that judges make a good-faith effort to effectuate legislation regardless of their agreement or disagreement with its means or ends, subject to constitutional and institutional limitations. In this respect their position is similar to that of military subordinates who may not share the strategic, tactical, or political goals of their superiors.

Third, and still related, it is not a legitimate criticism of my analogy to argue that if the platoon commander cannot decode the order he will just do what he thinks best, which a judge should not do. The platoon commander is a subordinate officer, like the judge, and one of the things he is subordinate to is a body of doctrine. It is not for a lieutenant to ᵈecide what shall be the offensive doctrine of the United States Army. No more is it for a judge interpreting a legislative text, even an unclear one, to decide the public policy of the United States in accordance with his personal conception of right and wrong, sound and unsound policy. (I thus reject Hamilton's suggestion that judges should try to "civilize" constitutional statutes.)

This point, and the military analogy generally, may help make clear that in arguing that judges have a duty to interpret, even when the legislative text is unclear, I am not arguing for judicial activism. The relationship between a military officer and his superiors and their doctrines, preferences, and values is, after all, the very model of obedience and deference. But the relationship does not entail inaction when orders are unclear. On the contrary, it requires "interpretation" of the most creative kind. And nothing less will discharge the judicial duty, even for those who believe, as I do, that self-restraint is, at least in our day, the proper judicial attitude. Creative and willful are not synonyms. You can be creative in imagining how someone else would have acted knowing what you know as well as what he knows. That is the creativity of the great statutory judge.

Another objection to my military analogy is that the real addressee of the legislative command, corresponding to the platoon commander, is not the judge but the executive or administrative officers, or private persons, whose conduct the statute regulates. If the command is garbled, it is they, not the judge, who, it can be argued, should have the power to act. But surely the command is addressed to both the regulated person and the judge. If the judge is to be placed outside the chain of command, as it were, it can only be because his competence is thought limited to interpreting clear commands. But as a trained and disinterested interpreter, the judge should be recognized to have a competence to interpret unclear, even garbled, commands, at least if I am right that interpretation is not impossible—only difficult—in such a case. On that issue my case studies may cast some light.

Before turning to them let me emphasize one more point. A theory of interpretation, such as I have been propounding, cannot in general be derived from the thing being interpreted. Few texts provide a guide on how to interpret them. This point is as true of the Constitution as of most of the statutes enacted pursuant to it. A theory of interpretation rests ultimately on political (in its philosophical, not partisan, sense) and epistemological premises. The theory I have sketched, for example, depends heavily on a conception of judges as properly subordinate to legislators, coupled with a rejection of extreme skepticism concerning the possibility of carrying out other people's unclearly formulated plans. Calabresi would, I suspect, reject the first premise (subordination); Easterbrook, the second (rejection of skepticism).

VII.   Some Exercises in the Reading of Statutes

Written by Justice Harlan for a unanimous Court, the opinion in *Moragne v. State Marine Lines*[38] is generally considered a model of sensitive and creative use of statutes, but it can be pulled apart and shown to be arbitrary and uninformed. The issue was whether the survivor of a longshoreman killed aboard a ship docked at a Florida port could sue the shipowner for wrongful death caused by the ship's unseaworthiness. If the accident had occurred farther out, on the "high seas," she could have sued for wrongful death under the federal Death on the High Seas Act.[39] If it had occurred in the coastal waters of almost any state except Florida, whose wrongful death statute happened to be inapplicable to unseaworthiness, she could have sued under state law by virtue of the federal "savings to suitors" clause.[40] And if the victim had been a seaman rather than a longshoreman, the suit could have been maintained under the Jones Act.[41] The plaintiff fell among all these stools. The only basis for suit was the judge-made federal admiralty law, which had never recognized liability for wrongful death.[42] The Supreme

---

38. 398 U.S. 377 (1970). Justice Blackmun did not participate in the decision.

39. 46 U.S.C. §§ 761-768 (1982).

40. 28 U.S.C. § 1333 (1982) (original and exclusive district court jurisdiction in admiralty or maritime, "saving to suitors . . . all other remedies to which they are otherwise entitled").

41. 46 U.S.C. § 688 (1982).

42. In this respect it resembled its common law cousin, tort law (I am using "common law" in its technical sense here, not in the broad sense of Parts I and II of this Article), which likewise had never recognized liability for wrongful death. Such liability is the product of statutes stretching back to Lord Campbell's Act. Fatal Accidents Act, 1846, 9 & 10 Vict. ch. 93.

Court, noting the law's trend toward liability for wrongful death in maritime law—a trend illustrated by the Death on the High Seas Act itself—held that the judge-made admiralty law would, from this case forward, impose such liability.

The analysis and conclusion are flawed in several respects. First, the Court treats wrongful-death statutes in general and maritime wrongful-death statutes in particular (the Jones Act and the Death on the High Seas Act) as if they reflected obviously sound public policy and hence provided solid premises for deducing new judge-made admiralty doctrine. But this view bespeaks a limited acquaintance with legal developments in the field of industrial (i.e., workplace) accident liability. The overall trend has been from tort law to workers' compensation law—the Jones Act (and by extension the Death on the High Seas Act) being regarded in many quarters as an anachronism. Furthermore, even if liability for wrongful death caused by industrial accidents is a good idea, the specific form of that liability incorporated in the Federal Employers' Liability Act,[43] on which the Jones Act and the Death on the High Seas Act are closely modeled, can be criticized for eliminating such defenses as assumption of risk and waiver of liability, and for diluting the requirement of proving negligence. The Court did not discuss these issues. Another wrinkle is that unseaworthiness is not negligence, but rather is akin to strict liability,[44] so that the Court was actually going beyond the Federal Employers' Liability Act and the Jones Act in making new admiralty doctrine. In doing so it conferred a windfall on Moragne's estate, since the widow's suit for wrongful death under Florida negligence law had failed for lack of proof that the defendant had been negligent.

Second, the Court's implicit assumption that it makes a difference whether longshoremen are entitled to sue for wrongful death is contestable. The Coase theorem (not mentioned by the Court, and not in the forefront of judicial awareness back in 1970—or today, for that matter) suggests that in the absence of such an entitlement,

---

43. 45 U.S.C. §§ 51-60 (1982).

44. See Seas Shipping Co. v. Sieracki, 328 U.S. 85, 93-94 (1946); Ryan Stevedoring Co. v. Pan-Atlantic S.S. Corp., 350 U.S. 124 (1956); Italia Societa per Azioni di Navigazione v. Oregon Stevedoring Co., 376 U.S. 315, 317, 322-24 (1964). In 1972, Congress substituted negligence for unseaworthiness as the standard of liability in suits by longshoremen against shipowners. See 33 U.S.C. § 905(b) (1982) ("The liability of the vessel under this subsection shall not be based upon the warranty of seaworthiness or a breach thereof at the time the injury occurred."); Scindia Steam Navigation Co. v. De Los Santos, 451 U.S. 156, 156-60, 162-69, 172 (1981); United States Fidelity & Guaranty Co. v. Jadranska Slobodna Plovidba, 683 F.2d 1022, 1024-25 (7th Cir. 1982).

longshoremen's wages will rise by an amount just sufficient to enable them to insure against the consequences of a fatal accident.[45]

Third, given the Court's emphasis on the Death on the High Seas Act as a source of guidance for judge-made admiralty principles, the decision, rather than expressing deference to legislative judgments, invites comparison to writing the age thirty-five provision out of the Constitution. Essentially the Court deleted the word "High" from the Death on the High Seas Act.[46] Congress thought it was legislating for the high seas. It thought wrong. The Court took the statute and applied it (the heart of it, at any rate) to coastal waters.

Fourth, by doing this the Court may have made it more difficult for Congress to enact such statutes in the future. If courts ignore the scope limitations built into statutes by using the statute minus the limitations as a model for a rule of judge-made law, a legislator can no longer defend a bill by reference to its limitations. A legislator who wanted a wrongful-death statute applicable to a particular activity but didn't want to universalize liability for wrongful death might vote against the statute out of fear that the statute would be used to do just that. The tradition of free-wheeling interpretation helped sink the Equal Rights Amendment, whose opponents conjured up all sorts of far-out interpretive possibilities.

These points do not prove that *Moragne* was decided incorrectly; indeed, words like "correct" and "incorrect" are generally misplaced when applied to hard questions of statutory interpretation. My view is that these points show that the Court did not have sufficient reason to overrule *The Harrisburg*,[47] which had held that wrongful death was not a part of maritime law. The creation of a remedy for wrongful death has traditionally been considered a legislative function, and no good reason for departing from that tradition was shown, especially since it was a workplace accident that did Moragne in. The enactment of the Death on the High Seas Act was not a good enough reason.

---

45. See Coase, *The Problem of Social Cost*, 3 J. L. & ECON. 1 (1960). On wage premia for dangerous jobs see references in R. POSNER, *supra* note 7, at 183 n.5. It is unimportant that Moragne was not the *defendant's* employee. He was an indirect employee in an economic sense. For the more dangerous his work was, the higher would be the wage that his employer (the stevedore company) would have to pay him; and the employer would demand compensation from the shipowner, who would therefore in effect be paying Moragne his wage premium for dangerous work.

46. Except that the details of the admiralty wrongful-death doctrine that the Court created in *Moragne*, as subsequently elaborated, are not identical to those of the statute. *See, e.g.*, Mobil Oil Corp. v. Higginbotham, 436 U.S. 618 (1978).

47. 119 U.S. 199, 213 (1886).

United States v. Locke[48] is another hard case that seemed easy to the Justices, though this time to only six of them. *Locke* involved a federal statute requiring a firm that has an unpatented mining claim on federal public lands to reregister the claim annually, "prior to December 31."[49] Claims not reregistered in time are forfeited. Mines are frequently abandoned; the requirement of annual registration provides an easy means of determining abandonment. The plaintiffs in *Locke* filed on December 31, and the government declared the plaintiffs' mine forfeited. The Supreme Court upheld this determination.

The decision is impeccable as a matter of lexicography: "prior to December 31" means no later than December 30. It seems more than probable, however, that the statute contains a drafting error and that what Congress meant was that you must file before the end of the year, i.e., on or before December 31. Further evidence of inadvertence in the use of "prior to" is that the same section of the statute distinguishes between claims "located prior to October 21, 1976" and claims "located after October 21, 1976," thus leaving a void for claims located on October 21, 1976—if "prior to" is read literally. No one has ever suggested a reason why Congress might have wanted the filings made before December 31. It is not enough to say that all deadlines are arbitrary and that if the plaintiffs in *Locke* had won, then the next plaintiff would file on January 1 and say that his filing was timely too. The end of the year is a natural and common deadline and is almost certainly what Congress intended, so a claim filed on January 1 would be too late. Anyone familiar with the workings of the legislative process knows how easily drafting errors are made and how frequently they escape notice. The statute as drafted by Congress and as enforced by the Supreme Court became a trap for the unwary, destroying valuable property rights (and thereby precipitating a constitutional controversy which the plaintiffs also lost) because of a natural and harmless inadvertence. Nor is there any reason to think the trap was set by some interest group. No purpose, whether self-interested or public-interested, can be ascribed to the December 30 deadline. Finally, no one relied on the December 30 deadline, as by snapping up the "abandoned" Locke mining claim.

What makes the case appear difficult, rather than plainly incorrect, is that the plaintiff seems not to have been asking the Supreme

48. 105 S. Ct. 1785 (1985).
49. Federal Land Policy and Management Act of 1976, § 314(a), 43 U.S.C. § 1744(a) (1982).

Court to interpret an ambiguity or fill in a gap, but to rewrite clear statutory language. The language is clear, however, only if significant contextual circumstances are ignored. The Court's approach was analogous to that of a platoon commander who (in a variant of my previous example), having received an order that is clear, but also clearly erroneous because of a mistake in transmission, nevertheless carries out the order as received, rather than trying to determine what response would advance the common enterprise.

Is my preferred interpretation of *Locke* consistent with refusing to read the Constitution's age thirty-five requirement nonliterally? I think so. As I said before, the framers' selection of a fixed age for eligibility, like a legislature's selection of a fixed age to denote the assumption of adult rights and responsibilities (or a fixed period for a statute of limitations), reflects a preference for a definite rule over a standard uncertain in application. To interpret age thirty-five to mean as mature as the average thirty-five year old would thus undo a choice deliberately made by the framers. The Federal Land Policy and Management Act of 1976 also reflects a preference for a fixed deadline but not necessarily for a fixed deadline of December 30 rather than December 31. Congress (by which I mean those members who took an interest in this provision of the Act) almost certainly thought it was making December 31 the deadline, even though it said December 30.[50]

Here is another example, this one decided in favor of the plaintiffs. The Federal Employers' Liability Act, which I mentioned in connection with the *Moragne* case, makes railroads liable to their workers for the negligence either of the railroad (meaning, the negligence of persons in positions of authority with the railroad) or the

---

50. With *Locke* compare Stock v. Department of the Air Force, 186 F.2d 968 (4th Cir. 1950). In 1948, the year following passage of the statute which made the Air Force a separate service, Congress provided that "the Articles of War and all other laws now in effect relating to" military injustice "shall be applicable to" the Air Force. Under those Articles, confirmation by the President was required for certain sentences imposed by courts-martial. Shortly before the statute quoted above was passed, Congress had passed an act substituting confirmation by the judicial councils of the services for confirmation by the President—but the alteration did not become effective until after the statute quoted above took effect. Stock's sentence was confirmed by a judicial council, not the President, and he argued that this was illegal, since the statute providing for confirmation by the President was "now in effect" when Congress made the laws relating to military justice applicable to the Air Force. The court rejected this argument, noting that Congress' purpose in enacting the statute was to provide uniformity among the services, rather than to freeze the rules of military justice for the Air Force in the form in which they existed at the date of the statute's enactment. This is a sensible result though it could be described as rewriting the words "now in effect."

railroad's other workers.[51] Thus, if worker A injures worker B through negligence, the railroad is prima facie liable to B; and since the Act abolishes the principal defenses in negligence cases, the railroad will find it difficult to escape liability once A's negligence is shown. In addition, only minimal negligence is required. But what if worker A injures worker B deliberately in circumstances where under ordinary principles of respondeat superior their employer would be liable for A's intentional tort? If the Act, which displaces these ordinary principles, is read literally, B is out of luck. Yet the Supreme Court held many years ago, with a minimum of fuss in an era by no means liberal, that such an accident is covered by the Act.[52] Any other result would be hard to understand, for the purpose of the FELA was not to cut back the railroad's common law liability but to expand it by abolishing various defenses and enlarging the plaintiff's choice of forum. (The Act entitles him to sue in either state or federal court, and denies the railroad any right of removal.) Perhaps, however, such result would be no harder to understand than the Court's result in *Locke.*

Can my analysis of the FELA case be reconciled with what I have suggested would have been the proper result in *Moragne?* I think so. In *Moragne,* Congress had legislated with regard to one class of accidents, those occurring on the high seas, and the Supreme Court in effect applied the legislation to another class of accidents. It is as if the Court had used the Federal Employers' Liability Act itself as the basis for creating a right of action for wrongful death in maritime cases. Since the whole idea of the FELA, however, was to curtail the railroad's defenses to personal injury suits by railroad workers, it is hard to imagine why Congress might have wanted to distinguish between intentional and unintentional torts in circumstances where at common law the railroad would have been liable for either type of tort under the doctrine of respondeat superior. Nothing in the legislative history of the Act suggests a desire to make such a distinction (whether based on a "deal" between the railroads and the unions or on any other circumstance). In these circumstances the most plausible interpreta-

---

51. Every common carrier by railroad . . . shall be liable in damages to any person suffering injury while he is employed by such carrier . . . for such injury . . . resulting in whole or in part from the negligence of any of the officers, agents, or employees of such carrier, or by reason of any defect or insufficiency, due to its negligence, in its cars, engines, appliances, machinery, track, roadbed, works, boats, wharves, or other equipment.

45 U.S.C. § 51 (1982).

52. *See* Jamison v. Encarnacion, 281 U.S. 635, 641 (1930).

tion of the statutory word "negligence" was wrongfulness under common law principles, not only carelessness.

Here is another example where the courts quite sensibly have overridden the "plain language" of a statute.[53] The Bankruptcy Act, until its overhaul in 1978,[54] allowed interlocutory as well as final orders by federal district courts in bankruptcy "proceedings" to be appealed; but in bankruptcy "controversies," only final orders.[55] A bankruptcy controversy is a discrete dispute within the overall framework of the bankruptcy proceeding; an example of such a controversy is a tort claim against the bankrupt. A bankruptcy proceeding is a stage in the administration of the bankrupt estate. Thus, an order appointing a trustee in bankruptcy would be an order in a bankruptcy proceeding, and though interlocutory would be appealable. The problem is that the courts of appeals would be flooded if they had to entertain appeals from every order issued in a bankruptcy proceeding. In a major reorganization there might be a thousand such orders. The courts of appeals therefore carved out an exception for "trivial orders," under which rubric most discovery orders, orders granting or denying continuances, and other routine nonfinal managerial orders were not appealable.[56] Nothing in the language of the statute gave any purchase for such a doctrine. On the other hand there were no outcries of judicial usurpation, and when Congress finally got around to revising the Bankruptcy Act, it simply struck out the provision allowing interlocutory appeals.[57] It may seem, however, that, sensible as it was, the "trivial orders" doctrine could not possibly be thought an exercise in interpretation. However, if I am correct that interpretation embraces efforts to repair a broken communication in the interest of the overall enterprise, the doctrine is a valid interpretation. No interest of Congress would be promoted by flooding the courts with trivial appeals in bankruptcy cases. That would merely slow down those cases, increase the expense of bankruptcy, distract the courts from enforcing other congressional legislation, and thus impede rather than advance the enterprise established by the enact-

53. For others, see Harris, *The Politics of Statutory Construction*, 1985 B.Y.U. L. Rev. 745, 770-73, 785-86.

54. Pub. L. No. 95-598, 92 Stat. 2549 (1978) (codified in scattered sections of 11 U.S.C.).

55. Bankruptcy Act of 1898 § 24(a), 11 U.S.C. § 47(a) (1976) (omitted in 1978 revision).

56. *See In re* Chicago, Milwaukee, St. Paul & Pac. R.R., 756 F.2d 508, 511-13 (7th Cir. 1985), and cases cited therein; 9 J. Moore, B. Ward & J. Lucas, Moore's Federal Practice ¶ 110.15 (2d ed. 1986).

57. *See* 28 U.S.C. § 158(d) (Supp. II 1984).

ment of bankruptcy laws and the creation of a federal judicial system.

The difference between *Locke* and the FELA and trivial-order cases, on the one hand, and *Moragne* on the other, is that the former cry out for judicial correction of a minor and fairly obvious oversight in the legislative drafting process, while the latter involves judicial legislation free of any substantial moorings in the legitimate legislative process. There is no evidence that Congress accidentally confined the Death on the High Seas Act to the high seas. Though there is an appealing symmetry in treating all maritime workers the same no matter where they are injured, doing so just aggravates the asymmetry in the treatment of railroad and maritime workers compared to other workers (I recognize that a similar argument can be made in the FELA case)—making the decision hard to defend as a pure exercise in common law reasoning either.

Lest the reader think me too cavalier about statutory language, I shall give a controversial instance where I believe that the pull of statutory language is so strong that it cannot be overcome once *some* rational purpose can be assigned to the literal interpretation. (This condition was not satisfied in *Locke*, and cannot be satisfied in the FELA or trivial-orders cases either.) I refer to Rule 35(b) of the Federal Rules of Criminal Procedure, which before its 1985 amendment provided, "The [district] court may reduce a sentence within 120 days after the sentence is imposed"[58] or becomes final on appeal. A number of courts read this language to require that the motion for reduction of sentence be filed within 120 days; if it was filed within that period, the court could act on the motion within a reasonable time, even if this meant acting after the 120 days had passed.[59] This interpretation, flatly contrary to the language of the rule, was motivated by an understandable concern that, if the rule were read literally, many defendants would lose their chance for a reduction in sentence merely because the district judge had not acted on their motion within the 120-day period. There was, however, an argument of policy for the literal reading: it served to enforce the division of responsibilities between the sentencing judge and the parole authorities.[60] If the judge waited to see how the defendant was adjusting to prison before the judge decided the Rule 35(b) motion (which was in fact a common reason for judges missing the 120-day deadline), he would be treading on the authority of

---

58. Fed. R. Crim. P. 35(b) (1983).
59. *See* FED. R. CRIM. P. 35(b), advisory committee's note on 1985 amendment.
60. *See* United States v. Kajevic, 711 F.2d 767, 770-71 (7th Cir. 1983).

the Parole Commission to fix—based in part on the defendant's behavior in prison—the actual length of the defendant's imprison-
ment. Maybe as an original matter this reason for a 120-day
deadline on reductions of sentence is overborne by other considerations; I don't mean to suggest that I disagree with the amendment
to the rule. But it is a sufficient reason to enforce the rule as written. For suppose the draftsmen of the original rule in fact wanted
to impose a 120-day deadline on the judge. How could they have
done it more clearly? By saying, "And we really mean it"? Or
(what is the same thing) by saying, "And the court shall have absolutely no authority to consider a motion to reduce sentence after
120 days"? But if draftsmen started adding emphatic language of
this sort, judges would wonder, whenever such language was missing, whether that meant that the interpretation of the provision was
up for grabs. The currency of communication would be devalued.
Perhaps, unlike *Locke*, the draftsmen did want to impose such a
deadline. With this a real possibility, the prudent judicial course
was to defer to the language of the rule and let those responsible for
promulgating rules change it if they so desired (as they subsequently
did with no great fuss).

My last example involves the Sherman Act.[61] It was enacted in
1890, but is interpreted today as if Congress had enacted the evolving economic analysis of monopoly and competition. Today the
Act means, not what its framers may have thought, but what economists and economics-minded lawyers and judges think.[62]

The Act makes it a crime to conspire in restraint of trade, or to
monopolize, attempt to monopolize, or conspire to monopolize.
The problematic terms are "restraint of trade" and "monopolize."
The legislative history makes clear that the Act was aimed at the
great trusts (cartels and monopolies) of the time, but is not single-
minded concerning what aspect of the trusts was reprobated. Some
members of Congress wanted to punish the trusts because the trusts
restricted output and raised price, and thus hurt consumers. Others
believed that the trusts, whether through economies of scale or

---

61. 15 U.S.C. § 1 (1982).
62. For a striking recent example, see Matsushita Electric Industrial Co. v. Zenith Ra-
dio Corp., 106 S. Ct. 1348, 1360 (1986). *See also* Broadcast Music, Inc. v. Columbia Broad-
casting System, 441 U.S. 1, 19-20 (1979); Reiter v. Sonotone Corp., 442 U.S. 330, 343 (1979);
Rothery Storage & Van Co. v. Atlas Van Lines, Inc., 792 F.2d 210, 228-29 (D.C. Cir. 1986);
Ball Memorial Hospital, Inc. v. Mutual Hospital Ins., Inc., 784 F.2d 1325, 1338 (7th Cir.
1986); *In re* Wheat Rail Freight Rate Antitrust Litigation, 759 F.2d 1305, 1315-16 (7th Cir.
1985); Products Liability Ins. Agency, Inc. v. Crum & Forster Ins. Cos., 682 F.2d 660, 663-
64 (7th Cir. 1982).

other efficiencies, produced a greater output at lower price, thus helping consumers (in both the short and long run) but hurting inefficient competitors.[63] Still other members of Congress relied on both reasons for supporting the Act, believing that it would both help consumers and help the trust's competitors. The modern economic analysis of monopoly has made the inconsistency of these two reasons transparent. But no one in 1890 understood the economic concept of efficiency; it hadn't been developed yet.

Although both restraint of trade and monopoly were concepts in the common law of unfair competition at the time, the statute would be nonsense if interpreted to forbid all agreements that would have been deemed restraints of trade at common law. Any covenant not to compete, however harmless and reasonable, given by the seller of a business to the buyer is a restraint of trade in the common law sense, though lawful if it is reasonable in extent and duration.[64] Indeed, an agreement between two partners not to compete while they are in partnership is a restraint of trade. The fact that the statute carried criminal penalties (though at first very weak ones) adds a further note of uncertainty about its intended meaning.

From these unpromising beginnings a vast decisional edifice has been constructed which at present is more or less committed to the economic-efficiency, as opposed to the competitor-protection, conception of the statute. A critical intermediate step was to perform reparative judicial surgery on the statute by inserting the word "unreasonable" in front of "restraint."[65] Is it a legitimate edifice? It cannot be shown to coincide with the intentions of a majority of the

---

63. For contrasting interpretations of the legislative history of the Sherman Act see Bork, *Legislative Intent and the Policy of the Sherman Act*, 9 J. L. & ECON. 7 (1966); L. Kaplow, Antitrust, Law & Economics, and the Courts 50-59 (Harv. L. School, unpublished; forthcoming, LAW & CONTEMP. PROBS.); Lande, *Wealth Transfers as the Original and Primary Concern of Antitrust: The Efficiency Interpretation Challenged*, 34 HASTINGS L.J. 65 (1982); W. LETWIN, LAW AND ECONOMIC POLICY IN AMERICA: THE EVOLUTION OF THE SHERMAN ANTITRUST ACT 53-99 (1965).

64. *See, e.g.*, Mitchel v. Reynolds, 1 P. Wms. 181, 197, 24 Eng. Rep. 347, 352 (K.B. 1711):

In all restraints of trade, where nothing more appears, the law presumes them bad; but if the circumstances are set forth, that presumption is excluded, and the Court is to judge of those circumstances, and determine accordingly; and if upon them it appears to be a just and honest contract, it ought to be maintained.

65. As Justice Stevens has explained with a candor uncharacteristic of judges, "One problem presented by the language of § 1 of the Sherman Act is that it cannot mean what it says. The statute says that 'every' contract that restrains trade is unlawful. But . . . restraint is the very essence of every contract; read literally, § 1 would outlaw the entire body of private contract law. Yet it is that body of law that . . . enables competitive markets . . . to function effectively." National Soc'y of Professional Engineers v. United States, 435 U.S. 679, 687-88 (1978) (footnotes omitted).

Congress that passed the Sherman Act or any of its subsequent amendments and elaborations (e.g., the Clayton Act,[66] or the 1950 amendments thereto), which are also now interpreted in conformity with the efficiency theory. Essentially the courts treat the Sherman Act as if Congress had dumped the trust problem in the lap of the courts and said, "You solve it." And they have done so, more or less. Is this a proper approach for the courts to have taken? I think it is. Setting a goal of promoting economic efficiency makes it possible to derive rules of antitrust law that are reasonably objective, that draw on a large body of economic learning, that are coherent, and yet that are related to the purposes, or some of the purposes, that animated the framers—so that it is not a case of looking for the lost coin where the light is good rather than where you dropped it. In contrast, if courts tried to create antitrust doctrine out of a judicious mixture of conflicting political and distributive goals that some legislators and commentators have assigned to antitrust law, they would be completely at sea and might also shipwreck the economy. Nevertheless, the statute does not purport to delegate a common law rulemaking power and it would be curious to find such a delegation in a criminal statute, though the mail- and wire-fraud statutes[67] come close. There is nothing unusually vague (by statutory standards) about such terms as "restraint of trade" and "monopolization," nor is there any evidence in the legislative history that Congress thought it was simply handing the courts a set of policy issues that it could not resolve itself. By making "*Every* contract, combination in the form of trust or otherwise, or conspiracy, in restraint of trade or commerce . . . illegal,"[68] Congress might have been thought to be limiting judicial discretion rather than conferring it.

It might seem that the present body of judge-made antitrust law could be tied to the purposes of Congress by noting that the main purpose, as expressed by statements made on the floor of Congress, was to help consumers, and modern economics teaches how to do this. But the limitation of this approach can be seen by imagining that modern economics shows that cartels and monopolies—the loose-knit and tight-knit "trusts" that Congress was worried about—actually benefit consumers on balance, by enabling cost reductions that more than offset the power over price created by elim-

---

66. Clayton Act, ch. 323, § 7, 38 Stat. 730, 731-32 (1914) (current version at 15 U.S.C. § 18 (1982)).

67. 18 U.S.C. §§ 1341, 1343 (1982).

68. 15 U.S.C. § 1 (1976) (emphasis added).

inating competition.[69] Then the Sherman Act would have no effect at all; it would have been repealed by economic theory. But it is hard to read the statute as a delegation to the courts to repeal it if and when expert knowledge teaches that the statute can no longer achieve its framers' purposes.

The Sherman Act is a standard instance of a statute that is poorly thought through, that is delivered to the courts in a severely incomplete state, that begs—though it doesn't actually ask—the courts to do what they can to make it reasonable. What the courts have done with the Sherman Act in reading "restraint" to mean "unreasonable restraint" is more aggressive—certainly as regards consequences—than what the Supreme Court would have done if it had read "prior to December 31" to mean "no later than December 31" in the *Locke* case. So I would have difficulty understanding a theory of statutory interpretation that approved both the currently dominant interpretation of the Sherman Act and the decision in *Locke*. The body of antitrust doctrine that the courts have developed in the name of the Sherman Act and the other antitrust statutes is best understood and justified as an effort to complete an enterprise set on foot, in the normally unclear fashion of major legislation, when those statutes were enacted.

VIII. THE ROLE OF POLICY IN INTERPRETATION: THE SEGREGATION DECISION

I have said that "legal formalism" and "legal realism" are not useful terms in which to discuss interpretation; interpretation is different from either logical deduction or policy analysis. Nevertheless it should be apparent from my discussion of cases that policy considerations affect the interpretation of unclear statutory and constitutional provisions. Notions of policy are part of the cultural setting in which interpretation takes place. The uncertainty that would be injected into the electoral process is one reason why a "literal" reading of the age thirty-five provision in Article II is the correct reading, or, stated otherwise, one reason why the provision means what it says. It is a policy reason.

---

69. A firm's profit-maximizing price is determined by the elasticity of demand facing the firm and by the firm's marginal cost. The lower the elasticity of demand, the higher the profit-maximizing price; the lower the marginal cost, the lower the profit-maximizing price. The formation of a monopoly or cartel will reduce the elasticity of demand facing the monopolist (or the cartel members) and thereby push up price. However, if marginal cost also falls, the monopoly or cartel price may turn out to be lower than the competitive price, and consumers will be better off than under competition.

The murkier a provision is, the more important policy considerations are in interpreting it. Indeed, when we say a provision is
"unclear" we mean that the elements in the linguistic and cultural
environment that enable us to get meaning out of words and
sentences are uncertain or contested, and often this is true because
of disputes over policy. Because such disputes can be extremely difficult to resolve, the interpretation of unclear statutory and constitutional provisions will never achieve the certainty of formalist
reasoning. So not only is logic misplaced in statutory analysis; interpretation of unclear provisions can never attain the certainty of
logical reasoning. This raises the question: how can we ever know
whether the interpretation of an unclear provision is the correct
interpretation?

I want to approach this question through a brief examination of
Brown v. Board of Education.[70] *Brown,* of course, held that racial
segregation in public schools denies black schoolchildren the equal
protection of the laws guaranteed by section 1 of the fourteenth
amendment even if the black schools are not demonstrably inferior
to the white ones. I have selected this example not because I disagree with the *Brown* decision—I do not disagree with it—but to
make clear that the Court's interpretation of equal protection does
not have the inevitability of the interpretation of the age thirty-five
provision as "meaning what it says." The *words* "equal protection"
are not incompatible with a system of segregated schools, provided
the black schools are as good as the white ones. If they are not as
good, the logical remedy, one could argue, would be to order them
improved. (I will not discuss the question whether the fourteenth
amendment's privileges and immunities clause would have provided
a firmer ground of decision.) It is no doubt true that since the motive for segregated schools is to keep blacks from mixing with
whites, segregation stamps the blacks with a mark of inferiority
which common sense suggests could be very damaging to them psychologically, although there is surprisingly little evidence of this
point and "separatist" blacks would disagree with it. Public school
segregation also denies black people the opportunity for associations that are more valuable to members of a minority than to members of the majority[71] and is likely to produce more racial
segregation than a free market would. Moreover, it had costly spil-
lover effects in the northern states to which blacks migrated. It is

---

70. 347 U.S. 483 (1954).

71. *See* R. POSNER, THE ECONOMICS OF JUSTICE 355 (1981) (criticizing Wechsler, *Toward Neutral Principles of Constitutional Law,* 73 HARV. L. REV. 1 (1959)).

also no doubt true that a white majority that insists on segregation will be unwilling to support truly equal public schools for the blacks and yet the disparity will be difficult to rectify by judicial decree, making a goal of "separate but equal" unattainable as a practical matter.

But against this powerful case for interpreting the equal protection clause to forbid public school segregation it can be argued that the framers of the fourteenth amendment did not intend to bring about true equality between the black and white races but merely wanted to give the blacks certain fundamental political rights which did not include equal education.[72] Many white Northerners, as well as almost all white Southerners, would have thought it right and natural in 1868 that black people should attend segregated and inferior schools (though as a result of Reconstruction many white Southerners did not participate in the decision to ratify the fourteenth amendment). In 1896, the Supreme Court decided that racial segregation in public facilities was constitutional.[73] The public institutions of the South were built in reliance on that ruling; any change, one could argue, should come from Congress. It is true that congressional action was blocked because of the domination of committee chairmanships by southern Democrats who had safe seats, but maybe this is not a proper thing for a court to consider.

The Supreme Court's unanimous decision to hold segregation unconstitutional was, despite the turmoil and delays encountered in effectuating the decision, politically right and even inspired, but it is not a *demonstrably* correct legal decision. It was not and could not have been derived by a process of logical deduction. Viewed as an effort to carry out the command of the framers of the equal protection clause, it runs up against the standard problem of interpretation—blockage of the channels of communication. The Supreme Court had to balance a variety of policies, including the policy of stare decisis, in order to decide what interpretation would advance the enterprise set on foot by the enactment of the fourteenth amendment. The ultimate justifications for the decision have to be sought in such essentially political or (what are not sharply distinct) ethical desiderata as: (1) improving the position of blacks, (2) adopting a principle of racial (and implicitly also ethnic and religious) equality to vindicate the ideals for which World War II had been fought, (3) raising public consciousness of racial injustice, (4) eradicating an institution that was an embarrassment to America's foreign policy,

---

72. *See* Bickel, *supra* note 25, at 56-59.
73. Plessy v. Ferguson, 163 U.S. 537 (1896).

(5) reducing the social and political autonomy of the South ("completing the work of the Civil War"), (6) finding a new institutional role for the Supreme Court to replace the discredited one of protecting economic liberty (a transformation begun in the second flag-salute case[74]), and (7) breathing new life into the equal protection clause. Some of the items on this list, such as "finding a new institutional role for the Supreme Court," I would rule out of bounds on the ground that they cannot be referred back to the enterprise set on foot by the enactment of the fourteenth amendment. Most of the items, though, seem relevant to the interpretation of an unclear text.

Among efforts to ground the decision in logic, I find Robert Bork's particularly interesting. His premise is that "Where constitutional materials do not clearly specify the value to be preferred, there is no principled way to prefer any claimed human value to any other. The judge must stick close to the text and the history, and their fair implications, and not construct new rights."[75] Applying this premise to the issue of public school segregation, he says that all that we as readers can get out of the equal protection clause and its history is that the clause "was intended to enforce a core idea of black equality against governmental discrimination."[76] A court, Bork continues, must avoid intruding its own values and "choose a general principle of equality that applies to all cases. For the same reason, the Court cannot decide that physical equality is important but psychological equality is not. Thus, the no-state-enforced-discrimination rule of *Brown* must overturn and replace the separate-but-equal doctrine of *Plessy v. Ferguson*."[77]

Bork uses a conception of the institutional limitations of courts (they mustn't intrude their own values) to precipitate a concept out of the equal protection clause, a concept from which the result in *Brown* can be deduced. But the logical form is deceptive. Bork assumes, rather than demonstrates, that the only way the Supreme Court could accommodate its institutional limitations to the "core idea of black equality" was to define the core as including psychological as well as physical equality. The Court could have said, however: "We do not know how large the core was supposed to be, so we will enforce only physical equality, which is easier to police and avoids our getting mired in psychological conjectures." This

---

74. West Virginia State Bd. of Educ. v. Barnette, 319 U.S. 624 (1943).

75. Bork, *Neutral Principles and Some First Amendment Problems*, 47 IND. L.J. 1, 8 (1971).

76. *Id.* at 14.

77. *Id.* at 14-15.

would not be a value judgment about the relative importance of physical and psychological equality. It would be a drawing in of the judicial horns, consistent with Bork's conception of a modest judicial role, one that avoids the making of value judgments.

Bork's second tacit premise is that achieving a better approximation to the (as Bork stresses) largely unknown intent of the framers of the equal protection clause is worth the sacrifice of the values of stare decisis that is entailed. Those values are not trivial, even in constitutional cases. The conventional view that the Supreme Court must feel free to correct its previous mistakes of constitutional (but not statutory) interpretation because of the difficulty of correcting them by a constitutional amendment is superficial. The correction itself may be mistaken, in which case the difficulty of passing a constitutional amendment will entrench the mistake. This point, by the way, undermines the even more deeply seated view that constitutional provisions should be more flexibly interpreted than statutory ones because it is difficult to adapt the Constitution to changing circumstances through the amendment process. Although the difficulty indeed makes the benefits of a correct flexible interpretation greater in the constitutional than in the statutory sphere, it makes the costs of an incorrect flexible interpretation greater, too, because Congress can't correct it, as it can correct an erroneous statutory interpretation.

Bork's third implicit premise is that courts should read "equal protection of the laws" more broadly than the words themselves might be thought to imply when taken in conjunction with the breakdown in law and order in the South following the Civil War. They imply merely that a state cannot discriminate in the provision of police, fire, and other protective services—cannot make black people (or members of some other unpopular group) outlaws, thereby exposing them to the tender mercies of private terrorist groups such as the Ku Klux Klan. Bork might reply that the words "equal protection of the laws" were deliberately chosen as a vague formula to give the courts maximum flexibility. But are they so vague?

The point of all this quibbling with Bork's ingenious analysis is not to question the soundness of the *Brown* decision but to suggest that its soundness is not demonstrable, whether by deductive logic, or by the "shock of recognition" test by which we comprehend clear communications, or by the slightly more elaborate process, illustrated by my discussion of the age thirty-five provision of Article II, by which one shows that policy and other environmental considerations on which almost everyone agrees demonstrate that the words of a text can be taken in only one sense. In other cases, illustrated by my examples in Part VII and most dramatically by *Brown* itself, the judge's task is inescapably problematic because it involves decoding the garbled communications of his constitutional superiors in circumstances where merely ignoring a garbled communication is not an adequate discharge of judicial responsibilities. The judge must examine the enterprise that the framers launched when they enacted the particular statute or constitutional provision in issue and then see what he can do to promote the enterprise, subject to the usual constraints. I wish I could be more precise about the nature of the inquiry in such cases but I am able to do no better than give examples of how I think it can be conducted.

This brings me to my final question, which is how judicial decisions in cases of garbled communications, of unclear commands, can ever be shown to be right. I believe, without being able to develop the point here, that the only test of correctness in such cases is the test of time. This is the same test by which great works of art, or for that matter of statesmanship, are validated.[78] It is the test used whenever the criteria of excellence are in dispute or the application of the criteria to specific works is highly uncertain. Judicial decisions that are overruled or ignored flunk the test of time. So far, *Brown* has passed it triumphantly. Whatever doubts may attend the soundness of the decision, and there are few, are confined to the academy. An even clearer example, however, is the "trivial orders" doctrine which, ratified by Congress after a successful trial period, has to my knowledge attracted no criticism.[79]

Although I believe that neither legal formalism nor legal realism, nor the art of interpretation, can be used to demonstrate—to prove—that the *Brown* decision is correct as a matter of law, I do not infer from this that the decision was lawless and can be justified, if at all, only on political grounds. The case studies in this Article show that it is possible to reason about difficult cases of interpretation even though it is not possible to arrive at irrefutable conclusions. The importance of the test of time is that it offers a method of verifying decisions that when rendered cannot be adjudged more than probably correct or probably incorrect.

---

78. *See* A. SAVILE, THE TEST OF TIME: AN ESSAY IN PHILOSOPHICAL AESTHETICS (1982).

79. *See supra* notes 54-57 and accompanying text.

COLUMBIA LAW REVIEW

| VOL. XXXIII | FEBRUARY, 1933 | NO. 2 |

CASE LAW AND STARE DECISIS:
CONCERNING *PRÄJUDIZIENRECHT IN AMERIKA**

When the great ʿOmar performed the *tawaf* around the Ka'ba in Mecca, and kissed the black stone there enshrined, he is said to have declared: "I know thou art a stone, powerless to help or hurt, and I would not have kissed thee, if I had not seen the Envoy of God kiss thee." This happened, if it happened at all, some thirteen centuries ago. It was currently believed before that time and it has especially been believed since, that lawyers and judges are very much in the case of the Caliph Omar, that they are principally engaged in doing things they know to be irrational for no better reason than that they have seen some one else do them. And of some lawyers and judges, it can surely be said that they faithfully perform the *tawaf,* that is, they walk around the Ka'ba seven times, doubtless to see whether there is some way of escape. This habit of following the lead of other men, sometimes with obvious reluctance, is a thing with which laymen have from time immemorial reproached lawyers, but only in the Common Law systems has it been openly accepted by lawyers as a rule and given a Latin dress in the famous maxim, *stare decisis et quieta non movere.*

The history of this expression, or rather of the rule it purports to embody, has been frequently examined, most recently perhaps by Mr. C. K. Allen,[1] but whatever its history, the existence of some such doctrine has for a long time been taken to be axiomatic in the Common Law and to constitute in practice a striking contrast between it and the Civil Law. None the less the exact extent of the rule is not quite clear. Courts have been restive under the angry criticism to which they have been subjected and have reacted in one of three ways: either by defiantly maintaining *stare decisis,* by painfully rationalizing it, or

---

* K. N. Llewellyn, Präjudizienrecht und Rechtsprechung in Amerika (1933).
[1] Law in the Making (1927) 147. There is a different presentation and approach in Oliphant, *A Return to Stare Decisis* (1928) 6 Am. Law School Rev. 215.

by boldly rejecting it. It often happens, further, that the defiant maintenance and the bold rejection are both merely screens behind which courts in fact do the opposite of what they declare.

What does the rule really mean? Professor Goodhart in an able paper[2] has given its precise content, as English courts have announced it, and has correctly come to the conclusion that those American courts which have varied this content have really to that extent abandoned the rule.

I shall confine myself to that element in *stare decisis* which is the most difficult for laymen to stomach—the doctrine that a court is bound by its own previous decisions. This is the rule of precedent proper, and the term "rule of precedent" will be used hereafter as a variant of the term *stare decisis;* although they are not really logically coextensive. Courts, I say, have been restive under the attacks made upon the rule of precedent, and in America those courts which have maintained it, have declared, first, that it is not absolute and, second, that in the main it is a good rule for a number of reasons. Most of those reasons are some forms of estoppel. Courts have allowed persons to assume that a certain legal doctrine would be applied. It is contrary to elementary justice to allow people to transfer property and obligate themselves on the faith of this expectation and then disappoint them. Or else, if precedents are followed the law is more readily discoverable than if they are not. The rule, we are told, makes for certainty. Other reasons are assigned but these two are the most important.

Evidently the rule of precedent is not to be confounded with deference to the authority of the wise and just who have preceded us. If we believe that Coke was infallible, to follow his judgment is not to apply the rule of *stare decisis,* but is a gesture of humility or piety, or an example of inertia. The law has already been discovered by a man better fit to find it out. It is certainly futile to rediscover America or to reinvent the steam engine. If a court follows a previous decision, because a revered master has uttered it, because it is the right decision, because it is logical, because it is just, because it accords with the weight of authority, because it has been generally accepted and acted on, because it secures a beneficial result to the community, that is not an application of *stare decisis.* To make the act such an application, the previous decision must be followed because it is a previous decision and for no other reason, and it becomes clear that we cannot be certain that the rule is being followed, unless it is *contre coeur,* just as Kant was undoubtedly

---

[2] *Case Law in England and America* (1930) 15 Corn. L. Q. 173. Reprinted in Goodhart, Essays in Jurisprudence and the Common Law (1931) c. 3.

right in holding that obedience to the categoric imperative is discernible only when something disagreeable is commanded.

That is to say, the rule of *stare decisis* is evidently and demonstrably being maintained only when the court declares that the conclusion to which the rule constrains it is one which it would not have reached except for the rule, a conclusion, in other words, of which the court does not morally approve, which cannot be rested on conscience, equity or the public welfare. If there is any additional reason for a decision besides the coercive precedent, the situation at once becomes obscured. *Stare decisis* may be operating but we cannot be sure of it. On the other hand, clearly if there is in fact a coercive precedent present, any further reason is quite irrelevant. *Stare decisis* is such a reason as will have no fellow. To say that a court reaches a conclusion partly because it is following a precedent and partly because the conclusion is just, is really impossible. We may say, if we choose, that the conclusion is just, and also happens to be in accord with precedent, or that the precedent is being followed and that it also happens to secure a just result. In either case the second clause adds nothing whatever to the reason for the court's action.

Something else must be added. It is quite common to find courts supporting their decision not by one, but by many citations of precedents. Can this be defended on strict principles? If the court is bound, it is bound by one decision. A second decision adds nothing. It may prove that the first decision was binding, but by hypothesis, we assumed it was. If a court is not bound except by a *longa series rerum similiter iudicatarum,* what binds it is not the precedent, but estoppel or the force of custom or something like that. We cannot make a rule stronger by adding another rule to it. We are following either the one rule or the other.

That may be called the strict, or the stark and naked, rule of *stare decisis,* and it is certainly the way it is commonly supposed to be applied. And in connection with this formulation we may ask, first, how does it work in detail, and second, can it be defended? To both questions the lawyer of a former generation would have brought an indifferent shrug. The rule works in the obvious way in which Caliph Omar's kissing of the fetish in the Ka'ba resembled that of his Master and the rule need not be defended, because the Common Law justifies itself. When one Common Lawyer talked to another, this did very well. One does not question what is obvious. And when a Common Lawyer addressed himself to the laity, he generally suggested that the beauty and effectiveness of the rule of *stare decisis* was a professional mystery with which the lay mind was unfit to grapple. It is only when lawyers were faced with the necessity of explaining the rule to Civilians, that the real difficulty became apparent. After all, these men were lawyers also, who on practical matters seemed to have largely the same goal and something of the same technique as themselves. And so far from finding the rule obvious, Civilians professed themselves unable to understand how it could be reconciled with reason or justice.

It thus comes about that the most thorough and exhaustive analysis of the rule in its American application is that which Llewellyn has prepared as a result of his recent experience as visiting professor in Leipsic. The book is the just published *Präjudizienrecht und Rechtsprechung in Amerika*. It is a formidable volume in two parts, of which the first is the general exposition and the much larger second part contains the "Materials," which in almost every instance is a case—usually condensed and supplied with comment and analysis; but among these cases, there are also selections from outstanding masters of American legal science, Pound, Cardozo, Holmes and a number of others. There is a selected bibliography at the end of Part I,[3] and a selection of extremely recent articles, at the end of Part II.[4] The net result is that German jurists have in easily accessible form a brilliant and complete presentation of a fundamental doctrine of American law, and American jurists can only trust that some one will do as much for them. Perhaps a visiting professor can be drafted for that purpose.

Evidently Llewellyn has a much larger task before him than that of merely expounding the American theory of precedent. He has to make clear to foreigners our intricate machinery of courts and to work out such theories as can be gathered of American justice. Since he has to do this for persons who are accustomed to subsume their ideas under broad principles, he can scarcely help examining such fundamental questions as sociological backgrounds, freedom of the will, and the psychological processes of which judicial thinking is a part. The whole book, therefore, is a great deal more than a presentation of a legal principle in its American application. It is a setting forth of a theory of law, in which the known breadth of view and keen critical sense of the author are splendidly evidenced.

What becomes at once apparent, as Professor Goodhart's analysis has already shown, is that the rule of precedent in the United States is very far from being what laymen suppose such a rule must be. Instead of being simply a mechanical device which forces a court in a given

---

[3] Pp. 120-2.
[4] P. 351.

direction, it turns out to be an instrument capable of a great many variations and allowing movement in ways that have little obvious relation to the direction indicated in the precedent. In the cases which Llewellyn analyzes, however, the precedent is never directly disregarded. It is always stated that under certain conditions—not now present, within certain limits—here transcended, the precedent would be in fact controlling.

Llewellyn has quite properly explained the character of the rule by analyzing a few cases in which a previous case was consciously followed, although it was not quite approved of, and a great many more in which the precedent was qualified or extended. In these latter cases, evidently something else was necessary to reach the judicial conclusion than the mere presence of the precedent and Llewellyn shows by means of these illustrations that the rule of precedent is far more flexible, at least in the United States, than it seems to the uninitiated.

That precedent law, and particularly the Common Law form of it, implies a closed system—*Geschlossenheitstheorie*[5]—may well be doubted. It has indeed been said of the Common Law—alas, how often!—that it was the "perfection of reason," but this grandiloquence is scarcely to be taken more seriously than the Palmist's statement that Jerusalem was the "perfection of beauty." Less partial observers might have reserved a doubt. Coke and Common Lawyers were jealous of statutes and regarded them as impertinent meddlings, but that does not quite establish a *Geschlossenheitstheorie*. One has only to remember that even the post-Coke Common Law recognized that there were cases of first impression, *"primae impressionis."* How little the earlier Common Law thought of itself as a closed system is now an historical commonplace. The matter is of moment particularly in the United States, since in most of the states, questions are constantly arising for which on any theory of precedent there is no binding authority. To be sure, "persuasive" precedents from other jurisdictions are generally available, but persuasion may be, and often is, resisted, and an independent conclusion is reached, without the aid of precedent of any kind.

The possibility that a case may be denominated a case of first impression is nothing less than the recognition that there may be gaps in the law. And, as in the *Freirecht* movement, the mere capacity to see gaps in what to others is a solid wall is enough to permit a wholly new attitude to the law to arise, if one chooses to have such an attitude. After all, in the case of a "gap" or in a "case of first impression"

---

[5] II, 4.

the really important thing is to find that the gap is there. There will be no lack of material to fill it.

German readers will thus get a realistic, subtle and acute discussion of just what *Präjudizienrecht* comes to in the United States, and will learn that there is no inherent reason why the wilderness of single instances, the lawless science of our law, if handled by wise and just men, should be incapable of securing any reasonable goal such men set themselves. As a matter of fact, Llewellyn might have gone farther. One would not fully realize from his presentation just how free American courts have felt themselves to overrule as well as to "distinguish" and to "gnaw" at an objectionable precedent. The term "overrule" deserves to have been more prominently brought out, if American law is to be expounded. Not only do we have the capital fact that the United States Supreme Court has formally and unqualifiedly rejected *stare decisis* and has frequently exemplified its rejection, but many state courts have overruled their precedents, although in general professing to accept the rule. There is that notable statement of the court, "Shall we stumble where they stumbled?" And in the case of *Alferitz v. Borgwardt,*[6] originally included in Llewellyn's materials[7] but crowded out by exigencies of space, we have the astonishing assertion made in 1899, that "a lawyer who could have advised his client to rely upon the *Berson* case[8] [decided in 1883] in making a loan would show his incapacity." It is not often, even in the wide open spaces, that courts open such a devastating fire on their own decisions.

Overruling is rare, of course, but it may be stated that it happens oftener than the other extreme, to-wit the slavish following of a decision against the court's own notion of right and wrong. This fact is obscured by a common formula like: "Whatever view we might have taken if the question were a new one, *etc.*" In most of these instances, it is easy enough to see that had the question been a new one, the decision would none the less have been the same. But the implied overruling that is done by means of "distinguishing" is a device with which scholasticism has long been familiar and which nowhere has been so freely, and we might almost say flagrantly, employed, as in Common Law courts. Then there is the almost desperate resource which may be called sterilization of the unwanted precedent. "The case of *Smith v. Jones* rests upon its own facts and is not to be extended." The precedent is allowed to live, but it shall have no progeny.

Declared from the start not to be absolute, subject to the reserved

---

[6] 126 Cal. 201, 58 Pac. 460 (1899).
[7] I, 6.
[8] Berson v. Nunan, 63 Cal. 550 (1883).

power to overrule, and to the frequently exercised power to sterilize and to distinguish, the American rule is even more different from the strict or stark rule of *stare decisis* than we might have supposed after reading Llewellyn. Would we be better served if we clung to the strict rule?

What is really done when a precedent is followed? Those who lean on metaphors think of treading in the still visible footsteps of a predecessor. But, of course, the process is not really like that at all. Perhaps we shall see it by observing its operation in a famous case, that of *MacPherson v. Buick Motor Co.*[9] decided in 1916, in which we have the advantage of a characteristically fine opinion of Judge Cardozo, then recently appointed to the Court of Appeals of the State of New York. It is especially apt for our present purpose because it is used by Llewellyn in his book,[10] together with a law review comment.[11]

The situation was simple and could not be better stated than in the words of the court. "The defendant is a manufacturer of automobiles. It sold an automobile to a retail dealer. The retail dealer resold it to the plaintiff. While the plaintiff was in the car it suddenly collapsed. He was thrown out and injured. One of the wheels was made of defective wood, and its spokes crumbled into fragments. The wheel was not made by the defendants; it was bought from another manufacturer. There is evidence, however, that its defects could have been discovered by reasonable inspection and that inspection was omitted. There is no claim that the defendants knew of the defect and wilfully concealed it."

Shall the Buick Company pay damages to MacPherson? I have presented this situation to some twenty laymen of various types and nearly all have immediately and without hesitation answered the question in the affirmative. It may be said that an affirmative answer accords with a generally accepted sense of right or justice, even among persons who would be quite incapable of formulating a "rule" or a "principle" or a "theory" which could cover it. It was also the answer of the majority of the court. One judge dissented. One judge did not vote.

Now, the majority opinion in the case is not, properly speaking, a statement of the reasons which led the court to this conclusion. It is a brief essay on a particular phase of the law of damages, on "a branch of the law" as the court directly calls it, and from every point of view it is an admirable essay. I venture to say that in both Germany and

---

[9] 217 N. Y. 382, 111 N. E. 1050 (1916).
[10] II, 174-87.
[11] II, 183; Note (1927) 40 Harv. L. Rev. 886.

France—to take two examples of Civil Law countries—the result would have been reached immediately and justified by a brief *"attendu"*—and a statement that when a loss must fall on one of two innocent persons, it is just that it be imposed on the one whose negligence contributed to the situation which caused the loss. I venture further to suppose that the result is one which the majority, and perhaps the entire court, desired to reach, the one which accorded with their almost immediate feeling of justice, just as it did with such a feeling among laymen. And it is with these two assumptions that I should like to look more closely at the decision.

There is not a word of the justice or the injustice of distributing the loss. There is instead a statement of a number of cases, which may be listed: (1) *Thomas v. Winchester,* 6 N. Y.[12]; (2) *Loop v. Litchfield,* 42 N. Y.[13]; (3) *Losee v. Clute,* 51 N. Y.[14]; (4) *Devlin v. Smith,* 89 N. Y.[15]; (5) *Statler v. Ray Co.,* 195 N. Y.[16]; (6) *Torgesen v. Schultz,* 192 N. Y.[17] The numbers of the reports indicate the approximate intervals that separated these cases. It is further stated that a number of cases between 89 N. Y. and 192 N. Y. have been passed over.

In all these cases, the issue was whether a manufacturer of an article or a sub-purchaser should bear the loss of an non-wilfully caused injury. In (1) the article was a package of belladona, misbranded as dandelion, in (2) it was a circular saw, in (3), a steam boiler, in (4), a painter's scaffold, in (5) a large coffee urn, in (6) a bottle of aerated water. In (1), (4), (5), (6) the manufacturer was held liable. In (2) and (3), he was exonerated and in both these cases there had been something very much like an assumption of risk by the original purchaser.

When the court decided in favor of the sub-purchaser, was it following (1), (4), (5), or (6), or even (2), or (3) on the principle of *exceptio probat regulam in causis non exceptis?* Evidently, elementary justice will allow that when the risk is assumed, the original manufacturer is not necessarily liable. I have suggested that by the strict or stark rule of *stare decisis,* it is inadmissible to say that it was following them all. Either (1) controlled (4), which controlled (5) and so following, or they were all independent and only one need be mentioned. It may be said that in all subsequent cases, (1) had been mentioned as a point of departure.

[12] 397 (1852).
[13] 351 (1870).
[14] 494 (1873).
[15] 470 (1882).
[16] 478, 88 N. E. 1063 (1909).
[17] 156, 84 N. E. 956 (1908).

Did (1) compel the decision in *MacPherson v. Buick Motor Co.?* The compulsion could not have been very strong, because in the mind of the defendant's attorneys and in that of Chief Judge W. Bartlett, (1) compelled the opposite result. The majority opinion in fact suggests that it is really following (4), and this can be met by the minority only by the assertion that (4) can be understood only as an attempt to follow (1), and that it is still (1), therefore, which must be kept in mind.

Now, what was decided in (1)? It was decided that a manufacturer who sold belladona in a package marked dandelion must pay the damages to any one who buys that package, no matter from whom he buys it. How can we follow that case, when we are dealing with automobiles? Evidently only if belladona and a Buick automobile resemble each other, so that either belladona or the Buick can symbolize the common class. If the class is (A) "obviously and necessarily dangerous substance," the belladona can symbolize it, but perhaps not the Buick, and it is this class which Judge Bartlett says it meant to symbolize. If the class is (B) "substances potentially dangerous if defectively made or mis-labelled," either can symbolize it. Judge Cardozo says this is the class. One could go further and say the class is (C) "any manufactured article which could possibly cause an injury," or that it is (D) "any manufactured article." Each one of these classes is a longer and larger generalization of the belladona in (1), a wider and wider determinable of which the belladona is the determinate. Judge Bartlett would stop at (A) and Judge Cardozo at (B). Neither apparently would go as far as (C), not to say (D).

As far as logic is concerned, the decision to stop at any particular generalization certainly is not derived from the decision in (1) quite by itself. The belladona could easily be classed under (A), (B), (C) or (D). Indeed, the generalization might have stopped long before that. The class symbolized might have been (a) "misbranded poisons capable of fatal results" or (b) "misbranded poisons." Even if the court in (1) had mentioned the class, and said, "We mean this decision to apply to this class only and to go no further," that would not have concluded us. It is very doubtful whether a court has a power to limit the process of generalization of its decisions. But if in case (4), the court had said, "the manufacturer is not liable because a painter's scaffold is not within class (A), *i.e.* is not an obviously and necessarily dangerous article," then we should have a real limitation. Case (1) allows of the progressive generalizations (a) (b) (A) (B) (C) (D). Case (4) would then have stopped it at (A), as Judge Bartlett wished to do in the case of the Buick. But, evidently, it must be such a negative decision which will check the generalization, and an affirmative decision, the mere fact that the court had held a painter's scaffold to belong to Class (A), would not have indicated that the process might not have gone on further.

Now, if (4) had been decided as suggested, what would the majority have done? If I am right in assuming that they desired to reach the result they did, they would certainly have imitated the Caliph Omar at least to the extent of performing the *tawaf,* and marching seven times around the situation. Perhaps then they would have resignedly kissed the fetish and reached what they thought an unjust result. Or, perhaps—who knows?—they might have fled as far from the Ka'ba and Mecca as they could. This sort of a Hegira is easy enough. All they would need to do is to decide that a Buick is in Class (A)—an obviously dangerous instrumentality—and the assumed decision in (4) is successfully circumvented and the fetish remains unkissed.

But, if we look at the majority opinion again, we must admit that they do not even assert that they are following (1). In fact, Judge Cardozo admits that (1) may have been limited to (A). "Whatever the rule in *Thomas v. Winchester*[18] may once have been, it has no longer that restricted meaning."[19] In other words, even if the law is that the process of generalization in (1) is not to go beyond (A), that law was changed. But just how is such a result effected on the principle of *stare decisis?* Assuming that (4) carried the generalization from (A), where (1) left it, to (B), what power had the court to do so, if (1) implied that it was to stop at (A)? In that case (4) has overruled (1), and there is nothing that need stop the *Buick* case from overruling (4).

But really Judge Cardozo is not basing his decision on any assertion that (4) has overruled (1). He examines (4), (5) and (6) and believes that they can be much more readily classified under (B) than (A), which, despite the minority, I think must be conceded. He sees no negative decision which expressly stops at (A). He is satisfied that modern conditions need this particular decision, and that the general opinion of courts and judges in 1916, when the *Buick* case was decided, would approve of making the manufacturers liable. All these conditions together create the law for him and not an auto-limitation of (1), so of its own momentum it will travel to (B) and go no further. Judge Bartlett who would like it to stop at (A), to do him justice, has also more practical and realistic grounds for his belief than any such auto-limitation.

---

[18] *Supra* note 12.
[19] *Supra* note 9, at 387, 111 N. E. at 1052.

Indeed, we must observe that although Judge Cardozo said he would not go as far as (C), there is nothing really to prevent the next court from doing so. He spoke, in fact, of a "trend" of decision and trends do not stop abruptly or by conscious limitation.

I think we can see from this how hard it really is to "follow" a precedent. We have experimented, not *in corpore vili* but *in corpore valde pretioso,* as every decision of Cardozo is. The single instance is capable of generalization, and the generalization will not stop at any particular place, unless by a negative decision, by a statement that a given situation is outside the genus, a subsequent court has deliberately attempted to stop it. Then the process begins all over again, because the excluded situation is itself capable of successive generalizations and we must know whether a large or a small genus is to be excluded from (A). A Buick car is not in (A). Is an automobile truck? An electric machine? A hypothetical new type of car driven by more explosive mixtures than gasoline, and so on?

From what has been said, our original assertion that the rule of *stare decisis* in its strict form assumes a single precedent and no more, needs revision. A single precedent, however binding, is merely the initiation of a process of generalization. If it is a negative decision, if it decides that situation (1) is not in class (B), it bars class (B), but leaves room for much generalization outside of it. If it is affirmative, if it decides that (1) is in class (B), it needs another decision to stop the generalization at (C) or (D) or (E).

We have been going on the assumption that if (4) had been negatively decided, the majority would have yielded to Judge Bartlett and decided in favor of the Buick Company. If they had, it would doubtless be said that they had allowed legal dialectic to overcome their sense of reality. Or better, they would have allowed one type of reality—since the existence and psychological effect of dialectic on a technical profession is a reality—to overcome other realities, those which relate to current non-professional social and business activities. It is, to say the least, unlikely that they would have done so, and it is likely that they would have evaded, distinguished, sterilized, or perhaps overruled, the hypothetical decision.

Modern lawyers and judges, it is hoped, do not enjoy moving exclusively in the attenuated atmosphere of dialectic. And the factor that most readily enables them to deal with their dialectical task—after they have accomplished their practical one—is something so far disregarded, the "opinion."

Llewellyn has made especially clear the functions of the opinion,

including the *dictum,* throughout his book.[20]   The confusion of the
opinion with the decision is an inveterate one, particularly with students,
and is in terms at least not unknown to judges themselves.

It is often said that the opinion gives the "reason" for the decision.   In the vast majority of cases, it does not really do that, but, as
in the instance of the *Buick* case, it is a brief essay, or series of essays,
on points of law.   These essays, to be sure, are rarely as good as Judge
Cardozo's.   In most instances they owe their existence to similar essays
presented in the contending briefs.   They are sometimes quite long
and frequently excellent in every way.   But there ought to be no question that it is not the opinion that is binding.   The rule is *stare decisis,*
not *stare opinionibus* or even *stare responsis.*

Not only has it been unqualifiedly held that it is the decision itself
which must be followed and not the opinion, but the whole technique
of applying the rule of precedent demonstrates it.   Opinions are not
legally required in most states, and, in these, a decision without an
opinion is none the less binding.   The opinion may not logically lead to
the decision at all.   There may be other and better reasons for the decision than those in the opinion.   There may be several different and
even contradictory opinions.   In all these situations, the decision is as
"binding" as it was before.

Whatever the opinions do, they do not add to the binding force of
the decision.   But evidently they have a force of their own.   And that
force is quite correctly and aptly described by the word "authority."

These little essays on the law possess authority in various degrees.   They derive it from the personality and character of the judge,
from the standing of the tribunal, from the inherent qualities of the
opinion.   But to yield to this authority or to resist it, is neither to follow nor to depart from the rule of *stare decisis.*   The position of the
opinion is almost exactly that of the *doctrine* of Continental jurisprudence.   Lawyers and judges read and perpend, but whether they will
be moved to act in accordance with the doctrine they are receiving, depends on a number of factors of which the general authority of the
opinion is only one.   It may be said that *all* opinions have no more than
"persuasive" force.   They can, in the nature of the case, have no more.

Our "doctrine" is scattered through the pages of thousands of reports instead of being concentrated in text books, but so is a great deal
of the "doctrine" of French courts, where the notes by distinguished
jurists in the pages of Dalloz, Sirey or the *Gazette du Palais,* enjoy a
real authority.   The doctrinal discussions in the many German legal

[20] And particularly in I, 14 ff.; II, 47 ff.

periodicals are studied by all German lawyers. We have merely taken the comment on the decision from the footnote into the text and have put it into the mouth of the judge himself. We have not transformed its *vis essentialis* into anything better than authority, but we have, it must be admitted, enormously enhanced that authority.

And there, of course, is the nub of the matter. In spite of what ought by this time to be the cornerstone of our legal concepts, we still speak of law as being in books or not being in books. We still hear it asserted that "the law" is this or that formulated doctrine. We know better in practice. Law books and living habits of communities, formulas and theories, common opinions and general notions, are possible sources of law, but law essentially is an expectation. It is a conjecture of what a court would do,—a particular, concrete, now existing court. It is the law that the minimum wage statute of the District of Columbia violates the Fifth Amendment of the Constitution, not because the Supreme Court said so in *Adkins v. Children's Hospital*,[21] but because it is likely they will say so again, although it is commonly believed that a majority of the present court think otherwise.

We owe this understanding particularly to Holmes and if we slip back into the phrases of the scholasticism from which his genius should have freed us, we ought to do it only in words and without blurring our realization of the facts. Since, therefore, our law *is* what courts *will* decide, it is evident that we must base our prophecies on our knowledge of the court. If French or German judges were doctrinal authorities, could anyone help estimating their decisions on the basis of the doctrines they had professed to be theirs? When both M. Aubry and M. Rau sat on the *Cour de Cassation,* was it not fairly evident that the *Cours de droit civil français d'après la méthode de Zacharie* was earnestly studied by men who had never been at Strasbourg?

So, if we have a little essay by Judge Smith, concurred in by his colleagues, on the law of personal injuries or the obligation of an indorser, we are certainly neglecting an important source of information, if we do not read it carefully, when we are asked what the law on that question is, in a jurisdiction in which Judge Smith will make the law. And, if Judge Smith is long dead, but it is certain that his successor will read Smith's opinion, we had better read it too.

The fact that in order to learn what our law is, we must study the opinions is one thing. The rule of *stare decisis* is another. And the fact that courts, as well as lawyers and writers on law, have confused these two things is also an important fact. The ideas could easily be

---

[21] 261 U. S. 525, 43 Sup. Ct. 394 (1923).

kept separate. As applied in the United States, the rule of *stare decisis* is a matter of technique. In whatever way courts reach their conclusion, they are expected to place the situation they are judging within the generalized class of some existing decision. In doing so, they may, if they choose, disregard the opinion-essay of that decision entirely.

If this were not, to a large extent, merely a technique of presentation, if the judicial process were not what Judge Cardozo has shown it to be in his classic little book,[22] if we did not possess the devices previously set forth, this might be a *Präjudizienkult,* a cult of precedents, the control of living realities by the casual acts of men long since dead. But, as Llewellyn has particularly shown, it need not be so and is not so in fact.

Still less is American preoccupation with "cases," *i.e.* opinions, such a control. It is simply a statement of the fact that in order to estimate the probable action of a court, it is well to read the books which the court will read and will study, and to refute, if we can, whatever we find in those books that runs counter to what we wish the law to be,—or, generally, to have been. Reading these books will be far indeed from making our prophecies of court action, our knowledge of the law, certain. But it will help.

And certainly reading Llewellyn's book will help to make us understand how our system functions.

MAX RADIN

UNIVERSITY OF CALIFORNIA
SCHOOL OF JURISPRUDENCE

---

[22] THE NATURE OF THE JUDICIAL PROCESS (1925).

TÛ-TÛ †

Alf Ross *

ON the Noîsulli Islands in the South Pacific lives the Noît-cif tribe, generally regarded as one of the more primitive peoples to be found in the world today. Their civilization has recently been described by the Illyrian anthropologist Ydobon, from whose account the following is taken.[1]

This tribe, according to Mr. Ydobon, holds the belief that in the case of an infringement of certain taboos — for example, if a man encounters his mother-in-law, or if a totem animal is killed, or if someone has eaten of the food prepared for the chief — there arises what is called *tû-tû*. The members of the tribe also say that the person who committed the infringement has become *tû-tû*. It is very difficult to explain what is meant by this. Perhaps the nearest one can get to an explanation is to say that *tû-tû* is conceived of as a kind of dangerous force or infection which attaches to the guilty person and threatens the whole community with disaster. For this reason a person who has become *tû-tû* must be subjected to a special ceremony of purification.

It is obvious that the Noît-cif tribe dwells in a state of darkest superstition. *"Tû-tû"* is of course nothing at all, a word devoid of any meaning whatever. To be sure, the above situations of infringement of taboo give rise to various natural effects, such as a feeling of dread and terror, but obviously it is not these, any more than any other demonstrable phenomena, which are designated as *tû-tû*. The talk about *tû-tû* is pure nonsense.

---

† This Comment was originally published in FESTSKRIFT TIL HENRY USSING (Borum & Illum ed. 1951). It will appear in the near future in the first issue of the forthcoming *Scandinavian Studies in Law*, a periodical designed to acquaint English-speaking scholars with developments in Scandinavian legal thought and jurisprudence.

* Professor of Law, University of Copenhagen. LL.B., University of Copenhagen, 1922, J.D., 1934; Ph.D., University of Uppsala, 1929.

[1] YDOBON, THE NOÎTCIFONIAN WAY OF LIFE: STUDIES IN TABOO AND TÛ-TÛ (1950).

Nevertheless, and this is what is remarkable, from the accounts given by Mr. Ydobon it appears that this word, in spite of its lack of meaning, has a function to perform in the daily language of the people. The *tû-tû* pronouncements seem able to fulfill the two main functions of all language: to prescribe and to describe; or, to be more explicit, to express commands or rules, and to make assertions about facts.[2]

If I say, in three different languages, "My father is dead," "Mein Vater ist gestorben," and "Mon père est mort," we have three different sentences, but only one assertion. Despite their differing linguistic forms, all three sentences refer to one and the same state of affairs (my father's being dead), and this state of affairs is asserted as existing in reality, as distinct from being merely imagined. The state of affairs to which a sentence refers is called its semantic reference. It can more precisely be defined as that state of affairs which is related to the assertion in such a way that if the state of affairs is assumed actually to exist then the assertion is assumed to be true. The semantic reference of a sentence will depend upon the linguistic usages prevailing in the community. According to these usages a certain definite state of affairs is the stimulus to saying "My father is dead." This state of affairs constitutes the semantic reference of the pronouncement and can be established quite independently of any ideas the speaker may possibly have concerning death — for example, that the soul at death departs from the body.

On the other hand, if I say to my son "Shut the door," this sentence is clearly not the expression of any assertion. True, it has reference to a state of affairs, but in a quite different way. This state of affairs (the door's being shut) is not indicated as actually existing, but is presented as a guide for my son's behavior. Such pronouncements are said to be the expression of a prescription.

According to Mr. Ydobon's account, within the community of the Noît-cif tribe there are in use, among others, the following two pronouncements:

(1) If a person has eaten of the chief's food he is *tû-tû*.
(2) If a person is *tû-tû* he shall be subjected to a ceremony of purification.

---

[2] On the distinction between prescriptive and descriptive language, see HARE, THE LANGUAGE OF MORALS (1952).

Now it is plain that quite apart from what "*tû-tû*" stands for, or even whether it stands for anything at all, these two pronouncements, when combined in accordance with the usual rules of logic, will amount to the same thing as the following pronouncement:

(3) If a person has eaten of the chief's food he shall be subjected to a ceremony of purification.

This statement obviously is a completely meaningful prescriptive pronouncement, without the slightest trace of mysticism. This result is not really surprising, for it is simply due to the fact that we are here using a technique of expression of the same kind as this: "When $x = y$ and $y = z$, then $x = z$," a proposition which holds good whatever "y" stands for, or even if it stands for nothing at all.

Although the word "*tû-tû*" in itself has no meaning whatever, yet the pronouncements in which this word occurs are not made in a haphazard fashion. Like other pronouncements of assertion they are stimulated in conformity with the prevailing linguistic customs by quite definite states of affairs. This explains why the *tû-tû* pronouncements have semantic reference although the word is meaningless. The pronouncement of the assertion "N. N. is *tû-tû*" clearly occurs in definite semantic connection with a complex situation of which two parts can be distinguished:

(1) The state of affairs in which N. N. has either eaten of the chief's food or has killed a totem animal or has encountered his mother-in-law, etc. This state of affairs will hereinafter be referred to as affairs 1.

(2) The state of affairs in which the valid norm which requires ceremonial purification is applicable to N. N., more precisely stated as the state of affairs in which if N. N. does not submit himself to the ceremony he will in all probability be exposed to a given reaction on the part of the community. This state of affairs will hereinafter be referred to as affairs 2.

Given the existence of these two states of affairs, the pronouncement that N. N. is *tû-tû* is assumed to be true. Thus, the combination of the two states, in consequence of the definition, is the semantic reference of the pronouncement. It is quite another matter that the members of the Noît-cif tribe are not themselves aware of this, but rather, in their superstitious imaginings, ascribe to the pronouncement the occurrence of a dangerous force, a different reference from that which it has in reality. This, however, does not prevent one from discussing quite reasonably whether or not a person in given circumstances really is *tû-tû*. The reasoning, then, sets out to show whether the person in question has committed one of the relevant infringements of taboo and whether the purification norm is applicable to him in consequence.

An assertion to the effect that N. N. is *tû-tû* can thus be verified by proving the existence of either the first or the second state of affairs. It makes no difference which, because according to the ideology prevailing in the tribe these two states of affairs are always bound up with one another. It is therefore equally correct to say "N. N. is *tû-tû*, because he has eaten of the chief's food (and therefore must be subjected to a ceremonial purification)" or "N. N. is *tû-tû*, because the purification norm is applicable to him (because he has eaten of the chief's food)." The latter does not preclude the possibility of also saying at the same time "The purification norm is applicable to N. N. because he is *tû-tû* (because he has eaten of the chief's food)." The vicious circle which apparently results here is in reality nonexistent, since the word "*tû-tû*" stands for nothing whatever, and there thus exists no relation, either causal or logical, between the presumed *tû-tû* phenomenon and the application of the purification norm. In reality all three statements — as indicated in the added parentheses — express, each in its own way, nothing more than that the person who has eaten of the chief's food shall undergo a ceremonial purification.

What has been said here in no way upsets the assertion that "*tû-tû*" is a meaningless word. It is only the statement "N. N. is *tû-tû*" to which, taken in its entirety, semantic reference can be ascribed. But there cannot be distinguished in this reference a certain reality or quality which can be ascribed to N. N. and which corresponds to the word "*tû-tû*." The form of the statement is inadequate in relation to what is referred to, and this inadequacy is of course a consequence of the superstitious beliefs held by the tribe.

Thus any attempt to ascribe to the word "*tû-tû*" an independent semantic reference in propositions like the following is doomed to failure:

(1) If a person has eaten of the chief's food he is *tû-tû*.
(2) If a person is *tû-tû* he shall be subjected to a ceremony of purification.

The attempt might be made in the following possible ways:

(*a*) In proposition (1), for *"tû-tû"* substitute affairs 2; and in proposition (2), for *"tû-tû"* substitute affairs 1. Each will then acquire a meaning on its own.[3] But this solution is inadmissible, because the two propositions constitute the major and minor premises for the conclusion that a person who has eaten of the chief's food shall be subjected to a ceremony of purification. The word *"tû-tû,"* therefore, if it means anything at all, must mean the same thing in both of them.

(*b*) In both propositions, for *"tû-tû"* substitute affairs 1. This will not do, for in that case proposition (1) becomes analytically void and without any semantic reference whatever. For the sense of it will be: "When a person has eaten of the chief's food, the state of affairs exists where he has either eaten of the chief's food or killed a totem animal or . . . ."

(*c*) In both propositions, for *"tû-tû"* substitute affairs 2. This will not do either, for in that case proposition (2) becomes analytically void, as can be demonstrated by exact analogy with the above paragraph.

Mr. Ydobon tells of a Swedish missionary who had worked for a number of years among the Noît-cif tribe, ardently endeavoring to make the natives understand that *"tû-tû"* signified nothing whatever and that it was an abominable heathen superstition to maintain that something mystical and indeterminable comes into being because a man encounters his mother-in-law. In this, of course, the good man was quite right. However, it was an excess of zeal which led him to denounce anyone who continued to use the word *"tû-tû"* as a sinful heathen. In so doing he overlooked what has been demonstrated, that quite apart from the fact that the word in itself has no semantic reference whatever and quite apart from the ideas of mystical forces attaching to it, pronouncements in which the word occurs can nevertheless function effectively as the expression of prescriptions and assertions.

Of course it would be possible to omit this meaningless word altogether, and instead of the circumlocution:

(1) He who kills a totem animal becomes *tû-tû*;
(2) He who is *tû-tû* shall undergo a ceremony of purification,

---

[3] Proposition (1) would mean, "If a person has eaten of the chief's food, he shall be subjected to a ceremony of purification"; and proposition (2), "If a person has either eaten of the chief's food or . . . , he shall be subjected to a ceremony of purification."

to use the straightforward statement:

> (3) He who has killed a totem animal shall undergo a ceremony of purification.

One might therefore ask whether — when people have realized that *tû-tû* is nothing but an illusion — it would not be advantageous to follow this line. As I shall proceed to show later, however, this is not the case. On the contrary, sound reasons based on the technique of formulation may be adduced for continuing to make use of the "*tû-tû*" construction. But although the "*tû-tû*" formulation may have certain advantages from the point of view of technique, it must be admitted that it could in certain cases lead to irrational results if against all better judgment the idea that *tû-tû* is a reality is allowed to exert its influence. If this should be the case, it must be the task of criticism to demonstrate the error and to cleanse one's thinking of the dross of such imaginary ideas. But even so, there would be no grounds for giving up the *tû-tû* terminology.

But perhaps it is now time to drop all pretense and openly admit what the reader must by now have discovered, that the allegory concerns ourselves. It is the argument concerning the use of terms such as "right" and "duty" approached from a new angle.[4] For our legal rules are in a wide measure couched in a "*tû-tû*" terminology. We find the following phrases, for example, in legal language:

> (1) If a loan is granted, there comes into being a claim;
> (2) If a claim exists, then payment shall be made on the day it falls due.

---

[4] The "Swedish missionary" of the fable refers to the late Professor A. V. Lundstedt. Throughout his writings, *e.g.*, 1 LUNDSTEDT, DIE UNWISSENSCHAFTLICHKEIT DER RECHTSWISSENSCHAFT (1932), he has emphasized that the only demonstrable reality in the so-called situations of rights consists in the function of the machinery of the law. Under given conditions a person can, according to the law in force, institute proceedings and thereby set the machinery of the law in motion, with the result that the public power is exercised for his benefit. He can achieve judgment and execution by force, creating for himself an advantageous position, a possibility of action, an economic benefit. And that is all. One can readily agree with the author up to this point. But then, instead of proceeding to ask what is characteristic of the situations designated as rights and how the concept of rights may be analyzed and used as a tool for the description of these situations, Lundstedt gives a peculiar twist to his critical account by saying that rights do not exist and that anybody using this term is talking rubbish about something that does not exist. Similar views have been defended by Léon Duguit, 1 DUGUIT, TRAITÉ DE DROIT CONSTITUTIONNEL (3d ed. 1927), and earlier by Jeremy Bentham, *e.g.*, BENTHAM, THE LIMITS OF JURISPRUDENCE DEFINED 57–88 (1945).

This is only a roundabout way of saying:

(3) If a loan is granted, then payment shall be made on the day it falls due.

The claim mentioned in (1) and (2), but not in (3), is obviously, like *tû-tû*, not a real thing; it is nothing at all, merely a word, an empty word devoid of all semantic reference. Similarly, our assertion to the effect that the borrower becomes pledged corresponds to the allegorical tribe's assertion that the person who kills a totem animal becomes *tû-tû*.

We too, then, express ourselves as though something had come into being between the conditioning fact (juristic fact) and the conditioned legal consequence, namely, a claim, a right, which like an intervening vehicle or causal connecting link promotes an effect or provides the basis for a legal consequence. Nor, really, can we wholly deny that this terminology is associated for us with more or less indefinite ideas that a right is a power of an incorporeal nature, a kind of inner, invisible dominion over the object of the right, a power manifested in, but nevertheless different from, the exercise of force (judgment and execution) by which the factual and apparent use and enjoyment of the right is effectuated.

In this way, it must be admitted, our terminology and our ideas bear a considerable structural resemblance to primitive magic thought concerning the invocation of supernatural powers which in turn are converted into factual effects. Nor can we deny the possibility that this resemblance is rooted in a tradition which, bound up with language and its power over thought, is an age-old legacy from the infancy of our civilization.[5] But after these admissions have been made, there still remains the important question — whether sound, rational grounds may be adduced in favor of the retention of a *"tû-tû"* presentation of legal rules, a form of circumlocution in which between the juristic fact and the legal consequence there are inserted imaginary rights. If this question is to be answered in the affirmative, the ban on the mention of rights must be lifted. I believe that this question must be

---

[5] Axel Hägerström has cited weighty arguments in support of the magical origins of Roman legal conceptions. HÄGERSTRÖM, DER RÖMISCHE OBLIGATIONS-BEGRIFF (1927). Modern research in sociology and history of religion also points in the same direction. See ROSS, TOWARDS A REALISTIC JURISPRUDENCE 214–44 (1946); MAX WEBER ON LAW IN ECONOMY AND SOCIETY 106 (Rheinstein ed. 1954).

answered in the affirmative and shall take the concept of ownership as my point of departure.

The legal rules concerning ownership could, without doubt, be
expressed without the use of this term. In that case a large number of rules would have to be formulated, directly linking the
individual legal consequences to the individual legal facts. For
example:

> If a person has lawfully acquired a thing by purchase, judg-
> ment for recovery shall be given in favor of the purchaser against
> other persons retaining the thing in their possession.
>
> If a person has inherited a thing, judgment for damages shall be
> given in favor of the heir against other persons who culpably dam-
> age the thing.
>
> If a person by prescription has acquired a thing and raised a
> loan that is not repaid at the proper time, the creditor shall be given
> judgment for satisfaction out of the thing.
>
> If a person has occupied a *res nullius* and by legacy bequeathed
> it to another person, judgment shall be given in favor of the legatee
> against the testator's estate for the surrender of the thing.
>
> If a person has acquired a thing by means of execution as a
> creditor and the object is subsequently appropriated by another
> person, the latter shall be punished for theft.

An account along these lines would, however, be so unwieldy
as to be practically worthless. It is the task of legal thinking to
conceptualize the legal rules in such a way that they are reduced
to systematic order and by this means to give an account of the
law in force which is as plain and convenient as possible. This
can be achieved with the aid of the following technique of presentation.

On looking at a large number of legal rules on the lines indicated, one will find that it is possible to select from among them
a certain group that can be arranged in the following way:

$$
\begin{array}{llll}
F_1 - C_1 & F_2 - C_1 & F_3 - C_1 \quad \ldots\ldots & F_p - C_1 \\
F_1 - C_2 & F_2 - C_2 & F_3 - C_2 \quad \ldots\ldots & F_p - C_2 \\
F_1 - C_3 & F_2 - C_3 & F_3 - C_3 \quad \ldots\ldots & F_p - C_3 \\
\quad \cdot & \quad \cdot & \quad \cdot & \quad \cdot \\
\quad \cdot & \quad \cdot & \quad \cdot & \quad \cdot \\
\quad \cdot & \quad \cdot & \quad \cdot & \quad \cdot \\
F_1 - C_n & F_2 - C_n & F_3 - C_n \quad \ldots\ldots & F_p - C_n
\end{array}
$$

The conditioning fact F_1 is connected with the legal consequence
C_1, etc. This means that each single one of a certain totality of

conditioning facts $(F_1 - F_p)$ is connected with each single one of a certain group of legal consequences $(C_1 - C_n)$; or, that it is true of each single F that it is connected with the same group of legal consequences $(C_1 + C_2 \ldots + C_n)$; or, that a cumulative plurality of legal consequences is connected to a disjunctive plurality of conditioning facts.

These $n \times p$ individual legal rules can be stated more simply and more manageably in the figure:

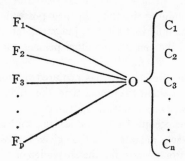

"O" (ownership) merely stands for the systematic connection that F_1 as well as F_2, $F_3 \ldots F_p$ entail the totality of legal consequences C_1, C_2, $C_3 \ldots C_n$. As a technique of presentation this is expressed then by stating in one series of rules the facts that "create ownership" and in another series the legal consequences that "ownership" entails.

It will be clear from this that the "ownership" inserted between the conditioning facts and the conditioned consequences is in reality a meaningless word, a word without any semantic reference whatever, serving solely as a tool of presentation. We talk as if ownership were a causal link between F and C, an effect occasioned or created by every F, and which in turn is the cause of a totality of legal consequences. We say, for example, that:

(1) If *A* has lawfully purchased an object (F_2), ownership of the object is thereby created for him.

(2) If *A* is the owner of an object, he has (among other things) the right of recovery (C_1).

It is clear, however, that (1) + (2) is only a rephrasing of one of the presupposed norms $(F_2 - C_1)$, that purchase as a conditioning fact entails the possibility of recovery as a legal consequence. The notion that between purchase and access to recovery something was created that can be designated as ownership is nonsense. Nothing is created as the result of *A* and *B* exchanging a few sentences legally interpreted as a contract of purchase. All that has occurred is that the judge will now take this fact into consideration and give judgment for the purchaser in an action for recovery.

What has been described here is a simple example of reduction by reason to systematic order. In the final instance it is, to be sure, the task of legal science to undertake this process of simplification, but this task has largely been anticipated by prescientific thought. The idea of certain rights took shape at an early stage in history. A systematic simplification can be carried out, of course, in more ways than one, and this explains why the categories of rights vary somewhat from one legal system to another, though this circumstance does not necessarily reflect a corresponding difference in the law in force.

The same technique of presentation can frequently be employed without the idea of an intervening right. In international law, for example, one series of rules may state which area belongs to a specific state as its territory. That this area has the character of "territory" is per se meaningless. This characterization has meaning only when taken together with another set of rules expressing the legal consequences that are attached to an area's character as territory. In this example it would also be possible to state the legal relations without using the interpolated concept "territory," although such a statement would undeniably be complicated.

Sometimes the intermediate link is not a single right, but a complex legal condition of rights and duties. This is the case, for example, when in family law a distinction is made between the conditions for contracting marriage and the legal effects of marriage, when in constitutional law a distinction is made between the acquisition of nationality and the legal effects of nationality, or in administrative law between the creation of civil-servant status and its legal effects. In these and similar situations it is usual to speak of the creation of a status. Whatever the construction, the reality behind it is in each case the same: a technique which is highly important if we are to achieve clarity and order in a complicated series of legal rules.

"Ownership," "claim," and other words, when used in legal language, have the same function as the word "*tû-tû*"; they are words without meaning, without any semantic reference, and serve a purpose only as a technique of presentation. Nevertheless, it is possible to talk with meaning about rights, both in the form of prescriptions and assertions.

With regard to prescriptions, this emerges from the foregoing. The two propositions "A person who has purchased a thing has the ownership of it" and "A person who has the ownership of a thing can obtain recovery of it" together produce the meaningful prescriptive rule that a person who has purchased a thing can obtain recovery of it.

With regard to assertions, the following holds good by exact analogy with the exposition given above in respect to *"tû-tû"* assertions: the assertion that *A* possesses the ownership of a thing, when taken in its entirety, has semantic reference to the complex situation that there exists one of those facts which are said to establish ownership, and that *A* can obtain recovery, claim damages, etc. It is thus possible with equal correctness to say:

> *A* has the ownership of the thing because he has purchased it (and can therefore obtain recovery, claim damages, etc.)

and

> *A* has the ownership of the thing because he can obtain recovery, claim damages, etc. (because he has purchased it).

The latter does not preclude its being possible also to say:

> *A* can obtain recovery of the thing and claim damages, etc., because he has the ownership of the thing (because he has purchased it).

Just as in the case of the corresponding *"tû-tû"* formulations, there is here no vicious circle, since "ownership" does not stand for anything at all, and there thus exists no relation, either causal or logical, between the supposed phenomenon of ownership and the legal consequences mentioned. All three pronouncements — as indicated by the added parentheses — express, each in its own way, nothing more than that the person who has purchased a thing can obtain recovery of the same, claim damages, etc.

On the other hand it is impossible to ascribe to the word "ownership" an independent semantic reference in the arguments operating with the word.[6] Any attempt to take it as a designation

---

[6] In an article published shortly after the original publication of the present Comment, but evidently without knowledge of it, Anders Wedberg arrived at conclusions similar to mine:

It may be shocking to unsophisticated common sense to admit such "meaningless" expressions in the serious discourse of legal scientists. But, as a matter

of either legal facts or of legal consequences, of both together, or of anything else whatever, is foredoomed to failure. Let us, for example, consider the following syllogisms:

(*A*) If there is a purchase, there exists also ownership for the purchaser. Here there is a purchase. Therefore there exists also ownership for the purchaser.

(*B*) If ownership exists, the owner can obtain recovery. Here there is ownership. Therefore recovery can be obtained.

Together (*A*) and (*B*) express the meaningful rule that a person who has purchased a thing can obtain recovery of it. This conclusion holds good whatever "ownership" may stand for, or even if it stands for nothing at all. For "ownership" there could be substituted "old cheese" or "*tû-tû*" and the conclusion would be just as valid.

On the other hand, it is impossible in this conclusion to ascribe to the word "ownership" a semantic reference such that each of the conclusions (*A*) and (*B*) considered in isolation can acquire meaning or legal function. The conceivable possibilities of such an attempt are the same as those given above in the analysis of the corresponding "*tû-tû*" propositions, and the results also correspond:

(*a*) If we substitute for "ownership" in (*A*) the cumulative totality of legal consequences, and in (*B*) the disjunctive totality of conditions, (*A*) and (*B*) each acquire meaning, but cannot be combined in a syllogism since the middle term is not the same.

(*b*) If in both cases we substitute for "ownership" the disjunctive totality of conditioning facts, the major premise in (*A*) becomes analytically void and thus without any semantic reference.

---

of fact, there is no reason why all expressions employed in a discourse, which as a whole is highly "meaningful," should themselves have a "meaning." It appears likely that many expressions employed by other sciences, especially the so-called exact sciences, lack interpretation and solely function as vehicles of systematization and deduction. Why should not the situation be the same within legal science?

Wedberg, *Some Problems in the Logical Analysis of Legal Science*, 17 THEÒRIA 246, 273 (Sweden 1951).

A similar view has since been expressed by H. L. A. Hart. It is possible, that author maintains, to define a term such as "right" not by substituting for it other words describing some quality, process, or event, but only by indicating the conditions necessary for the truth of a sentence of the form "You have a right." Hart, *Definition and Theory in Jurisprudence*, 70 L.Q. REV. 37, 41–42, 45–49 (1954).

(c) If in both cases we substitute for "ownership" the cumulative totality of legal consequences, then the major premise in (B) becomes analytically void.

I will leave it to the reader to work out for himself the correctness of these assertions by exact analogy with the analysis of the corresponding "*tû-tû*" pronouncements.

The observations I have made here are well fitted to throw light on a most interesting controversy conducted in recent years in Scandinavian literature between Per Olof Ekelöf and Ivar Strahl concerning the meaning in which the concept of rights is taken when used in legal reasoning.[7] Ekelöf started the discussion in an attempt to find out what states of affairs could be substituted in such reasoning for an expression couched in terms of rights. This attempt is the same thing as a quest for the semantic reference of the term. It is interesting to follow the course of the controversy, as it amusingly illustrates the correctness of what has been maintained here.

In broad outline, the course of the controversy was as follows. Ekelöf began by assuming that the term "claim" (this is the term he operated with in his examples, which in other respects were completely analogous to the (A) and (B) formulations adduced above) does not stand for the same thing in both (A) and (B), but respectively for the legal consequence and the legal fact. This corresponds exactly with the possibility marked by (a) in the experiment set out above. Strahl countered with the powerful argument that such an interpretation was inadmissible because the term must of necessity be used with one and the same meaning in both the (A) and (B) propositions because these constitute the premises of a conclusion. Strahl made himself the spokesman for the position that the concept of rights in both propositions stands for the juridical fact, the disjunctive totality of conditioning facts. This position corresponds to the possibility set out above under (b). To this Ekelöf replied with the argument that if that is so the major premise in case (A)′ becomes analytically void. Subsequently Ekelöf adopted Strahl's theory that the word must stand for the same state of affairs in both (A) and (B), but maintained that it did not follow as a matter of course that this state of affairs common to both was necessarily the juridical fact. He discovered that the con-

---

[7] The discussion was conducted in the Scandinavian legal reviews *Tidsskrift for Rettsvitenskap* and *Svensk Juristtidning* in the years 1945 to 1950.

clusion comprising (*A*) and (*B*) held good whatever was substituted for the "rights" concept — whether juridical fact, legal consequence, or both of them together. But he got no further. He did not realize that the conclusion would hold good even if for the concept of rights there were substituted "old cheese" or "*tû-tû*."

In this controversy it was Strahl who came closer to the truth, when he asserted that the concept of right in case (*A*) is used to designate the circumstance which in case (*B*) serves as juridical fact and went on to characterize this as a device serving the technique of presentation. But what Strahl did not see was that the concept of a right does not designate any "circumstance" at all, and that the right as "fact" is not a fact at all, and that it is hopeless to attempt to ascribe a meaning to the major premises in the (*A*) and (*B*) syllogisms when each of them is considered in isolation. For "the device serving the technique of presentation" means that the two propositions have meaning only as fragments of a larger whole in which they both occur, causing the concept of rights as the common middle term in a syllogism to vanish as completely meaningless.

In making these critical observations I have not in any way intended to belittle the value of the research undertaken by Ekelöf and Strahl. On the contrary, I think that Ekelöf's substitution method was a fortunate line to take and that it sharpened the issues; and I must add that it was along these lines that I was led to the view which I believe to be the true one, that the concept of rights is a tool for the technique of presentation serving exclusively systematic ends, and that in itself it means no more and no less than does "*tû-tû*." [8]

---

[8] I have tried elsewhere to show how the concept of rights can lead to errors and dogmatic postulates if it is wrongly taken, not merely as being the systematic unit in a set of legal rules, but as being an independent "substance." Ross, *op. cit. supra* note 5, at 189–202.

THE THEORY OF JUDICIAL PRECEDENTS.

THE importance of judicial precedents has always been a distinguishing characteristic of English law. The great body of the common or unwritten law is almost entirely the product of decided cases, accumulated in an immense series of reports extending backwards with scarcely a break to the reign of Edward I at the close of the thirteenth century. Orthodox legal theory indeed long professed to regard the common law as customary law, and the reported precedents as merely evidence of the customs and of the law derived therefrom. But this was never much better than an admitted fiction. In practice, if not in theory, the common law of England has been manufactured by the decisions of English judges. Neither Roman law, however, nor any of those modern systems which are founded upon it, allows any such place or authority to precedent. They allow to it no further or other influence than that which is possessed by any other expression of expert legal opinion. A book of reports and a text-book are on the same level. They are both evidences of the law; they are both instruments for the persuasion of judges; but neither of them is anything more [1]. English law, on the other hand, draws a sharp distinction between them. A judicial precedent speaks in England with a voice of authority; it is not merely evidence of the law but a source of it; and the courts are bound to follow the law that is so established.

It seems clear that we must attribute this feature of English law to the peculiarly powerful and authoritative position which has been at all times occupied by English judges. From the earliest times the judges of the king's courts have been a small and compact body of legal experts. They have worked together in harmony, imposing their own views of law and justice upon the whole realm, and establishing thereby a single homogeneous system of common law. Of this system they were the creators and authoritative interpreters. They did their work with little interference either from local custom or from legislation. The centralization and concentration of the administration of justice in the royal courts gave to the royal judges a power and prestige which would have been unattainable on any other system. The authority of precedents

---

[1] [This is so. But in point of fact the importance of reported decisions has been on the increase in both France and Germany for some time.—ED.]

was great in England because of the power, the skill, and the professional reputation of the judges who made them. In England the bench has always given law to the bar; in Rome it was the other way about, for in Rome there was no corporate body of professional judges capable of doing the work that has been done for centuries in England by the royal courts.

Declaratory and creative precedents.—In proceeding to consider the various kinds of precedents and the methods of their operation, we have in the first place to distinguish between those decisions which are creative of the law and those which are merely declaratory of it. A declaratory precedent is one which is merely the application of an already existing rule of law. A creative precedent is one which creates and applies a new rule. In the former case the rule is applied because it is already law; in the latter case it is law for the future because it is now applied. In any well developed system such as that of modern England, declaratory precedents are far more numerous than those of the other class; for on most points the law is already settled, and judicial decisions are therefore commonly mere declarations of pre-existing principles. Creative precedents, however, though fewer in number, are greater in importance. For they alone develop the law; the others leave it as it was, and their only use is to serve as good evidence of it for the future. Unless required for this purpose, a merely declaratory decision is not perpetuated as an authority in the Law Reports. When the law is already sufficiently well evidenced, as when it is embodied in a statute or set forth with fullness and clearness in some comparatively modern case, the reporting of declaratory decisions is merely a needless addition to the great bulk of our case law.

It must be understood, however, that a declaratory precedent is just as truly a source of law as is one belonging to the other class. The legal authority of each is exactly the same. Speaking generally, the authority and legal validity of a precedent do not depend on whether it is, or is not, an accurate statement of previously existing law. Whether it is or is not, it may establish as law for the future that which it now declares and applies as law. The distinction between the two kinds turns solely on their relation to the law of the past, and not at all on their relation to that of the future. A declaratory precedent, like a declaratory statute, is a source of law, though it is not a source of *new* law. Here, as elsewhere, the mere fact that two sources overlap, and that the same legal principle is established by both of them, does not deprive either of them of its true nature as a legal source. Each remains an independent and self-sufficient basis of the rule.

I have already referred to the old theory that the common law is customary, not case law. This theory may be expressed by saying that according to it all precedents are declaratory merely, and that their creative operation is not recognized by the law of England. Thus Hale says in his History of the Common Law:—

'It is true the decisions of courts of justice, though by virtue of the laws of this realm they do bind as a law between the parties thereto, as to the particular case in question, till reversed by error or attaint, yet they do not make a law properly so called: for that only the king and parliament can do ; yet they have a great weight and authority in expounding, declaring and publishing what the law of this kingdom is ; especially when such decisions hold a consonancy and congruity with resolutions and decisions of former times[1].'

Hale, however, is evidently troubled in mind as to the true position of precedent, and as to the sufficiency of the declaratory theory thus set forth by him, for elsewhere he tells us inconsistently that there are three sources of English law, namely, (1) custom, (2) the authority of parliament, and (3) 'the judicial decisions of courts of justice consonant to one another in the series and succession of time[2].'

In the Court of Chancery this declaratory theory never prevailed, nor indeed could it, having regard to the known history of the system of equity administered by that court. There could be no pretence that the principles of equity were founded either in custom or legislation. It was a perfectly obvious fact that they had their origin in judicial decisions. The judgments of each Chancellor made the law for himself and his successors.

' It must not be forgotten,' says Sir George Jessel, ' that the rules of courts of equity are not, like the rules of the common law, supposed to have been established from time immemorial. It is perfectly well known that they have been established from time to time—altered, improved, and refined from time to time. In many cases we know the names of the Chancellors who invented them. No doubt they were invented for the purpose of securing the better administration of justice, but still they were invented[3].'

But both at law and in equity this declaratory theory must be totally rejected if we are to attain to any sound analysis and explanation of the true operation of judicial decisions. We must admit openly that precedents make law as well as declare it. We must admit further that this effect is not merely accidental and indirect, the result of judicial error in the interpretation and autho-

[1] Hale's History of the Common Law, p. 89 (ed. of 1820).
[2] Ibid. p. 88.   [3] *In re Hallett*, 13 Ch. D. at p. 710.

ritative declaration of the law. Doubtless judges have many times altered the law while endeavouring in good faith to declare it. But we must recognize a distinct law-creating power vested in them and openly and lawfully exercised. While it is quite true that the duty of the courts is in general *jus dicere* and not *jus dare*, nevertheless they do in fact and in law possess both these functions. Creative precedents are the outcome of the intentional exercise by the courts of their privilege of developing the law at the same time that they administer it.

Authoritative and persuasive precedents. — Decisions are further divisible into two classes, which may be distinguished as authoritative and persuasive. These two differ in respect of the kind of influence which they exercise upon the future course of the administration of justice. An authoritative precedent is one which judges must follow whether they approve of it or not. It is binding upon them and excludes their judicial discretion for the future. A persuasive precedent is one which the judges are under no obligation to follow, but which they will take into consideration, and to which they will attach such weight as it seems to them to deserve. It depends for its influence upon its own merits, not upon any legal claim which it has to recognition. In other words, authoritative precedents are *legal* sources of law, while persuasive precedents are merely *historical*. That is to say, the former establish law in pursuance of a definite rule of law which confers upon them that effect. The latter, if they succeed in establishing law at all, do so indirectly, through serving as the historical ground of some later authoritative precedent. In themselves they possess no legal authority.

The authoritative precedents recognized by English law are the decisions of the superior courts of justice in England. The chief classes of persuasive precedents are the following:

(1) Foreign decisions, and notably those of American courts [1].

(2) The decisions of superior courts in other portions of the British Empire, for example, the Irish courts. 'Decisions of the Irish courts, though entitled to the highest respect, are not binding on English judges [2].'

(3) The decisions of the Privy Council when sitting as the final Court of Appeal from the colonies. In *Leask* v. *Scott* [3] it is said by the Court of Appeal, speaking of such a decision in the Privy Council : 'We are not bound by its authority, but we need hardly say that we should treat any decision of that tribunal with the greatest respect, and rejoice if we could agree with it.'

---

[1] *Castro* v. *R.*, 6 App. Cas. 249. [2] *In re Parsons*, 45 Ch. D. 62.
[3] 2 Q. B. D. 376, at p. 380.

(4) Judicial *dicta*, that is to say, decisions which go beyond the occasion, and lay down a rule wider than is necessary for the purpose in hand. We shall see later on that the authoritative influence of precedents does not extend to such *obiter dicta*, but they are not equally destitute of persuasive efficacy[1].

Absolutely and conditionally authoritative precedents.—Authoritative precedents are of two kinds, for their authority is either absolute or conditional. In the former case the decision is absolutely binding and must be followed without question, howsoever unreasonable or erroneous it may be considered to be. It has a legal claim to implicit and unquestioning obedience. Where, on the other hand, a precedent possesses merely conditional authority, the courts possess a certain limited power of disregarding it. In all ordinary cases it is binding, but there is one special case in which its authority may be lawfully denied. A precedent belonging to this class may be overruled or dissented from, when it is not merely wrong, but so clearly and seriously wrong that its reversal is demanded by the interests of the sound administration of justice. Where this is not so, the precedent must be followed, even though the court which follows it is persuaded that it is erroneous or unreasonable. The full significance of this rule will require further consideration shortly. In the meantime it is necessary to state what classes of decisions are recognized by English law as absolutely, and what as merely conditionally, authoritative.

Absolute authority is attributed to the following kinds :—

(1) Every court is absolutely bound by the decisions of all courts superior to itself. A court of first instance cannot question a decision of the Court of Appeal, nor can the Court of Appeal refuse to follow the judgments of the House of Lords.

(2) The House of Lords is absolutely bound by its own decisions. ' A decision of this House once given upon a point of law is conclusive upon this House afterwards, and it is impossible to raise that question again as if it was *res integra* and could be re-argued, and so the House be asked to reverse its own decisions[2].'

(3) The Court of Appeal is, it would seem, absolutely bound by its own decisions and by those of older courts of co-ordinate authority, for example, the Court of Exchequer Chamber[3].

In all other cases save these three, it would seem that the authority of precedents is merely conditional. That is to say, in

---

[1] Persuasive efficacy, similar in kind though much less in degree, is attributed by our courts to the civil law and to the opinions of the commentators upon it ; also to English and American text-books of the better sort.

[2] *London Street Tramways Company* v. *London County Council* [1898] A. C. 375, at p. 379.

[3] *Pledge* v. *Carr* [1895] 1 Ch. 51 ; *Lavy* v. *London County Council* [1895] 2 Q. B. at p. 581, per Lindley L.J.

all other cases a court is only conditionally bound by its own decisions, by the decisions of inferior, and by those of co-ordinate courts. It will be seen from these rules that the authority of a precedent depends not merely on the court from which it proceeds, but also on the court in which it is cited. Its authority may be absolute in one court, and merely conditional in another. A decision of the Court of Appeal is absolutely binding on a court of first instance, but is only conditionally binding upon the House of Lords.

In order that a court may be justified in disregarding a conditionally authoritative precedent, two conditions must be fulfilled. In the first place, the decision must in the opinion of the court in which it is cited be a *wrong* decision. A decision is wrong in two cases : first when it is contrary to law, and secondly when it is contrary to reason. It is wrong as contrary to law, when there is already in existence an established rule of law on the point in question, and the precedent fails to conform to it and accurately to express and apply it. We shall see later on that a precedent has no abrogative force. When the law is already settled, the sole right and duty of the judges is to follow it. A precedent *must* be declaratory whenever it *can* be, that is to say, whenever there is any law to declare. A decision which is wrong as being contrary to law is therefore one which is creative when it ought to have been merely declaratory.

But in the second place, a decision may be wrong as being contrary to reason. Where there is no settled law to declare and follow, the courts may make law for the occasion. In so doing it is their duty to follow reason, and so far as they fail to do so, their decisions are wrong, and the principles involved in them are of defective authority. Unreasonableness is one of the vices of a precedent, no less than of a custom and of certain forms of subordinate legislation.

It is not enough, however, that a decision should be contrary to law or reason. There is a second condition to be fulfilled before the courts are entitled to reject it. If the first condition were the only one, a conditionally authoritative precedent would differ in nothing from one which was merely persuasive. In each case the precedent would be effective only so far as its own intrinsic merits commended it to the minds of successive judges. But where a decision is authoritative, it is not enough that the court to which it is cited should be of opinion that it is wrong. It is necessary in innumerable cases to give effect to precedents notwithstanding such opinion. It does not follow that a precedent once established should be reversed simply because it is not as perfect and rational as it ought to be. It is often more important that the law should be certain than that it should be ideally perfect. These two requirements are to a great extent inconsistent with each other, and we must often choose between them. Whenever a decision is departed from, the certainty of the law is sacrificed to its rational development. The evils of the uncertainty thus produced may far outweigh the very trifling benefit to be derived from the correction of the erroneous doctrine. The precedent, while it stood unreversed, may have been counted on in numerous cases as definitely establishing the law. Valuable property may have been dealt with in reliance on it. Important contracts may have been made on the strength of it. It may have become to any extent a basis of expectation and the ground of mutual dealings. Justice may therefore imperatively require that the decision, though founded in error, shall stand inviolate none the less. *Communis error facit jus* [1]. 'It is better,' said Lord Eldon, 'that the law should be certain than that every judge should speculate upon improvements in it [2].'

It follows from this that, other things being equal, a precedent acquires added authority from the lapse of time. The longer it has stood unquestioned and unreversed, the more harm in the way of uncertainty and the disappointment of reasonable expectations will result from its reversal. A decision which might be lawfully overruled without hesitation while yet new, may after the lapse of a number of years acquire such increased strength as to be practically of absolute and no longer of merely conditional authority. This effect of lapse of time has repeatedly received judicial recognition.

'Viewed simply as the decision of a court of first instance, the authority of this case, notwithstanding the respect due to the judges who decided it, is not binding upon us; but viewed in its character and practical results, it is one of a class of decisions which acquire a weight and effect beyond that which attaches to the relative position of the court from which they proceed. It constitutes an authority which, after it has stood for so long a period unchallenged, should not, in the interests of public convenience, and having regard to the protection of private rights, be overruled by this court except upon very special considerations. For twelve years and upwards the case has continued unshaken by any judicial decision or criticism [3].'

'When an old decided case has made the law on a particular

---

[1] It is to be remembered that the overruling of a precedent has a retrospective operation. In this respect it is very different from the repeal or alteration of a statute.

[2] *Sheddon* v. *Goodrich*, 8 Ves. 497.

[3] *Pugh* v. *Golden Valley Railway Company*, 15 Ch. D. at p. 334.

subject, the Court of Appeal ought not to interfere with it, because people have considered it as establishing the law and have acted upon it [1].'

The statement that a precedent gains in authority with age must be read subject to an important qualification. Up to a certain point a human being grows in strength as he grows in age ; but this is true only within narrow limits. So with the authority of judicial decisions. A moderate lapse of time will give added vigour to a precedent, but after a still longer time the opposite effect may be produced, not indeed directly, but indirectly through the accidental conflict of the ancient and perhaps partially forgotten principle with later decisions. Without having been expressly overruled or intentionally departed from, it may become in course of time no longer really consistent with the course of judicial decision. In this way the tooth of time will eat away an ancient precedent, and gradually deprive it of all authority and validity. The law becomes animated by a different spirit and assumes a different course, and the older decisions become obsolete and inoperative.

To sum the matter up, we may say that to justify the disregard of a conditionally authoritative precedent, it must be erroneous, either in law or in reason, and the circumstances of the case must not be such as to make applicable the maxim, *Communis error facit jus.* The defective precedent must not, by the lapse of time or otherwise, have acquired such added authority as to give it a title to permanent recognition notwithstanding the vices of its origin.

The disregard of a precedent assumes two distinct forms. The court to which it is cited may either overrule it, or merely refuse to follow it. Overruling is an act of superior jurisdiction. A precedent overruled is definitely and formally deprived of all authority. It becomes null and void, like a repealed statute, and a new principle is authoritatively substituted for the old. A refusal to follow a precedent, on the other hand, is an act of co-ordinate, not of superior jurisdiction. Two courts of equal authority have no power to overrule each other's decisions. Where a precedent is merely not followed, the result is not that the later authority is substituted for the earlier, but that the two stand side by side conflicting with each other. The legal antinomy thus produced must be solved by the act of a higher authority, which will in due time decide between the competing precedents, formally overruling one of them, and sanctioning the other as good law. In the meantime the matter remains at large, and the law uncertain.

---

[1] *Smith* v. *Keal*, 9 Q. B. D. at p. 352. See also *In re Wallis*, 25 Q. B. D. 180; *Queen* v. *Edwards*, 13 Q. B. D. 590 ; *Ridsdale* v. *Clifton*, 2 P. D. 306.

D d 2

Precedents suppletory, not abrogative.—We have already seen the falsity of the theory that all precedents are declaratory. We have seen that they possess a distinct and legally recognized law-creating power. This power, however, is purely suppletory and in no degree abrogative. Judicial decisions may make law, but they cannot alter it. Where there is settled law already on any point, the duty of the judges is to apply it without question. They have no authority to substitute for it law of their own making. Their legislative power is strictly limited to supplying the vacancies of the legal system, to filling up with new law the gaps which exist in the old, to supplementing the imperfectly developed body of legal doctrine.

This statement, however, requires two qualifications. In the first place, it must be read subject to the undoubted power of the courts to overrule or disregard precedents in the manner already described. In its practical effect this is equivalent to the exercise of abrogative power. But in legal theory it is not so. The overruling of a precedent is not the abolition of an established rule of law. It is an authoritative denial that the supposed rule of law has ever existed. The precedent is so treated not because it has made bad law, but because it has never in reality made any law at all. It has not conformed to the requirements of legal efficacy. Hence it is that the overruling of a precedent, unlike the repeal of a statute, has retrospective operation. The decision is pronounced to have been bad *ab initio.* A repealed statute, on the contrary, remains valid and applicable as to matters arising before the date of its repeal. The overruling of a precedent is analogous not to the repeal of a statute, but to the judicial rejection of a custom as unreasonable or otherwise failing to conform to the requirements of customary law.

In the second place, the rule that a precedent has no abrogative power must be read subject to the maxim, *Quod fieri non debet, factum valeat.* It is quite true that judges ought to follow the existing law whenever there is any such law to follow. They are appointed to fulfil the law, not to subvert it. But if by inadvertence or otherwise this rule is broken through, and a precedent is established which conflicts with pre-existing law, it does not follow from this alone that such decision is destitute of legal efficacy. It is a well-known maxim of the law that a thing which ought not to have been done may nevertheless be valid when it is done. If, therefore, a precedent belongs to the class which is absolutely authoritative, it does not lose this authority simply because it is contrary to law and ought not to have been made. No court, for example, will be allowed to disregard a decision of the House of

Lords on such a ground; it must be followed without question, whether it is in harmony with prior law or not. So also with those which are merely conditionally authoritative. We have already seen that error is only one of two conditions, both of which are requisite to render allowable the disregard of such a precedent. And in this respect it makes no difference whether the error consists in a conflict with law or in a conflict with reason. It may well be better to adhere to the new law which should not have been made than to recur to the old law which should not have been displaced.

Grounds of the authority of precedents.—The operation of precedents is based on the legal presumption of the correctness of judicial decisions. It is an application of the maxim, *Res judicata pro veritate accipitur.* A matter once formally decided is decided once for all. The courts will listen to no allegation that they have been mistaken, nor will they reopen a matter once litigated and determined. That which has been delivered in judgment must be taken for established truth. For in all probability it is true in fact, and even if not, it is expedient that it should be held as true none the less. *Expedit reipublicae ut sit finis litium.* When therefore a question has once been judicially considered and answered, it must be answered in the same way in all subsequent cases in which the same question again arises. Only through this rule can that consistency of judicial decision be obtained, which is essential to the proper administration of justice. Hence the effect of judicial decisions in excluding the *arbitrium judicis* for the future, in providing predetermined answers for the questions calling for consideration in future cases, and therefore in establishing new principles of law.

The questions to which judicial answers are required are either questions of law or of fact. To both kinds the maxim, *Res judicata pro veritate accipitur*, is applicable. In the case of questions of law, this maxim means that the court is presumed to have correctly ascertained and applied the appropriate legal principle. The decision operates therefore as proof of the law. It is, or at all events is taken to be, a declaratory precedent. If the law so declared is at all doubtful, the precedent will be worth preserving as useful evidence of it. But if the law is already clear and certain, the precedent will be useless; to preserve it would needlessly cumber the books of reports, and it will be allowed to lapse into oblivion.

In the case of questions of fact, on the other hand, the presumption of the correctness of judicial decisions results in the creation of new law, not in the declaration and proof of old. The decision becomes, in a large class of cases, a creative precedent. That is to say, the question thus answered ceases to be one of fact, and becomes for the future one of law. For the courts are now provided with a predetermined answer to it, and it is no longer a matter of free judicial discretion. The *arbitrium judicis* is now excluded by one of those fixed and authoritative principles which constitute the law.

For example, the meaning of an ambiguous statute is at first a pure question of fact. When for the first time the question arises whether the word ' cattle ' as used by the statute includes horses, the court is bound by no authority to determine the matter in one way or the other. The occasion is one for the exercise of common sense and interpretative skill. But when it has once been judicially decided that ' cattle ' does include horses, the question is for the future one of law and no longer one of fact. For it is incumbent on the courts in subsequent cases to act on the maxim, *Res judicata pro veritate accipitur*, and to answer the question in the same way as has been done already [1].

The operation of creative precedents is, therefore, the progressive transformation of questions of fact into questions of law. *Ex facto oritur jus.* The growth of case law involves the gradual elimination of that judicial liberty to which it owes its origin. In any system in which precedents are authoritative the courts are engaged in forging fetters for their own feet. There is of course a limit to this process. It is absurd to suppose that the final result of legal development will be the complete transformation of all questions of fact into questions of law. The distinction between law and fact is permanent and essential. What then is the limit? To what extent is precedent capable of effecting this absorption of fact into law?

Rationes decidendi.—In respect of this law-creating operation of precedents, questions of fact are divisible into two classes. For

---

[1] It will be understood that the word *fact* is here used in a wide sense to include everything which is not *law*. A question of law means one which is to be answered in accordance with a fixed and predetermined principle authoritatively established, and excluding the liberty of judges to answer the question at their own free will. All others are questions of fact in the wide sense which is here adopted, and which indeed *must* be adopted if the distinction between questions of law and those of fact is to be regarded as logically exhaustive. Every question, therefore, in which the *arbitrium judicis* is not excluded by any authoritative and binding principle, is a question of fact in this sense, whether it is, or is not, one of fact in one or other of the narrower uses of this equivocal term.

The statement in the text that the meaning of an ambiguous statute is a question of fact, may seem paradoxical at first sight. It is, indeed, a question of law in that loose and illogical sense in which every question for the court, as opposed to the jury, is one of law. And it is also, of course, a question as to what the law is. But a question of law does not mean one as to *what the law is*, but one which must be answered by the courts *in accordance with a rule of law*.

some of them do, and some do not, admit of being answered *on principle*. The former are those the answer to which is capable of assuming the form of a general principle. The latter are those the answer to which is necessarily specific. The former are answered by way of abstraction, that is to say by the elimination of the immaterial elements in the particular case, the result being a general rule applicable not merely to that single case but to all others which resemble it in its essential features. The other class of questions consists of those in which no such process of abstraction, no such elimination of immaterial elements, as will give rise to a general principle, is possible. The answer to them is based on the total circumstances of the concrete and individual case, and therefore produces no rule of general application. Now the operation of precedent is limited to one only of these classes of questions. Judicial decisions are a source of law only in the case of those questions of fact which admit of being answered on principle. These only are transformed by decision into questions of law. For in this case only does the judicial decision give rise to a rule which can be adopted for the future as a rule of law. Those questions which belong to the other class are permanently questions of fact. Their judicial solution leaves behind it no permanent results in the form of legal principles.

For example, the question whether the defendant did or did not make a certain statement is a question of fact, which does not admit of any answer save one which is concrete and individual. It cannot be answered on principle. It necessarily remains, therefore, a pure question of fact; the decision of it is no precedent, and establishes no rule of law. On the other hand, the question whether the defendant in making such a statement was or was not guilty of fraud or negligence, though it may be equally a question of fact, nevertheless belongs to the other class of such questions. It may well be possible to lay down a general principle on a matter such as this. For it is a matter which may be dealt with *in abstracto*, not necessarily *in concreto*. If, therefore, the decision is arrived at on principle, it will amount to a creative precedent, and the question, together with every other essentially resembling it, will become for the future a question of law, predetermined by the rule thus established.

A precedent, therefore, is a judicial decision which contains in itself a principle. The underlying principle which thus forms its authoritative element is often termed the *ratio decidendi*. The concrete decision is binding between the parties to it, but it is the abstract *ratio decidendi* which alone has the force of law as regards the world at large. 'The only use of authorities or decided cases,' says Sir George Jessel, 'is the establishment of some principle, which the judge can follow out in deciding the case before him [1].' 'The only thing,' says the same distinguished judge in another case, 'in a judge's decision binding as an authority upon a subsequent judge is the principle upon which the case was decided [2].'

This is the true significance of the familiar contrast between authority and principle. It is often said by judges that inasmuch as the matter before them is not covered by authority, they must decide it upon principle. The statement is a sure indication of the impending establishment of a creative precedent. It implies two things: first, that where there is any authority on the point, that is to say, where the question is already one of law, the duty of the judge is simply to follow the path so marked out for him ; and secondly, that if there is no authority, and if, therefore, the question is one of pure fact, it is his duty if possible to decide it upon principle, that is to say, to formulate some general rule and to act upon it, thereby creating law for the future. It may be, however, that the question is one which does not admit of being answered either on authority or on principle, and in such a case a specific or individual answer is alone possible, no rule of law being either applied or created [3].

To avoid misapprehension, it may be advisable to point out that decisions as to the meaning of statutes are always general, and therefore establish precedents and make law. For such interpretative decisions are necessarily as general as the statutory provisions interpreted. A question of statutory interpretation is one of fact to begin with, and is decided on principle ; therefore it becomes one of law, and is for the future decided on authority.

Judicial dicta.—Although it is the duty of courts of justice to decide questions of fact on principle if they can, they must take care in such formulation of principles to limit themselves to the requirements of the case in hand. That is to say, they must not lay down principles which are not required for the due decision of the particular case, or which are wider than is necessary for this purpose. The only judicial principles which are authoritative are those which are thus relevant in their subject-matter and limited in their scope. All others, at the best, are of merely persuasive efficacy. They are not true *rationes decidendi*, and are distinguished from them under the name of *dicta* or *obiter dicta*, things said by the way. The prerogative of judges is not to make law by formulating and

---

[1] *In re Hallett*, 13 Ch. D. at p. 712.
[2] *Osborne* v. *Rowlett*, 13 Ch. D. at p. 785.
[3] It is clearly somewhat awkward to contrast in this way the terms authority and principle. It is odd to speak of deciding a case on principle because there is no legal principle on which it can be decided.

declaring it—this pertains to the legislature—but to make law by applying it. Judicial declaration, unaccompanied by judicial application, is of no authority.

The sources of judicial principles.—Whence then do the courts derive those new principles, or *rationes decidendi*, by which they supplement the existing law ? They are in truth nothing else than the principles of natural justice, practical expediency, and common sense. Judges are appointed to administer justice—justice according to law, so far as the law extends, but so far as there is no law, then justice according to nature. Where the civil law is deficient, the law of nature takes its place, and in so doing puts on its character also. But the rules of natural justice are not always such that he who runs may read them, and the light of nature is often but an uncertain guide. Instead of trusting to their own unguided instincts in formulating the rules of right and reason, the courts are therefore wisely in the habit of seeking guidance and assistance elsewhere. In establishing new principles, they willingly submit themselves to those various persuasive influences which, though destitute of legal authority, have a good claim to respect and consideration. They accept a principle, for example, because they find it already embodied in some system of foreign law. For since it is so sanctioned and authenticated, it is presumably a just and reasonable one. In like manner the courts give credence to persuasive precedents, to judicial *dicta*, to the opinions of text-writers, and to any other forms of ethical or juridical doctrine which seem good to them. There is, however, one source of judicial principles which is of special importance, and calls for special notice. This is the analogy of pre-existing law. New rules are very often merely analogical extensions of the old. The courts seek as far as possible to make the new law the embodiment and expression of the spirit of the old—of the *ratio juris*, as the Romans called it. The whole thereby becomes a single and self-consistent body of legal doctrine, containing within itself an element of unity and of harmonious development. At the same time it must be remembered that analogy is lawfully followed only as a guide to the rules of natural justice. It has no independent claim to recognition. Wherever justice so requires, it is the duty of the courts, in making new law, to depart from the *ratio juris antiqui*, rather than servilely to follow it.

It is surprising how seldom we find in judicial utterances any explicit recognition of the fact that in deciding questions on principle, the courts are in reality searching out the rules and requirements of natural justice and public policy. The measure of the prevalence of such ethical over purely technical considerations is the measure in which case law develops into a rational and tolerable system as opposed to an unreasoned product of authority and routine. Yet the official utterances of the law contain no adequate acknowledgment of this dependence on ethical influences. 'The very considerations,' it has been well said, 'which judges most rarely mention, and always with an apology, are the secret root from which the law draws all the juices of life [1].' The chief reason of this peculiarity is doubtless to be found in the fictitious declaratory theory of precedent, and in the forms of judicial expression and reasoning which such theory has made traditional. So long as judges affect to be looking for and declaring old law, they cannot adequately express the principles on which they are in reality making new.

The respective functions of judges and juries.—The division of judicial functions between judge and jury creates a difficulty in the theory of precedent which requires some consideration. It is commonly said that all questions of fact are for the jury, and all questions of law for the judge. But we have already seen that creative precedents are answers to questions of fact, transforming them for the future into questions of law. Are such precedents then made by juries instead of by judges? It is clear that they neither are nor can be. No jury ever answers a question on principle ; it gives decisions, but no reasons; it decides *in concreto*, not *in abstracto*. In these respects the judicial action of juries differs fundamentally from that of judges. The latter decide on principle, whenever this is possible ; they formulate the *ratio decidendi* which underlies their decision ; they strive after the general and the abstract, instead of adhering to the concrete and the individual. Hence it is that the decision of a judge may constitute a precedent, while that of a jury cannot. But in composite tribunals, where the jury decides the facts and the judge the law, how does the judge obtain any opportunity of establishing precedents and creating new law ? If the matter is already governed by law, it will of course fall within his province ; but if it is not already so governed, is it not a pure question of fact which must be submitted to the jury, to the total destruction of all opportunity of establishing any precedent in respect of it ? The truth of the matter is that, although all questions of law are for the judge, it is very far from being true that all questions of fact are for the jury. There are very extensive and important portions of the sphere of fact which fall within the jurisdiction of the judge. It is within these portions that the law-creating operation of judicial decisions takes place. No jury, for example, is ever asked to interpret a statute or, speaking

---

[1] Holmes, The Common Law, p. 35.

generally, any other written document. Yet unless there is already some authoritative construction in existence, this is pure matter of fact. Hence that great department of case law which has its origin in the judicial interpretation of statute law. The general rule—consistently acted on, though seldom expressly acknowledged—is that a judge will not submit to a jury any question which he is himself capable of answering *on principle.* Such a question he answers for himself. For since it can be answered on principle, it provides a fit occasion for the establishment of a precedent and a new rule of law. It *ought* to be a matter of law, and can only become what it ought to be, by being kept from the jury and answered *in abstracto* by the judge. The only questions which go to a jury are those questions of fact which admit of no principle, and are therefore the appropriate subject-matter for those concrete and unreasoned decisions which juries give.

I have said that this rule, though acted on, is not expressly acknowledged. The reason is that judges are enabled to avoid such acknowledgment through recourse to the declaratory theory of precedent. As between judge and jury this theory is still in full force and effect, although when the rights and privileges of juries are not concerned, the courts are ready enough at the present day to acknowledge the essential truth of the matter. As between judge and jury, questions of fact are withdrawn from the exclusive cognizance of the latter by means of the legal fiction that they are already questions of law. They are treated as being already that which they are about to become. In a completely developed legal system they would be already true questions of law; the principle for their decision would have been already authoritatively determined. Therefore the judges make bold to deal with them as being already that which they ought to be, and thus the making of law by way of precedent is prevented from openly infringing upon the rights of juries to decide all questions which have not been already decided by the law.

JOHN W. SALMOND.

The
University
of Chicago
Law Review

VOLUME 56   NUMBER 4   FALL 1989

© 1989 by The University of Chicago

The Rule of Law as a Law of Rules

Antonin Scalia†

Louis IX of France, Saint Louis, was renowned for the fair and evenhanded manner in which he dispensed justice. We have the following account from *The Life of Saint Louis* written by John of Joinville, a nobleman from Champagne and a close friend of the king:

> In summer, after hearing mass, the king often went to the wood of Vincennes, where he would sit down with his back against an oak, and make us all sit round him. Those who had any suit to present could come to speak to him without hindrance from an usher or any other person. The king would address them directly, and ask: "Is there anyone here who has a case to be settled?" Those who had one would stand up. Then he would say: "Keep silent all of you, and you shall be heard in turn, one after the other."[1]

The judgments there pronounced, under the oak tree, were regarded as eminently just and good—though as far as I know Louis IX had no particular training in the customary law of any of the

---

© Copyright 1989 Antonin Scalia

† Associate Justice, United States Supreme Court. This essay was first delivered as the Oliver Wendell Holmes, Jr. Lecture at Harvard University on February 14, 1989.

[1] Jean de Joinville, *The Life of Saint Louis*, in Margaret R. B. Shaw, transl, *Joinville & Villehardouin: Chronicles of the Crusades* 163, 177 (Penguin, 1963).

counties of France, or any other legal training. King Solomon is also supposed to have done a pretty good job, without benefit of a law degree, dispensing justice case-by-case.

That is one image of how justice is done—one case at a time, taking into account all the circumstances, and identifying within that context the "fair" result. It may not be as outmoded an image as one might think, considering the popularity of Judge Wapner.

And yet what would Tom Paine have thought of this, who said:

> [L]et a day be solemnly set apart for proclaiming the charter; let it be brought forth . . . [so] the world may know, that so far we approve of monarchy, that in America *the law is king.* For as in absolute governments the king is law, so in free countries the law *ought* to be king; and there ought to be no other.[2]

As usual, of course, the Greeks had the same thought—and put it somewhat more dispassionately. In his *Politics*, Aristotle states:

> Rightly constituted laws should be the final sovereign; and personal rule, whether it be exercised by a single person or a body of persons, should be sovereign only in those matters on which law is unable, owing to the difficulty of framing general rules for all contingencies, to make an exact pronouncement.[3]

It is this dichotomy between "general rule of law" and "personal discretion to do justice" that I wish to explore.

In a democratic system, of course, the general rule of law has special claim to preference, since it is the normal product of that branch of government most responsive to the people. Executives and judges handle individual cases; the legislature generalizes. Statutes that are seen as establishing rules of inadequate clarity or precision are criticized, on that account, as undemocratic—and, in the extreme, unconstitutional—because they leave too much to be decided by persons other than the people's representatives.

But in the context of this discussion, that particular value of having a general rule of law is beside the point. For I want to explore the dichotomy between general rules and personal discretion within the narrow context of *law that is made by the courts.* In a

[2] Thomas Paine, *Common Sense*, in Nelson F. Adkins, ed, *Common Sense and Other Political Writings* 3, 32 (Liberal Arts, 1953).

[3] Ernest Barker, transl, *The Politics of Aristotle*, book III, ch xi, § 19 at 127 (Oxford, 1946).

judicial system such as ours, in which judges are bound, not only by the text of code or Constitution, but also by the prior decisions of superior courts, and even by the prior decisions of their own court, courts have the capacity to "make" law. Let us not quibble about the theoretical scope of a "holding"; the modern reality, at least, is that when the Supreme Court of the federal system, or of one of the state systems, decides a case, not merely the *outcome* of that decision, but the *mode of analysis* that it applies will thereafter be followed by the lower courts within that system, and even by that supreme court itself. And by making the mode of analysis relatively principled or relatively fact-specific, the courts can either establish general rules or leave ample discretion for the future.

In deciding, for example, whether a particular commercial agreement containing a vertical restraint constitutes a contract in restraint of trade under the Sherman Act,[4] a court may say that under all the circumstances the particular restraint does not unduly inhibit competition and is therefore lawful; or it may say that no vertical restraints unduly inhibit competition, and since this is a vertical restraint it is lawful. The former is essentially a discretion-conferring approach; the latter establishes a general rule of law.

The advantages of the discretion-conferring approach are obvious. All generalizations (including, I know, the present one) are to some degree invalid, and hence every rule of law has a few corners that do not quite fit. It follows that perfect justice can only be achieved if courts are unconstrained by such imperfect generalizations. Saint Louis would not have done as well if he were hampered by a code or a judicially pronounced five-part test.

Of course, in a system in which prior decisions are authoritative, no opinion can leave *total* discretion to later judges. It is all a matter of degree. At least the very facts of the particular case are covered for the future. But sticking close to those facts, not relying upon overarching generalizations, and thereby leaving considerable room for future judges is thought to be the genius of the common-law system. The law grows and develops, the theory goes, not through the pronouncement of general principles, but case-by-case, deliberately, incrementally, one-step-at-a-time. Today we decide that these nine facts sustain recovery. Whether only eight of them will do so—or whether the addition of a tenth will change the outcome—are questions for another day.

---

[4] Sherman Act, 15 USC § 1 (1982).

When I was in law school, I was a great enthusiast for this approach—an advocate of both writing and reading the "holding" of a decision narrowly, thereby leaving greater discretion to future courts. Over the years, however—and not merely the years since I have been a judge—I have found myself drawn more and more to the opposite view. There are a number of reasons, some theoretical and some very practical indeed.

To begin with, the value of perfection in judicial decisions should not be overrated. To achieve what is, from the standpoint of the substantive policies involved, the "perfect" answer is nice—but it is just one of a number of competing values. And one of the most substantial of those competing values, which often contradicts the search for perfection, is the appearance of equal treatment. As a motivating force of the human spirit, that value cannot be overestimated. Parents know that children will accept quite readily all sorts of arbitrary substantive dispositions—no television in the afternoon, or no television in the evening, or even no television at all. But try to let one brother or sister watch television when the others do not, and you will feel the fury of the fundamental sense of justice unleashed. The Equal Protection Clause epitomizes justice more than any other provision of the Constitution. And the trouble with the discretion-conferring approach to judicial law making is that it does not satisfy this sense of justice very well. When a case is accorded a different disposition from an earlier one, it is important, if the system of justice is to be respected, not only that the later case *be* different, but that it *be seen to be so.* When one is dealing, as my Court often is, with issues so heartfelt that they are believed by one side or the other to be resolved by the Constitution itself, it does not greatly appeal to one's sense of justice to say: "Well, that earlier case had nine factors, this one has nine plus one." Much better, even at the expense of the mild substantive distortion that any generalization introduces, to have a clear, previously enunciated rule that one can point to in explanation of the decision.

The common-law, discretion-conferring approach is ill suited, moreover, to a legal system in which the supreme court can review only an insignificant proportion of the decided cases. The idyllic notion of "the court" gradually closing in on a fully articulated rule of law by deciding one discrete fact situation after another until (by process of elimination, as it were) the truly *operative* facts become apparent—that notion simply cannot be applied to a court that will revisit the area in question with great infrequency. Two terms ago, the number of federal cases heard by my Court represented just about one-twentieth of one percent of all the cases decided by federal district courts, and less than one-half of one percent of all cases decided by federal courts of appeals.[5] The fact is that when we decide a case on the basis of what we have come to call the "totality of the circumstances" test, it is not *we* who will be "closing in on the law" in the foreseeable future, but rather thirteen different courts of appeals—or, if it is a federal issue that can arise in state court litigation as well, thirteen different courts of appeals and fifty state supreme courts. To adopt such an approach, in other words, is effectively to conclude that uniformity is not a particularly important objective with respect to the legal question at issue.

This last point suggests another obvious advantage of establishing as soon as possible a clear, general principle of decision: predictability. Even in simpler times uncertainty has been regarded as incompatible with the Rule of Law. Rudimentary justice requires that those subject to the law must have the means of knowing what it prescribes. It is said that one of emperor Nero's nasty practices was to post his edicts high on the columns so that they would be harder to read and easier to transgress. As laws have become more numerous, and as people have become increasingly ready to punish their adversaries in the courts, we can less and less afford protracted uncertainty regarding what the law may mean. Predictability, or as Llewellyn put it, "reckonability,"[6] is a needful characteristic of any law worthy of the name. There are times when even a bad rule is better than no rule at all.

I had always thought that the common-law approach had at least one thing to be said for it: it was the course of judicial restraint, "making" as little law as possible in order to decide the case at hand. I have come to doubt whether that is true. For when, in writing for the majority of the Court, I adopt a general rule, and say, "This is the basis of our decision," I not only constrain lower courts, I constrain myself as well. If the next case should have such different facts that my political or policy preferences regarding the outcome are quite the opposite, I will be unable to indulge those preferences; I have committed myself to the governing principle. In the real world of appellate judging, it displays more judicial restraint to adopt such a course than to announce that, "on balance," we think the law was violated here—leaving ourselves free to say in

---

[5] *Annual Report of the Director of the Administrative Office of the United States Courts* 4, 7, 15 (GPO, 1988).

[6] See Karl N. Llewellyn, *The Common Law Tradition* 17 (Little, Brown, 1960).

the next case that, "on balance," it was not. It is a commonplace that the one effective check upon arbitrary judges is criticism by the bar and the academy. But it is no more possible to demonstrate the inconsistency of two opinions based upon a "totality of the circumstances" test than it is to demonstrate the inconsistency of two jury verdicts. Only by announcing rules do we hedge ourselves in.

While announcing a firm rule of decision can thus inhibit courts, strangely enough it can embolden them as well. Judges are sometimes called upon to be courageous, because they must sometimes stand up to what is generally supreme in a democracy: the popular will. Their most significant roles, in our system, are to protect the individual criminal defendant against the occasional excesses of that popular will, and to preserve the checks and balances within our constitutional system that are precisely designed to inhibit swift and complete accomplishment of that popular will. Those are tasks which, properly performed, may earn widespread respect and admiration in the long run, but—almost by definition—never in the particular case. The chances that frail men and women will stand up to their unpleasant duty are greatly increased if they can stand behind the solid shield of a firm, clear principle enunciated in earlier cases. It is very difficult to say that a particular convicted felon who is the object of widespread hatred must go free because, on balance, we think that excluding the defense attorney from the line-up process in this case may have prevented a fair trial. It is easier to say that our cases plainly hold that, absent exigent circumstances, such exclusion is a per se denial of due process.[7] Or to take an example involving the other principal judicial role: When the people are greatly exercised about "overregulation" by the "nameless, faceless bureaucracy" in a particular agency, and Congress responds to this concern by enacting a popular scheme for legislative veto of that agency's regulations—warmly endorsed by all the best newspapers—it is very difficult to say that, on balance, this takes away too much power from the Executive. It is easier to say that our cases plainly hold that Congress can formally control Executive action only by law.[8]

Let me turn, briefly, from the practical to the theoretical, to suggest that when an appellate judge comes up with nothing better than a totality of the circumstances test to explain his decision, he is not so much pronouncing the law in the normal sense as engag-

---

[7] *United States v. Wade*, 388 US 218 (1967).
[8] See *INS v Chadha*, 462 US 919 (1983).

ing in the less exalted function of fact-finding. That is certainly
how we describe the function of applying the most venerable totality of the circumstances test of them all—the "reasonable man"
standard for determining negligence in the law of torts. At the
margins, of course, that determination, like every determination of
pure fact or mixed fact and law, can become an issue of law—if, for
example, there is no evidence on which any jury can reasonably
find negligence. And even short of that extreme, the courts have
introduced some elements of law into the determination—the rule,
for example, that disregard of some statutorily prescribed safe-
guards is negligence per se,[9] or the opposite rule that compliance
with all the requirements of certain statutes precludes a finding of
negligence.[10] But when all those legal rules have been exhausted
and have yielded no answer, we call what remains to be decided a
question of fact—which means not only that it is meant for the
jury rather than the judge, but also that there is no single "right"
answer. It could go either way. Only, as I say, at the margins can
an appellate judge say that this determination *must* come out the
other way *as a matter of law.*

Why, one reasonably may wonder, should that not be the
status of all questions that do not lend themselves to further principled resolution? Why should the question whether a person exercised reasonable care be a question of fact, but the question
whether a search or seizure was reasonable be a question of law?
The latter, like the former, lends itself to ordination by rule *up to
a point.* We can say, as we have, that a search of a home is always
unreasonable, absent exigent circumstances, if a warrant is not obtained,[11] and that it is always unreasonable (apart from the field of
administrative searches)[12] where there is no probable cause to believe that a crime has occurred. But once those and all other legal
rules have been exhausted, and the answer is still not clear, why is
not what remains—the question whether, considering the totality
of the circumstances, this particular search was unreasonable—treated as a question of fact, as to which the law should not
expect, or seek to impose through de novo appellate review, a single, correct answer?

One conceivable answer to the riddle of why "reasonable care"

---

[9] See W. Page Keeton, et al, eds, *Prosser and Keeton on the Law of Torts* § 36 at 229-31 (West, 5th ed 1984).

[10] Id at 233.

[11] *Steagald v. United States*, 451 US 204, 211 (1981).

[12] *Camara v. Municipal Court*, 387 US 523, 535 (1967).

is a question of fact but "reasonable search" a question of law is that we do not trust juries to answer the latter question dispassionately when an obviously guilty defendant is in the dock. If that is the reason, it is not a reason that we apply consistently. We let the jury decide, for example, whether or not a policeman fired upon a felon in unavoidable self-defense, though that also is not a question on which the jurors are likely to be dispassionate. Perhaps, then, the answer is that "reasonable search" is a *constitutional* standard, and whether such a standard has been met *must* be left to the judges. Again, however, if that is the reason it is not one that we apply consistently. Prohibition on restraint of "the freedom of speech" is also to be found in the Constitution, but we generally let juries decide whether certain expression so offends community standards that it is not speech but obscenity.[13]

I frankly do not know why we treat some of these questions as matters of fact and others as matters of law—though I imagine that their relative importance to our liberties has much to do with it. My point here, however, is not that we should undertake a massive recategorization, and leave a lot more of these questions to juries, but simply that we should recognize that, at the point where an appellate judge says that the remaining issue must be decided on the basis of the totality of the circumstances, or by a balancing of all the factors involved, he begins to resemble a finder of fact more than a determiner of law. To reach such a stage is, in a way, a regrettable concession of defeat—an acknowledgment that we have passed the point where "law," properly speaking, has any further application. And to reiterate the unfortunate practical consequences of reaching such a pass when there still remains a good deal of judgment to be applied: equality of treatment is difficult to demonstrate and, in a multi-tiered judicial system, impossible to achieve; predictability is destroyed; judicial arbitrariness is facilitated; judicial courage is impaired.

I stand with Aristotle, then—which is a pretty good place to stand—in the view that "personal rule, whether it be exercised by a single person or a body of persons, should be sovereign only in those matters on which law is unable, owing to the difficulty of framing general rules for all contingencies, to make an exact pronouncement."[14] In the case of court-made law, the "difficulty of framing general rules" arises not merely from the inherent nature of the subject at issue, but from the imperfect scope of the materi-

---

[13] See *Jenkins v Georgia*, 418 US 153 (1974).
[14] Aristotle's *Politics*, ch xi, § 19 at 127 (cited in note 3).

als that judges are permitted to consult. Even where a particular area is quite susceptible of clear and definite rules, we judges cannot create them out of whole cloth, but must find some basis for them in the text that Congress or the Constitution has provided. It is rare, however, that even the most vague and general text cannot be given some precise, principled content—and that is indeed the essence of the judicial craft. One can hardly imagine a prescription more vague than the Sherman Act's prohibition of contracts, combinations or conspiracies in restraint of trade,[15] but we have not interpreted it to require a totality of the circumstances approach in every case. The trick is to carry general principle as far as it can go in substantial furtherance of the precise statutory or constitutional prescription. I say "substantial furtherance" because, as I suggested earlier, *no* general principle can achieve a perfect fit. It may well be possible to envision some divisions of territory between competitors that do not, in the peculiar circumstances, reduce competition—but such phenomena would be so rare that the benefit of a rule prohibiting divisions of territory far exceeds the harm caused by overshooting slightly the precise congressional goal. As we have correctly expressed the test for per se Sherman Act illegality, it is whether the type of conduct in question "would always *or almost always* tend to restrict competition and decrease output."[16] Such reduction of vague congressional commands into rules that are less than a perfect fit is not a frustration of legislative intent because that is what courts have traditionally done, and hence what Congress anticipates when it legislates. One can conceive of a statute in which Congress makes clear that the totality of the circumstances is always to be considered. (See, for example, § 2(b) of the Voting Rights Act.)[17] But unless such a statutory intent is express or clearly implied, courts properly assume that "categorical decisions may be appropriate and individual circumstances disregarded when a case fits into a genus in which the balance characteristically tips in one direction."[18]

Of course, the extent to which one can elaborate general rules from a statutory or constitutional command depends considerably upon how clear and categorical one understands the command to

---

[15] 15 USC § 1.

[16] *Broadcast Music, Inc. v CBS*, 441 US 1, 19-20 (1979) (emphasis added).

[17] Voting Rights Act of 1965 § 2(b), 42 USC § 1973(b) (1982) ("A violation of subsection (a) is established if, based on the totality of circumstances, it is shown that the political processes leading to nomination or election . . . are not equally open to participation by members of a class of citizens protected by subsection (a). . ..").

[18] *United States Dept. of Justice v Reporters Committee*, 109 S Ct 1468, 1483 (1989).

be, which in turn depends considerably upon one's method of textual exegesis. For example, it is perhaps easier for me than it is for some judges to develop general rules, because I am more inclined to adhere closely to the plain meaning of a text. That explains the difference between me and most of my colleagues in *Michigan v Chesternut*,[19] a recent case involving the question whether a defendant had been "seized" for purposes of the Fourth Amendment. The defendant was running away from a police car, which initially followed him and ultimately drove alongside him. While thus engaged in what must have looked like a foot race with a police cruiser, he dropped a packet of illegal drugs, which the police recovered. If these events amounted to a seizure, and if probable cause was lacking, the evidence was inadmissible and the conviction for unlawful possession would have to be reversed. The Court specifically declined to hold either that a chase without a stop was a seizure or that a chase without a stop could not be a seizure. Rather, the Court consulted the totality of the circumstances to determine whether a person in the defendant's position would have felt that he was free to disregard the police and go about his business. That sets forth a rule of sorts—it is much more precise than asking whether, considering the totality of the circumstances, the defendant had been seized. But I thought that the law could properly be made even more precise. I joined Justice Kennedy's concurrence, which said that police conduct cannot constitute a "seizure" until (as that word connotes) it has had a restraining effect.[20]

Just as that manner of textual exegesis facilitates the formulation of general rules, so does, in the constitutional field, adherence to a more or less originalist theory of construction. The raw material for the general rule is readily apparent. If a barn was not considered the curtilage of a house in 1791 or 1868 and the Fourth Amendment did not cover it then, unlawful entry into a barn today may be a trespass, but not an unconstitutional search and seizure.[21] It is more difficult, it seems to me, to derive such a categorical general rule from evolving notions of personal privacy. Similarly, even if one rejects an originalist approach, it is easier to arrive at categorical rules if one acknowledges that the content of evolving concepts is strictly limited by the actual practices of the society, as reflected in the laws enacted by its legislatures.

It is, of course, *possible* to establish general rules, no matter

---

[19] 486 US 567, 108 S Ct 1975 (1988).
[20] 108 S Ct at 1981 (Kennedy concurring).
[21] See *United States v. Dunn*, 480 US 294 (1987).

what theory of interpretation or construction one employs. As one cynic has said, with five votes anything is possible. But when one does not have a solid textual anchor or an established social norm from which to derive the general rule, its pronouncement appears uncomfortably like legislation. If I did not consider my judgment governed by the original meaning of constitutional text, or at least by current social practice as reflected in extant legislation, I would feel relatively comfortable deciding case-by-case whether, taking into account all of the circumstances, the death sentence for this particular individual was "cruel and unusual"—but I would feel quite uncomfortable announcing firm rules (legitimated by nothing but my own sense of justice) regarding the relevance of such matters as the age of the defendant, mental capacity, intent to take a life, and so forth.

Since I believe that the establishment of broadly applicable general principles is an essential component of the judicial process, I am inclined to disfavor, without clear congressional command, the acknowledgement of causes of action that do not readily lend themselves to such an approach. In the area of the negative Commerce Clause, for example, it seems to me one thing to undertake uninvited judicial enforcement of the principle (never enunciated by Congress) that a state cannot overtly discriminate against interstate commerce. That is a general principle clear in itself, and there can be little variation in applying it to the facts. It is quite something else, however, to recognize a cause of action to challenge state laws that do not overtly discriminate against interstate commerce, but affect it to an excessive degree, given the value of the state interests thereby protected. The latter can only be adjudged by a standardless balancing, and so I am not inclined to find an invitation for such judicial enforcement within Article I of the Constitution.[22]

The last point suggests a parenthetical observation regarding the recent elimination of virtually all of the Supreme Court's remaining mandatory jurisdiction.[23] Until coming to the Court, I had never noticed what a high proportion of its Commerce Clause cases—so popular in the law school casebooks—involved appeals

---

[22] See *Tyler Pipe Industries v Wash St Dept of Revenue*, 483 US 232, 254 (1987) (Scalia concurring and dissenting in part).

[23] Compare 28 USC § 1257 (1982) (providing for Supreme Court review, by appeal, of certain final judgments rendered by state supreme courts, including judgments concerning the validity of state statutes) with 28 USC § 1257 (1989 Supp) (eliminating review by appeal and providing for Supreme Court review by writ of certiorari).

rather than petitions for certiorari. The reason is understandable enough. To an inordinate degree, these cases involved state *statutes*, rather than administrative acts, that were challenged under the federal Constitution and upheld below—thus meeting the requirements for our former mandatory jurisdiction. It will be interesting to see whether our Commerce Clause jurisprudence will be as extensive in the future, when these cases can be avoided without determining that there is no substantial federal question involved. My guess (or perhaps it is just my hope) is that it will be considerably less extensive, particularly in the category of cases where we have called for a balancing of state interests against impairment of commerce—whether the good to the state done by the requirement of mud-guards on trucks,[24] or the limitation of truck lengths,[25] or whatever else, outweighs the burden on interstate commerce. For when balancing is the mode of analysis, not much general guidance may be drawn from the opinion—just as not much general guidance may be drawn from an opinion setting aside a single jury verdict because in that particular case the evidence of negligence was inadequate. Of course each opinion will straighten out the law of an entire state—but unless there has arisen a state-court federal-court conflict, I think we will be little tempted to intervene when the settled law below seems at least reasonable.

I may be wrong in that prediction. We certainly take, on certiorari, a number of Fourth Amendment cases in which the question seems to me of no more general interest than whether, in *this* particular fact situation, pattern 3,445, the search and seizure was reasonable. It is my inclination—once we have taken the law as far as it can go, once there is no general principle that will make this particular search valid or invalid, once there is nothing left to be done but determine from the totality of the circumstances whether this search and seizure was "reasonable"—to leave that essentially factual determination to the lower courts. We should take one case now and then, perhaps, just to establish the margins of tolerable diversity. But beyond that, just as we tolerate a fair degree of diversity in what juries determine to be negligence, I think we can tolerate a fair degree of diversity in what courts determine to be reasonable seizures.

Lest the observations in this essay be used against me unfairly in the future, let me call attention to what I have *not* said. I have not said that legal determinations that do not reflect a general rule

---

[24] See *Bibb v Navajo Freight Lines*, 359 US 520 (1959).
[25] See *Kassel v Consolidated Freightways Corp.*, 450 US 662 (1981).

can be entirely avoided. We will have totality of the circumstances tests and balancing modes of analysis with us forever—and for my sins, I will probably write some of the opinions that use them. All I urge is that those modes of analysis be avoided where possible; that the *Rule* of Law, the law of *rules*, be extended as far as the nature of the question allows; and that, to foster a correct attitude toward the matter, we appellate judges bear in mind that when we have finally reached the point where we can do no more than consult the totality of the circumstances, we are acting more as fact-finders than as expositors of the law. I have not even tried to address the hardest question, which is: When is such a mode of analysis avoidable and when not? To what extent do the values of the Rule of Law, which I have described, justify the imprecision that it necessarily introduces? At what point *must* the Rule of Law leave off and the rest be left to the facts?

The difficulty of answering those questions is well enough demonstrated by the conflicting opinions of two of our greatest Justices, with which I will conclude. They come from the days when the Supreme Court had enough time that it even took diversity cases. In *Baltimore & Ohio RR Co v Goodman*,[26] a suit for wrongful death of a driver whose truck was struck by a train, the railroad had (of course) lost a jury verdict, and was trying to get the judgment overturned on the basis of contributory negligence as a matter of law. It succeeded. Justice Holmes wrote as follows:

> When a man goes upon a railroad track he knows that he goes to a place where he will be killed if a train comes upon him before he is clear of the track. He knows that he must stop for the train, not the train stop for him. In such circumstances it seems to us that if a driver cannot be sure otherwise whether a train is dangerously near he must stop and get out of his vehicle, although obviously he will not often be required to do more than to stop and look. It seems to us that if he relies upon not hearing the train or any signal and takes no further precaution he does so at his own risk. If at the last moment Goodman found himself in an emergency it was his own fault that he did not reduce his speed earlier or come to a stop. It is true . . . that the question of due care very generally is left to the jury. But we are dealing with a standard of conduct, and when the standard is clear it should be laid down once for all

---

[26] 275 US 66 (1927).

by the Courts.[27]

Seven years later—after Holmes had left the Court—in *Pokora v Wabash Railway Co*,[28] another diversity case involving another truck driver struck by a train, Justice Cardozo wrote as follows:

> Standards of prudent conduct are declared at times by courts, but they are taken over from the facts of life. To get out of a vehicle and reconnoitre is an uncommon precaution, as everyday experience informs us. Besides being uncommon, it is very likely to be futile, and sometimes even dangerous. If the driver leaves his vehicle when he nears a cut or curve, he will learn nothing by getting out about the perils that lurk beyond. By the time he regains his seat and sets his car in motion, the hidden train may be upon him . . . .
>
> Illustrations such as these bear witness to the need for caution in framing standards of behavior that amount to rules of law. The need is the more urgent when there is no background of experience out of which the standards have emerged. They are then, not the natural flowerings of behavior in its customary forms, but rules artificially developed, and imposed from without. Extraordinary situations may not wisely or fairly be subjected to tests or regulations that are fitting for the common place or normal. In default of the guide of customary conduct, what is suitable for the traveler caught in a mesh where the ordinary safeguards fail him is for the judgment of a jury. The opinion in *Goodman's* case has been a source of confusion in the federal courts to the extent that it imposes a standard for application by the judge, and has had only wavering support in the courts of the states. We limit it accordingly.[29]

---

[27] Id at 69-70.

[28] 292 US 98 (1934).

[29] Id at 104-06 (citations omitted).

The
University
of Chicago
Law Review

VOLUME 58   NUMBER 3   SUMMER 1991

© *1991 by The University of Chicago*

Exceptions

Frederick Schauer†

It seems commonly supposed that exceptions are to law what electric windows are to automobiles—useful accessories but hardly central to the enterprise. Exceptions to statutes, regulations, common law rules, and constitutional tests are of course everywhere in the law, a few of the innumerable examples being the good faith exception to the Fourth Amendment exclusionary rule,[1] the collateral order exception to the final judgment rule,[2] the "capable of repetition, yet evading review" exception to the mootness doctrine,[3] the market participant exception to the constitutional ban on state protectionism,[4] the state action exemption in antitrust

---

† Frank Stanton Professor of the First Amendment, John F. Kennedy School of Government, Harvard University. Earlier versions of this Article were presented at the Association of American Law Schools Workshop on Constitutional Law, the Austinian Society, the Smithsonian Institution, The University of Chicago Law School, and the University of Kentucky College of Law. I am grateful to Alvin Goldman, Frank Michelman, and Cass Sunstein for their challenging and consistently useful comments on an earlier draft.
[1] See, for example, *United States v Leon*, 468 US 897 (1984).
[2] See, for example, *Firestone Tire & Rubber Co. v Risjord*, 449 US 368 (1981); *Cohen v Beneficial Industrial Loan Corp.*, 337 US 541 (1949).
[3] See, for example, *Roe v Wade*, 410 US 113 (1973); *Dunn v Blumstein*, 405 US 330, 333 n 2 (1972); *Southern Pacific Terminal Co. v ICC*, 219 US 498, 515 (1911), overruled on other grounds by *Arkadelphia Milling Co. v St. Louis Southwestern Railway*, 249 US 134 (1919).
[4] See, for example, *Reeves v Stake*, 447 US 429 (1980); *Hughes v Alexandria Scrap Co.*, 426 US 794 (1976).

245

law,[5] and the numerous exceptions to the hearsay rule.[6] But although exceptions are an omnipresent feature of the legal terrain, their very pervasiveness appears to prompt the view that exceptions are but adjuncts to what is really important. However useful it may be to consider specific exceptions in particular doctrinal realms, thinking about exceptions as such does not get us very far in thinking about law.

This view about the unimportance of the exception as a discrete jurisprudential phenomenon is never stated explicitly. Indeed, the exception is an invisible topic in legal theory, thus distinguishing it from such thoroughly analyzed concepts as precedent and legislative intent. Implicit in this lack of attention seems to be an understanding that no interesting generalizations are to be derived about the exceptions that surface almost everywhere throughout most legal systems.

I believe this understanding rests on a confused notion of the logical status of an exception. Probing that status prompts the realization that there is no logical distinction between exceptions and what they are exceptions to, their occurrence resulting from the often fortuitous circumstance that the language available to circumscribe a legal rule or principle is broader than the regulatory goals the rule or principle is designed to further. As products of the relationship between legal goals and the language in which law happens to be written, exceptions show how the meaning of a legal rule is related to the meaning of the language that law employs. This relationship is an important subject in its own right, and I will say something about it.[7] But the relationship is only one component of the even larger relationship between law and a background social landscape whose most important elements are the language a society uses and the categories it deploys to carve up the world. In important ways exceptions link law to its linguistic and categorial underpinnings, situating law in a world it both reflects and on which it is imposed.

The use (or not) of exceptions can thus tell us more than we have traditionally thought about how law is located in a linguistic and categorial world. But that location is contingent, and conse-

---

[5] See *Parker v Brown*, 317 US 341 (1943).

[6] See FRE 803, 804.

[7] See H.L.A. Hart, *Definition and Theory in Jurisprudence*, in H.L.A. Hart, *Essays in Jurisprudence and Philosophy* 21 (Oxford, 1983); Mary Jane Morrison, *Excursions into the Nature of Legal Language*, 37 Cleve St L Rev 271 (1989). For further discussion see text at notes 39-47.

quently what is at some time or place a broad rule with an accompanying exception is at other times a narrow rule having no need for an exception to perform the same prescriptive task. Failure to understand the contingency of this relationship, however, often leads substantive debates of policy or principle to hide behind pseudo-logical claims that one side or the other has, by urging an exception, taken the low road of ad hoc expedience rather than the high road of principle. Once we see the fortuity of exceptions and the contingency of the circumstances in which they exist, however, arguments about who is upholding the principle and who is urging an exception become trivial, and so áre less likely to obscure the substantive debate.

The lesson that comes from exposing the logical emptiness of exceptions is yet larger, because after that exposure it is no longer possible to believe that exceptions are epiphenomenal adjuncts to the rules they are exceptions to, such that the power to append an exception does not undercut the primary force of the rule itself.[8] But if the phenomenon of the exception is not logically distinct, and rules and their exceptions occupy the same plane, then we cannot view the power to create exceptions as marginal. Rather, the relationship between the power to create exceptions and the basis for doing so becomes an essential element of the extent of rule-based constraint itself. Much of the picture of a legal system, and much that makes some legal systems different from others, therefore hinges on the power to create exceptions, for that power turns out to be the power both to change rules and to avoid their constraints.

In supporting these claims, I will start with an example from the Securities Act of 1933, turn to the obsolete criminal law prohibition on fornication, and then move to some questions about the definition of First Amendment principles in the context of flag desecration, Nazi speech, and pornography. Drawing on such diverse areas, I hope to show the pervasiveness of the phenomenon I set out to explore.

I. WHEN THE RIGHT WORDS DON'T EXIST

According to § 5 of the Securities Act of 1933, it is "unlawful for any person . . . to sell [an unregistered] security through the use or medium of any prospectus or otherwise."[9] Yet pursuant to

---

[8] See H.L.A. Hart, *The Concept of Law* 136 (Oxford, 1961).
[9] 15 USC § 77e(a)(1) (1988).

§ 3(a)(11) of the same act, sales of securities that would in all respects otherwise qualify for inclusion within the requirements (or prohibitions) of § 5 need not be registered if they are "offered and sold only to persons resident within a single State or Territory, where the issuer of such security is a person resident and doing business within or, if a corporation, incorporated by and doing business within, such State or Territory."[10] When a pair of legal rules operates in the way that §§ 5 and 3(a)(11) do, we say that the latter constitutes an *exception* to the former.[11]

Now imagine a different exception to the registration requirements of the Securities Act of 1933. Suppose that, in addition to the exemption for intrastate sales of securities, we were to find that the Act contained an exemption for sales of lawnmowers, both interstate and intrastate. Were that the case, we would think the statutory structure bizarre, in a way that we do not think the existing intrastate exemption bizarre, because the sale of lawnmowers, unlike the intrastate sale of securities, is not a subclass of the class of sales of securities.

The very definition of an exception, therefore, presupposes that what is excepted is otherwise within the scope of the broader rule. Because intrastate sales are within the scope of "sales of securities," the intrastate exemption makes sense. The "exception" for lawnmower sales, on the other hand, is superfluous, or redundant, because the registration requirements of the Act already exclude lawnmower sales in the definition of the original scope-designating term, "sale of any security."[12] Only where the primary designation of the scope of a legal rule *in*cludes rather than excludes some item that its creators wish not to include is it necessary to add an exception.

We can now see how the necessity of an exception (or lack thereof) to some legal rule is largely a function of the array of linguistic tools then available to the drafter of the rule. Where the language in which the rule is written contains a word or a familiar phrase that itself excludes what the drafters wish to exclude from the scope of the rule, no exception is necessary. All that is required is to employ the appropriate word or phrase, and that which is to be excluded is excluded without the necessity of an exception. But

---

[10] 15 USC § 77c(a)(11) (1988).

[11] In this context, the exception is commonly referred to as the intrastate "exemption," but nothing in this Article turns on any difference between an exception and an exemption.

[12] The immediately preceding language is a slight modification of the exact statutory term, but the modification serves only stylistic purposes.

where language does not provide any word or phrase, the scope of some primary prescription or proscription will be defined in terms that are likely to be overinclusive, from the perspective of the goals of the legal rule. In order to tailor the rule to the legal goals, it then becomes necessary to create an exception.[13] Thus, if the English language contained a word—say, "intersale"—to designate sales that were interstate but not intrastate in the § 3(a)(11) sense, then we might have expected to see the primary prohibition in § 5 of the Securities Act couched simply in terms of a prohibition on the "intersale" of unregistered securities, with no exemption for intrastate sales then being necessary.[14]

II. When the Right Words *Can* be Found

The lesson that emerges is that the need for an exception is frequently not at all a matter of substance. Rather, exceptions often exist as a product of what is essentially a linguistic fortuity, the way in which a language may or may not happen to contain terms—such as "intersale"—excluding from coverage that which the regulatory apparatus seeks to exclude. Exceptions can be the product of linguistic circumstance, of the existing linguistic and categorial structure of society that precedes the use or non-use of an exception.

My claim that exceptions "often" result from linguistic fortuity is somewhat inaccurate. In fact exceptions always result from

---

[13] I assume here that nothing turns on the grammatical-statutory *structure* within which the exception is placed. That is, I assume there is no difference between an exception that reads, "Public sales of securities other than intrastate sales must be registered," and one in which one discrete section states the general rule and a subsequent section carves out an exception. The difference would be of greater moment if allocation of the burden of proof turned on the form of designation. It might be, for example, that placement of the exception within the original proscription would have the effect of placing the burden of proving the non-applicability of the exception on the state or on the plaintiff, but that placing it separately and subsequently would convert it into an affirmative defense. At times that placement may have constitutional ramifications. See, for example, *Martin v Ohio*, 480 US 228 (1987); *Patterson v New York*, 432 US 197 (1977); *Mullaney v Wilbur*, 421 US 684 (1975); Ronald J. Allen, *Structuring Jury Decisionmaking in Criminal Cases: A Unified Constitutional Approach to Evidentiary Devices*, 94 Harv L Rev 321 (1980); John Calvin Jeffries, Jr. and Paul B. Stephan, III, *Defenses, Presumptions, and Burden of Proof in the Criminal Law*, 88 Yale L J 1325 (1979); Charles R. Nesson, *Rationality, Presumptions, and Judicial Comment: A Response to Professor Allen*, 94 Harv L Rev 1574 (1981).

[14] Anyone familiar with the operation of § 5 and its accompanying definitions and exceptions would justifiably question my assumption that the drafters would have chosen the most linguistically or grammatically efficient course. Among the many cases on the exceptions to the exemptions from § 5, see, for example, *McDaniel v Compania Minera Mar de Cortes*, 528 F Supp 152 (D Ariz 1981); *Pawgan v Silverstein*, 265 F Supp 898 (S D NY 1967).

linguistic fortuity, but putting it in just that way is misleading because some seeming fortuities are explained by an available array of linguistic tools that is itself far from fortuitous. Rather, the fortuity of the existence of the appropriate term in a language will often reflect the categories and distinctions the language has previously found it necessary to employ. The way in which the preexisting language sometimes requires an exception and sometimes not thus tells us interesting things about the relation between legal rules and the language in which they are written.

In order to pursue this issue, let me step back to explore the relevance of the commonplace philosophical distinction between regulative and constitutive rules. According to the distinction, drawn by H.L.A. Hart,[15] John Rawls,[16] and Max Black,[17] but most commonly associated with John Searle,[18] certain rules regulate conduct defined without reference to that rule. "No killing" or "No driving in excess of 55 miles per hour" are good examples, because the activities of both killing and driving in excess of 55 miles per hour can exist and be described independent of any rule prohibiting them. In these cases, the description of the activity is one thing, and the regulatory posture toward that activity is something quite different.

Other rules, by contrast, do not regulate logically antecedent behavior, but create the very possibility of engaging in conduct of a certain kind. Such constitutive rules define activities that could not, absent the rule, even exist, or at least could not be described in those terms. The rules of games are archetypal, since rules create the very possibility of winning a *trick*, or scoring a *touchdown*, or hitting a *home run*, or *castling*. Without the rules of chess you cannot castle at all; without the traffic laws you can very well drive in excess of 55 miles per hour (although you cannot *speed*).[19]

---

[15] Hart, *Definition and Theory in Jurisprudence*, in Hart, *Essays in Jurisprudence and Philosophy* 21 (cited in note 7).

[16] John Rawls, *Two Concepts of Rules*, 64 Phil Rev 3, 19-29 (1955).

[17] Max Black, *The Analysis of Rules*, in Max Black, *Models and Metaphors: Studies in Language and Philosophy* 95 (Cornell, 1962).

[18] John Searle, *Speech Acts: An Essay in the Philosophy of Language* 33-42 (Cambridge, 1969).

[19] The distinction between regulative and constitutive rules is not totally unproblematic, see Joseph Raz, *Practical Reason and Norms* 108-13 (Hutchinson, 1975), because there is a real question whether the distinction is one between different kinds of rules or rather just one between different ways of describing acts. Still, even the latter version is sufficient for my purposes here; my point turns only on a distinction none deny—between those descriptions that presuppose the existence of comparatively discrete norm systems and those that do not.

The idea of a constitutive rule is closely connected to the way in which legal rules or doctrinal tests sometimes employ technical language, often referred to as "terms of art." Here it is useful to identify two forms of technical language. One form consists of the technical term with no ordinary language meaning, such as quark, isotope, habeas corpus, or assumpsit. Another form consists of terms with both ordinary and technical meanings, such as "solid" to the physicist, "slice" to the golfer, or "contract" or "party" to the lawyer.[20] But whether the term has an ordinary meaning or not, we would normally expect the technical term to incorporate within its meaning those doctrinal nuances that determine the coverage of the term.[21]

In other words, we would ordinarily expect exceptions to be built into the meaning of a primary technical term. Because foul balls are not home runs in the first place, it is odd to say that foul balls are exceptions to the rule defining home runs. Similarly, we do not normally say that contracts are enforced except those not involving a meeting of the minds, or those not made with consideration, because such arrangements are not contracts at all. The answer to the question, "What is a corporation?" is much of (all of?) the law of corporations, including all the exceptions built into the concept itself.[22]

---

[20] Or "speech" to the constitutionalist? Compare Frederick Schauer, *Rules, the Rule of Law, and the Constitution*, 6 Const Comm 69 (1989); Frederick Schauer, *Easy Cases*, 58 S Cal L Rev 399 (1985); and Frederick Schauer, *An Essay on Constitutional Language*, 29 UCLA L Rev 797 (1982), with Frederick Schauer, *Speech and "Speech"—Obscenity and "Obscenity": An Exercise in the Interpretation of Constitutional Language*, 67 Georgetown L J 899 (1979). In defense of my own inconsistency in at times stressing technical meaning and at other times emphasizing ordinary language, I should note that the question of the relationship between technical and ordinary language, a question of recurring importance, is quite difficult, although it has received surprisingly little attention in the literature. A noteworthy exception is Charles E. Caton, *Introduction*, in Charles E. Caton, ed, *Philosophy and Ordinary Language* v (Illinois, 1963).

[21] The interesting exception is where one part of the law, for its own purposes, uses terms found in other parts of the law having different purposes. In such cases, we best think of the two meanings as separate, and the meaning from the "other part of the law" as being equivalent for these purposes to ordinary language or at least pre-legal meaning. Consider in this connection *Ploof v Putnam*, 81 Vt 471, 71 A 188 (1908), in which the Supreme Court of Vermont held in essence that the ordinary rule against trespass contained a necessity exception. Had the court been starting anew, unconstrained by any definitions existing either in English or in legal understandings, it could have defined "trespass" in such a way that necessary dockings simply fell outside the coverage of the trespass rule. The fact that it did not do so is strong evidence of the entrenchment of the existing definition of trespass, such that stipulative redefinition was impossible, and appending an exception consequently necessary.

[22] See Hart, *Definition and Theory in Jurisprudence*, in Hart, *Essays in Jurisprudence and Philosophy* 21 (cited in note 7).

Thus, were law written entirely in constitutive terms of art, we would expect to see few exceptions; the stipulative definition of those terms would most likely build in those exclusions that we would otherwise see in the form of exceptions. But because law is written substantially in English rather than in Lawish, and is partly beholden to ordinary understandings of language, all legal terms are not (nor could they be) constitutive terms of art. A legal rule regulating conduct defined in terms antecedent to that regulatory scheme is thus at the mercy of those antecedent terms. Just as the term "sale" draws no distinction between interstate and intrastate sales, many terms existing antecedent to their legal manifestation fail to draw the distinctions or create the exceptions that track the goal of some regulatory scheme. On occasion some antecedent terms already exclude that which the drafters of the legal rule wish to exclude, as with the exclusion of lawnmowers from the class of securities, and then it is unlikely that the rule need be crafted so as to incorporate an exception. But should the antecedent terms not exclude that which the drafters wish to exclude, as with intrastate sales of securities, then an exception will be necessary. The existence of an exception will therefore be a function not so much of total linguistic fortuity, but rather of the way in which legal goals intersect with the linguistic products and manifestations of the extra-legal and pre-legal human categorization that provides much of the foundation on which legal regulation is erected.

A good example of this phenomenon is the traditional legal prohibition of fornication. Fornication is defined in Webster's Third New International Dictionary as "sexual intercourse other than between a man and his wife."[23] Thus, a statutory or common law prohibition on fornication excludes sexual intercourse between married persons without the necessity of a separate exception.[24] Were the word "fornication" absent from the language, however, or were the category of "sexual intercourse other than between married persons" absent from the antecedent conceptual apparatus of the society, then we would expect to see the same prohibition couched in terms of a primary prohibition on sexual intercourse with an accompanying exception for sexual intercourse between married persons.

---

[23] The sole purpose of this footnote is to distance myself from the sexist way in which Webster's defines the act.

[24] See, for example, *State v Sharp*, 75 NJ L 201, 66 A 926, 927 (1907), *State v Dana*, 59 Vt 614, 10 A 727, 731 (1887).

The relationship between law and the antecedent linguistic and categorial apparatus in which and with which law is written can tell us something about the various goals of legal regulation. At times legal regulation seeks to change the social landscape. Not only Prohibition but also more modern statutory regulation with respect to discrimination, consumer protection, workplace safety, the environment, and the preservation of endangered species are examples of law pressing against existing social practices. Insofar as such practices are likely to have their linguistic manifestation, that is, insofar as a distinction or category recognized by social practice will also be recognized by that society's language (and here the Inuit's numerous words for different types of snow is the classic if hackneyed example), then laws designed to move society rather than reflect it will often encounter (and I make no more than this probabilistic claim) the absence of any preexisting language with which easily to do so. When that is the case, we can expect to see exceptions and related linguistic devices used to draw the distinctions not currently recognized by the language in which the law is written.

By contrast, law sometimes seeks only to reinforce social practices or norms against the possibility of individual deviation or widespread shift. Consider in this regard those laws prohibiting activities that few of us would contemplate even absent legal regulation, such as child molestation, indecent exposure, and cannibalism.[25] Where laws serve this reinforcing function, as with the traditional conception of the fornication laws, the linguistic and categorical apparatus is likely already to be in place, and it is then more probable that the scope of a legal rule will track the scope of a social category, making the exception device less likely to be necessary.[26] It is just because the goal of fornication laws was to reinforce an existing social distinction that those laws were able to find a seemingly exceptionless word that drew just the distinction that the drafters wished to draw.

Moreover, when a regulatory scheme tracks existing social practices, the drafters may be more confident that widespread agreement will be sufficient to allow interpreters to locate approxi-

---

[25] Of course, the very fact that the activities are prohibited says something about the drafters' perception of possible behavior. It is not without interest that in Massachusetts, but in few other states, large signs prohibit drivers who have missed their exit from backing up on a divided interstate highway.

[26] I do not deny the possibility of a causal relation between the two categories, such that social aversions to public nudity or eating fellow human beings are partly or even largely a function of a social conditioning that itself employs legal or other norms.

mately the same range of implicit exceptions, and explicit ones will
be less necessary. The presence of an explicit exception, therefore,
is once again a signal that the law is operating less to reflect and
reinforce existing practice than to attempt to modify it.

III. EXCEPTIONS AND THE RHETORIC OF THE FIRST AMENDMENT

Both the Securities Act of 1933 and the statutory prohibitions
on fornication involve specific statutes written in canonical language. Often, however, exceptions arise not in the context of canonically inscribed rules, but rather with respect to common law or
constitutional rules. Such rules do not have a canonical inscription
in the strict sense, yet it is still often the case that certain understandings of those rules become so crystallized or entrenched that
those widely shared understandings operate in much the same way
as canonically inscribed rules. As a result, much about the contingent relationship of rules and exceptions with respect to statutory
rules applies outside the statutory context as well. In order to see
this, let us look now at claims about exceptions in a wide variety of
First Amendment debates. We can start with flag burning, and
consider not only the Supreme Court decision in *Texas v Johnson*,[27] but also the surrounding political/legal/constitutional controversy. This controversy largely revolved around the appropriate-
ness of creating an "exception" either to "the First Amendment"
(the alleged danger of which turned out to carry great rhetorical
force in debates about the wisdom of amending the Constitution to
reverse the rulings in *Johnson* and *United States v Eichman*[28]) or
to the principle, now well-established in the doctrine, that all viewpoint-based restrictions on the expression of political opinions in
the public forum are unconstitutional.[29]

Now that we have explored the logic of exceptions, we can see
that a great deal of the debate was not so much about the idea of
an exception as it was about the appropriate definition of the relevant principle. Justice Brennan's majority opinion in *Johnson* was
premised on the belief that Johnson's "political expression was restricted because of the content of the message he conveyed,"[30] and

---

[27] 491 US 397 (1989) (striking down state flag desecration statute under the First
Amendment).

[28] 110 S Ct 2404 (1990) (invalidating federal statute purporting to reverse *Johnson*).

[29] See, for example, *Boos v Barry*, 485 US 312, 321-22 (1988); *American Booksellers
Ass'n, Inc. v Hudnut*, 771 F2d 323 (7th Cir 1985), aff'd without opinion, 475 US 1001 (1986);
Geoffrey R. Stone, *Content Regulation and the First Amendment*, 25 Wm & Mary L Rev
189 (1983).

[30] 491 US at 412.

that "[i]f there is a bedrock principle underlying the First Amendment, it is that the Government may not prohibit the expression of an idea simply because society finds the idea itself offensive or disagreeable."[31] The relevant principle for Justice Brennan, analogous here to the initial specification of coverage in § 5 of the Securities Act of 1933 or to the existing definition of the practice of fornication, is thus that (my words, not his) "all political communication in the public forum is protected against viewpoint-based restrictions on either the content or the style of the communication." With that as the initial specification of the principle, it is no surprise that Justice Brennan would see Texas's arguments in *Johnson* as pleas for an exception to that principle. Twice he makes the argument in exactly this form: "We have not recognized an exception to this principle even where our flag has been involved."[32] "There is, moreover, no indication—either in the text of the Constitution or in our cases interpreting it—that a separate juridical category exists for the American flag alone. . . . We decline, therefore, to create for the flag an exception to the joust of principles protected by the First Amendment."[33] For Justice Brennan, the proponents of restrictions were seeking exceptions to an intrinsically exceptionless principle.

Chief Justice Rehnquist, by contrast, can now be seen as arguing that the relevant principle is that (my words) "all political communication in the public forum other than flag desecration is protected against viewpoint-based restrictions on either the content or the style of the communication." He wrote:

> For more than 200 years, the American flag has occupied a unique position as the symbol of our Nation, a uniqueness that justifies a governmental prohibition against flag burning.
> . . .
> [The flag] does not represent the views of any particular political party, and it does not represent any particular political philosophy. The flag is not simply another 'idea' or 'point of view' competing for recognition in the marketplace of ideas.
> . . .
> The Court decides that the American flag is just another symbol, about which not only must opinions pro and con be toler-

---

[31] Id at 414.
[32] Id.
[33] Id at 417, 418.

ated, but for which the most minimal public respect may not be enjoined.[34]

Thus, it is plain that Justice Brennan was saying that the relevant category is "political communication" and Chief Justice Rehnquist was saying that it is "political communication other than flag desecration." Although it is true that there is no single word for "political communication other than flag desecration," one way of seeing the Chief Justice's liberal use in his dissent of American history and patriotic poetry is as an attempt to support the argument that the category "political communication other than flag desecration" is an existing category in this culture. He is claiming that running through the history of the founding of the country, its battles to protect (and expand) its territory, and the songs and poetry that reflect this history is a consistent theme—that the flag and its preservation simply represent a category of understanding in this culture different from and lying outside any other category, including the category of political communication. Consequently, to the Chief Justice the pertinent and existing social category is not "political communication" but rather "political communication other than flag desecration."

The relevance of the Chief Justice's argument that "political communication other than flag desecration" is an existing category is that it can be seen as an attempt to rebut the claim that the dissent was in some way being ad hoc or unprincipled about its willingness to treat the flag as different or special. If we had a word for "political communication other than flag desecration"—"polation," for example—then the dissent might have said that the basic principle is that "polation is protected against viewpoint-based restrictions on either the content or the style of the communication," and that the majority was attempting to *engraft* ad hoc or unprincipled additions to that basic principle. Indeed, the Chief Justice specifically characterizes the majority's conclusions as an "extension of constitutional protection to the burning of the flag."[35] Implicit in this language is the view that "polation plus flag desecration" is no intrinsically neater than "political communication minus flag desecration."[36]

---

[34] Id at 422, 429, 435.

[35] Id at 435.

[36] See Richard Delgado, *Campus Anti-Racism Rules: Constitutional Narratives in Collision*, 85 Nw U L Rev 343, 345-48 (1991) (arguing in the context of sanctions on racist and therefore equality-denying speech that the current view of the First Amendment as limiting the principle of equality is no more inherently valid than a different view pursuant to which equality would limit the principle of freedom of speech).

So we now see that part of what transpired in *Johnson* was a potentially confusing rhetorical battle, with both sides claiming the high ground of the internally sound principle, and accusing the other of the aberrational attempt to pollute that principle. And we can see as well, from our beginnings with the Securities Act of 1933, that the battle was largely *just* rhetorical, for there is nothing more natural or intrinsically sound as a logical matter about Justice Brennan's category of political communication than there is about Chief Justice Rehnquist's of political communication other than flag desecration.[37]

But is the logical equivalence between the two arguments sufficient? What are we to make of the fact that "polation" is *not* a word in the language, and of the fact that there appears to be no existing simple phrase for "political communication other than flag desecration" other than "political communication other than flag desecration"? One answer would be that the lack of a single word or simpler phrase is indicative of a lack of a principled distinction between political communication via flag desecration and political communication using other methods, at least if we assume that those other methods might include harsh criticism of government by use of a method that offends many unwilling listeners or viewers.[38] Presupposed in this answer is the claim that there is a relationship between the intrinsic plausibility of a distinction and its existing economical embodiment in the language. Where we must resort to language as cumbersome as "political communication other than flag desecration," it might be said, we have good evidence that there is something unsound about the principle.

This position appears to evaluate the soundness of a principle according to the existence of an easy and brief way to characterize or reflect it. Yet surely the very enterprises of argument, analysis, and careful thought presuppose that we might be able to draw distinctions whose soundness is not undercut by the unavailability of a word or short phrase to reflect them. Were the existence of a single word or simple phrase dispositive, the absence of such a word or phrase would end discussion. But it does not, and that is

---

[37] Indeed, although I focus on a debate that took place in a judicial decision, the rhetorical force of exceptions language is far more prevalent outside of judicial opinions, and plainly, as the ensuing flag desecration debate demonstrated, much that I argue here about the distorting nature of "exceptions" rhetoric is far more applicable to public than to judicial debate.

[38] See, for example, *Cohen v California*, 403 US 15 (1971) (wearing of jacket emblazoned with "Fuck the Draft" in corridor of county courthouse protected by First Amendment).

why the names we give principles, names like the principle of equality or Rawls' Difference Principle, are only names, telling us virtually nothing about the actual contours of the principles.[39] Accordingly, the lack of a culturally assimilated simpler phrase for "political communication other than flag desecration" is at best weak evidence of the inability to draw a sound distinction described by the more cumbersome phrase, although it might be quite good evidence of whether some culture has already drawn it.

This does not mean, of course, that all distinctions are sound. I have claimed only that the non-existence of a single word or short phrase reflecting an articulable distinction is at best little evidence of the soundness of the distinction. But to articulate a distinction or to make an argument is not to prove the soundness of the distinction or the tenability of the argument. In fact, for reasons not germane here, I am not persuaded that the distinction drawn by Chief Justice Rehnquist is normatively sound, given the language and underlying purposes of the First Amendment. Nevertheless, let us suppose that the dissent in *Johnson can* support a distinction. Let us suppose that, given such factors as the historical place of the flag, the degree of offense and hurt involved (and there is of course nothing unprincipled about drawing a distinction based on differences of degree[40]), and the importance of a unifying national symbol, there is a plausible argument that the flag *is* different for First Amendment purposes.[41] If this argument for the distinctiveness of the flag were taken to be sound, then the fact of the socially extant linguistic and categorial apparatus becomes relevant in a different way. For now Justice Brennan might be saying something quite different. Conceding for the sake of argument the theoretical tenability of the flag/no flag distinction, he could be read as arguing that the lack of a social consensus as to the distinctiveness of the flag, however unfortunate that lack of a social consensus might be, is indicative of the likely fragility of the "political communication other than flag desecration" category.[42] Were there

---

[39] This is why we often use the words "concept" or "idea" to mark the fact that some word, like "law," is but the name of something far more complex. Consider why "the concept of law" or "the concept of equality" or "the concept of justice" do not sound as odd as "the concept of penguin" or "the concept of subway."

[40] See Frederick Schauer, *Slippery Slopes*, 99 Harv L Rev 361 (1989).

[41] For an example of such an argument, see Douglas W. Kmiec, *In the Aftermath of Johnson and Eichman: The Constitution Need Not be Mutilated to Preserve the Government's Speech and Property Interests in the Flag*, 1990 BYU L Rev 577, 587-91 (1990).

[42] Although Justice Brennan did not make this argument in this form in *Johnson*, there is a close parallel between my interpretation of what Justice Brennan might have said in a different *Johnson* and what he *did* say in *Paris Adult Theatre I v Slaton*, 413 US 49, 82

an entrenched term for that category, then our fears of further exceptions would have less basis. And, even without an entrenched term, were the distinction itself socially entrenched, then the social acceptance of the distinction would cast doubt on the fear that exceptions to "political communication other than flag desecration" would be just around the corner. And in response to this argument from the fragility in practice of a distinction that was sound in theory, the dissent could then be seen as attempting to demonstrate with its poetry and its history the in-place social entrenchment that provides the answer to the majority's fears. Although there is no one word for the category the Chief Justice seeks to defend, to him there exists a socially entrenched idea, much like "fornication," within which the relevant exception is already incorporated.

Curiously, therefore, it is the so-called "conservative" dissent in *Johnson* that is being theoretically modernist, in the sense of relying on a perspective recognizing the social, cultural, and historical roots of our categories, and the consequent contingency of any society's categorial understandings.[43] It is, intriguingly, the dissent that wishes to resist the idea that there is something natural or neutral about the category "political speech," and about its intrinsic or logical priority over the category "political communication other than flag burning." To the dissent, but arguably not to the majority, the relevant categories are not rigid or abstract or natural, but must be examined in light of historical practices and current understandings.[44]

(1973) (Brennan dissenting). In arguing that the obscenity laws were unconstitutional, Justice Brennan did not reject the principle of obscenity as "non-speech" that he had set forth in 1957 in *Roth v United States*, 354 US 476 (1957). He maintained that the principle had proved unworkable in practice, a function of the inability of some sound distinctions to be interpreted as such by those charged with applying them. See Schauer, 99 Harv L Rev at 373-83 (cited in note 40).

[43] What I call modernist, see also David Luban, *Legal Modernism*, 84 Mich L Rev 1656 (1986), others might call post-modernist, but nothing here turns on that distinction, which in any event varies among disciplines (post-modernist architecture, for example, is characterized by its incorporation of traditional forms within contemporary design). All I maintain is that a range of perspectives stressing categorial malleability and categorial contingency is more evident in the dissent, and that a range of perspectives stressing the fixity and natural necessity of social categories is more evident in Justice Brennan's majority opinion.

[44] I put the issue in this way not (only) to be tendentious, but to suggest what I have recently urged at some length, that the idea of the categorial protection of freedom of *speech* is itself, to the core, dependent upon a rule-based and "formalistic" understanding of the relevance of the category "speech." See Frederick Schauer, *The Second-Best First Amendment*, 31 Wm & Mary L Rev 1 (1989).

Chief Justice Rehnquist may be historically inaccurate in his claim about the place of the flag in American history or in his assessment of the categorial import of that history. And even if he is historically correct, that category may be normatively undesirable, in the same way that many other existing distinctions are normatively undesirable. Yet implicit in the Chief Justice's historical and cultural analysis is a recognition of the way in which the categories of the law, including the categories of the First Amendment, are not natural and fixed but are reflective of the kinds of distinctions that a society has drawn and is capable of defending. Insofar as it is "conservative" to urge the (at least presumptive) workability of socially extant categories, then explaining the historical pedigree of the "political communication other than flag desecration" category is part of an argument for taking that category as a given.[45] But insofar as it is "conservative" to take existing phrases such as "political speech" as more natural and unchangeable than contingent and movable, then it is the majority rather than the dissent that seems conservative.

We now see that, given the ability to draw a theoretical distinction, any doctrinal rule reflecting that distinction would have to be considered principled, for there is nothing to the idea of a principled decision other than the willingness to adhere to the previously drawn distinction.[46] Some distinctions, however, will build on and employ a culture's existing linguistic and categorial structure, and in such cases we have reason to suppose that the distinction will resist efforts to defeat it. Others, however, will challenge rather than build on the society's in-place linguistic and categorial apparatus, and in those cases there is cause for less confidence that the distinction will have the strength necessary to resist efforts to destroy it.

IV. The Contingency of First Amendment Categories: Racial Hatred and Pornography

Consider in this regard the contrast between the Skokie decisions in this country[47] and the existence of anti-Nazi legislation

---

[45] See Anthony T. Kronman, *Precedent and Tradition*, 99 Yale L J 1029, 1047-68 (1990).

[46] See Kent Greenawalt, *The Enduring Significance of Neutral Principles*, 78 Colum L Rev 982 (1978); M.P. Golding, *Principled Decision-Making and the Supreme Court*, 63 Colum L Rev 35, 40-42 (1963).

[47] *Collin v Smith*, 578 F2d 1197 (7th Cir), stay denied, 436 US 953, cert denied, 439 US 916 (1978); *National Socialist Party of America v Village of Skokie*, 434 US 1327 (1977) (Stevens denying stay); *National Socialist Party of America v Village of Skokie*, 432 US 43

and governmental practice in Germany. A recent German law, aimed at those who would deny the existence of the Holocaust, permits prosecution for insult "if the insulted person was persecuted as a member of a group under the National Socialist or another violent or arbitrary dominance."[48] Other laws, also commonly understood to be aimed primarily at Nazis, and enforced primarily against neo-Nazis, prohibit incitement to hatred against segments of the population and prohibit the instigation of race hatred.[49] And in 1986 the Administrative Court of Braunschweig upheld revocation of a doctorate on the sole grounds that the recipient, a former judge, had subsequently written a book questioning whether six million Jews had died in the Holocaust.[50]

Implicit in the German racial hatred laws is thus a constitutionally permissible intention to deal specially and specifically with Nazi speech, and to restrict inciters of racial hatred although not other offensive or harmful speakers. In this regard the German law plainly diverges from the American, as the Skokie cases make clear. But one way of explaining why both may be correct (even assuming otherwise equivalent understandings of and commitments to freedom of speech) is in terms of the divergent experiences of the two countries with respect to the relevant category.[51] Part of most arguments for restricting Nazi speech is the supposition that there exist principled categories (and again remember that arguments from differences in degree can still be principled[52]) such as "offensive political communication other than by Nazis" or

---

(1977) (per curiam). See generally David Goldberger, *Skokie: The First Amendment Under Attack By Its Friends*, 29 Mercer L Rev 761 (1978).

[48] Eric Stein, *History Against Free Speech: The New German Law Against the "Auschwitz"—And Other—"Lies"*, 85 Mich L Rev 277, 323 (1986) (quoting the West German Criminal Code, Art 194, 1985 BGBl 965).

[49] Id at 322-23. See also Donald P. Kommers, *The Jurisprudence of Free Speech in the United States and the Federal Republic of Germany*, 53 S Cal L Rev 657 (1980).

[50] Stein, 85 Mich L Rev at 280 & n 11 (cited in note 48).

[51] It is possible that the German tolerance for a Nazi or racial hatred exception simply reflects a constitutional document more tolerant of exceptions generally, for the German Basic Law, just like Article 10 of the European Convention on Human Rights, explicitly allows for exceptions to the principle of freedom of speech. See generally Ulrich Karpen, *Freedom of Expression*, in Ulrich Karpen, ed, *The Constitution of the Federal Republic of Germany: Essays on the Basic Rights and Principles of the Basic Law with a Translation of the Basic Law* 97 (Nomos Verlagsgesellschaft, 1988). Still, there seems no basis for supposing that the resultant doctrinal structure is in general more complex or exception-laden in Germany than in the United States, although in the United States that structure comes only from the case law and not from the text. See generally Frederick Schauer, *Codifying the First Amendment: New York v. Ferber*, 1982 S Ct Rev 285. As a result, the difference seems explainable more by cultural differences in viewing the Nazi experience than by different broad-based constitutional methodologies.

[52] See Schauer, 99 Harv L Rev 361 (cited in note 40).

"offensive political communication other than that involving racial hatred." Where such categories exist, free speech protection for the communications falling within them can theoretically as well as practically coexist with restrictions on the speech lying outside them.

When arguments in this form are made in this country they are commonly rejected, as is implicit in the Skokie decisions, in part because this country and its legal/constitutional culture have arguably not seen Nazis as dramatically different from other morally reprehensible and offensive groups, of which the Ku Klux Klan and those who would urge the physical degradation of women are perhaps the most obvious examples. In this country Nazis are less *sui generis*, and are instead part of a larger category, or at least less distinct from other members of a potentially larger class. Consequently, the First Amendment operates against the background of an antecedent linguistic and categorial structure in which an "exception" for Nazis would amount to a legal confrontation with the society's underlying conceptual apparatus, a confrontation that might cause us to predict the possibility that acceptance of the "offensive political communication other than by Nazis" category would lead to the creation of other exceptions.

Compare, however, the likely understanding of the same category within Germany. In light of the history of that country, and in light of the continuing effect of the Nazi experience on that society's self-understanding, the existence of a durable and entrenched distinction between Nazis and all other groups (or, more precisely, between inciters of racial hatred and other harmful and offensive speakers), no matter how offensive, harmful, and reprehensible those other groups may be, seems much more plausible.[53] And if that is the case, then it is possible that the categories "offensive political communication other than by Nazis" or "political communications other than those urging racial hatred" are already well-established categories in Germany even if they are not here. Should that be so, then a range of (contingently) valid-in-this-country arguments about the potential future implications of an

---

[53] Implicit in the foregoing argument is the claim that neither this country's war with Nazi Germany nor its legacy of slavery has, as a matter of social fact, influenced the self-understanding and national identity of the 1991 United States in the way that Germany's Nazi past has influenced the self-understanding of the 1991 Germany. My claim here is descriptive rather than normative, attempting only to explain the prevalence of "dangerous precedent" and "slippery slope" arguments that are made in the United States when restrictions on Nazi or racist speech are urged, but which are not made when such restrictions are urged, enacted, and enforced in Germany.

"offensive political communication other than by Nazis" category would be far less valid in Germany.

Indeed, the divergence between the two countries may be explained simply by a difference between what counts as "political." Decisions in this country relating to Nazis and other inciters of racial hatred are premised on the inclusion of such groups within the category of the political. Their exclusion would consequently represent an exception to an otherwise inclusive category of political speech, with the accompanying concerns about the possibility of further exceptions. But if it is the case that in some societies the very concept or category of "political" already excludes those who would incite racial hatred or who would overthrow the constitutional order,[54] and that the ideas of "political speech by Nazis" or "political speech urging racial hatred" are internally contradictory, then even a principle prohibiting content-based discrimination against political advocacy would not cover the communications of those whose advocacy of genocide or racial hatred would simply not count as "political" at all.

Even if it is correct that there now exists in this country neither a well-entrenched definition of the political that internally excludes urgings to racial hatred, nor a well-entrenched category of "political speech other than that urging racial hatred," it is possible that some day there might be such distinctions, and it is possible to argue that such distinctions are defensible and *ought* to be embodied in this society's linguistic and conceptual apparatus. Indeed, this seems an illuminating way of understanding contemporary arguments about anti-pornography regulation. The First Amendment-based invalidation of the Indianapolis anti-pornography ordinance embodied the view that the ordinance constituted a viewpoint-based restriction, as to which there existed no doctrinal basis for an exception.[55] I will concede the doctrinal plausibility of that conclusion (which is not to deny the plausibility, perhaps even the doctrinal plausibility, of the opposite conclusion[56]), but we can now appreciate that the non-existence of an exception to a prohibi-

---

[54] On the exclusion of those who would overthrow the constitutional order from political participation, see the Basic Law of the Federal Republic of Germany, Art 18 (forfeiture of basic rights), translated in Gisbert H. Flanz, *Federal Republic of Germany* 49, in Albert P. Blaustein and Gisbert H. Flanz, eds, 6 *Constitutions of the Countries of the World* (Oceana, 1985).

[55] *Hudnut*, 771 F2d at 328. The same argument undergirded the mayor's veto of a similar ordinance in Minneapolis in 1985, and the unreported invalidation of essentially the same ordinance in Bellingham, Washington in 1989.

[56] See Cass R. Sunstein, *Pornography and the First Amendment*, 1986 Duke L J 589.

tion on viewpoint-based restrictions and the non-existence of a category of "viewpoints other than the viewpoint that women are appropriate objects for sexual violence," as to which no exception would be necessary, are neither natural nor neutral. They merely reflect the contingent linguistic and categorial apparatus with which we view these ordinances.

From this perspective, proponents of anti-pornography legislation can be seen to urge the recognition and entrenchment of the "viewpoints other than . . ." category, the category that could form the basis for a First Amendment principle that would be without exceptions. Taken in the light most consistent with the existing doctrinal structure of the First Amendment, those arguments could still be viewed as acknowledgments that this category does not now exist, but as attempts, structurally analogous to Chief Justice Rehnquist's in *Texas v Johnson*, to create a world in which this category did exist. In this case, the assimilation of the category within the doctrinal structure of the First Amendment would cause no worry about exceptions. The category would simply exclude that lying without it, just as the category of sales of securities excludes the sale of lawnmowers. Once we recognize the oddness of the very idea of an exception, we recognize as well the contingent conditions under which an argument from the undesirability of exceptions has rhetorical and doctrinal appeal.

Thus, contemporary anti-pornography proposals can be seen to ask three closely related questions: Why is the relevant juridical category "viewpoints" rather than "viewpoints other than the viewpoint that women are appropriate objects of sexual violence"? Why does the category "viewpoint" include articulation of the position that women are appropriate objects of sexual violence? Finally, why does the category of "politics" or "political argument" include those who would urge sexual violence against women? The point is that the existing category, including sexual violence and therefore necessitating a potentially fragile exception in order to permit the restriction, is only contingent, and it is hardly inconceivable that there could be a world in which the initial category would exclude advocates of sexual violence just as there is a Nazi-excluding category in Germany. From this perspective the proposed anti-pornography legislation is more than just an attack on a certain variety of communication. It is an attack on a conceptual structure that puts that communication in the same class with communications of a dramatically different sort.[57]

V. THE FOUNDATIONS OF A CATEGORIAL STRUCTURE

Nothing in the foregoing denies the existence of natural kinds like tigers and titanium. Context may be a lot, but it is not everything. Although this is hardly the place for a discourse on metaphysics, even were I qualified to give one, I want to grant the arguments of metaphysical realists, who maintain that there are natural kinds whose physical delineation precedes the act of human categorization. Where the law operates on such natural kinds, as when for example it prohibits killing bald eagles, it operates on a world in which the antecedent linguistic and categorial structure frequently reflects the underlying physical reality of the world. In such cases the linguistic and social categories upon which the law operates are likely to be least contingent, and least likely to change. As a result, the need for an exception will often be the result not of linguistic or cultural fortuity, but of the natural terrain upon which the law operates and by which it is constrained.

At the other extreme, law sometimes operates on categories entirely of its own making, as we saw in the examination of constitutive rules and technical terms. In such cases the presence or absence of an exception is likely to be a function either of mere stylistic felicity or of procedural concerns such as those involving allocation of the burden of proof. Where law is the master of its categorial underpinnings, it can work in a world in which little of substance turns on whether a legal rule employs the logically empty device of an exception.

In most cases, however, law operates between these extremes, confronting and using antecedent social and linguistic categories that are neither natural nor of the legal system's own making. Then the distinction between what looks like a principle and what looks like an exception is likely to be deceiving. The distinction is now seen to be contingent and not fixed, empirical and not inexorable. To say this, of course, is not to commit the Realist and neo-

---

[57] I believe that all I have said in this section applies to contemporary debates about controls on racist speech on campus or in the public forum.. Compare Charles R. Lawrence, III, *If He Hollers Let Him Go: Regulating Racist Speech on Campus*, 1990 Duke L J 431; Mari J. Matsuda, *Public Response to Racist Speech: Considering the Victim's Story*, 87 Mich L Rev 2320 (1989); and Note, *A First Amendment Justification for Regulating Racist Speech on Campus*, 40 Case W Res L Rev 733 (1989-90), with Robert C. Post, *Racist Speech, Democracy, and the First Amendment*, 32 Wm & Mary L Rev 267 (1991); and Nadine Strossen, *Regulating Racist Speech on Campus: A Modest Proposal?*, 1990 Duke L J 484, 523-48.

Realist fallacy of supposing that the social contingency of the categories with which law deals is strong or even much evidence of the ability of legal actors to change them.[58] But recognition of those categorial contingencies enables us to see in a different light the continuing interplay between legal and social change. At times, more rarely than many suppose, legal change might produce social change, and thus alter the categorial structure that reflects a society's understandings.[59] For example, the pervasiveness within much of current social consciousness of the concept of sexual harassment owes its origins to a movement for legal reform.[60] More commonly, legal change is parasitic on social change. That is why it is possible to accept simultaneously the plausibility both of the Skokie decisions and of the German anti-Nazi laws, even with an assumption of otherwise identical free speech principles in the two countries; why it is possible simultaneously to acknowledge the doctrinal basis of the result in the pornography ordinance cases while envisaging a world in which the opposite result would be considered sound; and why we can see the opinions in *Texas v Johnson* as reflecting not so much differing views about the First Amendment as different understandings of the American experience. The use of an exception is a signal that the law and the society on which it presses are not in harmony. Whether this is a good or bad thing depends mostly on the particular substantive context, but it is likely that those who employ or urge what is *now* seen to be an exception are the ones who are urging change in the status

---

[58] And this is why the "dangerous precedent" argument surrounding the Skokie cases was a real argument. If law's ability to remake its categories were complete, then the concern that an extra-legal world might fail to appreciate the distinction drawn by the courts would be of no significance.

[59] I do not deny the phenomenon. I do, however, question the suggestion (see Anders Vilhelm Lundstedt, *Legal Thinking Revised: My Views on Law* (Almqvist & Wiksell, 1956); Robert W. Gordon, *Critical Legal Histories*, 36 Stan L Rev 57 (1984)) that this is the prevalent direction of law/culture interaction or that culture is so law-soaked as to make the law/culture distinction itself problematic. Although legal concepts and categories do often provide the conceptual apparatus with which people outside of the legal system think and talk (see Frances E. Olsen, *The Family and the Market: A Study of Ideology and Legal Reform*, 96 Harv L Rev 1497 (1983)), the prevalence of that phenomenon is likely to be overestimated by lawyers inclined to see the world through a legal lens, and to see the world in a way that overstates the law's importance in it. (Nor are lawyers any different in this regard from others, all of whom are likely to see a world in which they and those like them occupy a more prominent place than would be seen by others differently situated.) Ultimately these questions are empirical, and assessing the prevalence of a phenomenon that all acknowledge (or should acknowledge) requires resort to empirical techniques all too rare in legal scholarship.

[60] See especially Catharine MacKinnon, *Sexual Harassment of Women: A Case of Sex Discrimination* (Yale, 1979).

quo, while those who argue against exceptions are those for whom the society's existing linguistic and conceptual structure reflects the world as they wish it to be.

VI. EXCEPTIONS AND THE FORCE OF RULES

Taking these cases together demonstrates that there is nothing special or inexorable about the line between an exception and what it is an exception to. In the First Amendment context, the lesson of this is that arguments couched in the language of exceptions are usefully viewed as arguments over competing conceptions of the central principle itself. But if arguments about exceptions are in reality arguments about the rule itself, then in many other contexts it is important to resist the idea that exceptions exist apart from rules, and, consequently, that adding an exception is anything other than changing the rule. The corollary of recognizing that rule *R*, which internally excludes instance *I*, is no different from rule *R(1)*, which internally includes instance *I* but then contains an exception for *I*, is that there is also no difference between adding an exception *I* to rule *R* and *changing* rule *R*. Now that we know that exceptions are continuous with the rules they are exceptions to, however contingent that continuity may be, we can see that there is no difference between adding an exception to a rule and simply changing it. Consequently, a significant benefit of understanding the logical emptiness of the idea of an exception as an analytically distinct concept is that we can now understand the power to create an exception in a much less epiphenomenal light.

A legal rule instantiates some background goal, purpose, or justification. Thus "Speed Limit 55" and "No Vehicles in the Park" might reflect the purpose of promoting safety (or conserving fuel), "No Dogs Allowed" might reflect the background purpose of preventing disturbance of the patrons in a restaurant, and the specific language of Rule 11 of the Federal Rules of Civil Procedure might further the purpose of preventing the filing of frivolous pleadings. None of these rules contains an exception, but cases might arise in which some form of conduct literally within the language of the rule-formulation seems not to serve the rule's background purpose or justification, as with Fuller's statue of a vehicle and the "No Vehicles in the Park" rule,[61] or with a seeing-eye dog and the "No Dogs Allowed" rule.

---

[61] Lon L. Fuller, *Positivism and Fidelity to Law—A Reply to Professor Hart*, 71 Harv L Rev 630, 663 (1958), responding to H.L.A. Hart, *Positivism and the Separation of Law and Morals*, 71 Harv L Rev 593, 607 (1958).

The prevailing American view of such cases is that the literal language of the rule should yield to the purpose, especially where the language is overinclusive rather than underinclusive.[62] Where the literal language is overinclusive, a common view is that courts (or other interpreters) should recognize *exceptions* where application of the literal language would not serve the rule's purpose.[63]

What is going on here? Assuming the putative exception does not already exist in the law, in which case nothing interesting is going on at all, the interpreter is being asked to *create* an exception to a rule not literally already recognizing that exception, or to *recognize* a supposedly immanent exception not previously explicitly recognized. But where is the normative purchase for the recognition or creation (which may or may not be the same thing), for saying that this exception is necessary and that one is not? Presumably it comes from consulting the rule's purpose, and the recent American tradition can be described in terms of a principle that would allow (or require) the interpreter to create or recognize an exception to a literally exceptionless rule if not to do so would yield a result inconsistent with the rule's purpose.

But if the ground for creating or recognizing an exception and applying it to the very case that prompted creating it is that failure to do so would frustrate the rule's purpose, then applying the rule and reserving the power to fashion an exception whenever exceptionless application would not serve the rule's purpose is extensionally equivalent to simply applying the rule's purpose directly to particular cases. If inconsistency with purpose is a sufficient condition for modifying what was previously thought to be the rule in the instant case, then no case will exist in which application of the rule will differ from application of the purpose, and thus it is the purpose rather than the rule-formulation that in fact *is* the

---

[62] "Curing" an underinclusive rule by holding it applicable to a party not literally within the rule's terms involves problems of notice and assertion of judicial authority that are less serious with respect to curing an overinclusive rule by refusing to apply it. For examples of refusal to cure literal underinclusiveness, see *Pavelic & LeFlore v Marvel Entertainment Group*, 110 S Ct 456 (1990) (refusing to extend FRCP Rule 11 liability to law firms); *McBoyle v United States*, 283 US 25 (1931) (Holmes) (refusing to extend National Motor Vehicle Theft Act to airplanes).

[63] *California Federal Savings & Loan Ass'n v Guerra*, 479 US 272 (1987); *Steelworkers v Weber*, 443 US 193, 200-08 (1979); Henry M. Hart, Jr. and Albert M. Sacks, *The Legal Process: Basic Problems in the Making and Application of Law* (Cambridge tent ed 1957); William Eskridge, Jr., *Dynamic Statutory Interpretation*, 135 U Pa L Rev 1479, 1537-54 (1987); Cass R. Sunstein, *Interpreting Statutes in the Regulatory State*, 103 Harv L Rev 405, 419-20 (1989).

rule.[64] It thus turns out that in a quite different context the language of exceptions is more misleading than helpful. There is something seemingly benign about the ability to create exceptions, for something about an exception looks comparatively trivial. But if there is power to create exceptions in the name of purpose, and to apply those exceptions immediately, then the exception-creating power is identical to the power to apply the purpose rather than the rule, or to take the purpose as in fact being the rule. Now this too may be benign,[65] but my point here is that little more than deception is served by employing the language of exceptions. We already have the linguistic tools to talk about the ability to apply purpose directly to cases, and we already have the linguistic tools to talk about the ability of judges to modify rules as they go along. Given that in American legal culture neither of these is considered anathema,[66] little is served by the use of a term that suggests that something else is transpiring.

The risk of confusion is even greater if the reason for creating an exception is equity or justice rather than the single purpose behind a single rule.[67] For if a rule will be applied only when it is consistent with justice, then it turns out once again that talk of exceptions, or of the power to create them, is largely distracting. The power to create an exception to a rule when required by justice is equivalent to the power to do justice *simpliciter*. Again, to describe the role of the courts in such terms is hardly abhorrent these days,[68] but if that is so there is even less reason to disguise in

---

[64] I am intentionally collapsing the distinction among creation, modification, and recognition of the previously unrecognized, for the seemingly less intrusive practice of recognition is no different from the seemingly more intrusive practices of creation or modification *if* what is "recognized" has not been recognized before. None of this is to say that intrusiveness in this sense is necessarily or acontextually undesirable, but here again we may be witnessing a conflict between the desire to promote interpretive authority and the desire to mask its existence.

[65] But sometimes not. See Frederick Schauer, *Formalism*, 97 Yale L J 509, 538-44 (1988).

[66] See generally Guido Calabresi, *A Common Law for the Age of Statutes* 163-66 (Harvard, 1982); Donald C. Langevoort, *Statutory Obsolescence and the Judicial Process: The Revisionist Role of the Courts in Federal Banking Regulation*, 85 Mich L Rev 672 (1987); Note, *Intent, Clear Statements, and the Common Law: Statutory Construction in the Supreme Court*, 95 Harv L Rev 892, 912-15 (1982).

[67] See generally Alfred C. Aman, Jr., *Administrative Equity: An Analysis of Exceptions to Administrative Rules*, 1982 Duke L J 277.

[68] But see Robert H. Bork, *The Tempting of America: The Political Seduction of the Law* (Free Press, 1990); Antonin Scalia, *The Rule of Law as a Law of Rules*, 56 U Chi L Rev 1175 (1989).

the trivializing language of exceptions what is in reality a quite different mode of decisionmaking.

Consider in this light the following from H.L.A. Hart, as quoted and endorsed by Judge Posner:

> We promise to visit a friend the next day. When the day comes it turns out that keeping the promise would involve neglecting someone dangerously ill. The fact that this is accepted as an adequate reason for not keeping the promise surely does not mean that there is no rule requiring promises to be kept, only a certain regularity in keeping them. It does not follow from the fact that such rules have exceptions incapable of exhaustive statement, that in every situation we are left to our discretion and are never bound to keep a promise. A rule that ends with the word "unless . . ." is still a rule.[69]

Hart's claim, which at other times he characterizes in terms of the *defeasibility* of a legal rule,[70] is that legal rules are always subject to the addition of what Posner calls "ad hoc exceptions."[71] But if the basis for creating or adding that ad hoc exception is the judicial determination that it would be best, all things considered, to add it, then the result again turns out to be extensionally equivalent to a procedure pursuant to which the judge simply makes the best all things considered decision directly.[72]

Yet this is exactly what Hart denies in claiming that ad hoc exceptions can be added at the moment of application while still not being "left to our discretion." Hart is able to make this claim, however, because he confuses and conflates two distinct phenomena—creating an exception to a rule and overriding a rule. The phenomenon Hart describes, certainly common enough to the American constitutionalist familiar with "compelling interests" and "clear and present dangers," is that some rules or principles are not absolute, but rather are capable of being overridden in particularly exigent circumstances. Just as racial classifications may

---

[69] H.L.A. Hart, *The Concept of Law* 136 (Oxford, 1961), quoted in Richard A. Posner, *The Jurisprudence of Skepticism*, 86 Mich L Rev 827, 834-35 (1988).

[70] H.L.A. Hart, *The Ascription of Responsibility and Rights*, 49 Proc Aristotelian Soc 171, 175 (1949). See generally G.P. Baker, *Defeasibility and Meaning*, in P.M.S. Hacker and J. Raz, eds, *Law, Morality, and Society: Essays in Honour of H.L.A. Hart* 26 (Clarendon, 1977).

[71] Posner, 86 Mich L Rev at 834 (cited in note 69).

[72] The point I make here is similar to David Lyons's argument that act- and rule-utilitarianism are extensionally equivalent as long as rules are allowed to be of unlimited specificity and continuous malleability. David Lyons, *Forms and Limits of Utilitarianism* 115-18 (Oxford, 1965).

be employed if they are held to serve a compelling interest,[73] or constitutionally covered speech may be restricted in order to prevent the realization of a clear and present danger,[74] so too might the rule requiring the keeping of promises be overridden by the force of the principle, as applied in some case, that one should attend to those in distress.

Thus, the phenomenon that Hart describes is not that of the continuously malleable rule subject to modification in the service of the best judgment for the case at hand, all things considered, nor that of the rule subject to the adding of exceptions whenever it seems best (all things considered) to add them. Both of these methodologies are indeed equivalent to the simple grant of discretion that Hart wants to distinguish. Rather, Hart wants to capture the way in which rules can be overridden in particularly exigent circumstances and still be rules, even if it is impossible to predict or to specify in advance what those exigent circumstances will be. But what can and must be specified in advance to preserve the ruleness of the rule is the very standard of exigency, or its equivalent, for, if the reasons for overriding a rule need be no greater than the reasons that support the rule, there will be no case in which the existence of the rule makes a difference. If we clarify Hart's point, therefore, we cast doubt on his whole notion of defeasibility (as something different from overrideability). We can still, however, maintain that unless the reasons for creating an ad hoc exception are stronger than the mere divergence between rule and purpose, or stronger than the mere existence of a better all things considered decision if the exception is added, there is no difference between the power to create an ad hoc exception and the power to change the rule. Moreover, unless there exists this divergence in the strength of the relevant reasons, there is no difference between the power to make an ad hoc change in a rule based on X and the power to make decisions based on X. This, to repeat, is not necessarily to be condemned, but little other than deception seems served by describing the process in ways that oc-

---

[73] See, for example, *Loving v Virginia*, 388 US 1, 11 (1967); *Korematsu v United States*, 323 US 214, 216 (1944).

[74] *Schenck v United States*, 249 US 47 (1919). On the distinction between coverage and protection, a distinction that makes it possible to describe the way in which conduct may simultaneously be within the scope of a right yet be properly restricted under exigent circumstances, see Frederick Schauer, *Can Rights Be Abused?*, 31 Phil Q 225 (1981); Frederick Schauer, *Categories and the First Amendment: A Play in Three Acts*, 34 Vand L Rev 265 (1981).

clude appreciating the central connection between issues of rule change and issues of authority to make those changes.

CONCLUSION

The results of this analysis seem thus to trivialize the idea of an exception, but this is not to trivialize exceptions. On the contrary, we can now see that in a number of seemingly quite different domains much of import is taking place beneath the language of exceptions. When talking about the power of a judicial interpreter to append exceptions to rules in the service of purpose, policy, or equity, the language of exceptions is often used to disguise what is no different from a modification or repeal of the previously existing rule. Here the language of exceptions is used to diminish the import of the phenomenon. By contrast, the language of exceptions is commonly used in the First Amendment context not to diminish but to exaggerate the import of the phenomenon. The archetypal First Amendment libertarian, recognizing that the power to make exceptions is the power to change the rule, is wary of exceptions, although commonly unaware of the contingency of the linguistic and categorial underpinnings upon which this suspicion rests. Hart and his followers recognize this contingency, but use the exceptions language as a way of disguising the assertion of judicial authority to change the rule.

What these uses of the language of exceptions share, for all their differences, is a use of that language to mask issues that are seemingly more basic. When we are talking about statutory design, the idea of an exception is sometimes a linguistic fortuity, and sometimes only a reflection of the different roles that law serves vis-a-vis the pre-legal social and categorial structure on which it operates. When we are talking about common-law or constitutional principles, the idea of an exception is much the same, because the language with which we speak of some principles tracks a less canonically inscribed but equally contingent categorial structure. And when we are talking about the ability of judges to create exceptions, we are really talking more about the central question of common-law methodology, the ability of judges to modify rules in the process of application.[75] That question, as with all of these others, is an important one, but as with the others we must be wary of the distracting effect of the trivializing phrase.

Exceptions are everywhere in law, but everywhere they are part and parcel of the rules they are exceptions to. To say this is

---

[75] See Frederick Schauer, *Is the Common Law Law?*, 77 Cal L Rev 455 (1989).

not to make normative recommendations about whether exceptions should be employed more or less than they are now, nor about when and where they should be used. Nothing of the kind emerges from what I have said here. The lesson is only that the use or non-use of an exception is likely to reflect a substantive choice of some import, and so too with the use or non-use of the language of exceptions in legal debate. Once we see this, we have the tools available to pierce the rhetoric and fortuity of exceptions, and consider directly these questions of substantive principle and interpretive authority that the language of exceptions so often obscures.

THE ANALYSIS OF LEGAL CONCEPTS

THE positive aim of this article is to reveal and identify a recurrent error which has bedevilled the branch of study traditionally and somewhat misleadingly called analytical jurisprudence, which concerns itself with the analysis of legal conceptions. In order both to identify this error, and to show the consequences which flow from it, I shall discuss three jurisprudential theories, advanced by writers who were concerned to investigate the nature of legal conceptions, and analyse the supposedly peculiar logical function of legal language. The first of these is the theory put forward by Professor Ross in his entertaining article on the concept of " *tû-tû*," a concept which, we are to suppose, is in use amongst the unsophisticated islanders of the Noîsulli Islands, who have never been blessed with the gladsome light of jurisprudence.[1] The second is the theory advanced by Professor Hart in " Definition and Theory in Jurisprudence," [2] Professor Hart employing as a simple model not a mythical island but the language of cricket and other games.[3] The third is a theory put forward many years ago by Hohfeld.[4] I do not suggest that the views of these three writers are the same; they differ in many important respects, and each writer has in his different way done much to illuminate the problems of legal analysis, as I should be the first to admit. Nevertheless I hope to show that all three theories exemplify the same fundamental error.

I

The purpose of using fictional models, and this is particularly true of " desert island " examples of the technique, is that models are simple, and their simplicity can be used to reveal features of real life which the complexity of real life tends to conceal. Therein lies their danger also, as I hope to show. The use as a model of the notion of a game, a real game, is free from this danger, but also lacks the simplicity of an artificial model; the danger here is that the complexity of the model may be neglected, to the detriment of the analysis of the jurisprudential problem which the model is designed to illuminate. With these pontifical remarks in mind, let us now take a trip to the Noîsulli Islands.

---

[1] Alf Ross, " *Tû-tû*," 70 H.L.R. 812.
[2] H. L. A. Hart, " Definition and Theory in Jurisprudence," 70 L.Q.R. 37.
[3] Ross, *op. cit.* 822, note 6, noting the similarity between his own views and Hart's.
[4] W. N. Hohfeld, *Fundamental Legal Conceptions* (Yale, 1923) Chap. 1 (reprinted from 23 Yale L.J. 16).

Unfortunately we cannot do so; they do not exist. We must therefore confine our attention to the very limited amount of information given us by Mr. Ydobon. He reports as follows:

" The tribe, according to Mr. Ydobon, holds the belief that in the case of an infringement of certain taboos—for example, if a man encounters his mother-in-law, or if a totem animal is killed, or if someone has eaten of the food prepared for the chief —there arises what is called ' *tû-tû.*' The members of the tribe also say that the person who committed the infringement has become ' *tû-tû.*' It is very difficult to explain what is meant by this. Perhaps the nearest one can get to an explanation is to say that ' *tû-tû* ' is conceived of as a kind of dangerous force or infection which attaches to the guilty person and threatens the whole community with disaster. For this reason a person who becomes ' *tû-tû* ' must be subjected to a special ceremony of purification." [5]

And in addition we are told that:

" within the community of the Noît-cif tribe there are in use, among others, the following two pronouncements:

    (1) If a person has eaten of the chief's food he is ' *tû-tû.*'

    (2) If a person is ' *tû-tû* ' he shall be subjected to a ceremony of purification." [6]

On the basis of this information, Professor Ross draws the conclusion that the tribe:

" dwells in a state of darkest superstition. ' *Tû-tû* ' is of course nothing at all, *a word devoid of any meaning whatever.*[7] To be sure, the above situations of infringement of taboo give rise to various natural effects, such as a feeling of dread and terror, but obviously it is not these, any more than any other demonstrable phenomena, which are designated as ' *tû-tû.*' The talk about ' *tû-tû* ' is pure nonsense." [8]

Now with the general conclusion, that the tribe is superstitious, we may well agree. The reason why we can agree with this can easily be identified; *we* do not believe that communities are threatened with disaster, or that individuals are in any sense infected or invested with a dangerous force if such taboos as these are violated. We do not accept as true certain beliefs about natural events and processes which the islanders do accept as true, though

[5] Ross, *op. cit.* 812.
[6] Ross, *op. cit.* 813.
[7] My italics.
[8] Ross, *op. cit.* 812.

if we did accept these beliefs we would find their primitive legal rules rational enough. And granted their view of nature, these rules *are* rational enough.

But all this has nothing to do with the meaning of the word " *tû-tû*," for we must surely distinguish between the assertion that there is no such thing as " *tû-tû*," and the assertion that the *word* " *tû-tû* " is a word devoid of meaning. Similarly we must distinguish between saying that it is nonsense (which here only means untrue) to say that there really is a condition of " *tû-tû*," and saying that it is nonsense (which here can mean a number of different things) to talk about " *tû-tû* " at all. I currently believe, and the belief is shared, I think, by all who have given their attention to the matter, that unicorns (the philosopher's favourite animal) do not exist, and indeed, unlike great auks,[9] never have existed. But from this is does not in the least follow that the word " unicorn " has no meaning. A unicorn, as one of Thurber's characters sharply points out, is a mythical beast, and it is quite clear what is meant by the assertion that there is a unicorn in the garden. No doubt there are some difficult philosophical problems raised by unicorns and indeed great auks, problems which are indeed insoluble if one supposes that the only function of words is to stab at things, after the fashion of kebab skewers.[10] These problems are not, I suggest, illuminated simply by saying that such words are *meaningless*, for they are generated simply by the everyday observation that these words are not meaningless.

Ross indeed is estopped from asserting that the word" *tû-tû* " is meaningless, *for he tells us* what " *tû-tû* " means— it is " a kind of dangerous force or infection which attaches to the guilty person and threatens the whole community with disaster." [11] Thus it is easy to construct meaningful sentences containing the word " *tû-tû*," indeed sentences expressing propositions which are true; if an islander were to say, for example, " I believe in the existence of ' *tû-tû* ' " this sentence, if uttered with sincerity, would be both meaningful and true, just as it would be both meaningful and true for Mr. Ydobon to say that he did not believe in " *tû-tû*." We can well sympathise with the plight of Mr. Ydobon, who found it difficult to explain what is meant by " *tû-tû* "; his difficulty is commonly experienced by travellers.[12]

---

[9] *Pinguinis impennis*, which became extinct on June 3, 1844.

[10] For discussions see G. Ryle, " Imaginary Objects," *Proceedings of the Aristotelian Society*, Supp. Vol. XII (1933), 27; P. F. Strawson, " On Referring," *Essays in Conceptual Analysis*, ed. A. Flew (London, 1956) 21; J. L. Austin, *How to Do Things with Words* (Oxford, 1962) pp. 20, 47–52.

[11] Ross, *op. cit.* 812.

[12] The difficulty is not peculiar to travellers; I should find it hard to explain what is meant by saying a person is " square "; is " square " a " *tû-tû* " word?

But whatever force the allegory possesses is not increased by the injection of a vague and uncertain element into the account of the islanders' beliefs. We could alter the story, and make " *tû-tû* " mean something quite specific, and say that the islanders believe that a person who is " *tû-tû* " will die in a fortnight in horrible agony, and that all who touch a person who is " *tû-tû* " will die likewise; this change would not affect the argument. The vagueness of the concept of " *tû-tû* " only serves to make more plausible, though not convincing, the claim that " *tû-tû* " means nothing at all. It is true that we sometimes say a word is meaningless if its meaning is extremely vague; but this is quite a distinct point, and one which is irrelevant to the argument, for the concept of " *tû-tû* " is not so vague as to incur the charge of being meaningless upon this account, and the islanders possess quite easily workable tests for deciding if a man is " *tû-tû* "; there are recognised criteria for the proper application of the word.

Ross' claim that " *tû-tû* " is a meaningless word is connected by him with a general theory of meaning; according to this theory the two main functions of language are to describe and prescribe.[13] A modification of Ross' argument would be to say only that the word " *tû-tû*," when used in a sentence whose function it is to describe a state of affairs, is meaningless; in such a sentence the word is meaningless because it lacks any " semantic reference." [14] This, which I think would be a softened form of the thesis, would leave open the question whether the word is meaningless in sentences whose function was different; thus it would leave open the question whether the word is meaningless (or the sentences nonsense) when it occurs in Ross' article in the *Harvard Law Review*, for Ross is not there concerned to describe a state of affairs which

---

[13] Ross, *op. cit.* 813.
[14] I find some difficulty in following the argument here, for Ross maintains that although the word " *tû-tû* " is meaningless, since it lacks semantic reference, yet nevertheless sentences containing the word " *tû-tû* " which assert the existence of states of affairs are not meaningless since such sentences do have semantic reference, semantic reference here meaning the state of affairs to which a sentence refers. But if it is a feature of the word " *tû-tû* " that it is meaningless because it refers to something which does not exist (which Ross equates with not referring at all) how can the sentence " He is ' *tû-tû* ' " be in better case? To what state of affairs which does exist can it refer? Ross tries to explain that such sentences have semantic reference because they are not " made in a haphazard fashion. Like other pronouncements of assertion they are stimulated in conformity with the prevailing linguistic customs by quite definite states of affairs," but here he simply changes the meaning of " meaningless," for the same could be said of the word " *tû-tû*." There is a sense in which substantives on their own never refer—if I simply squawk " cat," or " *tû-tû*," will my utterance lack meaning? But this will depend on the context—consider the word DOG on a dog bowl—and I do not think that this is Ross' point. What is surely required is a more elaborate analysis of " referring," a term which Ross is here using in a special philosophical sense but which he does not explain fully.

has ever existed. But it does not seem that the thesis is tenable, even in this softened form, for to say that the word " *tû-tû* " in the sentence " a person who encounters his mother-in-law is ' *tû-tû* ' " is meaningless because there is no such thing as " *tû-tû* " is no different from saying that the proposition which the sentence asserts is not true. This may very well be the case, though Ross gives us no reason for scepticism about " *tû-tû*," and having invented an island and islanders, he could if he wished invent an infection too. But the logical status of the word " *tû-tû*," and the status of descriptive sentences containing the word, cannot depend upon hypothetical contingent facts about the existence of " *tû-tû* "; all that can be said, given the allegory, is that the proposition that a person who encounters his mother-in-law is " *tû-tû* " is (logically) *capable* of being true or false (this supposing it to fall into the category of propositions which describe states of affairs). We may compare the position of the gorilla. It is a purely contingent fact that gorillas exist, and it is a melancholy fact that these attractive and agreeable creatures are currently in danger of extinction. But if it happens that the last gorilla expires, and goes the way of the passenger pigeon, nothing of logical importance will have occurred, nor will the meaning of the word " gorilla " change in an instant of time, much less disappear.

A consequence of Ross' argument, and one which he stresses, is that since the word " *tû-tû* " has no semantic reference, the meaning of the two propositions:

(A) If a person has eaten of the chief's food he is " *tû-tû*."

(B) If a person is " *tû-tû* " he shall be subjected to a ceremony of purification.

amounts to no more than the meaning of the proposition:

(C) If a person has eaten of the chief's food he shall be subjected to a ceremony of purification.

Propositions A and B do no more than state, in a roundabout way, proposition C, which he admits to be a meaningful prescription. Now proposition A is presumably conceived of by the islanders, if they give their attention to these matters, as a statement of what is the case; at any rate this is how Ross conceived it, for he thinks that it is not true. This being so, it seems clear that a person who was acquainted with proposition C, but was ignorant of A and B, would be less well informed about the islanders than a person who did know about their acceptance of both A and B. Unlike Ross, he would be unable to say that the islanders were superstitious. He would also not know *why* a person who had eaten of the chief's food was thought to be suitable purification fodder.

Further to this, if a person knew propositions A and B, and in addition knew proposition AA, " If a person kills a totem animal he is ' *tû-tû*,' " he would be in a position to draw the conclusion that such a person should be subjected to a ceremony of purification. But a person who knew only proposition C and proposition AA would be unable to draw this conclusion. It seems obvious therefore that the " cash value " of the two propositions A and B is greater than the " cash value " of the single proposition C.

Here it might be objected that one who knew all the A-type propositions, and in addition knew proposition B, would be no better informed than one who knew all the possible C-type propositions, particularly since he could *deduce* the systematic connection, which, Ross claims, is the only reality expressed by the word " *tû-tû*." But this is not so, for he would not be able to tell that all persons who were to be subjected to purification under rules C, CC, etc., were thought by the islanders to need purification for the same reason—because they had become " *tû-tû*." It is perfectly possible, indeed, that there may be other reasons why islanders require purification, which are quite distinct from " *tû-tû* "; the presentation of island custom in C-type rules will conceal from us whether this is the case or not.

Notwithstanding his claim that " *tû-tû* " is a meaningless word, Ross nevertheless claims that the word has a perfectly useful job to do in the language of the tribe, in that it can be used as a tool of presentation, and it is this same function which he allows to legal words, and to the legal concepts which lie behind the use of legal words. The examples he gives of such words are these: " right," " duty," " claim," " ownership," " territory," " marriage," " nationality," " civil servant status "; I think that there is no doubt that his analysis is supposed to apply to all legal words (or if one prefers it, legal concepts). Other examples would be " contract," " possessions," " tort," " crime." (In passing, and I shall later return to this point, it is worth noticing that Ross gives no indication of any independent criteria by which it is to be decided whether a particular word is a " *tû-tû* " word or, as we might say a *legal* word.) The function which such words have is that they enable us to express the law in a neat and systematic way, and no more. Thus, Ross argues, it would be *possible* to express all the rules about " ownership " without actually using the word by compiling a list of rules in the following form:

(i) *If a person has lawfully acquired a thing by purchase*, judgment for recovery shall be given in favour of the purchaser against other persons retaining the thing in their possession.

(ii) *If a person has inherited a thing,* judgment for damages
shall be given in favour of the heir against other persons who
culpably damage the thing.

etc., etc.[15]

But this procedure would be excessively inconvenient and long-
winded; instead it is simpler to interpose a concept, the concept of
ownership, between the conditioning fact or facts (indicated by the
italics) and the legal consequence, and to state the law in the form
of a list of the circumstances which give rise to " ownership," and
a separate list of the consequences of " ownership." This technique,
the " *tû-tû* " technique, can be represented schematically in the
following form, where F represents a conditioning fact, and C a
legal consequence.

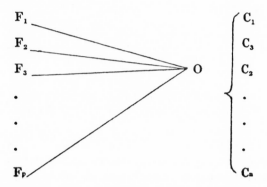

In such a scheme " ' O ' (ownership) merely stands for the systematic connection that F_1 as well as F_2, F_3 . . . F_p entail the totality
of legal consequences C_1, C_2, C_3 . . . C_n." [16]

II

An initial difficulty about the analysis is this: it is not clear that
Ross is correct in supposing that the function of the word " *tû-tû* "
in the allegory is the same as the function of such words as " ownership "; and if this is not the case then even if Ross' analysis of
" *tû-tû* " is correct, it would not follow that " ownership " (and
other " legal " words) were susceptible of the same analysis. This
is not a matter which is free from difficulty, and, to anticipate a
conclusion, I do not think that the question is soluble, *because of
our ignorance of the linguistic habits of the islanders.*[17] However,

[15] Ross, *op. cit.* 813; I have added the italics in order to make the argument
easier to follow.
[16] Ross, *op. cit.* 820.
[17] See below at section IV.

I think that an attempt to answer it, and an explanation of why it is unanswerable, may throw some light upon a matter which is of some general importance in analytical jurisprudence—the concept of a legal concept, or, what makes a concept a legal concept.

Now Ross tells us that [18]:

> " within the community of the Noît-cîf tribe there are in use, among others, the following two pronouncements:
>
> (1) If a person has eaten of the chief's food he is ' tû-tû.'
> (2) If a person is ' tû-tû ' he shall be subjected to a ceremony of purification."

This being so, it would seem that the first proposition, and such further propositions as:

> " Urk is ' tû-tû ' this morning, poor fellow ";
> " ' Tû-tû ' is rotting the fibres of our society,"

are all propositions which assert that something is the case, and are (logically) capable of being true or false. It would be natural to call them statements of fact. If we contrast such statements with these:

> " John Doe has just acquired ownership of Blackacre ";
> " Richard Roe has transferred ownership of Blackacre to John Style,"

there appears to be a difference, because, it has been suggested,[19] the propriety of making statements of this second class [20] *seems* to turn *both* upon the existence of certain states of affairs or the occurrence of certain events *and* upon the existence of certain rules, and for this reason the label " statement of fact " seems rather inappropriate. An equally inappropriate label would be " statement of law," for these statements do not simply (or indeed at all) tell us what the rule in question is; rather they apply the rule. Professor Hart, in " Definition and Theory in Jurisprudence," has both made this point and urges the importance of placing such statements in a separate conceptual compartment; such statements are *statements of legal conclusions*.

Hart's argument would suggest that " Urk is ' tû-tû ' " is a statement of fact, whilst " John Doe has acquired ownership of Blackacre " is a conclusion of law, and from this it would seem to follow that the function of the word " tû-tû " is different from the function of the word " ownership "; *ergo* Ross's use of the allegory

---

[18] Ross, *op. cit.* 813.
[19] By Prof. H. L. A. Hart, "Definition and Theory in Jurisprudence," 70 L.Q.R. 37.
[20] At least in legal contexts, a notion which is easy enough to understand though somewhat difficult to define.

is likely to mislead us. But this is not so obvious as it seems, for a difficulty centres upon the implications of saying, in this context, that a statement is a statement of fact. Now it may well be the case that both the significance of saying that a statement is a statement of fact, and the criteria by which it is decided that a statement is a statement of fact, vary according to the context in which the concept is used; for example, sometimes to say that a statement is a statement of fact means only that the statement is in fact true, whilst on other occasions the implication may be that the statement is capable (logically) of truth or falsity. In " Definition and Theory " " statements of fact " are contrasted with conclusions of law, and it is upon this contrast that we need to concentrate.

If I have followed Hart's reasoning correctly, the characteristic feature of a conclusion of law, as opposed to a statement of fact, is that it is a statement which applies a legal rule. As a simple model of such a statement Hart uses the statement " He is out," uttered in the context of a game of cricket. If the word " out " is to be used correctly in such a statement, not only must certain events have happened (the ball must have hit the wicket, or been caught without bouncing after having been struck whilst in play by the batsman's bat, or, I understand, wrist, etc.), but also whatever it is that has happened must count as being out according to the rules of cricket. With the conclusion " He is out " Hart contrasts the statement of fact " The ball has hit the wicket " (or whatever it is).[21] But this contrast is not easy to see, for just as " being out," cricket-wise, is *rule-defined*, so are " ball " and " wicket " *rule defined* by the laws of the game; not *any* object which could with linguistic propriety be called a ball counts as a cricket ball, but only certain balls made of certain materials of a certain size and weight. And the same is true of the wicket.[22] Now it is curious to find that Hart, when he applies his own theory to the simple model of cricket, classifies what surely ought to be a conclusion of law as a statement of fact. And perhaps the explanation is that the contrast which Hart is trying to identify has in reality nothing to do with a difference between the functions of sentences; instead the difference is that the word " possession " (or " ball ") when used on certain

---

[21] Hart, *op. cit.* 53.

[22] There is a difference here, for whereas the word "ball" has a use in other games, and outside the language of games, wickets do not, I think, feature in other games, and only rarely outside the game of cricket. There is an analogy here with the law, which employs some terms—"tenant in tail" for example—which seem peculiarly legal, and others, such as "possession," which have a use outside the law. Hence arise such expressions as "possession in fact" and "possession in law," but there are no "tenants in tail in fact," though it is a fact that there are tenants in tail.

occasions and for certain purposes is (legally) rule-defined, quite irrespective of the type or function of the sentence in which the word is used.

We can push the argument from cricket further. " He is out," viewed as a conclusion, depends upon " The ball has hit the wicket," which itself, according to the same criteria, is another conclusion. We could say that we have reached a statement of fact only when we reach a statement couched in words which currently are not rule-defined by the rules of cricket; something like this would serve: " a spherical object of such and such a weight, size and composition has hit (" hit " is not defined in the laws of cricket, or is it?) three cylindrical pieces of wood arranged in such a place in such a way." This technique of " pushing it back," which Hart's argument would require of us if we are to find a statement of fact, would be required also if, having accepted Ross's argument, we wanted to find a statement which did not employ a " tû-tû " (and therefore meaningless and dispensable) concept. This can be illustrated by examining one of the propositions in which Ross reformulates the rules about " ownership " without using the " tû-tû " concept of ownership:

> " *If a person has lawfully acquired a thing by purchase,* judgment for recovery shall be given in favour of the purchaser against other persons retaining the thing in his possession." [23]

If we take the clause italicised (though the same argument would apply to the rest), we find that this is said to be a statement of conditioning facts—" individual legal facts." But surely " person," " lawfully," " acquired," " thing " and " purchase " are all " tû-tû " words themselves, let alone " possession," which is as " tû-tû " as could well be. We should have to go much further [24] if we wish to reach a statement which avoids " tû-tû " like the plague.

The contrast which Hart makes between statements of fact and statements of legal conclusions, and the contrast in Ross's argument between " tû-tû " words and non-" tû-tû " words, is not essentially different from Hohfeld's neglected distinction between generic operative facts and specific operative facts, according to which the word " assault " in the statement " Smith assaulted Jones " is a word which describes generically certain facts, whilst the statement " Smith pointed a loaded gun at Jones," uttered in the same

[23] Ross *op. cit.* 819.
[24] Usually this would involve giving a more particular account of the facts.

context, describes the same facts more specifically.[25] Hohfeld engrafted this refinement upon an analysis of legal language in which the basic division was between words which referred to facts, and words which referred to legal relations, and although Hohfeld's reasoning may be open to various objections, he did succeed in identifying the root problem, which is the problem of putting one's finger upon precisely what is meant by saying that a concept is a legal concept (or a word a legal word).[26] For Hohfeld, like Hart and Ross, felt sure that there was something peculiar or special about the way in which lawyers used words, and he, too, attempted to construct a system of linguistic categories which would serve to reveal precisely where this peculiarity lay.

III

I suggest that the root of the difficulty can be exposed in the following way. Although it is common to talk of legal language or of legal words (or concepts), this way of talking must not be allowed to suggest the idea that legal language and ordinary language are distinct from each other in the way in which English, say, is distinct from German, much less that they are distinct in some stronger sense. For it is generally the case that the words used in stating and applying the rules of (for example) English law are words which are in current use in other contexts, contexts which are not legal contexts. Take the word " infant." We may say that in some contexts the correct use of this word is dictated by " ordinary " linguistic usage, and we can talk about the " ordinary " meaning of the word, so long as we do not suppose that " ordinary " means uncomplicated. It is a fact familiar to laymen that lawyers in legal contexts employ the word " infant " in a special way in stating and using certain legal rules; they say that a man of twenty is an infant, something which in a non-legal context could only be said as a joke, or for some satirical or offensive reason. But lawyers are neither joking nor satirising nor trying to be rude. We say that the word " infant " has a " legal use," or a " technical meaning," or that some people are " not *really* infants," but only infants " in the eyes of the law "; a whole range of expressions points to the existence of the familiar difference between the legal and extra-legal meanings of those words which are not the private property of lawyers. One of these expressions is the expression " legal concept," and what justifies us in saying

---

[25] Hohfeld, *op. cit.* 32 *et seq.* The same distinction may be used in connection with an analysis of the idea of " material facts " which is used in discussions of the doctrine of precedent.

[26] For an account of this see below at Section V.

that there is a *legal* concept of an " infant," or a " year," or of " murder," or " possession," or " trespass," is only that ordinary use and legal use diverge in some striking or important respect. Although it is usual to talk about a legal concept only when the divergence is striking or important, there is no difference in principle between considerable and minor divergences. But since ordinary use (and legal use) is often vague and uncertain, it is often difficult and sometimes impossible to say dogmatically whether there is or is not a divergence, and in such cases it is not usual to assert the existence of a legal concept or a legal usage. But whilst the existence of a legal concept of an " infant," of " cattle," of " consideration," or whatever it is, just means that there is a divergence between legal use and ordinary use (and nothing more), the usages are usually, and perhaps always, related and connected in a complex way, so that it is futile to attempt to prise apart the ordinary use from the legal use; they are dovetailed together in so complicated a way that separation will distort both. And this feature is just as important as the divergence.

The use of the word " infant " provides a simple example. A child of three counts as an infant both within the law and outside the law; my daughter, who is seven, is certainly an infant legally, but she is getting to an age when she might be rather cross if she were called an infant; following Hart, she is perhaps a penumbral infant. My pupils, some of whom are under twenty-one, are legally infants but certainly not infants in ordinary parlance. The legal concept of an infant might thus be said to *overlap* the ordinary concept of an infant. This is not unlike the concept of " being out " in cricket; if the meaning of being " out " were to be fully explained, one would have to explain the circumstances in which a batsman is " out " in cricket, and the consequences of being " out "; one would also have to explain that " being out " meant " being out of the game," and show how this concept was in use in other games (such as musical bumps) where the rules were different. In addition one would have to show how the concept of " being out " in games was related to " being out " in other contexts—consider the remark, " I hate being ' left out ' of things." Only by showing all this is it possible to see why cricketers came to use the word " out " instead of, say, " in " or, to use Ross's suggestion, " old cheese." [27]

On the divergence and relation between legal and ordinary concepts, certain general observations (which only remind us of what is already familiar) can be made.

---

[27] Offered as a substitute for " *tû-tû* " words.

(i) Some legal words or terms seem to have only a legal meaning—" tenant in tail after possibility of issue extinct," " entail "—English property law is rich in such words. Even here the legal meaning at one time was connected with an ordinary meaning. An example would be the word " tort," where the modern legal use cannot be understood unless it is realised that etymologically the word meant, vaguely, " wrong." The writing of a legal history has sometimes been distorted by a failure to see that words like " trespass " and " consideration " were originally used by lawyers in an untechnical way.

(ii) Where a word is used almost exclusively by lawyers *qua* lawyers,[28] the concept is both more precise and less amenable to change. Here again property law provides the classic example.

(iii) Where a word is current in ordinary language outside the law as well as within the law, the extra-legal concept may react upon the legal concept in a variety of different ways. Thus in *Derry* v. *Peek* [29] the legal concept of fraud was made to conform more closely to the ordinary concept of fraud, though previously there had been a marked divergence. In cases where the law is unsettled " what the layman would say " is always a respectable legal argument; cats and dogs have not become cattle, though geese, oddly enough, did. For although there may be divergence, there is also a pressure towards conformity also.

(iv) No word is immune from the hazard of legal definition, and once a word features in the formulation of a legal rule the danger is never far off; pass a Cats Act, and soon there is a legal concept of a cat. The word " signed " in the Statute of Frauds [30] is a classic example of the process. Nothing whatever turns here on whether the word is a word which stands for a tangible thing, or a fact, or whether the word is an abstract word, or a word which describes things, or one which typically or characteristically features in statements of fact or whatever.

---

28 One must not forget that lawyers are people, and legal English English; this may require an effort sometimes, but the effort is worth making.

29 (1889) 14 App.Cas. 337. See in particular, at p. 345, Lord Watson's reference to fraud " in the eyes of the law," and at p. 346 Lord Bramwell's discussion of the problem for decision in terms of a contrast between legal fraud and *actual* fraud. Similarly, see the remarks of Lord Herschell at p. 362, and note 22 above.

30 (1677) 29 Car. 2, c. 3.

(v) The reasons why legal and ordinary use diverge are often discoverable.[31] The primary reason is that the meaning given to a word in a legal rule has consequences of a special kind; men are hanged in the name of the meaning of " malice aforethought." But this is not the whole story; equally important are the desire to conceal change and the desire to conceal choice. Instead of inventing a new rule about geese, lawyers apply the old rule about cattle, and tell us that geese are cattle. Instead of saying to the prisoner, " You are to be punished because we think you should be punished," lawyers say, " You are to be punished because this is what the word means." And sometimes these things may be done consciously, and sometimes not.

(vi) Commonly enough a legal concept may be developed by accident; a court which is honestly trying to record and apply ordinary usage may introduce a special legal usage. There is a puzzle here about the logical status of legal definitions; indeed there is a puzzle about the distinction between legal rules and the rules of ordinary language. There is, in this area, no clear distinction between legal rules and rules of ordinary language, and further (and in consequence) no clear distinction between descriptions and prescriptions.

IV

This discussion of the nature of legal concepts [32] should makes it clear why it is impossible to determine whether the islander's concept of " *tû-tû* " is analogous to the legal concept of ownership; for we do not possess enough information about the linguistic habits of the islanders to enable us to tell whether there is a divergence between the meaning of " *tû-tû* " in law and its meaning outside the law; we cannot tell whether the pronouncement " He who kills a totem animal is ' *tû-tû* ' " defines a legal concept or not.[33] Further to this, theorists who attempt to explain the use of legal concepts and legal terms by supposing either that legal terms or the sentences in which they occur possess a peculiar logical function,

---

[31] For an example of an attempt to explain both the divergence and the connection see D. R. Harris, " The Concept of Possession in English Law," *Oxford Essays in Jurisprudence,* ed. Guest (Oxford, 1961) 69.

[32] For an elaborate account of the relevance of linguistic theory to the law see G. L. Williams, " Language and the Law, I–V," 61 L.Q.R. 71, 179 (esp. pp. 180–181), 293, 384 (esp. p. 390); 62 L.Q.R. 387. Though I should wish to disagree with some of Dr. Williams' views (and especially with his use of the notion of a verbal dispute), I only wish here to acknowledge indebtedness to these illuminating articles.

[33] Nor perhaps in a primitive society is there likely to be a divergence; the machinery for producing divergence does not exist. And the further back one goes into legal history, the less useful is the conceptual distinction between the " is " and the " ought."

are mistaken; the error is to suppose that a technical vocabulary must be linked to a logical function. To a motor-mechanic, *qua* mechanic, " sump " means a particular part of a car engine; to a speleologist " sump " means a passage filled with water for part of its length. But when a speleologist uses the word " sump " he does not necessarily or typically use the word in a *logically* different way from a motor mechanic; he simply uses the word with a different though related meaning. Of course the word " sump " might feature in the rules of a speleological society (" Nobody is to go through two sumps in one day, upon pain of expulsion ") or for that matter in an Act of Parliament, and there would be a difference in function between these *formulations of rules* and a statement made by a speleologist in the course of a caving expedition—" There is a sump ahead." But the difference in logical function has nothing to do with the existence of speleological, motor-mechanics and (let us suppose that there are legal decisions about sumps) legal meanings of the word sump, for the logical differences between prescriptions and descriptions would still exist even if everybody for all purposes made use of precisely the same conception of a sump. And in the same way, even if there were no legal concepts, and no divergence ever between the meaning which lawyers attached to words and the meanings which other folk attached to them, the logical difference between prescriptions and descriptions would remain.

V

The analyses of Hohfeld, Ross and Hart, I suggest all start from this same mistake, the mistake of attempting to link an explanation of the nature of legal concept to a theory of the logical function of words or sentences, though the conclusions reached are different.

Hohfeld

Hohfeld's view of language was essentially a crude one; words (he only considered substantives) point to or refer to or describe things. This being so, Hohfeld tried to identify the characteristic features of the facts or things to which those words which are the stock in trade of lawyers pointed. He embarked upon this undertaking because he wanted to analyse the fundamental legal conceptions which lay behind the use of these words; in this he could make no progress until he had separated the sheep from the goats, the legal conceptions from the non-legal conceptions.[34] Influenced

---

[34] Hence the first two sections of " Fundamental Legal Conceptions," which are entitled " Legal Conceptions contrasted with Non-legal Conceptions " and " Operative Facts contrasted with Evidential Facts " (Hohfeld, *op. cit.* pp. 27–35).

perhaps by the idea that it is the function of a legal system to
regulate and provide for situations in which one person's activities
affect some other person, Hohfeld propounded the theory that legal
conceptions were conceptions about the relationship between people,
and that the words which expressed these conceptions functioned
by referring to these relationships. But these legal relationships
were the creation of the law, and Hohfeld could not suggest that
the promulgation of a legal rule could alter the course of nature;
if you pass a law about people the people do not twitch. Hence
Hohfeld was led into a metaphysical solution; legal relations existed
only in some supersensible world, and their existence was not
perceptible to the senses. The metaphysical things to which legal
words referred *exist* all right, but unlike the things to which non-
legal words pointed they were intangible, invisible, etc.

Armed with this theory, Hohfeld then applied it to certain
words which possess a technical legal meaning—words like
" property," " contract," " power," " transfer." He admitted
that in fact such words were sometimes used to point to tangible
things; thus if Smith said, " Put my property on the 'bus " Hohfeld would admit that here the word " property " was being used
to perform the same function as the word " typewriter " (supposing
this to be the property in question). Hohfeld could only lament
this; such a usage, though current, was sloppy. Having disposed
of this difficulty, he faced up to another; it was hardly plausible
to say that all words which possessed a technical legal meaning
stood for relationships between people (or bundles of relationships).
For example Hohfeld did not think that the word " possession "
did, when used in a discriminating way, and perhaps here he had
in mind the enormous number of words which possess a technical
legal sense but which do not appear in jurisprudence. Yet Hohfeld
could hardly deny that there was something " legal " about such
words. To explain what this was he introduced a refinement. Such
words were *like* words which have no technical connection with the
law in that their function is to refer to things or facts which exist
in the real world. It is convenient, however, to use general terms
to refer generically [35] to classes of facts which have the same legal
force or effect, and this is the function of such words as " possession." Because the word describes generically a set of facts which
have the same legal consequence, it seems to have a special connection with the law. Hohfeld could then herd legal words into two
pens; in one went words whose function it is to refer to metaphysical things called legal relations, about which there existed *legal*

[35] Hohfeld could contrast general words with words which described facts (which
might be operative) more specifically.

conceptions, whilst in the other went words which referred to things or facts in the real world, about which there were no *legal* conceptions. The words in this second pen performed the same function as non-legal words, though their apparent connection with the law was explicable.[36] And after this *hors d'oeuvre*, Hohfeld could then address himself to the main task—to develop an atomic theory of legal conceptions.[37]

Hohfeld was forced by his own reasoning to refuse to admit the existence of legal concepts of " offer," " acceptance," " possession " and a host of others; his analysis is not therefore an analysis of the concept of a legal concept as that concept is in fact used; he failed to attach any importance to the divergence between the legal sense of words like possession and the extra-legal sense of the word, and did not see that it is this divergence which is the key to the identification of legal concepts. His attempt to link the identification of legal conceptions with the logical function of words led him into metaphysics; it also led him into regarding as improper uses of legal words which are both current and accurate (unless the typewriter is not mine, what *is* improper in saying, " Put my property on the bus, and by my property I mean that typewriter " ?) It further led him into making a purely arbitrary division into the two pens; no reason whatever is given for the decisions he makes. Such are the results of linking the notion of a legal concept to the function of words.

Ross

Ross's theory is not unlike Hohfeld's, with the difference that since Ross is anti-metaphysical, legal words refer not to metaphysical realities, but, somewhat startlingly, to nothing at all. Yet something is saved from the wreck, for these " meaningless " words are nevertheless, as we have seen, given their humble but dispensable job to do as organising concepts. But even in this humble role, arbitrary squiggles or " old cheese " would do the job as well. A theory of this kind again neglects to attach any importance to the fact that legal rules and legal talk is not conducted in a private set of squiggles, but in words which are part of a language —be it English, French or Tamil—and further that the use of words by lawyers is related to the extra-legal use, although it may

---

[36] Although Hohfeld concentrates upon the functions of individual words, his theory could equally well be presented as a theory about different types of statement; indeed at times he does so present it.

[37] Hohfeld's analysis of what he called the " fundamental " legal conceptions cannot very well be separated from his theory of meaning and his explanation of the function of legal concepts; customarily it is, inevitably at the price of distortion.

diverge from it. To substitute " old cheese " for " ownership "
would sever this relationship, and the operation would only leave the
position as it was, if it was understood that for " old cheese " one
must read " ownership." Consider how else would one translate
an English law book into French.[38] Ross's argument further
suggests that a knowledge of all the legal rules about " ownership "
(notice his inability to identify these rules without using the
concept !), these rules being expressed without using the term,
would be equivalent to a knowledge of these rules expressed in
terms of ownership. An argument which claims that a concept is
redundant but which can only be advanced by using the same
concept has gone wrong somewhere; the only terms upon which
we can discard a classifying concept are that we abandon the
classification, for we cannot at one and the same time maintain that
the concept of an elephant is unnecessary whilst we continue to
talk about elephants. Again it can be seen to what lengths Ross
is driven through his initial attempt to identify legal concepts by
reference to a theory about the logical function of legal words.[39]

Ross's attempt to explain the humble function of legal concepts
as organising concepts forms the positive part of his argument;
words which function in this way are contrasted with words which
describe facts. The word " ownership " (" O " in the scheme
reproduced) [40] " merely stands for the systematic connection that
F_1 as well as F_2, F_3, . . . F_p entail the totality of legal consequences
C_1, C_2, C_3, . . . C_n." To this analysis a number of objections can be
made.

  (a) This analysis fails to explain why the word " ownership "
      is used—why not " old cheese "? Indeed why not " *tû-tû* "?
  (b) It is not clear that to say that a person is owner does entail
      all the legal consequences of " ownership." Or take the
      concept of a contract. We may list the circumstances which
      give rise to a contract—offer, acceptance, consideration and
      perhaps intent to create legal relations—but when we list the
      consequences we have to hedge our list with words like
      " usually," " unless," " sometimes." Indeed we may find
      it necessary to do the same with the circumstances which give
      rise to a contract. The function of the word " contract "
      and of the word " ownership " cannot therefore be explained
      so simply as Ross suggests. And the reason for this is that

[38] See generally the essay on " Ownership " by Mr. A. M. Honoré, *Oxford
Essays in Jurisprudence*, 107.
[39] Ross, like Hohfeld, advances a theory which can be indifferently presented
as a theory about the function of individual words or a theory about particular
types of sentence.
[40] See above, p. 541.

legal rules commonly have exceptions to them, and in turn the reason for this is that legal rules are expressed in general words which classify, but unfortunately overlap. This over-lapping of categories would produce contradictions between different legal rules, which cannot be tolerated, and we avoid this by exceptions. An example may make this clear. Suppose we think it convenient or just (or whatever it is) that agreements should in general, but not always be action-able, and that one sort of agreement which we think should not be actionable is one entered into under duress. We have two categories—*agreements*, and *agreements entered into by duress*. Clearly the first category includes the second, and there happen to be no two words in the language which precisely fit the two categories we wish to demarcate; we solve the problem by expressing our rule (" agreements are actionable ") and adding an exception (" but not when entered into by duress "). An alternative technique is to express the rule, and define " agreement " in a special way —" an agreement in the eyes of the law does not include an agreement entered into under duress "; the substance remains the same.

(c) Sometimes a decision that a certain result ought to follow turns upon the question, " Is X owner ? " How can this be explained if the application of the word " owner " depends upon the consequences ?

It seems therefore that Ross's attempt to show that legal words have a peculiar logical function both fails and leads him into an untenable position.

Hart

In " Definition and Theory " the attempt to link the elucidation of legal concepts to a theory about their function takes on a much more elaborate form, and with many of the incidental conclusions which Professor Hart expresses I should not wish to disagree. Hart is concerned to argue that legal notions or conceptions can be elucidated (notwithstanding the rather discouraging history of earlier attempts) by " methods properly adapted to their special character." [41] This leads him into an attempt to identify what is special about " legal words " as opposed to " ordinary words," and he claims to have identified two features. The first is that some legal words (the example given is " law ") apply to such a wide range of cases that it is difficult to extract any principle

---

[41] Hart, *op. cit.* 37.

behind the use of the word, though reasonable enough to suppose
that some principle exists. The second, which he calls the " great
anomaly " of legal language, is that legal words

> " do not have the straightforward connexion with counterparts
> in the world of fact which most ordinary words have and to
> which we appeal in our definition of ordinary words." [42]

A *consequence* of this second feature, Hart argues, is our inability
to provide synonyms or expressions synonymous with legal words:
this looks like a separate feature of legal words, but Hart does not
present it as one.

Now Hart is here trying to lay a basis for the main argument
by suggesting that legal words are peculiar, or different from
ordinary words; he is trying to drive a wedge between legal language
and ordinary language. The attempt seems to me to fail. If we
take his first point, true it is that words like " law " apply to a vast
range of cases, and he is surely right in suggesting that this makes
it difficult to define the meaning of such words satisfactorily. But
this is not a peculiarity of legal words; it is just as true of a word
like " cat " though more obviously true of what we call abstract
terms like " life." As for the second point, this depends upon the
very large assumption that ordinary words (let us again take " cat "
as an example) do have a straightforward connection with counterparts in the world of fact. True it is that we can point to particular
cats, and we cannot point to particular rights, but pointing does not
catch the meaning of the word " cat." For suppose that I have a
cat called Mandragora, an ostensive definition of the word " cat "
will be indistinguishable from an ostensive definition of the word
" Mandragora," but " Mandragora " does not mean the same as
" cat." Indeed one point which I should have thought centuries
of philosophical effort had established is that there is nothing
straightforward about the connection between words and things.
In addition there are legal concepts (for example the concept of
an " infant ") where an ostensive definition (for what it is worth)
is possible. Further to this, the words which do seem to have a
straightforward connection with factual counterparts are proper
names, yet in the case of proper names the task of definition, so
far from becoming easy, becomes inappropriate.[43] Nor is it easy to

---

[42] Hart, *op. cit.* 38; compare Hart's " world of fact " with Hohfeld's " real
  world." But Hart, unlike Hohfeld, will at no price allow himself to be
  forced into a metaphysical explanation.

[43] Hart suggests that " it would be patently absurd to ask for elucidation of
  the principle in accordance with which different men are called Tom." Is
  this really so? One can give casual explanations of why different men are
  called Tom, and state the conventions, elaborate though they may be, which
  govern the use of proper names and the customs which influence the choice

see that the difficulty of finding synonyms (or substitute expressions) to which Hart attaches importance is either a difficulty peculiar to legal words, or that it is a consequence of " the great anomaly of legal language." For it seems to be quite a general feature of language that although one word will do as well as another in a particular context (" Put out the cat " is as good as " Put out Mandragora ") yet we cannot find substitutes which will do duty in all contexts. It is as though every word has its own job to do; there are no spare parts in the linguistic stores. If we expect that definitions of words, whether those words are legal words or ordinary words, can be used as substitutes we expect too much of definition. The conclusion from all this is that Hart's attempt to show that legal words are " anomalous " in these respects is not convincing.

Hart then goes on to develop in a wholly novel way a suggestion which Bentham made: that in elucidating legal concepts attention ought to be focused not upon single words, but upon sentences in which legal words appear. This raises a problem: what sort of sentence to choose? Hart selects sentences whose function it is to draw conclusions from legal rules, and goes on to make a number of illuminating observations upon the logic of such sentences, contrasting the logic of sentences of this type with the logic of sentences whose function it is to state or describe facts. In choosing such sentences he claims that he has chosen sentences in which legal words have their " typical " or " characteristic " role, and it is at this point, I suggest, that the argument goes wrong, for although it is true that legal words often feature in sentences of this type, they feature just as typically in other types of sentence. For example the word " possession " is just as at home in a statement of a legal rule, a statement about a legal rule or indeed in any sort of sentence one cares to think of, as it is in a conclusion drawing sentence. One cannot link particular words to particular sentence functions by the device of the typical or paradigm case, nor argue that the peculiarity of legal words can be explained by reference to the logical function of the sentences in which they " typically " appear.

The consequence is that although Hart purports to be identifying what is peculiar about legal words, what he contributes is an analysis

of particular names; surely this would be elucidation. Furthermore, the sort of elucidation which is possible here is not radically unlike the sort of elucidation which is possible in the case of legal concepts. It is true that a " definition " of a proper name, or the provision of a synonym, hardly makes sense; such notions are inappropriate here. Nor will elucidation produce a single princple, but at best a set of principles; explaining this would form part of the elucidation.

of the peculiarities of conclusion drawing sentences, and an analysis
of how legal terms function in sentences of this type, but not an
analysis of how legal terms function generally. And this, I suggest,
is why Hart's suggested technique for the elucidation of legal words
—which is offered in reply to such questions as " What is possession ? "—is only of limited utility. For if we reply to such an
inquiry by rehearsing the rules of English law, and show how the
word " possession " can be used in sentences which draw conclusions
from these rules in particular cases, and exhort the inquirer to see
that to ask " What is possession ? " is, as Hart says, to pursue a
" fruitless question," [44] I think our inquirer would go away only
partly satisfied, and would feel, with justice, that certain of his
difficulties had not been solved. And these difficulties might include
all or any of the following:

(a) He might be puzzled as to why " possession " was thought
to be a " legal concept."

(b) He might feel that although he now understood the meaning
of the word " possession " when used to draw conclusions
from rules, he has still received no explanation of how it was
used in the rules themselves.

(c) He might know that the concept of possession was used in
Roman law too, and further know that the rules of Roman
law differed from the rules of English law. But Hart's
elucidation would seem to suggest that knowing the meaning
of the word " possession " just consisted in knowing the
rules of a particular legal system in which the word was
used. And yet his instinct would tell him that there was
some sense in which " possession " was a word which means
the same as " *possessio* " (just as " law " means, in the
same elusive sense *the same* in England and Canada or the
U.S.A. although the legal rules about what counts as a law
differ). But Hart's explanation would not explain how this
can be so.

(d) He might have noticed that the word " possession," besides
being used by lawyers, was also used meaningfully by laymen
who know nothing of the law, and having noticed this he
might want to know whether this lay use is functionally
different, or whether the word has a different meaning in lay
use. And if the answer to this was yes, he might be puzzled
as to why it should be that lawyers give the word a different
meaning; why are lawyers not content to leave meanings
alone ?

[44] Hart, *op. cit.*, 59.

(e) He might, having learnt the rules, wonder why it is that the word " possession " is used in this area, and not some other words, like " old cheese."

(f) He might wonder why the search for a definition of possession is called a futile question, when so much apparently beneficial simplification of the law has been produced through attempts to define legal concepts, to substitute principles for lists.   And he might be led to suspect that the division between legal words which it is futile to attempt to define, and those it is not futile to attempt to define requires further elucidation.

It is because of the existence of difficulties like these that Hart's method of elucidation can only provide a partial answer to the various questions which lie concealed in the " What is . . . ? " questions of jurisprudence.

But besides being only apt to provide an answer to one of these lurking questions, Hart's attempt to link " legal words " with sentences of a particular logical type leads him into difficulty, a difficulty which stems from the fact that no such link exists.   We have seen how, in using his model of a game of cricket, Hart contrasts the factual statement that the ball has hit the wicket with the conclusion drawing statement that the batsman is out, and I have suggested that since " ball " and " wicket " are both rule defined notions it is difficult to see why the statement that the ball has hit the wicket is itself not classed as a conclusion drawing statement.   Pursuing this reasoning further, we saw that in order to reach a statement which is really a statement of fact we must describe what has occurred on the cricket field in words which are not currently rule defined by the rules of cricket, keeping one jump ahead of the M.C.C.   The hallmark of a statement of fact ceases to be the job the sentence does, but the words which appear in it; sentences which contain words which happen to be legally defined are classified as conclusion drawing sentences, and Hart's argument is reduced to the truism that when a legally defined word is used in a sentence which is uttered in a context in which the legal definition is relevant, the meaning of the word is determined by the rules which define the meaning.

This survey of these three attempts to elucidate the nature of legal concepts by reference to the function of legal words or the function of sentences suggests that such attempts are misdirected, and that if we are to understand what is peculiar about the way in which words are used in the law we would do better to investigate the way in which the meaning of legal terms both diverges from and is related to the extra legal meaning, concentrating our attention upon explaining how, when, why and with what consequences this comes to happen.

This surely is not a revolutionary programme; legal historians and critical writers expounding contemporary law have been investigating these matters for a very long time with much profit. There is no separate or distinct activity which we can label analytical jurisprudence which can throw some new and special light upon the concepts of the law. Only a pedagogic convention requires us to label Salmond's discussion of possession " jurisprudence " whilst denying the label to Maitland's investigations into the concept of seisin. The convention may have its uses, but it also has its dangers.*

A. W. B. Simpson.

---

* I am indebted to Professor G. V. V. Nicholls of the Dalhousie Law School for reading this article in typescript and making various suggestions for its improvement.

FALLACIES OF THE LOGICAL FORM IN ENGLISH LAW
A Study of *Stare Decisis* in Legal Flux
By *Julius Stone* *

PART I

Can the Common Law Theory of Precedent be Reconciled with the English Judicial Achievement?

It scarcely requires demonstration that the assumption of the necessary pre-existence of 'legal propositions,' that is, of given premises, from which the particular decision is to be derived, is still common in English legal thought, though these entities go under the name of 'the principles of law.' The idea is also not uncommon that further propositions can properly be arrived at on the basis of deductions from these first propositions. Language to both these effects teems in the reports and in the books. Yet there is much language to the contrary as well. 'We have in England a deep distrust of logical reasoning; and it is for the most part well-founded. Fortunately our judge-made law has seldom deviated into that path; but on some of the rare occasions when it has done so the results have been disastrous.'[1] This statement perhaps underrates the extent to which 'logical' (in the sense obviously intended of syllogistic deduction from existing legal propositions) is sought by our courts. Lord Wright has recently pointed out[2] that the use of 'fundamental rules of law' by later generations of judges as the basis of logical development is an important part of the common law judicial process; and this surely accords with the general view. But in its main assertion Judge Konstam's assertion cannot, with respect, be disputed. Many such highly authoritative admissions will be found in the English literature.[3]

What seems lacking is the will of lawyers to address themselves to the difficulties consequential on such admissions, so well posed in recent years by Lord Wright.[4] 'I have often wondered,' he has asked, 'how this perpetual process of change can be reconciled with the principle of authority and the rule of *stare decisis.*'[5] A similar penetrating observation had been made long before by another scholar as critical of logicism as Lord Wright himself. Eugen Ehrlich expressed the view in 1913 that the English system of precedent is a supreme example of the 'free finding of law' by the judges. Professor Ehrlich concluded that English judges had to a remarkable degree used this power to endow with the force of 'legal propositions' the actual rules of behavior which from time to time sprang from the inner ordering of English social groupings.[6]

No doubt, in some degree, Professor Ehrlich writing as he was, at a distance and in general terms, overlooked the many examples of judicial con-

* Substantially the same material is covered by chapter vii of Professor Stone's forthcoming book, *The Province and Function of Law,* to be published by Associated General Publications, LTD., Sydney, Australia.

duct which showed no consciousness of its creative function. But when this and other [7] allowances have been made, the main point which he shares with Lord Wright remains. It is the case, whatever the form behind which it has been concealed, that the work of English courts from the medieval period onwards represents a great achievement in legislation by reference to the changing facts of social life as seen in the actual behavior of associations of men for the time being.[8] And it is also the case that this was achieved and continues to be achieved not because of, but rather in spite of, the apparent reliance on legal conceptions and propositions and on pure deductions from them. The real grounds of this judicial activity have been the stuff on which all legislation proceeds. In Holmes' still apt words:[9]

> The actual life of the law has not been logic; it has been experience. The felt necessities of the time, the prevalent moral and political theories, intuitions of public policy, avowed or unconscious, even the prejudices which judges share with their fellow-men, have had a good deal more to do than the syllogism in determining the rules by which law shall be governed.

And what Holmes in 1881 asserted for the past, a learned Lord Justice has also recently asserted for our own age, claiming that the organic growth of the common law has continued 'in the last 100 years at an ever-increasing rate of progress, as new cases, arising under new conditions of society, of applied science, and of public opinion, have presented themselves for solution by the Courts.'[10]

This state of affairs raises a question of capital importance. What are the features of the English system of precedent which can give an appearance of stability and continuity and, nevertheless, permit constant change to take place, new propositions to be established, old ones discarded in whole or in part, and permit all this to proceed seemingly on the basis of logical deduction from pre-existing premises? Not the least reason for this capital importance is this. If it be the case, as is here submitted, that the determinative factors lie in experience of the actual world and the search for justice or 'convenience' in new situations,[11] it would follow that adequate attention to these matters in juristic discussion and judicial decision would become an urgent practical necessity. This urgency would be increased by the fact that in legal education little or no attention is given to them;[12] and, as will appear in the following pages, the amount of conscious judicial attention seems limited.

1. How Far Is This Achievement Based on Logical Deduction from Existing Principles of Law?

If the modern view of the limitations of merely deductive techniques be sound, we are immediately challenged to reconcile it with this undoubted English judicial record of sound adaptation of law to social change. That, too, is the conundrum propounded by Lord Wright. 'One cannot,' said Professor Ehrlich, speaking of the comparable problem for the continent, 'solve a difficulty of this nature by closing one's eyes to it.'[13] Nor is it sufficient to point out that the logic on which decisions claim to be based is often far less impressive than the concrete decision in relation to the situation before the court.[14]

Lord Wright thought that the answer to this question was to be looked for in the 'logical process implicit in judicial reasoning when it deals with the law of the case,' as modified by the special 'empirical methods of the common law and its reliance on a mass of authoritative decisions,' and by 'temperament and social predispositions.'[15] He commended a clarification of this process to 'some ingenious and learned writer.' This may be taken as a high warrant of the importance of this inquiry.[16]

The dualism is, without doubt, a deep reality. Most British judges and lawyers all the time, and all of them some of the time, do regard judicial decisions as either direct applications of existing law, or logical deductions from some existing principle. When, with his wonted spirit the late Mc-Cardie J. ventured to observe[17] that the object of the common law was to solve difficulties and adjust relations in social and commercial life, grow with the development of the nation, and deal with changing and novel circumstances, and added that an expanding society demands an expanding common law, this ground of decision was not received with acclaim or even tolerance. It was indeed strongly disapproved in the Court of Appeal.[18] While the utterances of a Lord Wright cannot so lightly be repudiated by colleagues, it must be admitted, with respect, that even Lord Wright's decisions seem sometimes to proceed on the orthodox assumptions.[19]

Even where it is recognized that there is some field for decision left free of logical compulsions, this field tends to be regarded as somewhat anomalous and still capable of occupation by judicial 'development' of existing principles. And this is confirmed by the fact, well known to counsel, that even in cases of first impression they are likely in most courts to fare better with holdings *sub silentio,* tenuous *dicta,* verbal analogies, and syllogistic deductions, than with a straightforward argument based on the social facts to be regulated and the policies applicable thereto.[20] Yet, if logic does not compel, on what else can sound decision be based?

In support of these inconsistencies it is often argued that certainty of result is as important as justice of result, or better, that certainty is an important element of justice.[21] 'It would,' it is said, 'be unendurable for a man to have to rely on his own moral judgment in order to know what view a court would take of his actions.'[22] The assumption, it will be observed, is that the growth of the common law in the past has not required such endurance—an assumption in itself presupposing independence of variable moral judgment, but dictated by the logical eking out of existing legal principles.

2. Uncertainty of Operation of Syllogistic Logic in the Judicial Process

Lawyers readily admit today that cases do *occasionally* arise requiring a judicial choice free of logical compulsions, either because a substantial part of the facts are of first impression or because there is square conflict of pre-existing authority. We are not here concerned with this narrower field, but rather with the much wider one in which decisions and commentation on them still take the form of logical derivation and logical testing. It is, it is believed, in this wider field that our system of precedent determines whether the common law shall or shall not grow into adequacy for contemporary problems. And in this wider field the question is: How is it possible for courts by supposedly necessary logical deduction from non-contemporaneous premises and apparently without entering upon social and ethical inquiries to reach conclusions well adapted to contemporary problems? It is assumed in the following discussion that the judicial achievement in this regard justifies the common estimate.[23]

The answer has repeatedly been made, especially since Holmes, that on the one hand the 'logical form' is often 'fallacious'; and on the other, the exclusion of considerations of social needs, social policies, and personal evaluation by the court is correspondingly illusory. And Lord Wright has recently said that 'judging is an act of will' and that 'notwithstanding all the apparatus of authority, the judge has nearly always some degree of choice.'[24] It is believed that this answer is substantially correct.[25] To leave the answer in this form is, however, to invite for this truth the same theoretical agreement and practical neglect that men habitually devote to great moral truths abstractly formulated. It is proposed, therefore, in this study to seek to separate in recent English case-law some of the more important 'fallacies of the logical form'; and to show how they serve as devices permitting a secret and even unconscious exercise by courts of what, in the ultimate analysis, is a creative choice. In other words, it is proposed to show that the logical forms identified, since they do not yield any one necessary answer in logic, both invite and compel the court to an answer based on the evaluation of the social situation confronting it.

The kind of logical deduction and demonstration which is in question in the judicial process, and in these pages, means that granted a certain major premiss a certain conclusion follows with regard to the facts at bar (the minor). For the purpose of this discussion we shall refer to a major premiss for judicial reasoning; that is, a supposed distinction, rule, principle, standard, or conception, from which a rule for the present case is to be derived, as a 'legal category.'

3. The Legal Category of Meaningless Reference

If the supposed principle by reference to which a case is decided has no possible meaning, then even though the court purports to derive its decision logically therefrom, it must be obvious that the real determinant of the decision must lie elsewhere. Such instances are not rare in the reports. Thus, a doctrinal basis of the rules in regard to the burden of proof is a supposed distinction between, on the one hand, a rule defined so as to exclude a given situation, and on the other, a rule defined without reference to that situation.[26] It is the distinction between a rule containing its qualification within itself and a rule the qualification upon which proceeds from a proposition outside the rule. Which party has the burden of proof of Fact A depends upon whether Fact A is included among the facts defining the scope of the general rule, or is merely contained in an exception to that rule. How are we to determine whether a particular fact which will defeat the opponent's claim is to be regarded as a fact defining the limits of the rule of law on which he relies, or whether it is to be regarded as merely setting in operation an exception to this rule?

The difficulties in which this distinction has caused the courts to labor suggest that a preliminary consultation with the logicians may be appropriate. What is the difference in logic between a quality of a class as contained in the definition of the class and a quality of a class as contained in an exception to the class? The answer appears to be—none at all.[27] Every qualification of a class can equally be stated without any change of meaning as an exception to a class not so qualified. Thus, the proposition 'all animals have four legs except gorillas' and the proposition 'all animals which are not gorillas have four legs,' are, so far as their meanings are concerned, identical.[28]

If the distinction between an element of the rule and an exception to it does not represent any distinction in meaning, it may still remain a valid distinction for legal purposes. In that case, however, it must turn upon something other than the meaning of the propositions involved. It may turn, for instance, merely upon their relative form or order. It may resolve itself into this—does the qualification *happen* to be stated in the body of the rule? Or does it *happen* to be stated as a separate exception? [29]

This seems, in fact, to have been the distinction in the rule that when the statutory definition of a crime includes a ground of excuse within itself in the same section, then the burden is on the Crown to negative the excuse; *aliter* if it be contained in a separate section. As would be expected, the results of such a criterion, dependent as it often might be on accidents of draftsmanship, by no means assured a just or a convenient result. It was, indeed, departed from both at common law and by statute.[30] In other fields the fallacious belief in a logical distinction still remains, having in particular cases a strong flavor of the magical, of a grin without a cat.[31]

That illusion of a logical distinction, based only on the order in which words are used, can, however, only be maintained if the rules of law to which it is to be applied are embodied in an authoritative form of words. This is so in the case of an offense defined by statute, or a liability defined by statute or contract, or, more doubtfully, in a statutory derogation from a common-law liability, and a common-law derogation from an expressed contractual liability.[32] The graver difficulties have arisen where both the rule and the exception, being common-law creations, are nowhere to be found in an authoritative form of words, and where, therefore, not even the formal distinction based on the order of the words constituting the rule and exception is of any use.[33] And where the substantive rule of law involved is comparatively new and its ramifications comparatively unexplored, the traditional divining rod must prove to be utterly and patently impotent.[34]

The Constantine Case [35] was just such a case. There the question arose on a plea of frustration whether the burden of showing that his fault *had not* induced the frustration, rested on the defendant who pleaded frustration. Or, alternatively, whether it rested on the plaintiff resisting the plea of frustration to show that the defendant's fault *had* induced the frustration.[36]

Atkinson J. in the lower court held that the burden was on the plaintiff denying frustration.[37] He relied on the analogy of exceptions to the shipowners' immunity in charter parties,[38] of exceptions to liability for negligence at common law,[39] and of the statutory exception under the Merchant Shipping Act, 1894, s.502.135. But these analogies cannot serve until it is first decided that absence of self-inducement is an exception to the plea of frustration rather than a part of the requirements of that plea; and since this distinction as a legal category is itself meaningless, no *necessary* conclusion can be based on it. The Court of Appeal, holding that absence of fault was part of the requirements for the plea of frustration, reversed the decision of Atkinson J. The defendant appealed to the House of Lords, which in turn reversed the decision of the Court of Appeal.

It was stressed by all the Lords that the question 'has not as yet . . . been the subject of a direct decision,' [40] and indeed that there was not 'a single case in which the question of onus appears to have been distinctly raised.' [41] Yet as I have shown,[42] the House purported to reach its decision by deduction from this same meaningless category. Indeed, Lord Wright even implied that while the Court of Appeal's decision changed the law, the reversal by the House of Lords merely applied existing law.[43]

It is believed, though the basic research is still required to be done, that other difficult branches of the law also center around meaningless categories.[44] In all such cases the present submission is not that the court's decision is meaningless or even unsound. I have shown, indeed, that the view arrived at by the Lords in the Constantine Case would probably have been arrived at if all attention had been concentrated on the social facts and the interest involved. The present submission is that if the legal category is meaningless from which the courts purport to deduce their decision, the decision must be attributed in practice, if not in so many words, to some other mental process than that within which the orthodox English view would seek to restrain judicial decision.

4. The Legal Category of Concealed Multiple Reference

Where the category is meaningless, the legislative act proceeds, well or ill, while the verbal formulation bemuses all concerned. Similar in effect but for a different reason is the category of concealed multiple reference where the verbal entity, V, for which a rule is prescribed may refer to any of several sets of facts, that is, real entities, E_1, E_2, and E_3, are such as in effect to give opposite results in the particular case according to whether V is taken to mean E_1 or E_2 or E_3. In that case since the legal category as it stands will logically justify opposite conclusions on the same facts the court's decision in favor of one or the other must be determined other than by mere deduction from the category.

When Lord Tomlin declared [45] of the *res gesta* doctrine that 'it has never so far as I am aware, been explained in a satisfactory manner,' he was directing attention to what must surely come to be recognized as the classic example of a category of concealed multiple reference. The present writer has pointed out [46] that it was the insistent attempt to draw from a single conception rules for a great variety of types of situations which had made the law as to *res gesta* what it is; namely, the lurking place of a motley crowd of distinct conceptions operating in the cases in mutual conflict and reciprocating chaos. The books, I there showed, were filled with the most self-contradictory propositions concerning a single category of evidence termed 'the *res gesta*.' They solemnly told us that declarations, to be part of the *res gesta*, must be contemporaneous with the act they explain; [47] and at the same time that they need not be contemporaneous,[48] each seeking to force all the conceptions constituting *res gesta* under one rule or the other. The less conscientious eclectics [49] cheerfully treated of complaints made after an act to illustrate the necessity for contemporaneity. So also, one was told that declarations to be part of the *res gesta* must be made by the person doing the act, and yet that they need not be, since a bystander's exclamations may be 'relevant and admissible.' [50] So also, one was told that the act which the declaration accompanies must itself be in issue and relevant, and that the declaration must be a part of it: and yet that an entire stranger's utterance may be admitted under the *res gesta* doctrine.[51] Finally, but without purporting to exhaust the examples, it was frequently said that declarations under the *res gesta* doctrine were not admitted as hearsay to prove what they assert but as original evidence to explain the act they accompany, and, yet, that declarations of mental or physical condition were admitted to prove what they assert under the *res gesta* doctrine.[52]

It was there sought, following the pioneering work of Dean Wigmore, to identify the plurality of conceptions in play and attribute to each rules which might be appropriate. It was possible to show that so-called *res gesta* evidence fell, on analysis, into at least seven distinct categories each with its own rules. First, the facts in issue; second, facts relevant to the facts in issue; third, declarations not in themselves in issue or relevant, but constituting a verbal part of either a fact in issue or a relevant fact; fourth, facts of all kinds, which, though not facts as issue or relevant, are so inextricably bound up with either that effective proof of the one cannot be made without proof of the other; and fifth, sixth, and seventh, statements admitted as hearsay under what constitute in effect three exceptions to the hearsay rule.

So long, however, as the courts and writers failed to recognize that the *res gesta* doctrine (V) covers not only factual situation E_1, but also situations E_2 to E_7, they were able in effect to reach pseudo-logically a wide variety of conclusions on any single set of facts by treating any of the inconsistent *res gesta* rules as applicable to any of the varied *res gesta* situations. Since many solutions can equally be reached by this logical mode it must be apparent extra-logical factors determine the issue in a particular case.

The examples of such multiple reference in legal categories are legion. The court in *Phillips* v. *Eyre*[53] laid down that for an action on a foreign tort to be in England it must *inter alia* be 'not . . . justifiable' by the *lex loci commissi*. Since that time the courts and the writers have been preoccupied with the effort to reconcile views which respectively treated this verbal entity (V) of 'justifiability' in the category as referring to no-civil-actionability (E_1),[54] no-common law-actionability (E_2),[55] no-civil-and-no-criminal-actionability (E_3).[56] In many situations opposite conclusions will be available as a matter of logic by the application of this apparently single category of 'justifiability' precisely by choosing one or the other of its concealed alternatives. The choice between alternative major premisses as has been sufficiently stressed cannot be a logical process. Willy-nilly it confronts the court with a problem of evaluation until the category is split into its alternatives.[57]

5. *Legal Categories of Competing References*

The simplest and the most spectacular type of 'fallacy of the logical form' is where two or more legal categories or their respective logical consequents, each prescribing different rules, overlap on their application to a particular situation.

In *Haseldine* v. *Daw*,[58] if the controller of a lift was assimilated to an occupier of realty one result followed; if to a common carrier another. The categories of occupier and common carrier competed for governance of the novel relation of business visitor and lift controller. In the *Springboard Case*[59] the property-law category of fixtures, and the category of a public river competed to decide the status of the deceased as he stood on the springboard, a few feet above the river. In *Southern Foundries* (1926) *Ltd.* v. *Shirlaw*[60] the categories of corporate powers and of contractual obligations competed to decide whether a director having an employment contract with Company A, could enforce his contract against Company B to whom as between Companies A and B all the rights and obligations of Company A had been validly transferred. The categories of 'substance' and 'procedure' compete to control a vast variety of matters, producing a confusion, in at least one field[61] which led the Law Revision Committee to refrain *sine die* from proposing reforms on the singular ground that 'it is a problem of considerable difficulty.'[62] The categories of 'illegality,' 'incapacity,' 'formalities'[63] have been in fierce competitions for generations to control the validity of voidity of many marriages. The comparatively late Anglo-American discovery of the problem of 'classification' in the conflict of laws, is, in the writer's suspicion, but a prelude to the even more belated discovery of the competition of categories; that is, of premisses for reasoning throughout our municipal law.

In the simple form of competition of two or more categories, both abstractions from a solution of an earlier actual problem, both fit, but neither exactly, a problem different from the earlier one. If both categories yield the same result we have the phenomenon, which need not be considered in the text, of converging categories.[64] If they yield different results they must compete *inter se*.[65] The choice between them, and, therefore, the result reached, is innovatory.

It has well been pointed out that at a certain point when the courts declined to enforce contracts for the benefit of third parties they rejected the competing category of trust and fastened on that of contract.[66] Willy-nilly, the courts, not the syllogism, are responsible for that act. In a late cognate case, the House of Lords and the Court of Appeal, as if to stress the point, chose the former, the trust category, and the latter, the contract category.[67] But perhaps the most interesting modern example is the latent competition, which has continued for more than a generation, between the principle of frustration that the loss must lie where it falls,[68] and the quasi-contractual principle that money paid may be recovered on a total failure of consideration. The authorities on the two categories proceeded side by side until the House of Lords in the *Fibrosa Case*[69] chose the quasi-contractual category and extended it into the field formerly occupied by the 'loss lies where it falls' category.[70]

6. The Single Legal Category with Competing Versions of Reference

Closely similar in legislative effect is the judicial choice between competing versions of a single category. The writer, in another place,[71] has traced the cause of the confused and fluid state of the rule of exclusion of similar fact evidence to an interplay of competing versions of that rule. Again Professor A. D. McNair was able in 1940[72] to draw out of the cases no less than three versions of the scope of the category of frustration of contract, all of them sanctified by authority. For many cases, no doubt the variations were immaterial.[73] But in circumstances falling within one version and not within others, the court would have to choose, and its choice would be necessarily a creative one. The point is well seen in *Perrin* v. *Morgan*[74] where the House of Lords gave what is hoped may have been a *coup de grâce* to the supposed rule of construction under which the term 'money' in a will has long been given a restricted 'legal' meaning, despite the apparent contrary intention of testators. The majority condemned the supposed rule of construction as 'a blot on our jurisprudence.' Their decision was as clearly a creative act as a statutory repeal would have been. A minority, however, Lords Russell and Romer, both primarily equity lawyers, reached the same result by preserving the old rule of construction and redefining its scope.[75] Choice between competing versions of a single category is equally innovatory with a choice between two competing categories.[76]

7. Competing Versions of a Single Category as a Normal Product of the British Judicial Process

It is important at this point to observe that competing versions of even the most everyday legal categories, far from being unusual, are constantly produced by our entire system of precedent. The large discretion left to a single judge for discussion of his reasons, and for *obiter dicta,* the separate opinions habitually given by the members of appellate courts and of the House of Lords, whether concurring or dissenting, are all productive of numerous versions of the legal category under examination. Even where all the decisions concur for the instant facts, the differing versions are liable to be brought into bitter competition by the slightly different state of facts of a future case. It is essentially from this feature of House of Lords decisions that there derives its wide freedom of action, despite the rule that it is bound by its prior decisions. For, since no sanctity attaches to one set of concurring reasons as against another, one may be preferred to another or even used merely to neutralize it, leaving the field clear.[77] This technique of distinguishing is often regarded as in the nature of an evasion of the system of precedent.[78] It is respectfully submitted that, on the contrary, it affords a deep insight into its essential nature. 'Competing versions' of a legal category are a normal feature of the authoritative materials: wherever they exist, a set of facts will sooner or later arise which stands between the competing versions, and can only be dealt with by a fresh creative decision. The system of separate speeches merely sets this aspect into relief.[79] And it is no less prominent in the Court of Appeal's persistent failure to bring itself finally into line with the text writer's assertions that it is bound by its own decisions.[80] The uncertainty which enshrouded the degree of binding force of decisions of the Court of Appeal and the House of Lords in Dominion Courts is a similar excellent medium for competing categories and competing versions of single categories.[81]

8. The Legal Category of Concealed Circuitous Reference: 'Duty' in Negligence and Remoteness of Damage

Even where the legal category in use has meaning, is single in character, and is unchallenged by competing categories, it may still be incapable of yielding any result in a particular case by mere logical deduction from it. In particular, we find that an essential role is played by categories of concealed circuitous reference and by categories of indeterminate reference. The line between these is by no means always clear, and different views may be held as to some of the categories hereafter classed as one or the other without affecting the present thesis. As here used both these types of categories are indeterminate in the sense that they cannot in themselves yield any definite result in a concrete case; but the 'circuitous' category conceals this indeterminacy by the addition of a question-begging form of words.

The requirement that the defendant shall have been under a duty towards the plaintiff to take care as a prerequisite of liability towards him in respect of negligence [82] constitutes, it is submitted, an outstanding example of the circuitous reference which Lord Wright aptly terms a mere 'proceeding of *idem per idem.*' [83] The nearest approach of the courts to a clear formulation of the criterion for deciding whether such a duty exists is perhaps that of Lord Atkin in *Donoghue* v. *Stevenson.*[84] He said that we owed a duty to persons in the position of 'neighbour' to us with regard to the subject matter, and that all those were 'neighbours who are so closely and directly affected by my act that I ought reasonably to have them in contemplation as being so affected when I am directing my mind to the acts or omissions which are called into question.' [85] A duty towards the plaintiff then means that the defendant ought reasonably to have him in contemplation as likely to be affected by the conduct in question, in short, the defendant ought reasonably to have anticipated injury to him. But is not that in any case one essential element of what is meant by the requirement of 'negligence' itself? It remains necessary even today to repeat the almost fifty-year-old comment of the late Mr. Justice Holmes that the prerequirement of duty in the given sense is an empty form of words, tautologous with the definition of negligence itself.[86]

If the 'duty' requirement is merely tautologous with the 'negligence' requirement, and if courts do nevertheless still purport to relieve some defendants of the consequences of 'negligence' by holding that there is no duty,[87] it must be obvious again that there is some determinant of the actual decision other than can be drawn by deductive logic from the category ostensibly used.[88]

One other example of the circuitous reference may be mentioned in the text. The doubts and disputations which have preceded and followed *Re Polemis* [89] as to the limit of a man's responsibility for the consequences of his wrongful act are well known. The version of the 'natural and probable' test, which before that case limited responsibility to what was reasonably foreseeable, was not (in one version of its meaning, at least) merely circuitous. The test of 'directness,' according to the common version of *Re Polemis,* was also not circuitous, for, as Lord Wright has pointed out,[90] it invites attention to everything which followed from the operation of the act of negligence immediately upon the plaintiff's property or person. Both these tests, however, are indeterminate (see above) and consequently divergences of opinion on a concrete situation, as well as variations of application to different situations, are to be expected.

Re Polemis involved physical damage to a physical object flowing from physical impact with it. It suggested in such a case that *all* consequences were 'immediate' or 'direct.' The *Liesbosch Case* [91] involved economic damage flowing from physical impact with the physical object. The House of Lords cut off the plaintiff's claim at the point where loss followed onto the plaintiff's 'delicate financial position,' [92] which prevented his fulfillment of a profitable contract by purchase in another dredge. Lord Wright comments on this that it is impossible by any 'logical' reason to demonstrate this limi-

tation, or to distinguish this financially delicate condition from the physi-
cally-delicate condition of an injured plaintiff, which would not cut off the
claim.[93] The writer, respectfully agreeing, would point out that this follows also from the *indeterminacy* of the category of directness: it is not
'logic,' but 'practical reasons'[94]—assessment of the social facts and what justice requires—which determine the result.

When, however, Lord Wright seeks to clarify the matter and to bring
such diverse holdings under a single head by defining liability by reference
to those consequences of which the wrongful act was 'a legal cause'[95] or to
those which are not 'too remote,'[96] it is submitted that he is merely creating
a further circuitous category which, as he says elsewhere of the 'implied contract,' in quasi-contract may be 'innocuous,' but is certainly 'unnecessary' and
possibly 'misleading.'[97] Above all, it should not conceal the important point
made by Andrews J. in the very American case he cites[98] that such terms
tend to conceal the process of evaluation which is at the heart of the inquiry.

9. *Circuitous Reference: Quasi-Contract*

It was Holmes again who drew attention to another outstanding modern
example of the category of circuitous reference. As to 'implied conditions'
in the law of contract, Holmes tersely commented in 1897: 'You can always
imply a condition in a contract. But why do you imply it?'[99] At almost
every main point in modern English law where the courts have resorted to
the device of an 'implied term' or 'implied contract' to the problems before
them, doubt hovers like a mist among the restless tossings of judicial and
juristic disagreements. Outstanding is, of course, the law of quasi-contract.
It is perhaps not an over-simplification to suggest that the 'implied contract'
fiction was first indulged, as so many fictions in our law have been, to
obtain the advantage of a form of procedure, the *indebitatus assumpsit*.[100]
Recovery was not allowed because the court implied a contract, much less
because the court believed there had actually been a contract; it was rather
that the court *pretended* there was a contract because it was thought there
ought to be a recovery. In short, it was not the category of implied contract
which determined the view of the court. Another way of saying this is that
that legal category was of circuitous reference: it threw the court back on
the question, ought there to be recovery? When, in *Sinclair* v. *Brougham*,[101]
several Lords suggested that recovery would not lie at law against a building society in respect of unjust enrichment, where the money was not traceable and where the contract to be implied would, if actually made, have
been *ultra vires* of the Society, this circuitousness was to that extent broken.
To the extent that it was broken, decisions could be deduced logically from
the category; but by general agreement such deductions would be less just
by reason of this deduction.[102] A learned writer[103] has detected three conflicting points of view among contemporary English judges on this 'implied contract': first, that the implied term is the test of recovery, natural
justice being irrelevant;[104] second, a middle view, that though a contract

must be capable of being implied, natural justice determines whether it will be;[105] third, the view that the implied contract is otiose, the true and only basis of decision being whether it is unjust and unreasonable for the defendant to retain the benefit he had acquired.[106]

We are not here concerned to discuss which of the proferred rules constitute the law of England.[107] We are concerned rather to show their respective relations to the use and abuse of logic in the judicial process. On the first view, that recovery proceeds exclusively from the implied contract, Holmes' observation is decisive. You can always imply a contract but 'why do you imply it?' The implied contract must be a mode of stating the result, not a mode of reaching it. It is a category of circuitous reference concealing the legislative choice which decides the case. As to the middle view, the category is similarly circuitous but its circuity is no longer concealed. Decision still lies outside the category and its logic.[108] In the third view, that of Lord Wright, it will be observed that the 'implied contract' category has entirely disappeared. The judging process goes direct from the creative evaluation of the fact situation to the decision. The evaluation which was present in the first two rules, but there more or less concealed, is consciously made and exposed for examination.

The English law of frustration[109] represents a largely analogous field of logical doubt, and therefore of judicial creativeness, gravitating around the proposed use of an implied term in circumstances where its reference is mainly circuitous. Here again, Lord Wright's view[110] exposes the real nature of the judicial activity involved and the mainly circuitous nature of the implied term.

10. *The Legal Category of Indeterminate Reference*

The 'legal standard' as opposed to the 'legal rule' is the typical category of indeterminate reference.[111] Its requirement that the courts shall evaluate the concrete situation rather than apply a formula mechanically is so well recognized today[112] as to require only brief discussion. When courts are required to apply[113] such standards as fairness, reasonableness and not arbitrariness, conscionableness, clean hands, *just* cause or excuse, due care or adequacy, judgment cannot turn on logical formulations and deductions, but must include a decision as to what justice requires in the context of the instant case. This is recognized, indeed, in regard to such standards as 'reasonableness,' which has been aptly defined as 'a convenient summary of the dominant considerations which control in the application of legal doctrines'[114] and 'the legal counterpart to the philosophical conception of justice.'[115] But it has been pointed out that the same observation may well apply to standards which, on their face, are not evaluative; such as 'proximate' or 'remote' as a test of liability for consequences of an act.[116] To say that damage is too remote may be in the last resort but to say that on the court's evaluation of the concrete situation there ought to be no recovery. It is possible that some of the difficulties arising from the test of 'directness' proposed in

Re Polemis[117] arise precisely from the fact that, in so far as that is not a mere synonym for 'not too remote' and therefore merely circuitous, its operation by deductive logic would produce such a wide range of responsibility for unlawful acts as revolts the judicial sense of justice, as well as the common sense of men generally.[118]

11. *The System of Precedent Itself as Based on a Legal Category of Indeterminate Reference, Namely, the Ratio Decidendi of a Case*

The illusory nature of many supposed compulsions of logical consistency in the judicial process has also been stated in terms of logical theory itself.[119] The orthodox English theory of precedent as formulated, for instance, by Professor Goodhart imports that the particular decision is explained by a *ratio decidendi,* or a general proposition of which the particular decision is an application,[120] and which is 'required' or 'necessary' to explain that particular decision. Moreover this general proposition is to be drawn from the particular decision itself.[121]

In the logician's sense, however, it is possible to draw as many general propositions from a given decision as there are possible combinations of distinguishable facts in it. By looking at the facts it is impossible *logically* to say which are to be taken as the basis for the *ratio decidendi.* If there are ten facts, 1, 2, 3, etc., to 10, as many general propositions will explain the decisions as there are possible combinations of those facts. The question, What principle does a particular case establish? is, it has been said, 'strictly nonsensical; that is, inherently incapable of being answered.'[122]

Donoghue v. *Stevenson,* standing alone, could yield logically a range of propositions (quite apart from the diverse reasoning of the speeches) concerned with at least any or any combination of the following facts:

(1) *The Presence of* dead snails, or any snails, or any unpleasant foreign body, or any foreign body, or any unexpected quality,

(2) *in* opaque bottles of beverage, or in any bottles of beverage, or in any chattels for human consumption, or in any chattels for human use, or in any objects whatsoever (including land or buildings)

(3) *caused by the negligence of the defendant* who is a manufacturer whose goods are distributed to a wide and dispersed public by retailers, or of any manufacturer, or of any person working on the object for reward, or of any person working on the object, or of anyone dealing with the object,

(4) *provided* the object may reasonably be expected to be rendered dangerous by such negligence, *or* whether or not this is so,

(5) *if* it results in physical injury to the plaintiff, *or* nervous *or* physical injury to the plaintiff, *or* any injury whatsoever to the plaintiff,

(6) *the plaintiff being* (a) a Scots widow, or a Scotswoman, *or* a woman, *or* any adult or any human being, *or* any legal person (b) who is a purchaser for value from a retailer who bought directly from the defendant, *or* a purchaser for value from such, *or* a purchaser for value from anyone, *or* a person related to such purchaser, *or* any person into whose hands the object rightfully comes, *or* into whose hands it comes at all,

(7) *provided that* no intermediate party (a) could physically inspect and discover the defect without destroying the saleability of the commodity, *or* (b) had any duty to inspect and discover the defect, or (c) could reasonably be expected by the defendant to inspect and discover the defect, *or* (d) could reasonably be expected by the court or a jury to do so, is

(8) *and provided that* the facts complained of occurred in 1932 *or* any time before 1932, or after 1932, or at any time

(9) will render the Defendant liable to the Plaintiff in damages.

Most of these alternatives and any combination of them were, logically speaking, possible elements in any principle framed on the facts and speeches of *Donoghue* v. *Stevenson* alone.[123] Moreover, even should a subsequent case have arisen identical in all other particulars it would still be logically not *necessarily* within its principle since one of the facts would *ex hypothesi* be different, namely, the time of the occurrence. And if the reader be tempted to say illogically that the time factor, at any rate, is immaterial, he will be guilty of a *petitio principis;* for let him ask himself whether he really thinks that *Donoghue* v. *Stevenson* would have been so decided in 1800.[124] It follows that logically there was no *logical* compulsion on courts subsequently to *Donoghue* v. *Stevenson* to impose liability under it in any case where only some of the above possible material facts were found in combination.[125]

'Nothing,' an orthodox English writer has said,[126] 'can make the process of "binding" merely automatic and mechanical, for the judge has first to decide, according to his lights, whether the illustration is really opposite to the principle he is seeking. The humblest judicial officer can disregard the most authoritative declaration of the House of Lords unless he considers that the precedent cited is "on all fours." ' While this learned English writer follows a different course of demonstration, and though he refrains from drawing all the conclusions, his direction at least is similar to that of some American writers whose work he has unkindly described as 'jazz jurisprudence.'[127] He points out that 'all precedents, all arguments and all principles, must subserve' the doing of 'justice between litigants,' and that if justice is not attainable through precedents, judges in the last resort must turn to 'the principles of reason, morality and utility,'[128] to the 'general ethical principles'[129] with which 'express decisions' seldom conflict.

PART II

RELATION OF LOGICAL INDETERMINACY TO JUDICIAL CREATION OF LAW

All this is not to say that courts do not follow precedents, derive *rationes decidendi* from cases and decide subsequent cases in accordance with such *rationes*. They do so by saying that some of the facts in the prior case are 'material' or 'important' and that others are 'immaterial' or 'unimportant.' This discrimination is not a logical one but is ethical (in the broad sense of a creative evaluation as opposed to a mechanical application); and courts which purport to make it on logical grounds are not, by that, escaping responsibility for the result, or the liability to have their judgment submitted to ethical criticism. They cannot correctly plead that the law left them no choice. Each choice made by the court in the process of trial and error, by which a common law rule is defined, is an ethical choice, declaring, in effect, that some of the facts of prior cases were ethically material and others were ethically immaterial. In so far as these successive choices are made in the consciousness of their nature, the principle of *stare decisis* may be ethically justified as conducing to certainty and economy. But when a 'rule of law,' so defined by precedent, will be subject in its further extension to continual review, not merely in the light of the logical analogies and differences of facts and concepts involved in the new case, but in the light of the import of these analogies and differences, in terms of what is it just for the case at bar?

If this logical indeterminacy of the *ratio* of any particular decision be recognized, the role of a course of decisions in giving predictability to the law becomes apparent. Such decisions, as has frequently been observed, plot some of the outer limits of possibilities left indeterminate by the leading case. They also give clues in regard to the judicial views of the social facts and of the values to be applied. But what is not frequently observed in British countries is that, though the element of indeterminacy is thus reduced, it is never eliminated. Ultimately, it is not by achievement of logical certainty that the system of precedent is to be justified, but by the insistence on regarding particular situations in the contexts for which experience in administering justice already exists in the form of precedents. The contexts rarely provide a ready-made answer in a novel case; indeed, they often provide conflicting answers. The contexts do usually ensure that what official experience there is relevant to such situations is examined; but they do not themselves logically compel any particular answer in a new case.[130]

1. *Spurious Nature of the Ideals of Logical Consistency of Legal Propositions as a Basis of Decision*

What the Romans called *elegantia,* what the common lawyer often protects when he appeals to 'the principles of the common law' and their logical consequences, and when he objects to statutes in derogation of the common law, is, therefore, not logical in the syllogistic sense. Analogical extension or the refusal to extend is not, as we have seen, an operation demanded by logic; logic in no way restricts the introduction of new premises for new subject matters; logic in no way requires that the premises applicable to different subject matter shall be identical or mutually consistent; nor that the whole legal system shall be deducible from one or a few main principles. Since there is no logical compulsion about these matters it is apparent that, even in the everyday view of the practitioner, courts exercise a wide freedom of choice regarding which way they shall go. Ideally in that sphere their theory of justice, whatever it be, should prevail. What this dictates in the infinite variety of emerging circumstances will not, except by chance, coincide with the tendencies to extend conceptual analogies, to restrict the introduction of new premises in new situations, to keep premises in different subject matters logically consistent; or to keep the body of legal rules in a form deducible from a few main principles. To the extent, then, that the latter tendencies dominate decisions to the exclusion of due consideration of the social facts,[131] and of the problem of values, which is an essential prerequisite to the creation of a rule for a new situation, the court is indulging a spurious substitute for its true judicial activity.

This spurious substitute for judgment [132] is the more dangerous, since the search for symmetry and consistency in a body of legal propositions, regardless of their correspondence or relevance to actual human relations, appears to have a curious fascination for the human mind.[133] 'Juristic science,' wrote Professor Ehrlich,

although it is basically different from mathematics,[134] has at all times had a strange power to charm mathematical minds. A juristic mathematician is not endeavouring by means of juristic science to satisfy the needs for which the latter really exists, but to secure the high intellectual enjoyment which analytical mathematics or the theory of numbers could afford in a less questionable manner.

Such a tendency was perhaps, with respect, apparent in Sir Frederick Pollock's reference to the law as 'a work of art,' [135] implying that law had its own autonomous standards of beauty and proportion and harmony. In the comparative legal and social stability in which Pollock wrote, such a conception may be innocuous, and may, indeed, have corresponded in some degree to what was demanded of law. But to remain bemused by it in a transition period like the present easily leads to neglect of the fuller ideal of the law as a just arbiter between men living amid the conflicts of a real society.[136] And what is so for an ideal of logical consistency of the whole body of propositions is so in lesser degree for any reliance on logical deduction from existing propositions as a sufficient basis of judgment.[137]

2. Precedent as a Practical Means of Marshaling Past Experience for Present Choice

It is not the intention of the present paper to suggest that all judicial decisions should be cast in the language of justice, public policy, values, and the like, and the traditional language of conceptions, categories, doctrines, principles, and rules abandoned. In most cases these serve well enough. Admitting the full reality of judicial legislation, it still remains the case, as Dicey long ago stressed, that often a change in the rule consecrated by precedent can only be changed by Act of Parliament. To invite courts to consider anew every question before them in the light of social facts would be to invite them to a monstrous waste of time and energy, and in an impossible cause at that.[138] Nor, indeed, is it the intention to invite courts to decide any question involving criteria of justice or values at all, in any situation other than those in which they already, and inevitably, do at present decide such questions. What is invited is, first, a recognition that nothing in the law compels the application of categories or conceptions beyond the limits of the contexts in which they have already been applied; and second, a readiness to review any past applications when experience suggests serious error.

Precedent has played and will continue to play a most important part in common-law judicial achievement. In the first place precedents present for the instant case a rapid if incomplete review of social contexts comparable to the present, and of a rule thought suitable for that context by other minds after careful inquiry. In the second place, precedents serve to indicate what kind of result will be reached if a particular premiss or category is chosen for application in the instant case, and permit comparison with the results if some other premiss or category is adopted, either drawn from other cases, or judicially invented. In *Haseldine* v. *Daw* the common-carrier cases gave the court a ready view of the results for the lift passenger if that analogy were followed, as well as of the context in which courts in the past had regarded such results as just for an injured plaintiff. The cases on occupiers of premises afforded another glimpse of other results deemed just in another context. But the court had still to make up its mind that it wished to reach one or other result, or some result quite different from either in the context that was actually before it in *Haseldine* v. *Daw*. 'A good judge is one who is the master, not the slave, of the cases.' [139]

At the point, indeed, when a precedent ceases to be used to illustrate a probably just result in other contexts for comparison with the present, and is taken as an ultimate formulation independent of their former context to be transposed as a premiss for deductions to the present context, precedent ceases to be a rational means towards judgment. It becomes a symbol, and a device which conceals rather than determines the process of judgment.[140] Precedents become rather pegs on which to hang judgment than an explanation of the process of reaching it. While this is not in itself an evil, it is likely to become one at the point when the peg chosen for hanging the present decision was manufactured in a different factual context and with a different purpose from the instant case. And, as has been seen, assessment whether contexts are sufficiently similar to justify use of the same peg for decision is essentially a process of evaluation.[141]

3. Scope for Judicial Creativeness in the Interpretation of Legislation

The frequently illusory character of the compulsive forces of precedent is also found in the interpretation of statutes by common law courts. We do not refer here to the influence of the courts' own outlook on life, fixed naturally by the education, training, experience and associations of judges, so frankly and moderately stated by Holmes and Cardozo in America, by Scrutton, L. J.[142] and others in England. This influence is of course considerable, as the history of judicial interpretation of statutes for the emancipation of trade unions, and of married women, to mention no others, seems to show.[143] We refer rather, as in the preceding paragraphs, to the contrast even in more technical fields between the logical forms and the creative substance which the form conceals.

The central illustration concerns, perhaps, certain traditional principles of interpretation of statutes. The first is that 'policy' of any kind may not be referred if the provision is clear and unambiguous in its ordinary sense. A second is that even when 'policy' may be referred it shall not be 'policy' as it emerges from a present inquiry into the relevant facts and a judicial evaluation on their bases, but 'the policy of the act' alone, to be inferred from the evil in the pre-existing state of the law which the statute, by its terms, seems intended to remedy. These principles imply that the line between 'clear and unambiguous' and 'unclear and ambiguous' words is itself clear.[144] Because this is not so, it is easy to show that in practice courts regularly have resort to policy outside these limits in statutory interpretation.

In the much-debated Liversidge Case [145] Regulation 18 (b) of the English Defence (General) Regulation, 1939, provided that:

If the Secretary of State has reasonable cause to believe any person to be of hostile origin or associations, or to have been recently concerned in acts prejudicial to the public safety or the defence of the realm or in the preparation or instigation of such acts, and that by reason thereof, it is necessary to exercise control over him, he may make an order against that person directing that he be detained.

The question before the House was whether the courts were entitled to know the cause of the Secretary of State's belief, and to determine its reasonableness. Were the words 'has reasonable cause to believe' ambiguous or not? Virtually the entire eighty pages of the report were devoted to this question. Lord Atkin took the strong view that 'the words in question have a plain and natural meaning, that that meaning has invariably been given them in many statements of the common law and many statutes, that there has been one invariable construction of them in the courts. . .' [146] On the other hand the majority (Viscount Maugham, Lords Macmillan, Wright, and Romer) regarded them as ambiguous, since they might equally mean either (1) that the Secretary of State must have reasonable cause, or be 'satisfied' that he has reasonable cause so to believe.[147] In the context and in the light of the policy of the Regulation they preferred the latter, and held, therefore, that the good faith of the Minister being admitted, the court could not inquire into the reasonableness of his belief.

Theoretically, the canons of construction forbade consideration of policy until the words were found doubtful or ambiguous. What is here interesting is that despite these canons, assessments of policy seemed to base both the minority and majority decisions *ab initio,* in determining the very question whether there was ambiguity.[148] Lord Atkin stressed the disastrous effects upon liberty if, in the many statutes in which a similar formula was used, judicial inquiry was barred. He viewed gravely judicial attitudes towards liberty 'more executive-minded than the executive,' [149] and stressed on this account the special obligation to give words their natural meaning. On the other hand, the majority's finding of 'ambiguity' was aided, patently, by solicitude for England's critical military situation.[150] Lord Macmillan went so far as to say that if the Regulation had been framed to mean 'if the Secretary has such cause of belief as a court of law would hold to be reasonable,' that would not have been an acceptable emergency measure since courts may differ as to what is an emergency.

Nor is this an isolated case of resort to 'policy' in order to decide whether policy may be resorted to. In *Nokes* v. *Doncaster Amalgamated Collieries*[151] the House of Lords had to consider whether a statutory provision empowering the court to transfer from one company to another, in the course of statutory amalgamation, all its 'property' and 'liabilities,' included a power to transfer the rights and obligations under contracts of service of employees. The same section defined 'property' to include 'property, rights, and powers of every description,' and 'liabilities' to include 'duties.' By the orthodox canon, then, until property and liabilities as thus defined were found unclear or ambiguous in their application to employment contracts, there was no room for resort to the policy of the act, much less to policy in general.

Yet the speeches addressed themselves with little ado to the policy that English servants should not be reduced to 'serfs,'[152] that a workman's free choice of his employer is 'fundamental' in the common law.[153] They thereupon found the meaning given by the six judges below to 'property' to be incorrect, since even the comprehensive statutory definition was, *in view of this fundamental principle,* ambiguous; since, if the Legislature really desired to contravene that principle, it could devise 'plainer words.'[154] Lord Atkin thought[155] that 'it has been the duty of the court on countless occasions to construe general words cutting down the generality to the obvious [*sic*] intention of the legislature'; while Lord Porter came to the same conclusion, protesting that he was not concerned with the intention of the legislation since 'primarily . . . the question is one of construction.'[156]

This paper is not concerned with the merits of such decisions, but only to point out that the processes involved, however valiant be the efforts to give them an appearance of logical validity or even compulsiveness,[157] are, in fact, the result of a choice by judges based more or less consciously on ideas of justice applied to the facts before them. What the House did in the *Nokes Case,* it has been aptly said,[158] was 'to interpret a technical section of the Companies Act in the light of an unwritten principle of our social constitution, much in the same spirit in which they would have declared the section unconstitutional, if there was a written constitution embodying the freedom of the contract of employment.'

4. *Effects of Lack of Conscious Attention to the Non-Syllogistic Elements in Judicial Reasoning*

Failure to attend consciously to the non-compulsive nature of judicial reasoning cannot free courts from the responsibility for what Lord Wright termed the 'act of will' involved in many, perhaps in most, appellate decisions. What it may and does do is to cause important factors for decision

319

to be ignored, and encourage those tendencies towards the less perplexing path which judges share with other men. This, perhaps, is the reason why, despite general recognition that logical deduction from existing premisses cannot conclusively decide cases, reliance on this device is still too often a cause of miscarriage of justice. Holmes warned in 1897[159] that judges themselves have failed adequately to recognize their inevitable creative responsibility, with the result that 'the very ground and foundation of judgment' was left 'inarticulate and often unconscious.' He thought that greater awareness would lead lawyers to hesitate often where now they are confident, and to realize that they were really taking sides upon debatable and even burning questions. In the English literature, it was no other than John Austin himself, who three generations before, defending judicial law-making from Bentham's attacks, anticipated Holmes' point:

Notwithstanding my great admiration for Mr. Bentham, I cannot but think that instead of blaming the judges for having legislated he should blame them for the narrow, timid and provincial manner in which they have legislated and for legislating under cover of vague and indeterminate phrases. . .

The essential nature of the abuse of logic thus involved has already been explored. It must suffice here to show briefly that this abuse is no more absent from common-law legal reasoning than from that of other systems.

A first main type of abuse is the making of logical deductions from existing legal propositions and assuming, without more, that these are law. The so-called problem of *Rose* v. *Ford*,[160] which has plagued the courts in recent years, springs, it is respectfully believed, from such a fallacy. In terms of deductive logic the reasoning may well be unexceptionable.[161] But the actuality is that expectation of life, while the deceased lives, represents an actual human interest of the deceased. After his death *his* interest ceases. Any interest which his dependents have in his death is quite distinct in fact, if not in logic, and is already provided for, more or less, by the Fatal Accidents Act.[162] Further, it can scarcely have been the intention of the legislator in 1934 to allow this speculative action for the benefit of the general creditors. The 1934 Act did not explicitly cover the matter and was open to be interpreted so as to exclude it;[163] and we have been authoritatively informed that the Law Revision Committee, pursuant to whose recommendations the 1934 Act was passed, did not intend to recommend that actions for pain and suffering and shortened expectation of life should survive.[164] It is, moreover, scarcely necessary to document the unhappiness and embarrassments of the judges in enforcing this survived action.[165] In short, by a supposedly compulsive deduction from existing propositions which did not compel it and which no one intended should compel it, there have resulted embarrassments for the courts and little justifiable benefit to anyone else.

Another type of abuse is the transposition of legal conceptions or propositions from an old subject matter to a new one, from one part of the law to another, or even one period to another, and the assumption that the results represent without more, the law for the new subject matter; 'hasty generalisation' it has been called.[166] The use of the classes of charities set out in a statute of Elizabeth were never designed as a basis for the entire modern law of charitable gifts in a long-standing instance, and is perhaps to no small extent responsible for what has been aptly termed 'the wilderness of legal charity.' [167] A recent example, I have elsewhere submitted, with respect, was the effort by the House of Lords in the *Constantine Case* to transpose the concept of 'automatic' operation of frustration from its purpose as fixing at some given moment the rights and liabilities of the parties to the newly-arisen problem of determining the burden of proof as to the cause of frustration,[168] which no one had in contemplation when the 'automatic termination' concept was devised. It may further be suggested, though left for argument elsewhere,[169] that the unfortunate judicial history of the civil action for conspiracy is, in part, due to a judicial assumption that one single principle must be applicable to all associations, regardless of the variations of conflicting interests as between, for instance, traders *inter se,* workmen *inter se,* employees and workmen in combination, and non-trading associations. The injustices in the law of construction of documents, especially wills, which have agitated law reformers for more than a century, are attributable, in part at any rate, to such a pseudo-compulsive transposition of concepts. The 'rule of construction,' by which generations of judges have felt compelled to give the word 'money' as used by testators the meaning of a legal category of 'money,' instead of that intended by the testator, has survived long enough to earn a severe condemnation from the House of Lords and the title of a 'blot on the history of justice.' [170] The relation of the doctrine of consideration to both the transpositive and deductive forms of legal abuse of logic emerges so clearly from recent English critiques of great authority [171] that it is unnecessary to do more than stress its relevance at this point.[172] The doctrine of common employment has been so grievously and consistently beset by English courts, and even by sedate English legal journals in recent years, that, in mercy, this writer leaves the reader to draw for himself its significance for the present thesis.

5. *Special Effects on Judicial Interpretation of Statutes*

The civilian variety of abuse of logic in statutory interpretation has been flavored in England by the deep-rooted common-law tradition of judicial hostility to legislation.[173] It has indeed been suggested that this hostility itself derived from an aesthetic ideal of logical symmetry, *elegantia,* with which the court identifies the common law, and which it regards as disturbed when the legislature intervenes. It is certainly clear that there has long been a canon of construction requiring within vague limits, that statutes 'in derogation of' the common law shall be strictly construed. However that be, and however harmless such a canon might have been in former times when legislation was but a rare footnote to the law developed by the courts, the effects today when legislation is a major (perhaps the major) source of law, must, obviously, be serious.[174]

These effects have been the subject of critical comment in connection with

321

many major fields of legislation, as, for instance, public health,[175] the eman-cipation of married women,[176] and the related matter of family life-insurance policies,[177] road traffic legislation, workmen's compensation legislation,[178] in-dustrial re-organization legislation,[179] trade-union legislation,[180] and many others. We are more concerned here to understand the relation of the syl-logism to these alleged frustrations than to make or judge the catalogue.

It is submitted, first of all, that it is in professional thought rather than in mere unconscious personal or even class prejudice that the main root of this phenomenon is to be sought,[181] though the other causes cannot, as Scrutton L. J. has observed, be lightly dismissed. Before the remarkable case of *R. v. Donoghue*,[182] it has been well pointed out,[183] common-law judges had pressed for three quarters of a century for legislation to relieve them of the 'solemn mockery' of condemning to death (knowing that re-prieve would follow) mothers who, during post-natal unbalance, killed their child. Yet, in that case, common-law judges so emasculated the resulting statute that they had to repeat the 'solemn mockery' after the Act. Only some fundamental deficiency of technique, such as Professor Pound has sug-gested, can explain such incidents.[184] The whole past training of the com-mon lawyer, and, in large part, the present training of the future English lawyer, is in the manipulation of case materials. That manipulation admits growth and adaptation behind pseudo-logical treatment of judicial prece-dents, just as the French lawyer's training admits them behind pseudo-logical treatment of legislative provisions. But the common lawyer, despite the growing importance of legislation, has not acquired the techniques of handling legislative materials in a similarly creative manner to that in which he handles case law. Our judges do not yet argue by analogy from statutes as they do from cases.[185]

Exaggerating this deficiency is the still strong dominant fallacy that words, especially words of statutes, have meaning in themselves apart from what the makers intended. On no other assumption is it possible to explain the rigid British canon (not followed in the United States,[186] or on the Conti-nent),[187] that *travaux preparatoires*, however clear and decisive on the point at issue, are never to be consulted in aid of interpretation—a canon recently applied by the Australian High Court on a constitutional issue of major im-portance.[188] On no other basis is it explicable that lawyers can regard with equanimity cases in which judges may pronounce, *ex cathedra*, that so-and-so clearly *could not* have been in the legislator's mind when the Parliamentary debates ready at hand (but judicially unopened) might show that that was precisely what was in his mind.[189] Rationalizations by academic lawyers who, it has been well said, are beset by a 'vague sense of discomfort' when-ever they are close to legislation,[190] do not help the matter.[191] It is be-lieved, however, that the most important single factor in the frequent judi-cial frustration of statute law is the lack of conscious recognition of the degree of creative choice, which is so often present in the process of judg-ing. This lack of consciousness, with the resulting tendency to pursue methods which give the illusion of freedom from the responsibility of choice, encourages concentration on words, purports normally to exclude consideration of the policy of the act, and foreshortens the inquiry into policy even when it is admitted. Yet not only is it unavoidable that the legislator's silence or equivocation should leave responsibility for choice to the court in such cases. Often, indeed, as Professor Ehrlich pointed out, such matters are so left precisely because of the difficulty of weighing in advance the interests involved; a difficulty which may be either inherent, or by reason of the absence of a decisive value-judgment either way in the community.[192]

6. Examples of the Consciously Creative Judicial Process

A judge, said Oliver Wendell Holmes, Jr., who believes that his decision is absolutely right and that a dissent is wrong, is proceeding on the fallacy that judgment consists of 'adding up his sums correctly.'[193] The conscious recognition of the non-syllogistic evaluative nature of the judicial process, for which Holmes called, had had many other distinguished common-law judges and jurists including Brandeis, Cardozo, and Roscoe Pound in the United States, and Lord Wright in England, for its advocates. It is important at this stage to point out that that call does not ask for the impossible, and that examples of its fulfillment may be found in the English reports, and even, perhaps increasingly, at the present day. The English Committee on Law Reporting in 1940 decided, indeed, that no advantage, and possibly great disadvantage, might ensue from attempting to render collection of reports of cases complete. This view scarcely comports with the idea that legal development springs inexorably from decided cases: for, if that were so, then incomplete reporting would mean a constant loss of necessary basic material.[194]

Numerous cases may be found in which the courts, faced with unanswerable arguments based on logical deduction from existing categories, have in effect declined to accept the deduction, or have created a new category in their view more apt for the case before them. They have said with Lord Wright that 'the excellence of the logic will not justify the rule if that is based on a fundamental premiss which is bad.'[195] The courts are in fact working out distinct premisses for determining whether damage is too remote in different kinds of cases—differentiating physical damage from economic loss, and from nervous shock, and contract claims from tort claims.[196] In the *Fibrosa Case,* Viscount Simon[197] declined to treat the giving of a promise as constituting a consideration for the purposes of the law of quasi-contract merely because it was such for the purpose of formation of contract.[198] And when in the same case the House overturned the principle of *Chandler* v. *Webster* for most contracts, it preserved the similar rule for the special class of cases dealing with prepaid freight.[199] Judicial creation of categories could scarcely be more patently displayed[200] except perhaps in Lord Wright's view of the implied term in quasi-contractual recovery.[201]

In *Nelson* v. *Cookson*[202] the court was confronted by the argument that the medical officers of County Council Hospital, because for other purposes they had been held not to be servants, must be independent contractors whose torts were not within the protection of the Public Authorities Protection Act. The Court declined to be caught in such a cleft stick of counsel's creation. The cases holding that for various specific purposes the court will 'lift the corporate veil,' that is, not begin with the premiss of the separate corporate personality, are, it is believed, examples of the same frankly creative approach.[203] And, finally, but without seeking to exhaust the examples,[204] it is submitted that the line of cases still proceeding, plotting the limits of the *Donoghue* v. *Stevenson* principle, would be shown by further basic analysis to contain a prominent element of conscious trying-out of the suitability of possible premisses.[205] These examples must suffice to suggest that English courts are not entirely unaware that often the application of law to actual problems may require 'the multiplication of concepts and working categories' and not the logical working-out of the one first discovered.[206]

7. Nature of the Law of Tort in Relation to Creative Judicial Law-Making

Recognition, indeed, of this growing consciousness in the judicial process is also implicit in the now inveterate debate among distinguished academic lawyers as to the nature of the law of torts. This debate seems to center around the question whether it is accurate to speak of a broad principle of liability for damage done without just cause or excuse, or whether we should rather speak of a definite number of classes of acts within one of which the plaintiff must bring the case in order to recover. It is to be observed that the first view does not assert that there is to be liability for all damage done. It merely asserts that there is a residuary power of judicial legislation to meet new situations. The qualification 'without just cause of excuse' is a typical category of circuitous reference which throws the court back upon a creative choice. The opposed view,[207] indeed, admits that the courts have in the past created new torts and may do·so in the future. It denies, however, that courts in the past were 'consciously' creating new torts, and denies for the future their right deliberately to create new ones.

It is respectfully submitted that the controversy cannot fruitfully be pursued as if it concerned the existence or non-existence of the supposed general principle as a principle of the law of torts itself. A more apt universe of discourse is in terms of the actual law applying behavior of courts. In these terms both sides are in agreement that in the field of torts the courts, consciously and openly or not, have in the past created and still continue to create, new heads of liability. This actual nature of the judicial process is in no sense peculiar to the law of torts. It is only more prominent there because of the immediate impact of social change upon that comparatively new field. The same need for increased consciousness and awareness of the responsibility for choice applies in this as well as in all other fields.[208]

324

8. *Relation of Conscious Creativeness in the Judicial Process To Logical Form and Legal Certainty*

Behind the use of legal principles, standards, and conceptions lie what Lord Wright terms 'acts of will.' 'Notwithstanding all the apparatus of authority, the judge has nearly always some degree of choice.' A tentative answer has here been sketched to Lord Wright's question how 'this perpetual process of change can be reconciled with the principle of authority and the rule of *stare decisis.*' That answer, it is believed, lies in the creative judicial choice permitted and even dictated by the use of legal categories of meaningless, or competing, or multiple, or circuitous, or indeterminate reference; as well as in the nature of our judicial process, which is almost a perfect medium for the creation of multiple and competing references. The logical form has not one but many fallacies.

It must now be clear that the defense of legal 'certainty,' in so far as it assumes that certainty, can be attained by continuing to adhere closely to logical development of the 'principles of law,' is defending what has never existed. The appearance of certainty and stability in legal rules and principles conceals existing uncertainty. 'We may think the law is the same,' wrote the late Benjamin Cardozo, 'if we refuse to change the formulae. The identity is verbal only.' [209]

The fallacy of the logical form . . . flatters that longing for certainty and repose which is in every human mind. But certainty generally is an allusion and repose not the destiny of man. Behind the logical form lies a judgment as to the relative worth and importance of competing legislative grounds, often an inarticulate and unconscious judgment it is true, and yet the very root and nerve of the whole proceeding. You can give any conclusion a logical form.[210]

What Professor Ehrlich said a generation before concerning the principle of 'the stability of legal norms generally' is equally applicable to that supposed permanent body of 'principles of the common law,' from which traditional thought supposes to be the sufficient source of the remarkable extension of our law. Apparently stable principles, he wrote, 'have become so general by the uninterrupted process of extension and of enrichment of their content in the course of millennia, that they are adaptable to the most diverse situations. . . In actual fact it is not the same norm at all; it has remained unchanged in appearance only; it has received an entirely new inner content.' [211]

The magnificent achievement of the English courts in evolving great bodies of rules reasonably adapted to changing conditions, cannot, therefore, be explained as the fruits of the kind of logical deduction with which the analysts have familiarized us. The term 'logic' is, indeed, often applied to this other creative type of mental activity, but it is not 'logic' in the Austinian or even the Kelsenite sense or in the sense understood by lawyers generally. Professor Dewey has described 'logic' in this creative sense as working not from a given major premiss to a conclusion, but as a gradual drawing of the premiss from 'the total situation'; that is, the finding of 'statements of general principle and of particular fact, which are worthy to serve as premisses,' syllogistic logic and deduction, being merely an aid in the search.[212] Perhaps, no better example can be found of this mental process, made explicit in the English reports, than in the judgment of Mackinnon L. J. in *Heap* v. *Ind Coope:* [213]

As far as I am concerned, freely avow that inasmuch as in common sense and in all decency Heap ought to be able to recover against somebody, and in the circumstances of this case . . . in all common sense and decency he is able to recover against these defendants, if the law allows it; [214] my only concern is to see whether, upon the cases, the law does allow him so to recover.

But, after all, 'logic' in this sense is but a description of the psychological process of reaching decisions, and the inquiry what is the role of 'logic' in this sense in judicial reasoning answers itself. 'Logic' in this sense would be 'judicial reasoning.' [215]

In this study we have, therefore, kept to Holmes' narrower meaning of 'logic,' which is also its traditional scholastic meaning and its common meaning in lawyer's usage.[216] It was in this sense that Holmes used it when he said that 'the whole outline of the law is the resultant of a conflict at every point between logic and good sense—the one striving to work fiction out to consistent results, the other restraining and at last overcoming that effort when the results become too manifestly unjust.' If 'good sense' be taken as a shorthand expression for the complex process of assessment of contemporary facts and of conscious or unconscious decision of what is a just result for that class of facts, the foregoing pages may have added some English footnotes to Holmes' point. But its main purpose was something more. It was to display the devices and techniques whereby English judges can live and work by the creative light of this 'good sense,' even while they render homage to the authoritative premise and the syllogistic deduction. It was to display how they are able to promote legal flux under the very banner and in the very stronghold of *stare decisis.*

NOTES

1. Judge Konstam, Note (1944) 60 *Law Q. Rev.* 232.
2. Op. cit. xxv.
3. See e.g. F. Pollock, 'Judicial Caution and Judicial Valour' (1929) 45 *Law Q. Rev.* 293; Lord Macmillan, *Law and Other Things,* 1937, 76 ff.
4. Ibid. *passim,* esp. Preface.
5. Ibid. xvi.
6. See Ibid. 131, the whole of c. xii on 'Juristic Science in England' and cf. c. xi on 'Juristic Science in Rome.' See also generally ibid. c. vi, esp. 124-5, 127-8, and c. xvii, esp. 392.
7. For instance, he concentrated on the historic role of the judges in the past growth of common law and equity and underrated the degree to which, with the decadence of equity and the rise of the modern legislature, modern courts have regarded their task as the mechanical application of pre-existing legal propositions.
8. Professor Ehrlich (ibid. c.v., esp. 85 ff.) reduced the facts dealt with by rules of social behavior to the categories of 'usage, domination, possession, declaration of will.'

9. In *The Common Law*, 1881.

10. Scott L. J. in *Haseldine* v. *Daw* (1941), 1· All. E. R. 525, rev. (1941) 2 K.B. 353, Lord Wright's estimate (op. cit. 345) that 'reported cases, with comparatively few exceptions become obsolete in fifty years' is a startling measure of this constant change. See also ibid. 381-6, and *passim*.

11. Cf. ibid. xvii.

12. See J. Stone, 'The Province of Jurisprudence Redetermined,' 1944, of *Mod. L. Rev.* 97.

13. Ibid. 131.

14. Though this is certainly often the case. See e.g. J. Stone, 'Res Gesta Reagitata' (1939), 55 *Law Q. Rev.* 61; J. Stone, 'Burden of Proof and the Judicial Process' (1944), 60 *Law Q. Rev.* 262, *passim*, esp. 268-9, 277-8.

15. Ibid. xxiv-xxv.

16. But in engaging briefly upon it, the present writer claims neither to have fulfilled the commission, nor to have the qualities rightly stipulated for its fulfillment. The inquiry has, of course, long been opined up in continental countries and the United States.

17. In *Prager* v. *Blatspiel . . . Ltd.* (1924), 1 K.B. 566, 570.

18. See e.g. the comments of Scrutton, L. J., in *Jebara* v. *Ottoman Bank*, 1927, 2 K.B. 254 at 271. Contrast the view of R. S. T. Chorley, 'Liberal Trends in Commercial Law' (1940), 3 *Mod. L. Rev.* 258, 276.

19. See e.g. his position in the Constantine Case (1942); J. Stone, 'Burden of Proof' in op. cit. at 272-3, 276-7. Cf. his position in the Liversidge Case, *infra*. Cf. in Australia a somewhat similar uncertainty of position in, for instance, the assertion of Dixon J. in *Waghorn* v. *Waghorn* (1942), 65 *C. L. R.* 289, 295-9, that the word 'desert' had an indubitable meaning from which indubitable logical consequences could there be drawn without reference to 'social or sociological conceptions or preconceptions.' And cf. his discussion of the applicability of English C. A. decisions in Australia, also purporting to proceed without reference to the social issues in the law of marriage there involved.

20. I have respectfully submitted elsewhere ('Burden of Proof' in op. cit. 109) that the confusions of the Constantine Case exemplify this state of affairs.

21. See for a very confident recent formulation in H. W. R. Wade, 'The Concept of Legal Certainty' (1941), 4 *Mod. L. Rev.* 183. The over-simplicity of this article is perhaps mitigated by the fact that it is apparently designed (somewhat belatedly) to rebut the equally over-simple thesis of J. Frank, *Law and the Modern Mind*, 1930.

22. H. W. R. Wade, in op. cit. 187. There is a countervailing complaint equally vehement and of partial truth that rules of law become by logical development so artificial that the moral judgment of ordinary men is unable to follow them. We are not here concerned with the degree of merit in each complaint, which will certainly vary for different parts of the law and conditions of society.

23. At the outset of our attempted reply two caveats are necessary. In part at least the question above is as strictly unanswerable as the inquiry of the henpecked husband: how often do you beat your wife? For in important measure judicial conclusions may not be well adapted to contemporary problems. That measure cannot be here considered. A second caveat is that voiced by Professor Ehrlich. In some degree the apparent consistency of logically deduced rules with social needs may be a mere delusion. If, as he urges, the rules of law applied by courts and officials (as distinct from the living rules actually observed by men in society) have little effect in society, even 'the most unjust decisions' may cause little harm and be little noticed. To that extent rules of law in the books and their manipulation may maintain themselves and even win praise as a ritual of decision precisely because they do not seriously affect what actually happens in society. See E. Ehrlich, op. cit. 135. It is believed that the rules for exercise of discretion in favor of an adulterous petitioner in divorce might provide an illustration.

24. Ibid. xxv. B. Cardozo, indeed (*Paradoxes of Legal Science*, 1928, 10), regarded

the judge's function as merely 'administrative' if the applicable rule were clear and regarded the judicial function as beginning only 'where doubt enters.'

25. The literature on the judicial process, especially in the United States, is too voluminous and too well known to list here. The writer recommends the brief selections in R. Pound, *Outlines of Lectures on Jurisprudence* (5th ed. 1943), 120, 122-3, which he assisted in making.

26. For a fuller discussion of the matters here touched upon and for the authorities, see J. Stone, op. cit. n. 109, 262, 270-84, of which the account above is a résumé.

27. Lord Wright's use of both formulas (1942, A.C. at 192) without suggesting any difference in meaning, is notable in this regard. Contrast with Lord Wright's apparent indifference to the form, the manner in which Lord Esher, M. R. in *The Glendarroch* (1894, 226, 230-31, C.A.) based his decision precisely on the form in which he felt compelled to frame an 'implied' exception.

28. Pace, Bailhache J.'s attempted contrary demonstration in *Munro Brice & Co.* v. *War Risks Association Ltd.* (1918), 2 K.B. 78, 88, 89, relied on by G. G. Webber, *Effect of War on Contracts* (1940), 423, to support the decision of the Court of Appeal in the Constantine Case.

29. This degeneration from meaning to formal order is strikingly seen in Lord Esher, M. R.'s efforts in *The Glendarroch* (op. cit.) to decide on whom to place the burden as to negligence impliedly excepted from the 'perils of the sea' exception, by deciding at what point in the clauses the implied exception should be read.

1879, s. 39 (2), re-enacting with some change the similar Act of 1848, s. 14, and the Licensing Act, 1872, s. 51 (2).

30. See e.g. Turner's Case (1816) 5 M. & S. 206; and *Summary Jurisdiction Act,*

31. See e.g. my comments in 'Burden of Proof' (op. cit.), at 282 ff., on the Privy Council's advice in Official Assignee of *Cheah Soo Tuan* v. *Khoo Saw Cheow* (1931) A.C. 67; and on the same puzzling assumption of logical dictation even as to an 'implied exception' in *The Glendarroch* (op. cit.). Cf. similar doubts as to non-statutory documents, for instance whether, in a covenant for power to convey and quiet enjoyment covering acts of the covenantor 'or any through whom he derives title otherwise than by purchase for value,' the covenantor or covenantee has the burden as to purchase for value. In *Stoney* v. *Eastbourne* R.D.C. (1927), 1 Ch. 367 (C.A.), it was held that the clause was a compendious way of enumerating the class and that the burden was on the covenantee, citing *David* v. *Sabin* (1893), 1 Ch. 523, and distinguishing *The Glendarroch*. The reversal was on another point. The writer is reluctantly compelled to avow that the distinctions taken on pp. 374-6 to support the holding leave him unrepentant of his skepticism.

32. *Lennard's Carrying Co. Ltd.* v. *Asiatic Petroleum Co. Ltd.* (1915) A.C. 705, esp. Viscount Haldane L.C. at 714.

33. *Jackson* v. *Union Insurance Co.* (1874) L.R. 10 C.P. 125.

34. Even here the shadow of a 'grin' may continue where the rule of law is old and has acquired a virtually agreed formulation, as with certain exceptions to liability for negligence. See cases cited in J. Stone, 'Burden of Proof,' op. cit. at 271 and 283 n.

35. (1942) A.C. 154.

36. For discussions of this aspect of the case see G. G. Webber, *Effect of War on Contracts* (1940), 411-23 (written before the decision of the House of Lords); and brief comments of Professor Chorley in (1942) 4 *Mod. L. Rev.* 63; G.L.W. Note 5 *Mod. L. Rev.* 135, 138, and Note in (1941) 58 *Law Q. Rev.* 13 (an uncritical statement of the Court of Appeal holding).

37. *The Glendarroch* (1894) 226.

38. See his elaborate discussion of these in (1940) 1 K.B. 812, at 821 ff.

39. *Lennard's Carrying Co. Ltd.* v. *Asiatic Petroleum Co. Ltd.* (1915) A.C. 705.

40. Viscount Simon at 160.

41. Viscount Maugham at 169.

42. 'Burden of Proof,' op. cit. at 270-84.

43. Ibid. at 277.

44. The following list is suggested for further work: (a) The distinction from Pothier between mistake as to person, which invalidates an executory contract, and mistake that does not, adopted and ostensibly acted upon in *Smith* v. *Wheatcroft* (1878) 9 Ch.D. 223, 230 (per Fry J.), and *Gordon* v. *Street* (1899) 2 Q. B. 641, per A. L. Amith L.J., and by the House of Lords per Viscount Haldane in *Lake* v. *Simmons* (1927) A.C. 487. Cf. the comments of A. L. Goodhart, 'Mistake as to Identity . . .' (1941) 57 *Law Q. Rev.* 228, 236-44, with reference to the use of Pothier's test in the Potter Case (1940) K.B. 271. F. H. Lawson's criticism of the Pothier test, 'Error in Substantia' (1937) 52 *Law Q. Rev.* 79, on the ground of differences between English and French law would be subsidiary if the category were meaningless. (b) The problem of *Smith* v. *Hughes* (1871) L. R. 6 Q. B. 597; (c) The distinction between *Williams* v. *Jones* (1865) 3 H. & C. 602 and *Jefferson* v. *Derbyshire Farmers* (1921) 2 K.B. 281, as to the scope of employment for purposes of vicarious liability, and possibly the corresponding distinction in the Workmen's Compensation Act cases; see now *New Century etc.* v. *Northern Ireland etc.* (1942) A. C. 509 (JS); (d) The distinction between intent to injure another and the intent to further one's own trade interests long dominant in the cases on civil conspiracy; see now the Harris Tweed Case (1942) A. C. 435. (e) The distinction in the law of frustration between an assumed state of facts which is 'the substance of the contract' (Vaughan Williams L.J. in *Krell* v. *Henry* (1903) 2 K.B. 740, 749) and failure of which will frustrate, and a mere motive or inducement to enter into the contract (ibid. applied in *Herne Bay Steamboat Co.* v. *Hutton* (1903) 2 K.B. 683) which will not; (f) (with more doubt) the distinction between findings of inferior courts on jurisdictional facts 'collateral' to the 'merits' which were said to be not conclusive and its findings on other facts going to the 'merits' which were. (*Bunbury* v. *Fuller* (1853) 9 Exch. 111, 140, on which see *Tithe Redemption Co.* v. *Wynne* (1943) 1 K.B. 756 (C.A.) and learned comment by D. M. Gordon, sub. nom. 'Tithe Redemption Commission *v.* Gwynne' (1944) 60 *Law Q. Rev.* 250); (g) (with similar doubt) the distinction between acceptance by a landlord of 'mesne profits' from a tenant holding over after notice to quit which does not revive the tenancy and payment of rent which does. (Lord Kenyon in *Doe* v. *Calvert* (1810) 2 Camp. 387, on which see Judge Konstam's Note (1944) 60 *Law Q. Rev.* 232.

45. In *Homes* v. *Newman* (1931) 2 Ch. 112, 120.

46. 'Res Gesta Reagitata' (1939) 55 *Law Q. Rev.* 66.

47. E.g. S. L. Phipson, *Evidence* (6 ed. 1921) 59.

48. I. Pitt Taylor, Evidence (12 ed. 1931), para. 588.

49. E.g. Powell, Evidence (10th ed.) 61-2. Cf. S. L. Phipson, op. cit. 65, as to declarations showing knowledge.

50. E.g. S. L. Phipson, op. cit. 59.

51. Ibid.

52. See e.g. S. L. Phipson, op. cit. 61-5, esp. 61. This learned author's proposition amounted to this: that when a witness testifies from the box as to his state of mind, that is testimonial evidence, but when the identical assertion is made by him out of court, its later use is original evidence.

53. (1870) 6 Q.B. 1.

54. E.g. Dr. Cheshire's tendency, as well as that of the American courts. See generally on the position in English law, G. C. Cheshire, *Private International Law* (2nd ed. 1938), 302 ff.; A. H. Robertson, 'The Choice of Law for Tort Liability' (1940) 4 *Mod. L. Rev.* 27.

55. *McMillan* v. *Canadian Northern Rly.* (1923) A. C. 120, and the Walpole Case, (1923) A.C. 113.

56. *Machado* v. *Fontes* (1897) 2 Q. B. 231. To be exhaustive other possibilities, such as 'no-moral-culpability' either cumulatively with any of E_1-E_3 (making E_4, E_5, and E_6) or independently (E_7) would have to be included.

57. Other legal categories which it is believed might be shown by further basic work to have concealed multiple references are (1) the category *'personalis'* in the

maxim *actio personalis moritur cum persona;* and of course, as has repeatedly been demonstrated, (2) the category of 'a right,' e.g. in *ubi ius ibi remedium,* and (3) the category of malice in the law of torts and crimes.

58. *Supra* n. 13.

59. *Hynes* v. *N.Y.C.R.R.* (1921) 231 N.Y. 229.

60. (1940) A.C. 701, (1940) 2 All. E. R. 445.

61. As to limitation of actions.

62. *Fifth Interim Report* (Dec. 1936, Cmd. 5334) 35. See generally on the English position, W. E. Beckett, *British Year Book of International Law,* 1934, 76.

63. Omitting refinements on the categories, such as whether a putative spouse is English, or the marriage is English.

64. The student will readily identify 'converging reference' if he recalls his difficulties and that of his teachers in distinguishing at many points of application the exact limits of the torts of negligence, trespass off the highway, breach of statutory duties, *Rylands* v. *Fletcher,* liability for animals, fire, dangerous things, dangerous premises, and nuisance. For some recent cases suggesting these problems see *Hanson* v. *Wearmouth Coal Co.* (1939) 55 T.L.R. 747; *Wrings* v. *Cohen* (1940) 56 T.L.R. 101; *Sedleigh-Denfield* v. *St. Joseph Society* (1940) K.B. 2; (1940) 3 All. E.R. 3491.

And see the provocative 'Nores' by W. Friedmann (1940) 3 *Mod. L. Rev.* 305, and 4 id. 139. The learned writer contends vigorously that all the above-mentioned torts are merely applications of one common principle, and that 'the maintenance of hypertrophy of torts with the corresponding waste of mental energy involved in maintaining and elaborating more and more meaningless distinctions . . . is a luxury which no modern body politic . . . can afford' (4 id. 144). It is respectfully believed, however, that the evil of this situation lies not so much in the fact that the categories are numerous as that they depend in considerable part on historical accident (e.g. the old forms of action) and often do not correspond to the actual conflicts of interests in play in twentieth-century society. Besides wasting time they tend to conceal the real problem for judgment. A single principle is not desirable for its own sake but only as a step in the abandonment of the present inappropriate categories and the construction of others more appropriate. Conversely, it is not the multiplication or perpetuation of numerous categories *per se,* but when they are unrelated to the substantial questions of justice in the actual situation, which is harmful.

Cf. M. Franklin's criticism of the number of overlappings and conflicting definitions in the various American *Restatements of the Law* on this account (article cited *supra* at 1385-91). M. Franklin's discussion (especially his ambiguous idealization (1388, 1391) of 'broad-based . . . conceptualism' on the analogy of the civilian 'legal transaction') is even more subject to the caveat made upon Mr. Friedmann. It is of interest that both writers have special experience of traditional civil-law techniques.

Cf. also generally and esp. as to public and private nuisance, trespass, *Rylands* v. *Fletcher* and *Donoghue* v. *Stevenson,* liabilities, P. H. Winfield, *Torts* (1st ed. 1937), 140-41, 146.

65. They should also compete with newly devised categories. For an impressive argument that the House of Lords in the Fibrosa Case merely substituted one arbitrary rule for another through failure in effect to devise new categories, see G. L. Williams, 'The End of Chandler v. Webster' (1942), 6 *Mod. L. Rev.* 46, 57.

66. See e.g. A. M. Finlay, *Contracts for the Benefit of Third Persons,* 1939.

67. *Naas* v. *Westminster Bank Ltd.* (1940) A.C. 366, 1 All. E.R. 485 (C.A.).

68. Proceeding through *Chandler* v. *Webster* (1904) 1 K.B. 493.

69. (1943) A.C. 32.

70. And see the admirable analysis of G. L. Williams, 'The Coronation Cases' (1941) 4 *Mod. L. Rev.* 241, 5 id. 1 and Note, 5 id. 135; also R. G. McElroy and G. L. Williams, *Impossibility of Performance,* 1942.

71. See J. Stone, 'The Rule of Exclusion of Similar Fact Evidence in England' (1933) 46 *Harv. L. Rev.* 954, and 'The Rule of Exclusion of Similar Fact Evidence: America' (1938) 51 *Harv. L. Rev.* 988.

72. 'Frustration of Contract by War' (1940) 56 *Law Q. Rev.* 173.

73. See e.g. Lord Finlay's concurrent use of them as if they were synonymous in *Larrinaga* v. *Société Franco-Américaine* (1923) 29 Com. Cas. 1, at 7, on which see A. D. McNair, op. cit. 177.

74. (1942) Ch. 345, sub. nom. *Perrin* v. *Morgan* (1943), A.C. 399.

75. By indicating that the rules of construction should only be resorted to when other means of ascertaining the testator's meaning fail.

76. Cf. the diverse meanings given before *Re Polemis* to the apparently single category of 'natural and probable,' and the continued diversity as to 'direct' after that case. See *infra*.

77. See the recently much-discussed treatment by the House in the Fibrosa Case (1943) A.C. 32, of its earlier decision in the French Marine Case (1921) 2 A.C. 494. Cf. the acute analysis by G. L. Williams, 'The End of Chandler v. Webster' (1942) 6 *Mod. L. Rev.* 46-57. The above is respectfully suggested as an additional explanation for the fact observed by Lord Wright, op. cit. xxv, that 'the higher the court . . . the freer the choice. . . The House of Lords' foes generally or frequently take a broad and common-sense view of the law.'

78. See e.g. the overtones in G. L. Williams, op. cit.

79. The often-expressed desire that the House should emulate the Privy Council in giving a single joint opinion (which it has recently done) may assist harassed searchers after the *ratio decidendi,* and, certainly, it would probably not assist the flexible development of the law. It is noteworthy that able commentators attribute some of the maladjustment of the Canadian constitution to modern conditions to the single anonymous opinions given by the Privy Council. See e.g. J. R. Mallory, 'The Courts and the Sovereignty of the Canadian Parliament,' *Can. Jo. Econ. Pol. Sci.,* May 1944.

80. *Dicta* for the court being bound include Lord Herschell L.C. in *Pledge* v. *Carr* (1895) 1 Ch. 51; Lindley L. J. in *Lavy* v. *L.C.C.* (1895) 2 Q.B. 577, 581; Scrutton L. J. in *Newsholme Bros.* v. *Road Transport Co.* (1929) 2 K.B. 356, 375; Greer L. J. in *Sigley* v. *Hale* (1938) 2 K.B. 630. *Contra* include Cotton L.J. in *Mills* v. *Jennings* (1880) 13 Ch.D. 639, 648; and the decision in *Wynne-Finch* v. *Chaytor* (1903) 2 Ch. 475. And see a valuable Note (1939) by E. W. White (1939) 3 *Mod. L. Rev.* 66. But see now *J. S. Young* v. *British Aeroplane Co.* (1944) 60 T.L.R. 536.

81. See the recent discussion in *Waghorn* v. *Waghorn* (1942) 65 C.L.R. 289. Cf. the problem as to House of Lords decisions: see *Piro* v. *W. Foster Ltd.* (1943) 68 C.L.R. 313.

As a learned writer (M. J. Adler, 1931, 31 *Col. L. Rev.* 91, 102) has said: 'the structure of the law itself is a plurality of legal doctrines or theories, one of which affords the rationalization [demonstration] of the propositions expressed by a given decision as a rule of law, and another of which similarly supports its contradiction. Thus, the probability of any prediction is in part conditioned upon the alternative rationalizations which are provided by the pluralistic logical structure of the law as a body of general propositions grounded in sub-systems, which are competing or alternative legal doctrines.' It may be added that it is an unstable plurality, which can acquire stability only at the sacrifice of its real goal of doing justice between living men in a living society.

In the light of this, Lord Wright's view (op. cit. 345) that decisions of 'a single judge should be more sparingly cited,' and that 'citations should generally be limited to judgments of the Court of Appeal and of the House of Lords' gains, it is believed, a new and vivid significance.

82. See e.g. Lord Wright's late formulation, op. cit. 118 ff. and 102, where he squarely asserts the existence of a 'duty' to be 'a prerequisite to negligence.'

83. (1932) A.C. 562, 580.

84. Op. cit. 259.

85. There are interesting philosophical linkages of this formulation, notably with R. Stammler, which must be left for another place.

86. O. W. Holmes, 'The Path of the Law' (1897) 10 *Harv. L. Rev.* 457, 472. Cf. Lord Wright, op. cit. 26, who terms the fictitious contract in restitution and impliedly the 'duty' requirement in negligence 'innocuous' but 'unnecessary' and possibly 'misleading.' Yet in his treatment of the Liesbosch Case (1933) A.C. 449 (ibid. 118 ff.) he treats the duty requirements as independent, defines it in the above terms, and assumes to regard it as independent of the negligence issue. The reasoning seems therefore, with respect, not to answer Holmes' point. Yet in ibid., 360 ff. Lord Wright's discussion seems to treat negligence as identifiable with the breach of duty, though he immediately reverts (363) to the view which Holmes criticized. A similar difficulty may be seen, ibid. 403-6. *Aliter* of course insofar as rules are laid down in advance giving a definite legal meaning to the range of duty. But in that case the range of duty is defined by reference to the existing legal rules and not to what a reasonable man ought to foresee.

87. As Lord Wright seems to assume they do, ibid. 118 ff.

88. It is believed that a precisely similar situation exists in the law of estoppel based on negligent misrepresentation, where, as here, the insusceptibility of the decisions to satisfactory logical analysis lends support to the main point.

89. (1921) 3 K.B. 560.

90. Op. cit. 100 ff.

91. (1933) A.C. 449.

92. Lord Wright, op. cit. 113.

93. Ibid. 100-101, 112-13.

94. Lord Wright, in the Liesbosch Case (1933) A.C. at 460-61.

95. E.g. op. cit. 113, 117.

96. Ibid. 104.

97. See next §.

98. *Palsgraf* v. *Long Island R.R.* (1928), 248 N.Y. 338.

99. Article cited *supra* at 466.

100. Cf. Lord Wright, op. cit. 18-21, 356-60.

101. (1914) A.C. 398.

102. Cf. Lord Wright, op. cit. 24-5. Lord Wright well points out (ibid. 18) that these parts of the speeches in *Sinclair* v. *Brougham* were unnecessary to the decision which as a whole (ibid. 1-15) was an admirable example of adaptation of existing precedent to do justice in the particular case.

103. D. W. Logan, Note (1938) 2 *Mod. L. Rev.* 153, 158.

104. E.g. Greene M.R. in *Morgan* v. *Ashcroft* (1938) 1 K.B. 49-62.

105. E.g. Lord Dunedin in *Sinclair* v. *Brougham, supra,* at 427 ff., Sir W. Holdsworth, *Jo. Soc. Pub. Teachers of Law,* 42.

106. This is the view consistently taken by Lord Wright. See e.g. his opinion in Brooks' *Wharf* v. *Goodman Bros.* (1937) 1 K.B. 534, 545; *Legal Essays and Addresses* (1938) 18 ff., 356-60, and see the earlier judicial views to the same effect there cited, and the literature and discussion in c. ii.

107. Though it will be clear that the writer respectfully follows Lord Wright's view, and agrees with Mr. Logan's analysis, op cit.

108. To the extent that these two views require in addition that the parties shall have been capable of making an actual contract identical with that to be implied, the circuitousness is of course broken. Logic may to that extent operate but usually at the cost of arbitrary deprivation of a just remedy. Cf. D. W. Logan, op. cit.

109. Other examples of the circuitous category will, it is believed, be revealed by basis analysis of (1) 'the proper law of a contract' as a governing law in private international law. See e.g. G. C. Cheshire, op. cit. c. viii; in J. H. C. Morris and G. C. Cheshire, 'The Proper Law of a Contract' (1940) 56 *Law Q. Rev.* 320, the exposition tends to be less circuitous but only by dint of the interposition of independent rules as to 'intention' and 'closest factual connection' delimiting the concept; (2) the basis of recovery in *Upton-on Severn R.D.C.* v. *Powell* (1942) 1 All. E. R. 220, implying a contract to pay for the services of a fire brigade summoned from outside the fire district, both sides erroneously believing that the fire was within the district, and

neither intending that there by a charge; (3) the implied assumption of risk 'leg' of the common employment doctrine; (4) the implied term as a means of deciding whether, where the employment contract is silent, weekly wages are or are not to be paid during the employee's sickness (*Morrison* v. *Bell* (1939) 2 K.B. 187, (1939) 1 All. E. R. 745; (5) the use of the category of 'justification' in the suggested principle underlying the law of torts (P. H. Winfield, *Law of Tort*, 1937, 15) that 'all injuries done to another person are torts, unless there is some justification recognised by law.' The only effect of the category of 'justification' is to leave the field free for non-deductive judicial creation of law; (6) Bowen L. J.'s formula in the Mogul SS. Co. Case (1889) 23 Q.B.D. 598 'without just cause or excuse,' approved in the House of Lords (1892) A.C. 25 at 37, 49, 51, 57, as a part of a rule for determining the actionability of damage done by numbers; (7) statutory rules for relief of trustees or others embodying the criterion that in the court's view the person liable 'ought fairly to be excused.' (See e.g. the English Trustee Act, 1925, s.61.)

110. See his *Legal Essays and Addresses* (1938) 255, 284-5. At 259 he expressly characterizes such implications as 'proceeding on the basis of *idem per idem.*' Cf. Lord Wright, ibid. 379-80 as to the 'implied term' in the law of mistake.

111. Roscoe Pound's clarification of the nature of the legal 'standard' as contrasted with the legal 'rules,' 'principles,' and 'conceptions,' and his setting off against all of them of the authoritative materials and techniques and the received ideals of the legal system, are among the achievements which rank but small in his own *curriculum vitae*, but would loom large in that of many of his distinguished contemporaries. See R. Pound, 'The Theory of Judicial Decision' (1923) 36 *Harv. L. Rev.* 641; 'The Administrative Application of Legal Standards' (1919) 44 *Am. Bar Ass. Jo.* 440.

112. For a recent judicial statement see Sir Wilfrid Greene, M.R., in *Knightsbridge Estates Trust Co.* v. *Byrne* (1938) 55 T.L.R. 196, 198.

113. Cf. what R. Stammler terms the 'lenient' provisions of the German Civil Code. He also termed them 'abstract' as distinct from 'casuistic' rules. See the *Lehre*, pt. i, c. iii. Cf. 'the rule of reason' under U.S. anti-trust decisions; 'detriment of the public,' 'advantageous to the Commonwealth,' in the Australian Industries Preservation Act, 1906.

114. Stone J. in *U.S.* v. *Trenton Potteries Co.* (1927) 273 U.S. 392, quoted in E. N. Garlan, op. cit. 57.

115. E. N. Garlan, op. cit. 56.

116. Cf. Andrews J. in *Palsgraf* v. *Long Island R.R.*, cited *supra* n. 98.

117. (1921) 3 K.B. 560.

118. 'Too remote' could perhaps also be regarded as a category of circuitous reference. Lord Wright, op. cit. 258-9, regards the 'reasonableness' in the court's reading-in of terms such as 'reasonable time,' when the parties are silent, as circuitous, proceeding merely 'on the basis of *idem per idem.*' Lord Atkins' 'my neighbor' concept (*Donoghue* v. *Stevenson,* cited *supra*) may perhaps be equally regarded as a category of indeterminate reference.

119. Roscoe Pound has repeatedly stressed that only a line of decisions can give even an approximation to a definite rule. The best short account from the present standpoint is in F. S. Cohen, *Ethical Systems and Legal Ideals* (1933), 33-40.

120. A. L. Goodhart, 'Determining the Ratio Decidendi of a Case' (1931) 40 *Yale L. Rev.* 161, reprinted in *Essays in Jurisprudence and the Common Law;* cf. J. C. Gray, *Nature and Sources of the Law* (1909), s. 555; Salmond, *Jurisprudence* (3rd ed. 1910), 67, esp. 176.

121. It is as to the mode of drawing it that there is controversy and that Professor Goodhart's theory is far from universally accepted. It is challenged with particular vehemence by the American realists. This matter is not here under discussion, since the present thesis would hold in most respects, even if the courts behaved (which they clearly do not) in accordance with Professor Goodhart's theory.

122. H. Cairns, *The Theory of Legal Science* (1941), 80.

123. Some, no doubt, may have been virtually foreclosed by earlier decisions but that does not affect the present point.

124. Cf. the analyses by F. S. Cohen, 'Transcendental Nonsense and the Fundamental Approach' (1935), 35 *Col. L. Rev.*, 809, and by Oliphant, 'The Return to Stare Decisis' (1928), 14 *Amer. Bar Ass. Jo.* 71, 159, both discussed in E. N. Garlan, *Legal Realism and Justice* (1941), 26-9.

125. C. K. Allen, *Law in the Making* (1st ed. 1927), 164.

126. Not so convincing in some respects, for instance, his example on 165 (repeated in the 3rd ed., 1938, at 250-51) of a House of Lords decision given in ignorance of an applicable statute not being binding on lower courts because it is 'not a correct statement of the law' is unconvincing. The lower court's power to ignore the House of Lords case seems sufficiently explained by the fact that on any view a statutory rule prevails over one judicially created.

127. See his Introduction to the 3rd ed. (1938). Professor Simpson fails to drive this 'contradiction' quite home in his severe 'Review' (1940) 4 *Mod. L. Rev.* 121.

128. P. 167.

129. P. 193.

130. Cf. W. H. Hamilton, 'Preview of Justice' (1939), 48 *Yale L. Jo.* 819; E. N. Garlan, op. cit. 23-5.

131. The desirability of proceeding by this syllogistic method in so far as it may conduce to certainty is one social fact more or less important, to be weighed with others in making this choice. And as in the law of property, this fact may outweigh the rest so far as to give dominance to these tendencies. But it probably arises not from the method itself, but from the fact that laymen more frequently take legal advice before acting in property matters. The difference in this respect, e.g. between the law of property and the law of torts, has frequently been pointed out, for instance, by Roscoe Pound. Cf. also E. N. Garlan, op. cit. 46-52.

132. There are, of course, others, for instance, head-counting under the Roman *Law of Citations,* 426, A.P., and the practice of some common-law courts, and it is sometimes alleged in criticism, to some extent, in the American *Restatements of the Law.*

133. The story of the fascination of the western mind by the concept in 'indivisibility' might introduce a visitor from Mars to more of the main political, legal, and theological issues of western civilization. F. Gény, *Méthode . . .*, pt. ii, c. ii, enumerates a striking list of the applications of the concept with numerous attendant consequences in French jurisprudence alone.

134. In that its premisses or 'conceptions' or 'propositions' should be selected by reference to existential facts and not regardless of them.

135. *Essays in the Law,* 273.

136. These are ample signs that Pollock himself did not so remain bemused: see e.g. op. cit.; E. Ehrlich, op. cit. 331. Cf. F. Gény, *Méthode . . .*, pt. ii, c. ii; F. S. Cohen, op. cit. 56-61, and ibid. 251 ff. for the relationship of this matter to the limits of effective legal action. Cf. E. N. Garlan, op. cit. 46 ff.; B. Cardozo, *The Paradoxes of Legal Science* (1928), and *Nature of the Judicial Process* (1922), *passim.* F. S. Cohen, op. cit. 58, makes the *reductio ad absurdum,* that the qualities of consistency and harmony and simplicity and the like would still be preserved if we were to transpose all rewards and punishments, and all commands and prohibitions.

137. See e.g. *supra* n. 195 as to *Sinclair* v. *Brougham,* and the typical argument of counsel in *Nelson* v. *Cookson* (1940), 1 K.B. 100, that since the medical officer of a County Hospital had been held in earlier cases on other issues not to be a servant, he must therefore on the present issues, be an independent contractor, as if these two categories (a) exhausted all the possibilities and (b) were valid for all purposes.

The fascination is, of course, shared to some extent by draftsmen and legislators. Why, for instance, should a workman claiming under the Compensation Acts be debarred after recovery from proceeding at common law for any excess which the common-law action if brought first, would give him? Cf. A. Russell Jones, Note (1944) 7 *Mod. L. Rev.* 13 at 23.

138. E. Ehrlich, who was a vigorous advocate of open recognition of the 'free finding of law' which goes on in courts, long ago stated this impossibility (op. cit. 135, and see generally c. vi).

139. Lord Wright, op. cit. 341 ff. esp. 348-50.

140. Cf. E. N. Garlan, *Legal Realism and Justice* (1941), 35 ff.

141. 'The Work of the Commercial Courts' (1923), 1 *Camb. L. Jo.* 1, 7-8.

142. See Stone, *The Province and Function of Law,* op. cit. Ch. XXIII as to the first mentioned.

143. See *Haseldine* v. *Daw* cited *supra.*

144. Ultimately, it is believed, and the writer hopes in other places to show, they probably presuppose that words have meaning in themselves as distinct from their meaning to the transmitting and receiving human beings—a fallacy challenged by modern work on the theory of meaning.

145. *Liversidge* v. *Anderson* (1942), A.C. 207.

146. He cited numerous examples of this usage on 225-36.

147. Viscount Maugham, at 220. Cf. Lord Wright's formulation in the *Green Case* (1942), A.C. at 307.

148. Cf. A. L. Goodhart's Note (1943), 58 *Law Q. Rev.* 3, who regards the case as in effect discarding the traditional canons of interpretation; and C. K. Allen, 'Regulation 18B and Reasonable Cause' (1942) 58 *Law Q. Rev.* 232, 240-41. Both writers seem, with respect, too readily to assume that the canon as formulated in words has in the past invariably controlled judicial action.

149. Pp. 244, 225-36.

150. Thus, Viscount Maugham, at 221, said that the Secretary of State would risk prejudicing his future efforts for the defense of the realm if he had to disclose his sources; that, in any case, it would be impossible for the court to come to a different view from the Secretary; and that he could not believe that those responsible intended to expose the Secretary's action to judicial control. Cf. Lord Macmillan, at 254.

151. (1940) A.C. 1014.

152. Lord Atkin, at 1026.

153. Viscount Simon L.C., at 1020.

154. Viscount Simon L.C., at 1024.

155. Lord Atkin, at 1031.

156. At 1049.

157. A distinguished academic commentator (A. L. Goodhart, Note (1942) 58 *Law Q. Rev.* 1, 5-6) has characteristically pushed this further than judges themselves. Lord Atkin had argued in the Liversidge Case (227-8) that whether the Secretary of State had reasonable cause was 'as much a positive fact capable of determination by a third party as was a broken ankle or a legal right.' Professor Goodhart, in supporting the majority, was even willing to argue that 'if A has a broken ankle' is identical in meaning with 'if A thinks he has a broken ankle.' Cf. the comment by G. W. Keeton, Note (1941) 5 *Mod. L. Rev.* 173, to which I would add that the point in any case is not whether all 'facts' are only opinions after all, but *whose opinions?* Have courts in determining whether a defendant in malicious prosecution had 'reasonable cause' been determining a merely nonsensical question? Cf. C. K. Allen, 'Regulation 18B and Reasonable Cause' (1942) 58 *Law Q. Rev.* 232; Professor Goodhart's 'Replication,' ibid. 265, does not, with respect, support the 'broken ankle' argument.

158. O. Kahn-Freund, Note (1941) 4 *Mod. L. Rev.* 221, 223. And Cf. Lord Wright, op. cit. 226-7 on judicial treatment of the Statute of Frauds.

159. 'Path of the Law' (1897) 10 *Harv. L. Rev.* at 467.

160. (1937) A.C. 826.

161. That since a cause of action for shortened expectation of life inheres in an injured person during his life (*Flint* v. *Lovell* [1935] 1 K.B. 354) and since by the Law Reforе (Miscellaneous Provisions) Act, 1934, pre-existing causes of action survive his death, damages in respect thereof may be recovered on behalf of his estate in respect of such shortened expectation.

162. This, indeed, is recognized by the courts which did not permit recovery under both: *Davies* v. *Powell Duffryn Ass. Collieries* (1942), 1 All. E. R. 657. Cf. Goddard L. J. in *Banham* v. *Gambling.* (1941) A.C. 157: 'One is in effect, though I agree not in theory, merely giving a solatium to the parent for the loss of a child.'

163. Cf. O. Kahn-Freund, 'Expectation of Happiness' (1941) 5 *Mod. L. Rev.* 81.

164. J. Foster (Secretary of the Committee) 'Law Revision' (1938) 2 *Mod. L. Rev.* 14, 15.

165. *Benham* v. *Gambling,* cited *supra,* brought some of them to a head without, however, settling them.

166. F. S. Cohen, op. cit. 38.

167. N. Beratwich, 'The Wilderness of Legal Charity,' 1933, 49 *Law Q. Rev.* 520.

168. (1942) A.C. 154, Viscount Maugham at 17 ff., Lord Wright at 181 ff. Nonetheless so because as I have there submitted, it could not even after transportation yield the result arrived at. See my analysis, cited *supra* at 274-5.

169. And cf. W. Friedmann, Harris Tweed Case and 'Freedom of Trade' (1942) 6 *Mod. L. Rev.* 1, 5.

170. *Perrin* v. *Morgan* (1943) A.C. 399, per Viscount Simon L.C. at 406, quoting Lord Green M.R. in the C.A. (1942) Ch. 345, 346. Lords Russell and Romer sought to reframe the rule, see *supra* nn. 169, 170. Though the matter cannot be pursued, it is believed that there were, even before this decision, alternative premisses for reasoning which would have yielded just results if the courts had not felt themselves under the compulsion of the concept. Contemporary academic writing which sought to rationalize the old rule, e.g. C. K. Allen, *Law in the Making* (3rd ed., 1938), 400, will no doubt be rewritten.

171. Lord Wright, 'Ought the Doctrine of Consideration to be Abolished. . .' (1936), 49 *Harv. L. Rev.* 1225, repr. op. cit. 287; Law Revision Committee, *Sixth Interim Report* (May 1937, Cmd. 5449) 12-30. As with so many rules 'deductively' reached many 'applications' of the doctrine are well suspected to be logically unsustainable: see Lord Wright, op. cit. 305-7. The point is as to bilateral (i.e. executory) contracts, that each promise to be a valuable consideration and not mere words must have some binding force. Neither, then, can have binding force until and unless the contract itself binds. Lord Wright draws attention to the fine example in Bosanquet and Puller's Note to *Wennall* v. *Adney* (1803) 3 Bos. & P. 247 (C.P.), of what he calls 'the method of reasoning of the common lawyer of that period' (op. cit. 314). It is, indeed, a rich example of 'the fallacy of the logical form' in general, nor has it been limited to that period.

172. Cf. for an account of some only of the frustrations involved, A. M. Finlay, *Contracts for the Benefit of Third Persons,* 1939.

173. On common-law statutory interpretation generally, see C. K. Allen, op. cit. 396 ff.; J. S. Landis, 'A Note on Statutory Interpretation' (1930) 43 *Harv. L. Rev.* 886, and 'Statutes and the Sources of Law' in *Harvard Legal Essays* (1934), 213; R. Pound, 'Common Law and Legislation' (1908) 21 *Harv. L. Rev.* 383.

174. W. I. Jennings, 'Judicial Process at Its Worst' (1937) 1 *Mod. L. Rev.* 111.

175. Cf. Lord Wright, op. cit. 334-9, on this shift to the legislative form; and ibid. 336-7: 'The judges have to [*sic*] interpret statutes on common law principles and thus the common law plays a great part in the actual effect of the statutes.' But see ibid. 395-7, where he describes as inadequate the principle of holding in statutes 'in days of modern legislation.'

176. See *Edwards* v. *Porter* (1925) A.C. 1, *per* Birkenhead L. C. and Viscount Cave on *Seroka* v. *Kattenburg* (1886), 17 Q.B. D. 177.

177. See A. M. Finlay, cited *supra,* c. viii.

178. See e.g. A. Russell-Jones, 'Workmen's Compensation. . .' (1943) 7 *Mod. L. Rev.* 13. Cf. Scrutton L.J. quoted *supra.*

179. See the Nokes Case, *supra.*

180. S. Webb, *History of Trade Unionism* (1920 ed.); cf. Scrutton L.J. *supra.*

181. Scrutton L.J.

182. (1927) 20 Cr. App. Rep. 132.

183. D. Seaborne-Davies, 'Child-Killing in English Law' (1937) 1 *Mod. L. Rev.* 203, 269.

184. R. Pound, 'Common Law and Legislation' (1907) 21 *Harv. L. Rev.* 283. And see Davies, 'Interpretation of Statutes in the Light of their Policy by the English Courts' (1935) 35 *Col. L. Rev.* 519; M. Franklin, 'The Historic Function of the American Law Institute. . .' (1934) 47 *Harv. L. Rev.* 1367, 1376-82.

185. See *supra* nn. 261a, 272.

186. For a brief account see Note (1937) 50 *Harv. L. Rev.* 822.

187. See H. Lauterpacht, 'Preparatory Work in the Interpretation of Statutes' (1935) 48 *Harv. L. Rev.* 549, 558-62.

188. *The Uniform Tax Case, S. Australia v. Commonwealth* (1942) 65 *C.L.R.* 373, esp. Latham C.J. at 409-10.

189. See the remarkable example in *Murphy* v. *N. Ireland Transport Board* (1937) N.I. 22, and the learned Note by J. A. Coutts, 1 *Mod. L. Rev.* 166.

190. M. Finer, Note (1941) 5 *Mod. L. Rev.* 120.

191. E.g. C. K. Allen, op. cit. 404 ff., on which see S. P. Simpson's sharp criticism in 'English Law in the Making' (1940) 4 *Mod. L. Rev.,* at 125-6. For critical English views of traditional approaches, see also Sir M. Amos, 'The Interpretation of Statutes' (1934) 5 *Camb. L. Jo.* 163; W. I. Jennings, cited *supra,* and 'Courts and Administrative Law' (1936) 49 *Harv. L. Rev.,* 426; and H. J. Laski's contribution to the *Report of the Committee on Minister's Powers* (1932) Cm. 4060, 135-7. Lord Wright, e.g. op. cit. 377-8, occasionally writes as if he unqualifiedly accepts the traditional assumptions. But this, in view of his analysis of the judicial process, cannot, it is respectfully believed, be the case. The query is given piquancy by some hints at 395-7.

192. Op. cit. 199, 200.

193. *Path of the Law,* op. cit. 456-66.

194. As indeed Professor Goodhart, dissenting, implied when he proposed that there should be central deposition of all decisions (including reasons) of all courts of record. This attitude fits perfectly, of course, into Professor Goodhart's mechanical theory of precedent. And see the pertinent remarks of R. O'Sullivan, 'Committee on Law Reporting' (1940) 4 *Mod. L. Rev.* 104, esp. 107.

195. Op. cit. xviii.

196. See Lord Wright's essay on the Liesbosch Case. Controversies such as that between Professor Goodhart and Professor Winfield on this seem, however, with great respect, to proceed mainly within a pre-Holmesian universe of discourse. For a late example with references, see A. L. Goodhart, Book Review of P. H. Winfield, *Law of Torts* (2nd ed. 1944) 7 *Mod. L. Rev.* 81, 88.

197. (1943) A.C. 32 at 154; (1943) 2 All. E. R. 112 at 129.

198. Lord Atkin's refusal to admit this, while arriving at the same result by saying that the promise totally failed (at 131-2) points the matter nicely. Cf. G. L. Williams, 'The End of Chandler v. Webster' (1943) 6 *Mod. L. Rev.* 46-57.

199. On the basis of the exception see G. L. Williams, op. cit. 55.

200. It should be compared, for instance, with the Law Revision Committee's recommendation (Cmd. 6009, 1939), and Law Reform (Frustrated Contracts) Act, 1943, that the rule abolished for general purposes should be preserved in certain cases of carriage of goods by sea where it conformed to the expectations of merchants.

201. Cf. Viscount Haldane's view of the ground of discharge of frustration in the Tamplin Case (1916) 2 A.C. 397 at 406, 411. And cf. apart from quasi-contract Mackinnon L. J.'s approach in *Heap* v. *Ind Coope and Allsop* (1940) 2 K.B. 676 (C.A.) 3 All. E. R. 634 at 636-7.

202. (1940) 1 K.B. 100.

203. See e.g. *Smith* v. *Birmingham Corp.* (1939) 4 All. E. R. 116.

204. Cf. Sir W. Greene M.R.'s view of the judicial task in applying the standard of 'reasonableness' in the Knightsbridge Case, cited *supra;* the much disapproved but

none the less significant views of McCardie J. in *Prager* v. *Blatspiel,* cited *supra;* Goddard L.J.'s penetration to the substance of the surviving cause of action for loss of expectation of life cited by Viscount Simon L.C. in *Benham* v. *Gambling* (1941) A.C. 157, 165. And see generally the speeches in *United Australia Ltd.* v. *Barclay's Bank Ltd.* (1941) A.C. 1, esp. of Lords Atkinson and Wright; and cf. the latter's comment cited *infra* n. 296.

The use of technical concepts to limit the scope of doctrines generally disapproved is also notable. On common employment see e.g. *Radcliffe* v. *Ribble Motor Co.* (1939) A.C. 215; on the husband's liability for the wife's torts, see *Edwards* v. *Porter* (1925) A.C. 1.

As to the statement of Hamilton L.J. in *Baylis* v. *Bishop of London* (1913) 1 Ch. 127, 140, that 'we are not now free in the twentieth century to administer that vague jurisprudence which is sometimes attractively styled "justice between man and man," ' see Lord Wright, op. cit. 25-6.

205. For instance, as to the exact limits of discoverability by intermediate inspection which will defeat liability; see *Dransfield* v. *British Insulated Cables, Ltd.* (1939) 54 T.L.R. 11, and cf. with *Herschtal* v. *Stewart & Ardern* (1939) 56 T.L.R. 48, and *Paine's Case* (1939) 160 L.T. 24. Cf. Lord Atkin's qualified reference to the doctrine of the case in *East Suffolk Rivers Catchment Board* v. *Kent* (1941) A.C. 74 (1940) 4 All. E. R. 527. And see the continuing controversies, e.g. P. A. Landon, Note (1941) 57 *Law Q. Rev.* 185; W. Friedmann (1941) 5 *Mod. L. Rev.*

206. Cf. E. N. Garlan, op. cit. 11 and *passim.* One of the valuable emphases of the American realistic approach is upon the need for juristic and judicial readiness to multiply categories when new situations require it, rather than the torture to submit to old ones. And cf. Lord Wright, *United Australia Ltd.* v. *Barclay's Bank Ltd.* (1941) 57 *Law Q. Rev.* 184, 198.

207. See Professor Goodhart's latest formulation, 'The Foundations of Tortious Liability' (1938) 2 *Mod. L. Rev.* 1, esp. 8 ff., where references to the English literature will be found. It would of course be singular to deny it in face of the fact of growth without major legislative intervention, and the known creation of particular torts by cases such as *Pasley* v. *Freeman* (1789) 2 T.R. 51 (fraud); or *Lumley* v. *Gye* (1853), 2 F. & B. 216 (inducement of breach of contract) or *Rylands* v. *Fletcher* (1868) L.R. 3 H.L. 330 (escape of dangerous things).

208. Cf. Lord Wright, op. cit. 341-2. The following further comments may be ventured: (1) Professor Goodhart's assumption that the creative nature of judicial activity is disposed of by purporting to prove that the creativeness is unconscious seems linked with his theory of precedent and open to all the difficulties of that theory; (2) his point (op. cit. 8-9) that a discreet lawyer would not, on the strength of gradual change in the law of torts, advise a client at appeal on the chance of establishing a new tort seems of limited importance. For first, the problem is of far wider import than that affecting the minority of persons who litigate their rights. And second, if sufficient were at stake and the client of sufficient means a discreet lawyer might be very neglectful of his client's interests if he did not advise appeal in those many cases on which the law is formative. Mr. Justice Holmes, indeed, thought that a hard-headed practitioner should always regard his task as one of prediction of the probabilities of the court's behavior. The 'precedent system,' S. P. Simpson has recently said (cited *supra*), is '[a] process of progressive revelation, it is a process of unevenly created becoming.'

209. *Paradoxes of Legal Science* (1928) 10. Cf. on the main point Lord Wright, op. cit. xvi-xvii, 342-4.

210. O. W. Holmes, op. cit. *supra* n. 193, 457, 466, 468.

211. E. Ehrlich, op. cit. 132-4.

212. J. Dewey, 'Logical Method and Law' (1924) 10 *Cornell L. Qu.* 17 ff., quoted in J. Hall, *Readings in Jurisprudence* (1938), 345, 349.

213. *Supra* n. 290. Lord Atkin's speech in *Donoghue* v. *Stevenson,* cited *supra,* at 583, that he did not 'think so ill of our jurisprudence as to suppose "that our law

would" deny a legal remedy where there is so obviously a social wrong,' is on one, and perhaps the more likely interpretation, a generalization of the attitude concretely manifested by Mackinnon L.J. Cf. the Lord Chancellor's speech in the United Australia Case, cited *supra*.

214. In the context this appears to mean 'inasmuch as the defendants are so placed financially as to be able to pay Heap any sum likely to be awarded to him.'

215. The 'total situation' from which, it is said, premisses gradually emerge, includes (1) the syllogistic reasoning which may be involved in criticizing or verifying tentative conclusions on the basis of existing or assumed legal propositions; (2) the impress upon the judicial mind of the actual situation with which the court is faced, including the state of the authoritative legal materials in regard thereto; and (3) the standards of value or justice with which the court approaches the situation, standards which may derive from his membership in the community generally, or some section of it, from his training in legal traditions and materials, or (more rarely) from his own personality.

216. No use of the word need be caviled at provided it is consistently adhered to. The sense used in the present study besides being that of Holmes' 'fallacy of the logical form' is general in professional and judicial usage. See also B. Cardozo, *Nature of the Judicial Process* (1922), 38-9; and *Growth of the Law* (1924), 79-80; L. Brandeis, 'The Right of Privacy' (1890) 4 *Harv. L. Rev.* 193. The dangers sensed by F. S. Cohen, op. cit., in this usage as meaning 'consistent with existing premisses' as distinct from 'logically compelling' have, it is believed, not been incurred in the present study.

REASONING IN A CIRCLE OF LAW*

*Roger J. Traynor***

THERE are few great pioneers in any field, for greatness is by definition rare. In law as in other fields, however, we do not lack priests of high fashion who reject established ways to establish their own for slavish followers. Once it was high fashion to endorse the status quo automatically, too often without rhyme or reason. The conventional wooden square was in, and woe befell any lawyer or judge who did not fit his decision or brief squarely within its straight lines. Everyone who counted knew where he stood, even if he only stood in a corner. As for anyone who wanted to know where *she* stood, she soon learned. She usually stood outside the pale of the laws of descent or ascent or dissent. All that remained to her was dissolution in tears. Hardly anyone dreamed that some day one of her kind, preoccupied with bearing children, preferably male for property relevance, would walk into a Yankee legislature and bear tidings that began: "Brothers, I have news for you." Hardly anyone dreamed that some day the rights of people in general would cease to be only on the periphery of a worm's-eye view of property rights.

Now, the sedentary squares of the status quo are put down if not out, and the floating circles of law reform are in, hanging loose. Their pitchmen proclaim the absence of dust-collecting corners in the new products and guarantee them for at least ninety days. Best of all, these novel circles can stretch into other sizes and shapes. There are few to question the new dogma that ascribes to them an automatic relevance to current problems. The very term, *law reform*, evokes the mystique of relevance. It conveys assurance, like a miracle fabric, that all will be well as soon as it is pressed or unpressed into service. If one fabric fails, there is always another and another ready for use, and failures disappear from view in the endless busyness of fabrication.

As one receptive to change but wary of dogma in old forms or new,

*Law Day address delivered at the University of Virginia on May 2, 1970. In developing the theme of this address the author found it relevant to invoke at various junctures some reflections that he has set forth in previous addresses. Interestingly enough, time has made them more timely than ever.

**James Monroe Visiting Professor of Law, University of Virginia. Chief Justice of California (Retired). A.B., 1923; Ph.D., 1927; J.D., 1927, University of California.

I view with interest the production of contemporary circles, well-rounded or stretched out into new patterns, and stand ready to heed prosaic or well-rhymed reasoning on behalf of their miracle fabrics. Nonetheless you will note alternate warnings throughout the comment I now undertake on how lawmakers can best reason amid the new circles of law. The first warning, not always agreeable to the old, is that there is no assurance of continuing virtue in age and custom per se. The second warning, not always agreeable to the young, is that there is no assurance of full-blown virtue in youth and innovation per se.

With these warnings in mind, we can now proceed to note a salient change in lawmaking. Once the province mainly of courts, which brought to it slow, old-fashioned, often inefficient ways, it is now the province mainly of legislatures, of Congress and state assemblies and town councils, which bring to it newfangled ways that at worst breed new inefficiency or engender an efficiency at odds with reason. The hyperproductivity of this expanding field of lawmaking carries the mark of an age of plenty and the attendant risks of pollution.

Receptive we may be to an abundance of new riches in the law, but we cannot let them accumulate in such haphazard heaps that they confuse the law at the expense of rational reform. Hence, as legislatures increase their already formidable output of statutes, courts must correspondingly enlarge their responsibility for keeping the law a coherent whole.

It is no secret that a legislature usually makes much more law in a session via statutes than a court does over a long period of time via the painstaking application or adaptation of common-law rules and the occasional innovation of a new one. Legislators are free to experiment, to draft laws on a massive scale or ad hoc in response to what they understand to be the needs of the community or the community of interests they represent. The legislators themselves are experiments of a sort; they are on trial until the next election and must prove in the interim that they can make laws acceptable to their time and place, even though many of them may not be lawyers.

What a legislature does, however, it can undo without much ado. If some of its purported miracle fabrics fail to prove miraculous, they need no longer remain on the shelves. We can lament that they sometimes do, but we need not despair; they rarely survive indefinitely. Bumbling though the legislative process may be, it is more readily self-correcting than the judicial process. Given its flexibility, we can accept amiably that when a legislature is good, it can be very, very good, but

that when it is bad, it is horrid. We can also in some measure resign ourselves to how ingeniously it sometimes abstains from any action, how
mysteriously it sometimes moves its wonders not to perform. We can
reconcile ourselves to its swings of quality so long as the people exercise
responsibly their power to keep it in fact a do-gooder, a reformer of
the law.

It could not be otherwise in the modern world that for better or
worse the legislatures have displaced courts as our major lawmakers.
We have come a long way from the time when courts were on guard
to keep statutes in their place, in the shadow of precedent. In most of
their affairs people who seek out new rules of law now look to the next
legislative session, not to the day of judgment. In street wisdom, it is easier
to legislate than to litigate. A legislature can run up a law on short notice, and when it has finished all the seams, it can run up another and
another. It is engaged in mass production; it produces piecework of its
own volition or on order. The great tapestry of Holmes' princess, the
seamless web of the law, becomes ever more legendary.

Whatever our admiration for ancient arts, few of us would turn the
clock back to live out what museums preserve. The law of contracts
was once well served by delightful causeries of learned judges that
clarified the meaning of obligation. Such causeries, however, proved inadequate to provide an expansion and diversification of words to correspond with that of business enterprise. Thus it fell to the legislators
to spell out whole statutes such as insurance codes and the uniform
laws dealing with negotiable instruments, sales, bills of lading, ware-
house receipts, stock transfers, conditional sales, trust receipts, written
obligations, fiduciaries, partnerships, and limited partnerships.

There followed in the United States another development, a state-
by-state adoption of the Uniform Commercial Code, the culmination
of years of scholarly work sponsored by the American Law Institute
and the Commissioners on Uniform State Laws. Such statutes can take
a bird's-eye view of the total problem, instead of that of an owl on
a segment. They can encompass wide generalizations from experience
that a judge is precluded from making in his decision on a particular
case. Legislatures can break sharply with the past, if need be, as judges
ordinarily cannot. They avoid the wasteful cost in time and money of
piecemeal litigation that all too frequently culminates in a crazy quilt
of rules defying intelligent restatement or coherent application. They
can take the initiative in timely solution of urgent problems, in contrast with the inertia incumbent upon judges until random litigation

brings a problem in incomplete form to them, often too soon or too late for over-all solution.

As the legislators tend their factories replete with machinery for the massive fabrication of law, judges work away much as before at the fine interweaving that gives law the grace of coherent pattern as it evolves. Paradoxically, the more legislators extend their range of lawmaking, of statutory innovation and reform at a hare's speed, the more significant becomes the judge's own role of lawmaking, of reformation at the pace of the tortoise. Even at a distance from the onrushing legislators they can make their presence felt. It has been known since the days of Aesop that the tortoise can overtake the zealous hare; La-Fontaine has noted that it does so while carrying a burden. The frailty of the hare is that for all its zeal it tends to become distracted. The strength of the tortoise is its very burden; it is always in its house of the law.

Unlike the legislator, whose lawmaking knows no bounds, the judge stays close to his house of the law in the bounds of stare decisis. He invariably takes precedent as his starting-point; he is constrained to arrive at a decision in the context of ancestral judicial experience: the given decisions, or lacking these, the given dicta, or lacking these, the given clues. Even if his search of the past yields nothing, so that he confronts a truly unprecedented case, he still arrives at a decision in the context of judicial reasoning with recognizable ties to the past; by its kinship thereto it not only establishes the unprecedented case as a precedent for the future, but integrates it in the often rewoven but always unbroken line with the past.

Moreover, the judge is confined by the record in the case, which in turn is confined to legally relevant material, limited by evidentiary rules. So it happens that even a decision of far-reaching importance concludes with the words: "We hold today only that . . . . We do not reach the question whether . . . ." Circumspectly the weaver stops, so as not to confuse the pattern of transition from yesterday to today. Tomorrow is time enough for new weaving, as the facts of tomorrow come due.

A decision that has not suffered untimely birth has a reduced risk of untimely death. Insofar as a court remains uncommitted to unduly wide implications of a decision, it gains time to inform itself further through succeeding cases. It is then better situated to retreat or advance with a minimum of shock to the evolutionary course of the law, and hence with a minimum of shock to those who act in reliance upon judicial decisions. The greatest judges of the common law have proceeded in this way, moving not by fits and starts, but at the pace of the tortoise that steadily makes advances though it carries the past on its back.

The very caution of the judicial process offers the best of reasons for confidence in the recurring reformation of judicial rules. A reasoning judge's painstaking exploration of place and his sense of pace, give reassurance that when he takes an occasional dramatic leap forward he is impelled to do so in the very interest of orderly progression. There are times when he encounters so much chaos on his long march that the most cautious thing he can do is to take the initiative in throwing chaos to the winds. The great Judge Mansfield did so when he broke the chaos of stalemated contractual relations with the concept of concurrent conditions. Holmes and Brandeis did so when they cleared the way for a liquidation of ancient interpretations of freedom of contract that had served to perpetuate child labor. Cardozo did so when he moved the rusting wheels of *Winterbottom v. Wright*[1] to one side to make way for *MacPherson v. Buick Motor Co.*[2] Chief Justice Stone did so, in the chaotic field of conflict of laws, when he noted the leeway in the United States Constitution between the mandate of the full faith and credit clause and the prohibition of the due process clause.[3]

To a reasoning judge, each case is a new piece of an ever-expanding pattern, to be woven in if possible by reference to precedent. If precedent proves inadequate or inept, he is still likely to do justice to it in the breach, setting forth clearly the disparity between the expansively novel facts before him and the all too square precedents that now fail to encompass them. He has also the responsibility of justifying the new precedent he has evolved, not merely as the dispossessor of the old, but as the best of all possible replacements. His sense of justice is bound to infuse his logic. A wise judge can strengthen his overruling against captious objections, first by an exposition of the injustice engendered by the discarded precedent, and then by an articulation of how the injustice resulted from the precedent's failure to mesh with accepted legal principles. When he thus speaks out, his words may serve to quicken public respect for the law as an instrument of justice.

He is hardly eager to take on such tasks if he can do otherwise. He knows that a new rule must be supported by full disclosure in his opinion of all aspects of the problem and of the data pertinent to its solu-

---

[1] 152 Eng. Rep. 402 (Ex. 1842).

[2] 217 N.Y. 382, 111 N.E. 1050 (1916).

[3] Yarborough v. Yarborough, 290 U.S. 202, 214 (1933) (dissenting opinion).

tion. Thereafter the opinion must persuade his colleagues, make sense to the bar, pass muster with scholars, and if possible allay the suspicion of any man in the street who regards knowledge of the law as no excuse for making it. There is usually someone among them alert to note any misunderstanding of the problem, any error in reasoning, any irrelevance in data, any oversight of relevant data, any premature cartography beyond the problem at hand. Every opinion is thus subject to approval. It is understandable when a judge, faced with running such a gantlet, marks time instead on the line of least resistance and lets bad enough alone.

Moreover, he may still be deterred from displacing an inherently bad or moribund precedent by another restraint of judicial office—the tenet that the law must lag a respectful pace back of popular mores, not only to insure its own acceptance, but also to delay formalization of community values until they have become seasoned.

The tenet of lag, strengthening the already great restraints on the judge, is deservedly respected. It bears noting, however, that it is recurringly invoked by astute litigants who receive aid and comfort from law that is safely behind the times with the peccadillos of yesteryear and has not caught up with their own. At the slightest sign that judge-made law may move forward, these bogus defenders of stare decisis conjure up mythical dangers to alarm the citizenry. They do sly injury to the law when the public takes them seriously, and timid judges retreat from painstaking analysis within their already great constraints to safe and unsound repetitions of magic words from antiquated legal lore.

Too often the real danger to law is not that judges might take off onward and upward, but that all too many of them have long since stopped dead in the tracks of their predecessors. They would command little attention were it not that they speak the appealing language of stability in justification of specious formulas. The trouble is that the formulas may encase notions that have never been cleaned and pressed and might disintegrate if they were. We might not accept the formulas so readily were we to realize what a cover they can be for the sin the Bible calls sloth and associates with ignorance. Whatever the judicial inertia evinced by a decision enveloped in words that have lost their magic, it is matched by the profession's indifference or uncritical acceptance. Thus formula survives by default.

Stare decisis, to stand by decided cases, conjures up another phrase dear to Latin lovers—*stare super antiquas vias*, to stand on the old paths.

One might feel easier about that word *stare* if itself it stood by one fixed star of meaning. In modern Italian *stare* means to stay, to stand, to lie, or to sit, to remain, to keep, to stop, or to wait. With delightful flexibility it also means to depend, to fit or to suit, to live and, of course, to be.

Legal minds at work on this word might well conjecture that to *stare* or not to *stare* depends on whether *decisis* is dead. or alive. We might inquire into the life of what we are asked to stand by. In the language of *stare decisers*: *Primo*, should it ever have been born? *Secundo*, is it still alive? *Tertio*, does it now deserve to live?

Who among us has not known a precedent that should never have been born? What counsel does not know a precedent worn so thin and pale with distinctions that the court has never troubled to overrule it? How many a counsel, accordingly misled, has heard the court then pronounce that the precedent must be deemed to have revealed itself as overruled *sub silentio* and ruminated in bewilderment that the precedent on which he relied was never expressly overruled because it so patently needed to be?

The notion yet persists that the overruling of ill-conceived, or moribund, or obsolete precedents somehow menaces the stability of the law. It is as if we would not remove barriers on a highway because everyone had become accustomed to circumventing them, and hence traffic moved, however awkwardly. The implication is that one cannot render traffic conditions efficient without courting dangers from the disturbance of established habit patterns. We have reached such a pass, we are wont to say, that it is for the legislature and not the court to set matters aright. No one says it more than the courts themselves.

Why? One speculation is that the popular image of the legislature as the lawmaking body, in conjunction with a popular notion of contemporary judges as primarily the maintenance men of the law, has engendered an auxiliary notion that whatever incidental law courts create they are bound to maintain unless the legislature undertakes to unmake it.

One can speculate further that the occupational caution of judges makes them reluctant to take the initiative in overruling a precedent whose unworthiness is concealed in the aura of stare decisis. It takes boldness to turn a flashlight upon an aura and call out what one has seen, at the risk of violating quiet for the benefit of those who have retired from active thought. It is easier for a court to rationalize that less shock will result if it bides its time, and bides it, and bides it, the while it awaits legislative action to transfer an unfortunate precedent unceremoniously to the dump from the fading glory in which it has been basking.

Thus courts have maintained their own theatre of the absurd. For generations since the 1787 rule of *Jee v. Audley*,[4] for example, they earnestly pretended that ancient crones could have babies. Again, even after the advent of conclusive blood tests to the contrary, they could still pretend that anyone might be a father.[5] Flattering though it may have been to a crone to be viewed as a possible mother of the year though she would never have a child to show for it, it can only have been disquieting to a man to be named as an actual father of someone who was no child of his.

Fortunately all is not saved. In retrospect we come to see how well courts now and again do clear a trail for those who come after them. They have significantly expanded the concept of obligation. They are recognizing a much needed right to privacy.[6] They are recognizing a right to recovery for prenatal injuries[7] and intentionally inflicted mental suffering.[8] They are also recognizing liability once precluded by charitable[9] or governmental immunities.[10] Their now general acceptance of the manufacturer's liability to third persons for negligence has stimulated inquiry into appropriate bases for possible strict liability for injuries resulting from defective products.[11] There is more and more open preoccupation with compensation for personal injuries, which is bound in turn to augment the scope of insurance.[12]

Courts are also recognizing new responsibilities within the family

---

[4] 29 Eng. Rep. 1186 (1787).

[5] Arais v. Kalensnikoff, 10 Cal. 2d 428, 74 P.2d 1043 (1937); Berry v. Chaplin, 74 Cal. App. 2d 652, 169 P.2d 442 (Dist. Ct. App. 1946), *overruled by statute*, CAL. CIV. PROC. CODE §§ 1980.1-.7 (West 1955).

[6] Griswold v. Connecticut, 381 U.S. 479 (1965); *cf.* Stanley v. Georgia, 394 U.S. 557 (1969). *See generally* Prosser, *Privacy*, 48 CALIF. L. REV. 383 (1960).

[7] Woods v. Lancet, 303 N.Y. 349, 102 N.E.2d 691 (1951).

[8] State Rubbish Collectors Ass'n v. Siliznoff, 38 Cal. 2d 330, 240 P.2d 282 (1952).

[9] Malloy v. Fong, 37 Cal. 2d 356, 232 P.2d 241 (1951).

[10] Muskoph v. Corning Hosp. Dist., 55 Cal. 2d 211, 359 P.2d 457, 11 Cal. Rptr. 89 (1961).

[11] Seely v. White Motor Co., 63 Cal. 2d 9, 403 P.2d 145, 45 Cal. Rptr. 17 (1965); Greenman v. Yuba Power Prods., Inc., 59 Cal. 2d 57, 377 P.2d 897, 27 Cal. Rptr. 697 (1962); Henningsen v. Bloomfield Motors, 32 N.J. 358, 161 A.2d 69 (1960).

[12] *See* A. EHRENZWEIG, "FULL AID" INSURANCE FOR THE TRAFFIC VICTIM: A VOLUNTARY COMPENSATION PLAN (1954); L. GREEN, TRAFFIC VICTIMS: TORT LAW AND INSURANCE (1958); R. KEETON & J. O'CONNELL, BASIC PROTECTION FOR THE TRAFFIC VICTIM: A BLUEPRINT FOR REFORMING AUTOMOBILE INSURANCE (1965).

as well as new freedoms. They are recognizing the right of one member of the family to recover against another.[13] They are recognizing women as people with lives of their own, transcending their status as somebody else's spouse or somebody else's mother, transcending somebody else's vision of what nonentities they should be.[14]

In conflicts of law, wooden rules are giving way as surely as wooden boundary lines.[15] Comparable changes are on the horizon in property law that will reflect new ways of holding and transferring property, and evolving concepts of land use, zoning, and condemnation.[16] Criminal law is beginning to reflect new insights into human behavior.[17] Landmark cases in constitutional law evince major changes in the relation of the federal government to the states.[18]

A judge participates significantly in lawmaking whether he makes repairs and renewals in the common law via the adaptation of an old precedent or advances its reformation with a new one. He does so on a variety of fronts, in the interpretation of statutory or constitutional language as well as in the analysis of traditional common law problems.

Rare are the statutes that rest in peace beyond the range of controversy. Large problems of interpretation inevitably arise. Plain words, like plain people, are not always so plain as they seem. Certainly a judge is not at liberty to seek hidden meanings not suggested by the statute or the available extrinsic aids. Speculation cuts brush with the question: What purpose did the legislature express as it strung its word into a statute? An insistence upon judicial regard for the words of a statute does not imply that they are like words in a dictionary, to be read with no ranging of the mind. They are no longer at rest in their alphabetical bins. Released, combined in phrases that imperfectly communicate the thoughts of one man to another, they challenge men to give them more

---

[13] Self v. Self, 58 Cal. 2d 683, 376 P.2d 65, 26 Cal. Rptr. 97 (1962); Emery v. Emery, 45 Cal. 2d 421, 289 P.2d 218 (1955).

[14] People v. Pierce, 61 Cal. 2d 879, 395 P.2d 893, 40 Cal. Rptr. 845 (1964).

[15] Reich v. Purcell, 67 Cal. 2d 551, 432 P.2d 727, 63 Cal. Rptr. 31 (1967); Babcock v. Jackson, 12 N.Y.2d 473, 191 N.E.2d 279 (1963); Bernkrant v. Fowler, 55 Cal. 2d 588, 360 P.2d 906, 12 Cal. Rptr. 266 (1961); Grant v. McAuliffe, 41 Cal. 2d 859, 264 P.2d 944 (1953).

[16] The American Law Institute is currently at work on a Model Land Development Code.

[17] People v. Conley, 64 Cal. 2d 310, 411 P.2d 911, 49 Cal. Rptr. 815 (1966); People v. Baker, 42 Cal. 2d 550, 268 P.2d 705 (1954).

[18] Miranda v. Arizona, 384 U.S. 436 (1966); Fay v. Noia, 372 U.S. 391 (1963); Baker v. Carr, 369 U.S. 186 (1962); Brown v. Board of Educ., 347 U.S. 483 (1954).

than passive reading, to consider well their context, to ponder what may be their consequences.[19] Such a task is not for the phlegmatic. It calls for judicial temperament, for impassive reflection quickened with an awareness of the waywardness of words.

There are times when statutory words prove themselves so at odds with a clear legislative purpose as to pose a dilemma for the judge. He knows that there is an irreducible minimum of error in statutes because they deal with multifarious and frequently complicated problems. He hesitates to undertake correction of even the most obvious legislative oversight, knowing that theoretically the legislature has within its power the correction of its own lapses. Yet he also knows how cumbersome the legislative process is, how massive the machinery that must be set in motion for even the smallest correction, how problematic that it will be set in motion at all, how confusion then may be worse confounded.

With deceptively plain words, as with ambiguous ones, what a court does is determined in the main by the nature of the statute. It may be so general in scope as to invite judicial elaboration. It may evince such careful draftsmanship in the main as to render its errors egregious enough to be judicially recognized as such, inconsistent with the legislative purpose.

The experienced draftsmen of tax laws, among others, find it impossible to foresee all the problems that will test the endurance of their words. They did not foresee, for example, the intriguing question whether the United States is a resident of the United States, which arose under a revenue act taxing interest received by foreign corporations from such residents. What to do when a foreign corporation received interest from the United States? Mr. Justice Sutherland decided that this country resided in itself. He found a spirit willing to take up residence though the flesh was weak, if indeed not entirely missing. The ingenuity of the solution compels admiration, whatever misgivings it may engender as to our self-containment.[20]

So the courts now and again prevent erratic omissions or errant words from defeating legislative purpose, even though they thereby disregard conventional canons of construction. We come upon an intriguing but quite different problem when we consider what should be the fair import of legislative silence in the wake of statutory interpretation em-

[19] People v. Knowles, 35 Cal. 2d 175, 182, 217 P.2d 1, 5 (1950).
[20] Helvering v. Stockholms Enskilda Bank, 293 U.S. 84 (1934).

bodied in the occasional precedent that proves increasingly unsound in the solution of subsequent cases. Barring those exceptional situations where the entrenched precedent has engendered so much reliance that its liquidation would do more harm than good, the court should be free to overrule such a precedent despite legislative inaction.

It is unrealistic to suppose that the legislature can note, much less deliberate, the effect of each judicial interpretation of a statute, absorbed as it is with forging legislation for an endless number and variety of problems, under the constant pressure of considerations of urgency and expediency. The fiction that the failure of the legislature to repudiate an erroneous judicial interpretation amounts to an incorporation of that interpretation into the statute not only assumes that the legislature has embraced something that it may not even be aware of, but bars the court from reexamining its own error—consequences as unnecessary as they are serious.

It is ironic that an unsound interpretation of a statute should gain strength merely because it has stood unnoticed by the legislature. It is a mighty assumption that legislative silence means applause. It is much more likely to mean ignorance or indifference.[21] Thus time after time a judicial opinion calls out loud and clear that there is an unresolved problem or patent injustice that can be remedied only by the legislature. The message may be heard round the world of legal commentators who listen intently for such reports. Rarely, however, does it reach the ears of legislators across the clamor and the static of legislative halls. It would be high comedy, were it not for the sometimes sad repercussions, that we are wont solemnly to attribute significance to the silence of legislators. There can be idle silence as well as idle talk.

In spelling out rules that form a Morse code common to statutes and judicial decisions, and in the United States common even to the Constitution of the country and the constitutions of the states, courts keep the law straight on its course. That high responsibility should not be reduced to a mean task of keeping the law straight and narrow. It calls for literate, not literal, judges.

Hence we should not be misled by the half-truth that policy is a matter for the legislators to decide. Recurringly it is also for the courts to decide. There is always an area not covered by legislation in which they must revise old rules or formulate new ones, and in that process policy may be an appropriate and even a basic consideration. The

---

[21] *See* Boys Market, Inc. v. Retail Clerks Local 770, 38 U.S.L.W. 4462 (U.S. June 1, 1970).

briefs carry the first responsibility in stating the policy at stake and demonstrating its relevance; but if they fail or fall short, no conscientious judge will set bounds to his inquiry. If he finds no significant clues in the law books, he will not close his eyes to a pertinent study merely because it was written by an economist or perhaps an anthropologist or an engineer.

We need not distrust judicial scrutiny of such extralegal materials. The very independence of judges, fostered by judicial office even when not guaranteed by tenure, and their continuous adjustment of sight to varied problems tend to develop in the least of them some skill in the evaluation of massive data. They learn to detect latent quackery in medicine, to question doddered scientific findings, to edit the swarm spore of the social scientists, to add grains of salt to the fortune-telling statistics of the economists. Moreover, as with cases or legal theories not covered by the briefs, they are bound in fairness to direct the attention of counsel to such materials, if it appears that they may affect the outcome of the case, and to give them the opportunity to submit additional briefs. So the miter square of legal analysis, the marking blades for fitting and joining, reduce any host of materials to the gist of a legal construction.

Regardless of whether it is attended by abundant or meager materials, a case may present competing considerations of such closely matched strength as to create a dilemma. How can a judge then arrive at a decision one way or the other and yet avoid being arbitrary? If he has a high sense of judicial responsibility, he is loath to make an arbitrary choice even of acceptably rational alternatives, for he would thus abdicate the responsibility of judgment when it proved most difficult. He rejects coin-tossing, though it would make a great show of neutrality. Then what?

He is painfully aware that a decision will not be saved from being arbitrary merely because he is disinterested. He knows well enough that one entrusted with decision, traditionally above base prejudices, must also rise above the vanity of stubborn preconceptions, sometimes euphemistically called the courage of one's convictions. He knows well enough that he must severely discount his own predilections, of however high grade he regards them, which is to say he must bring to his intellectual labors a cleansing doubt of his omniscience, indeed even of his perception. Disinterest, however, even distinterest envisaged on a higher plane than the emotional, is only the minimum qualifications of a judge for his job. Then what more?

He comes to realize how essential it is also that he be intellectually interested in a rational outcome. He cannot remain disoriented forever, his mind suspended between alternative passable solutions. Rather than to take the easy way out via one or the other, he can strive to deepen his inquiry and his reflection enough to arrive at last at a value judgment as to what the law ought to be and to spell out why. In the course of doing so he channels his interest in a rational outcome into an interest in a particular result. In that limited sense he becomes result-oriented, an honest term to describe the stubbornly rational search for the optimum decision. Would we have it otherwise? Would we give up the value judgment for an abdication of judical responsibility, for the toss of the two-faced coin?

In sum, judicial responsibility connotes far more than a mechanical application of given rules to new sets of facts. It connotes the recurring formulation of new rules to supplement or displace the old. It connotes the recurring choice of one policy over another in that formulation, and an articulation of the reasons therefor.

Even so much, however, constituting the judicial contribution to lawmaking, adds up to no more than interweaving in the reformation of law. If judges must be much more than passive mechanics, they must certainly remain much less than zealous reformers. They would serve justice ill by weaving samplers of law with ambitious designs for reform. Judges are not equipped for such work, confined as they are to the close work of imposing design on fragments of litigation. Dealing as they do with the bits and pieces that blow into their shop on a random wind, they cannot guess at all that lies outside their line of vision nor foresee what may still appear.

As one who has declared himself against the perpetuation of ancient fabrics that no longer shield us from storms, if they ever did, I should like now to voice a cautionary postscript against judges rushing in where well-meaning angels of mercy tread, hawking their new methods of fabrication. The zealots of law reform too often are as indifferent to exacting standards of quality control as the mechanics of the status quo. Moreover, we cannot be so tolerant of heedless ventures in new directions in courts as in legislatures, given the constant risk that judicial error will become frozen as stare decisis.

We could wish that modern legislatures, often abundantly equipped to carry the main responsibility for lawmaking, would be weaving grand designs of law as informed and inspired reformers. Instead we must rue with Judge Friendly: *The Gap in Lawmaking—*

Judges Who Can't and Legislators Who Won't.[22] He laments that "the legislator has diminished the role of the judge by occupying vast fields and then has failed to keep them ploughed."[23]

Certainly courts are helpless to stay the maddening sequences of triumphal entry and sit-in. What is frustration to them, however, could be challenge to the scholars. Steeped in special knowledge of one field or another, they can well place their knowledge at the service of legislatures for the plowing of the fields, for their sowing and their care. Who but the scholars have the freedom as well as the nurturing intellectual environment to differentiate the good growth from the rubbish and to mark for rejection the diseased anachronism, the toadstool formula, the scrub of pompous phrases?

There is a tragic waste in the failure to correlate all our machinery for vigil to maximum advantage. Is it not time to break the force of habit that militates against steady communication between legislators in unplowed fields and scholarly watchbirds in bleachers? It is for no more sinister reason than lethargy that we have failed in large measure to correlate the natural resources of legislators who have an ear to the ground for the preemption of new fields and of scholars who have an eye on their long-range development.

Perhaps we can make a beginning by calling upon legislators to take the initiative in establishing permanent lines of communication. The scholars can hardly take that initiative, for they are not lobbyists. Why not invite their ideas through the good offices of a legislative committee that can insure their careful consideration? Why not, particularly when some legislatures are now equipped with permanent legislative aids, and here and there law schools have now set up legal centers, and there remains only to set up permanent lines of communication between them? The natural agency for such communication is a law revision commission such as those long since established in New York and California or the ones established for England and Scotland by the 1965 Law Commissions Act.

A law school offers an ideal environment for such a commission. It could there devote itself wholeheartedly to the formulation and drafting of statutes as well as to continuing re-examination of their fitness for survival. It could withstand the prevailing winds of pressure groups as it made timely use of the abundant wasting assets of scholarly studies. One can hardly imagine more valuable interchange for the law than that

[22] 63 COLUM. L. REV. 787 (1963).
[23] *Id.* at 792.

between those entrusted to review it critically and those entrusted to draft proposals for its revision. On a wide front they could collaborate in long-range studies of legal needs that would richly complement the applied research that legislatures recurringly ask of their legislative aids. In turn the work of the commissions would offer hearty sustenance not only to the law reviews but to all the other projects of a law school, not the least of which is the classroom. Such permanent relationships between law schools and law revision commissions, going far beyond today's occasional associations, would strengthen their beneficent influence on legislation.

Perhaps the story of law reform would get better as it went along if scholars steadily established quality controls for the weaving of law, spurring legislators to legislate when necessary and to legislate well, and untangling the problems that advance upon courts, to smooth the task of judicial decision. There comes to mind a story of pioneering times called *The Weaver's Children*, which begins: "Many years ago a little wooden mill stood in a ravine. . . . The little mill filled the space between a rushing stream and a narrow road."

The mill might symbolize the world of scholars, in law schools or on law revision commissions, in legislatures or courts, as well as in public or private practice. The weavers in the mill would keep a weather eye out for the volume and course of the rushing stream, of life itself, to calculate the tempo for the weaving of statutes. They would also keep a weather eye out for traffic conditions on the narrow road, estimating therefrom the tempo at which motley caravans could unload their variegated sacks of litigation. The mill would be a model of rational methods of weaving.

There was not such a model in an age when a narrow version of reasoning, the mechanical logic grounded in old forms of action, served as a quality control on a mean plane. Even today there is not such a model. We have yet to attain the ideal quality control, a tradition of reasoning on a noble plane that would still foster alertness in both the mass producers and the interweavers of law against excesses or deficiencies in their work.

We could come to the pessimistic conclusion that we have little basis for believing in any new circle of law as a miracle, however theatrical its initial twists and turns. I have not come full circle round, however, only to yield to pessimism. I like to believe instead that in time the children of weavers would bring such reasoning into the design and fabrication of the circles as to keep them on course for the long run, without ever boxing them in. Even in the absence of any clear and convincing evidence, I shall continue to believe that, not as a matter of logic, but as an act of faith.

Vagueness in Law and Language: Some Philosophical Issues

Jeremy Waldron†

INTRODUCTION

This Article is devoted to a philosophical account of the various problems with meaning that lawyers associate with the "void-for-vagueness" doctrine. I shall not attempt any detailed consideration of the doctrine itself. Apart from some comments in the concluding section, my contribution is intended to set the conceptual stage for, rather than preempt, the substantive discussion of problems of vagueness in the law. I am employed here, in John Locke's words,

> as an underlabourer in clearing ground a little, and removing some of the rubbish that lies in the way of knowledge; which certainly had been very much more advanced in the world, if the endeavours of ingenious and industrious men had not been so much encumbered with the learned but frivolous use of uncouth, affected, or unintelligible terms.[1]

I
A PRELIMINARY POINT ABOUT MEANING

Scholars in the Critical Legal Studies movement tell us that jurisprudence used to be dominated by "formalism," which is the doctrine that words determine their own applications to the objects to which they apply. It is difficult to state this formalist doctrine coherently (which is probably one of the reasons why, despite CLS claims, no legal philosopher ever held it), but Margaret Jane Radin's statement is typical of many:

> In the traditional conception of the nature of rules, a rule is self-applying to the set of particulars said to fall under it; its application is thought to be analytic. It is often said that rules are logically prior to the particular cases that fall under them. Another way of

---

† Associate Dean and Professor of Law and Philosophy, Jurisprudence and Social Policy Program, Boalt Hall School of Law and Department of Philosophy, University of California, Berkeley. B.A. 1974, LL.B. (Hons.) 1978, University of Otago; D.Phil. 1986, University of Oxford.

1. 1 JOHN LOCKE, AN ESSAY CONCERNING HUMAN UNDERSTANDING at xxxv (J. Yolton ed., 1978) (quote from Locke's introductory "Epistle to the Reader").

putting this is to think that somehow the applications to particulars are already present in the rule itself.[2]

This traditional view, Radin goes on, is mistaken: as a matter of fact, there is no way of telling deductively or analytically when a rule is being followed.[3] Words do not determine meanings, people do. No amount of staring at the words of a rule, then staring at the world, then staring at the words again, will tell us when we have a proper application. Radin's observation is true but trivial, and my preliminary claim in this Part is that it has nothing to do with the issue of vagueness.

Think of the least vague expression you can imagine being used in legislation—say, "less than twenty-one years old" in an ordinance prohibiting serving alcohol to minors. The phrase itself does not light up in the presence of an infant and then go out in the presence of a forty year old, like an ultra-sensitive neon sign at the doorway to a bar. The rule about not serving people under twenty-one is not like a geiger counter that emits a loud clicking whenever a teenager enters the premises. Even when expressions are precise, it is people who must apply the words.

True, people do so by using analytic meaning rules. "X is n years old" means the same as "A period of time which is no less than n years, and less than $n+1$ years, has elapsed since the beginning of the day on which X was born." If someone wants to know the meaning of "year," we define it analytically in this context as "a period of time equal to one year of the Gregorian calendar but beginning [possibly] at a different time."[4] We can go on, if necessary, to define the Gregorian system of 365 and 1/4 days, the meaning of "day" in terms of hours, minutes, seconds, and so on. But these are analytic connections between words and words, not between words and things. Eventually, if we are dealing with a complete neophyte who asks "But what is a second?" we may have to define some period of time ostensively: taking the neophyte to the Greenwich observatory and saying "Listen!—the length in time of *this* tone is a second."[5] That observation is a relation between a word and a thing, but it is not analytic or deductive.

---

2. Margaret J. Radin, *Reconsidering the Rule of Law,* 69 B.U. L. REV. 781, 795 (1989).

3. *See id.* at 798 (interpreting Ludwig Wittgenstein in *Philosophical Investigations*).

4. WEBSTER'S NINTH NEW COLLEGIATE DICTIONARY 1366 (1991) [hereinafter WEBSTER'S] (definition 2(b) of "year").

In addition, there is a whole array of considerations about the analytic/synthetic distinction that I cannot go into here. Clearly, there are circumstances imaginable in which we would modify the connection between "year," the Gregorian system, and our statistical understanding of the time it takes the earth to circle the sun. Does this show that the meaning I have given for year is a synthetic (e.g., astronomical) claim, rather than an analytic (e.g., verbal) claim? *See* W.V.O. QUINE, FROM A LOGICAL POINT OF VIEW at v (2d ed. 1961) (criticizing the "analytic/synthetic" distinction); *see also* SAUL A. KRIPKE, NAMING AND NECESSITY 3-15, 61-164 (1980) (discussing "rigid designators").

5. Or we may have to start all over again in the higher reaches of the language and say a second is the "unit of time equal to the duration of 9,192,631,770 periods of the radiation corresponding to the transition between the two hyperfine levels of the ground state of the cesium-133 atom." WEBSTER'S, *supra* note 4, at 1060 (definition 1(b) of "2 second").

Moreover, a whole apparatus of social practice, about the word "this" and about what it means for time to elapse, is presupposed in this ostension. If the neophyte has not grasped all that, no amount of hand-waving in the presence of tones will help.

Since words do not apply themselves, since it is we who apply them to cases, of course we may need further rules for their application, and of course we will eventually run out of analytic meaning-rules before a precise application is determined. There cannot be a rule to tell us how to apply every rule: sooner or later one simply makes a judgment.[6] Ludwig Wittgenstein, in his later work, is responsible for the insight that judgment cannot itself amount to "following a rule" in one's own mind; in the end, it must come down simply to participating with others in a form of life.[7]

My point is this: these difficulties and considerations concerning how words "have" meanings are independent of and prior to any issue about vagueness. For suppose words and rules were as the formalists thought they were: suppose they lit up like a neon sign or clicked like a Geiger counter in the presence of the objects to which they applied. Even if that were how meanings worked, there would still be the problem of how to interpret a slight, hesitant clicking or a dull flickering of the word in the presence of borderline cases. In fact, words are not Geiger counters and no one ever thought they were. We have to give an alternative account—say, a sociological account, along Wittgenstenian lines—of how words have the meanings they do. It is important, moreover, to see that unless the problem of meaning is solved, the issue of vagueness cannot even arise. We cannot know that a word is vague, unless we know something about its use. So although vagueness is a problem for the theory of meaning, the very postulation of the problem assumes that the basic question—of what it is for a word to have meaning—has in some way or another been settled.

---

6. See, for example, Kant's construction of the role of judgment:

> For a concept of the understanding, which contains the general rule, must be supplemented by an act of judgment whereby the practitioner distinguishes instances where the rule applies from those where it does not. And since rules cannot in turn be provided on every occasion to direct the judgment in subsuming each instance under the previous rule (for this would involve an infinite regress), theoreticians will be found who can never in all their lives become practical, since they lack judgement.

Immanuel Kant, *On the Common Saying: "This May be True in Theory, But It Does Not Apply in Practice,"* in KANT: POLITICAL WRITINGS 61, 61 (Hans Reiss ed. & H.B. Nisbet trans., 2d ed. 1991).

7. LUDWIG WITTGENSTEIN, PHILOSOPHICAL INVESTIGATIONS paras. 66-276, at 31e-96e (G.E.M. Anscombe trans., 1974). For a convincing argument that there is no warrant in Wittgenstein's theory for a greater indeterminacy in the use of language than traditional legal scholars have supposed, see Brian Bix, *The Application (and Mis-Application) of Wittgenstein's Rule-Following Considerations to Legal Theory,* in WITTGENSTEIN AND LEGAL THEORY 209 (Dennis M. Patterson ed., 1992).

II
SOME DEFINITIONS

Let us turn now to the specific problems about meaning with which the "void-for-vagueness" doctrine is concerned. In the philosophical literature, *ambiguity* is different from *contestability,* and both are different from *vagueness.* If we want a general term to cover all three, we may use "indeterminacy."

The term "blue" is *ambiguous* because it is used sometimes to indicate a color and sometimes to indicate a mood. Accordingly, we may be unclear what someone means when she says, "His smile was happy and his eyes were blue." Further, even if we are sure that "blue" is being used to describe a color, we know that it suffers from *vagueness:* there are shades of turquoise that we might classify as blue or green, and there are shades of lavender that we might classify as blue or purple.

The phrase "due process" has long been *ambiguous* in America: constitutional lawyers find they have to affix additional terms as in "substantive due process" and "procedural due process" to sort the ambiguity out. In addition, each of those terms is contested.[8] Some say, for example, that "procedural due process" requires municipal agencies to hold public hearings in response to planning applications; others deny this. Such disagreement is a dispute about the social norms and moral standards that are or ought to be embodied in the phrase. The existence of those disputes makes the meaning of the phrase *contestable.* Contestability, then, is different from the uncertainty we might have about "his eyes were blue" or about the classification of a certain shade of turquoise: the latter uncertainties are not in and of themselves uncertainties about norms (other than norms for the use of language).

Let me propose some preliminary definitions, which will serve as points of reference, and some examples of the application of the definitions:

(i) *AMBIGUITY:* An expression X is ambiguous if there are two predicates P and Q which look exactly like $X,$ but which apply to different, though possibly overlapping, sets of objects, with the meaning of each predicate amounting to a different way of identifying objects as within or outside its extension.

Example: "Blue" is ambiguous for there are two predicates—"blue"(-colored) and "blue" (melancholy)—which look the same but apply to different objects. As a matter of meaning, the application of the first of these predicates is determined by looking at an object's color; the application of the second is determined by looking at the object's mood.

---

8. And so, perhaps, is the existence of the ambiguity: some say that "substantive due process" is an oxymoron, and "procedural due process" a pleonasm; they deplore the fact that this distinction has found a place in constitutional jurisprudence.

(ii) *VAGUENESS:* A predicate *P* is vague if there are objects or instances x_1, x_2, etc. within the domain of the normal application of terms of this kind such that users are characteristically undecided about the truth or falsity of "x_1 is *P*," "x_2 is *P*," and they understand that indecision to be a fact about the meaning of *P* rather than about the extent of their knowledge of x_1, x_2, etc.

> *Example:* "Blue"-colored is vague because, although the predicate is supposed to apply to and discriminate among color patches, most of us would hesitate about saying of certain shades of turquoise and lavender either that they were blue or that they were not blue. We would regard them as borderline cases, perhaps undecidable except by arbitrary stipulation. Our hesitation would not be because we had only had a glimpse of the patches in question and needed a closer look. We would say rather that even under optimal conditions of perception the meaning of the word "blue" did not determine an answer.

(iii) *CONTESTABILITY:* A predicate *P* is contestable if (1) it is not implausible to regard both "something is *P* if it is *A*" and "something is *P* if it is *B*" as alternative explications of the meaning of *P;* and (2) there is also an element *e** of evaluative or other normative force in the meaning of *P;* and (3) there is, as a consequence of (1) and (2), a history of using *P* to embody rival standards or principles such as "*A* is *e**" and "*B* is *e**."

> *Example:* The term "democracy" is contestable, because (1) while it is plausible to explicate its meaning in terms of representation, it is also not implausible to explicate its meaning in terms of direct participation in government; (2) the term has a favorable evaluative meaning ("*e**" = "ought to be promoted," etc.); and (3) there is, as a consequence of (1) and (2), a history of using the term "democracy" to embody rival political principles such as "Every political system should have a representative structure" and "We ought to encourage direct popular participation in government."

The term "vagueness" in the "void-for-vagueness" doctrine is almost certainly indeterminate in all the ways mentioned above.[9] Its meaning certainly comprises both vagueness in the strict sense and ambiguity, and in a

---

9. The terms "vagueness," "contestability," and "ambiguity" are themselves vague, contestable, and ambiguous. For example, it is not clear when the metaphorical use of a term becomes ambiguity; certainly a metaphor is different from a homonym. The vagueness of a term like "torture" (Is sensory deprivation torture?) may well become contestability, or the vehicle for contestability, to the extent that "torture" is used to articulate normative standards such as those laid down in Article 3 of the European Convention on Human Rights. The European Court of Human Rights held, for example, in Ireland v. United Kingdom, 25 Eur. Ct. H.R. (ser. A) at 65, 67 (1978), that certain interrogation techniques used by the security forces in Northern Ireland, though they caused intense physical and mental distress to the

legal context, either of those forms of indeterminacy is likely to become contestability if there is a history of political argumentation about the meaning of the term.[10] Maybe "vagueness" is supposed to refer to any form of indeterminacy that encourages unwarranted discretion or leaves the citizen without reasonable notice of what is required of her. But even if we sort out its ambiguity using phrases like "arbitrary discretion" and "reasonably clear guidelines," the meaning of those phrases is likely in turn to be both vague and contested.

The definitions I have offered should be treated with some care in a legal context. In defining a strict philosophical sense of "vagueness" and distinguishing it from other forms of indeterminacy, it is not my intention to pin down the true meaning of the "void-for-vagueness" doctrine. The fact that philosophers have given "vagueness" a reasonably precise definition does not at all imply that constitutional lawyers should attach the same meaning to the term. Precision, as Aristotle reminded us, is always relative to a subject and the purpose for which it is undertaken.[11] I am drawing these distinctions—following general philosophical usage—only so that we can see and understand the diverse sources of indeterminacy that flow from the use of natural language in both descriptive and normative contexts.

I now want to develop some detailed comments on the various types of indeterminacy that I have defined.

---

persons subjected thereto and led to acute psychiatric disturbances during interrogation, "did not occasion suffering of the particular intensity and cruelty implied by the word torture as so understood."

Some writers deny that there is a phenomenon of conceptual contestability distinct from ambiguity and persuasive definition; others have responded that the idea of contestability is itself contestable. *See, e.g.,* WILLIAM E. CONNOLLY, THE TERMS OF POLITICAL DISCOURSE (2d ed. 1983); John Gray, *On Liberty, Liberalism and Essential Contestability,* 8 BRIT. J. POL. SCI. 385 (1978); Alasdair MacIntyre, *The Essential Contestability of Some Social Concepts,* 84 ETHICS 1 (1973).

Thomas Hobbes is famous for the suggestion that all verbal indeterminacy is in the end contestability: people only care about definitions when interests are at stake.

Which is the cause, that the doctrine of Right and Wrong, is perpetually disputed, both by the Pen and the Sword: Whereas the doctrine of Lines, and Figures, is not so; because men care not, in that subject what be truth, as a thing that crosses no mans ambition, profit, or lust. For I doubt not, but if it had been a thing contrary to any mans right of dominion, or to the interest of men that have dominion, *That the three Angles of a Triangle should be equall to two angles of a Square;* that doctrine should have been, if not disputed, yet by the burning of all books of Geometry, suppressed, as farre as he whom it concerned was able.

THOMAS HOBBES, LEVIATHAN ch. XI, at 73-74 (Richard Tuck ed., 1991) (1651).

10. Ambiguity, it can be argued, is a special case of vagueness, *see* ISRAEL SCHEFFLER, BEYOND THE LETTER: A PHILOSOPHICAL INQUIRY INTO AMBIGUITY, VAGUENESS AND METAPHOR IN LANGUAGE 37-40 (1979), and perhaps the first condition in the definition of contestability depends on vagueness also. Contestability will behave like ambiguity in certain contexts, and ambiguity can become contestability when something moral or political seems to be at stake in a discussion about the proper meaning of a term.

11. ARISTOTLE, NICOMACHEAN ETHICS 1.3 1094b23-28 (Martin Ostwald ed. & trans., 1962) ("For a well-schooled man is one who searches for that degree of precision in each kind of study which the nature of the subject at hand admits: it is obviously just as foolish to accept arguments of probability from a mathematician as to demand strict demonstrations from an orator.").

III

AMBIGUITY

Most of my remarks will be devoted to *vagueness* and *contestability*. This is not because *ambiguity* is unimportant but because it is the most easily understood of the three, and the most amenable to simple resolution. When our friend says "His smile was happy and his eyes were blue," we can simply ask her what she means: "Blue-colored or blue melancholy?"

In most cases of ambiguity, the look-alike predicates are so divergent in meaning that context will make it clear which one was intended. If the context does not make it clear, we may be faced with such a spectacular failure of communication as to make the interpretive enterprise all but impossible. Suppose the legislature has presented us with a provision setting up an agency to supervise "banks," and a court really is unsure, both from context and from legislative history, whether it is dealing with financial matters or riparian matters. Suppose also that there is now no way of asking the legislators what they meant—banking institutions or riverbanks? Since it is clear they meant one or the other—for there is, fortunately, no third homonym in play—someone may suggest that the two meanings of "bank" define the limits of our interpretive freedom: by choosing one meaning or the other, we have a greater probability of according with legislative intentions than if we simply write a new law ourselves.

But there is something ludicrous about this choice. If the legislators really did mean riverbanks, then an "interpretation" that focuses on financial institutions is about as far as could be imagined from their intentions and could not possibly be regarded as an instance of institutional deference. We should not think that by pursuing one or the other meaning of this string of letters (b-a-n-k), we are deferring to the legislature in a way that we would not be if, for example, we developed a general policy of our own about land use in place of the problematic provision. Another way of putting this is to insist that the problem of interpretation cannot get underway until we have at least a ball-park sense of the sort of message intended to be conveyed by the sounds and inscriptions that the legislature used.[12]

Not all ambiguity is homonymy. Occasionally the look-alike predicates will be so related to one another, semantically or etymologically, that some sort of interpretive exercise will be appropriate. Two cases spring to mind.

Sometimes ambiguity arises because of different levels of generality at which a term is used.[13] A term in my lease may read "Animals are prohibited on the premises except cats and dogs." Now my pet, Baby, is a cat; but she is a full-grown leopard rather than a small mouse-chasing animal of the

---

12. See the discussion of "the preinterpretive stage" in RONALD DWORKIN, LAW'S EMPIRE 65-66 (1986).

13. *See* SCHEFFLER, *supra* note 10, at 14-15.

species *felis catus.* We may wonder whether my landlord really meant to include all animals of the *Felidae* family within her general permission. There may be intermediate cases: suppose I manage to tame a small ocelot. If it is size and behavior rather than strictly speaking *species* that my landlord wanted to exempt from the prohibition, the ocelot may be permissible. But then what about a slightly larger member of the *Felidae* family? Clearly what is going on here is a slip from ambiguity into vagueness.

Another sort of non-homonymous ambiguity arises from the fact that some terms have technical meanings as well as natural meanings, and some terms with technical meanings have several inconsistent or equivocal technical meanings depending on which technician you listen to. A notorious example is "economic efficiency." Because economists have developed subtly different theories to address overlapping problems, we find that "efficiency" is used to characterize the pursuit of Pareto-optimality, the maximization of wealth, the use of the Kaldor-Hicks criterion, the maximization of utility in the traditional Benthamite sense, and the cost-effective pursuit of public policy.[14] The matter is not helped by the fact that earlier transfers of jargon from economics to ordinary language have given us a meaning of efficiency that refers ambiguously to the profitable operation of a business, to a certain sort of no-nonsense briskness, and to the clear-headed pursuit of any goals by anyone.[15] What we see in this case is a transformation of ambiguity into contestability: a technical term, defined initially in an ill-coordinated way, takes on an evaluative force which other definers seek to capture and exploit for the purposes of social and economic theories. Much of what I later say about contestability will apply to this species of ambiguity.

IV
THE PHILOSOPHERS' CONCEPT OF VAGUENESS

In defining vagueness, I used a color-word as an example. Colors seem particularly liable to vagueness. The difficulty seems to be that, in the case of colors, we use *classificatory* terms to divide up a sensory *continuum.* In general, problems of vagueness will arise whenever we confront a continuum with terminology that has, or aspires to have, a bivalent[16] logic. On the one hand, there is this subtle gradation of hues; on the other hand, surely something either is blue or is not blue. On the one hand, humans

---

14. For an excellent discussion, see JULES L. COLEMAN, MARKETS, MORALS AND THE LAW 95-132 (1988).

15. For litigation in England in which the meaning of "efficiency" was crucially at issue, see Bromley London Borough Council v. Greater London Council, [1982] 1 All E.R. 129 (C.A. & H.L.). There is a discussion of this case and its implications for interpretive disputes in JEREMY WALDRON, THE LAW 117-50 (1990).

16. "Bivalent" meaning "two-valued." Most if not all of our logic depends on our being able to assign just one of two truth values (true or false) to each proposition. So a statement like "The sky is blue today" is either (1) true or (2) false; there is, in a bivalent framework, no third alternative.

range imperceptibly in age from zero to more than a hundred years old; on the other hand, surely it is either true or false, at a given time, that Sam is a youth and not an adult. And so on for all sorts of terms: "short" and "tall" classifying persons on the continuum of height; "village," "town," and "city" classifying communities on the continuum of population; "rich" and "poor" classifying individuals on continua of wealth and income; "careful," "negligent," and "reckless" classifying behavior on a continuum of attentiveness.[17]

The philosophical significance of this sort of vagueness is symbolized by the Sorites Paradox:

> A series of things could be arranged in such a way that the first consists of a large heap of grains of some kind and each subsequent member consists of grains of the same kind but contains, in each case, one less grain than the one before. . . . The last member, which consists of a single grain, is obviously not a heap. But if any member of the series is a heap, then it would surely remain so if just one grain were subtracted. The application conditions for the predicate ["heap"] are not sharp enough to distinguish heaps from non-heaps on the basis of the difference of a single grain so if one member of a (suitably gradated) series is a heap, so is the next. Since the first member is certainly a heap, all the subsequent members are also, including the last.[18]

An illustration is baldness: If a man with n hairs on his head is bald, then surely so is a man with just $n+1$. The same is also true of numbers: "0 is [a] small [number]. If [some number] n is small, then $n+1$ is small: Therefore every number is small."[19] It is important to indicate to non-philosophers that such puzzles are not just a tease. There is no clever answer that all the professionals know; among philosophers there is no widely accepted resolution to the Sorites Paradox.

Though Sorites-vagueness is important, it would be a mistake to confine the concept of vagueness to this model of classificatory terms confronting a given continuum. A second type of vagueness attends complex predicates whose meaning is understood in terms of the application of other predicates. Philosophically, the most famous discussion of this second type of vagueness is Wittgenstein's:

> Consider for example the proceedings that we call "games." I mean board-games, card-games, ball-games, Olympic games, and so

---

17. I don't want to give the impression that it is only nouns, adjectives, and, in general, classificatory terms that are vague. Prepositions can be vague too. See the excellent discussion of "The cat is on the mat" in JOHN R. SEARLE, EXPRESSION AND MEANING: STUDIES IN THE THEORY OF SPEECH ACTS 121-22 (1979) ("If the cat was half on and half off the mat we might not know what to say . . . .") (I am obliged to Meir Dan-Cohen for this reference.).

18. LINDA C. BURNS, VAGUENESS: AN INVESTIGATION INTO NATURAL LANGUAGES AND THE SORITES PARADOX 5 (1991).

19. Michael Dummett, *Wang's Paradox*, 30 SYNTHESE 301, 303 (1975).

on. What is common to them all?—Don't say: "There *must* be
something common, or they would not be called 'games' "—but
look and see whether there is anything common to all.—For if you
look at them you will not see something that is common to *all*, but
similarities, relationships, and a whole series of them at that. To
repeat: don't think, but look!—Look, for example, at board-games,
with their multifarious relationships. Now pass to card-games; here
you may find many correspondences with the first group, but many
common features drop out, and others appear. When we pass next
to ball-games, much that is common is retained, but much is lost.—
Are they all "amusing"? Compare chess with [tic-tac-toe]. Or is
there always winning and losing, or competition between players?
Think of patience. In ball games there is winning and losing; but
when a child throws his ball at the wall and catches it again, this
feature has disappeared. Look at the parts played by skill and luck;
and at the difference between skill in chess and skill in tennis.
Think now of games like ring-around-the-rosy; here is the element
of amusement, but how many other characteristic features have disappeared! . . .

And the result of this examination is: we see a complicated
network of similarities overlapping and criss-crossing: sometimes
overall similarities, sometimes similarities of detail.[20]

"Game" is a particularly rich example, but this sort of vagueness crops up
whenever there is a term with a number of independent conditions of application, some but not all of which need be satisfied. "Religion" is another
example. Roman Catholicism and Islam are certainly religions, and they
exhibit certain features each of which seems relevant to the application of
the term. These features include: (1) belief in supernatural beings or gods;
(2) identification of certain objects or places as sacred; (3) rituals and cere-
monies oriented towards the gods and/or towards what is sacred; (4) a
moral code believed to be sanctioned by the gods; (5) feelings of awe and
mystery associated with sanctity; (6) prayer and other modes of communication with the gods; (7) a world view, including perhaps a general teleol-
ogy, a cosmology, and an eschatology; and so on.[21] However, we would
not hold that a belief-system was not a religion simply because one of the
above features was not present. If a belief-system failed to associate its
theology with a morality, i.e., simply because (4) did not apply, we would
not, without more, say that the system was not a religion. Hinyana Bud-
dhism, for example, is usually regarded as a religion even though there is no
specific ontological commitment to a supernatural being.

---

20. WITTGENSTEIN, *supra* note 7, para. 66, at 31e-32e.

21. This example is drawn from William P. Alston, *Vagueness, in* 8 THE ENCYCLOPEDIA OF
PHILOSOPHY 219 (Paul Edwards ed., 1967).

Multiple criteria do not necessarily lead to vagueness. "Square" applies to any figure that is (1) a rectangle and (2) has all sides equal. In this case, however, there are definite requirements for the application of the conditions: (1) and (2) are both necessary; neither alone is sufficient.[22] The problem in the case of "religion" is that it is not clear which of the seven conditions, if any, is necessary, and which subset, if any, is sufficient.[23]

Following Wittgenstein, philosophers use the term "family resemblance" to characterize these concepts.[24] For example, one member of a family may have the Churchill nose and the jowls, another the Churchill complexion and the dimple, another the nose and the cherubic expression but without the dimple: there may be no feature they all have in common, but still they share the Churchill family face. Schematically, we may envisage a set of five objects each with four properties:

1	2	3	4	5
A	B	A	A	A
B	C	C	B	B
C	D	D	D	E
E	E	F	E	F

There is no property or subset of the properties A-F that the objects 1 through 5 have in common. Even so, there may be a predicate P that applies to 1 through 5 by virtue of their possession of some of the features A-F. Now suppose object 6 has properties A, F, G, and H. Does P apply to 6? If users of P characteristically hesitate, and if they do not call for further information about 6, then P is vague in the Wittgensteinian sense.

Sometimes the two types of vagueness combine.[25] Some of the criteria for religions or for games or for being P may be vague in the classification/continuum sense: at the margin it may be hard to say whether an activity is competitive or noncompetitive, whether the Virgin Mary is sup-

---

22. This example is also taken from Alston. See id.

23. See also supra note 4 (discussing the analytic/synthetic distinction). One might ask: How many of these criteria are supposed to be definitive of "religion" in the sense of telling us about the meaning of a word, and how many of them are supposed to be general sociological theorems about religion? And how, at the margin, can we tell the difference? Notice, however, that though the issues mentioned in this footnote are important, they are not themselves issues of vagueness. It may be possible to show that a given criterion is linked analytically rather than synthetically with "religion" without being able to specify its place in a precise array of necessary and sufficient conditions for the use of the term.

24. WITTGENSTEIN, supra note 7, para. 67, at 32e.

25. There is also a third form of vagueness: vagueness with respect to the bounding and thus the individuation of objects. How many mountains are there in the Alps? How many clouds can one see in the sky at a given moment? Where does one cloud end and another begin? How many episodes of pain did I have today? How many offenses has a continual polluter committed? How many conurbations are there in the Bay Area: one or three (centered around Oakland, San Jose, and San Francisco)? In these cases, continuum/classification problems in boundary determination give rise to problems about identity and counting. See Alston, supra note 21, at 220.

posed to be natural or supernatural, whether an object like 6 is A or is not A.

It is tempting to explain vagueness in terms of the "borderlines" of a concept's application. However, the existence of the Wittgensteinian cases means that we must be careful when characterizing vagueness in this way. The image of borderlines suggests a circle with a center, where everything is clear, and a circumference where things become uncertain. It suggests that some cases just are core cases—in law, perhaps, "easy cases"—and others just are penumbral cases—in law, "hard cases." But people may disagree about how to draw the circle. In our schematic example above, someone who takes object 5 as a core case may regard object 1 as penumbral, and she may think that object 6 is obviously *P* if object 5 is. Someone else who takes object 2 as her core case will draw the circle differently and offer a different assessment of object 6.

The same is true of what we regard as paradigm cases. The idea of a paradigm case is the idea of a case by reference to which one learns the use of a term.[26] A child who learns to use the word "machine" in his parents' kitchen will have a different paradigm than one whose mother is a mechanic and who learns the word in her workshop. Someone who grows up in India may distinguish core and penumbral cases of "religion" quite differently from a person who grows up in an Episcopal vicarage.

These examples indicate that it may be wrong to regard vagueness as a property of words. Instead, it would appear that vagueness is a property of words' meanings. If we take "meaning" to connote the way a term is used, this suggests that vagueness is relative to users. We are all familiar with pedants who insist on great determinacy in the use of terms whose vagueness the rest of us take for granted: they refuse to say "It's freezing" unless the ground temperature is at or below 32° Fahrenheit. For such a person, the term "freezing" is less vague than it is for us.[27]

Vagueness may be relative to other things as well:[28] the purpose for which a term is being used, the time available for determining its applicability, the instruments used, and so forth. "Shorter than Clinton" may be a vague phrase if used on the basis of a quick glance at persons between 5'11" and 6'1", and a perfectly precise phrase if there is all the time in the world to make one's measurements and no one grows in the meantime.

There is another aspect to be careful about in the borderlines model. Lawyers sometimes talk as though fact-situations could be divided into three classes in relation to a given rule: (1) easy cases where the rule obviously does apply; (2) easy cases where it obviously does not apply; and (3)

---

26. The paradigm case of the concept "paradigm case" is the use of a particular Latin noun such as "mensa" as a basis for learning the case-endings for the First Declension.

27. Though it may be vague for him in other dimensions: Exactly where is the ground temperature to be measured? For how long must it dip below 32° Fahrenheit?

28. *See* SCHEFFLER, *supra* note 10, at 49.

hard cases or borderline cases, where it is both arguable that the rule does apply and arguable also that it does not. Similarly, logicians sometimes suggest that vague predicates might be understood in terms of a clear trichotomy of cases: a statement of the form "*x* is *P*" may be (1) clearly true, (2) clearly false, or (3) clearly undecidable. Both suggestions appear to instill a form of exactness into our use of vague predicates, though of course they will pose difficulties for contexts—like courts—where a bivalent rather than a trivalent logic is required. However, the trivalence idea does not do justice to the sort of vagueness that is really troubling for philosophy, science, and law.

Indeed if the division into these three categories is clear and uncontroversial, we are arguably not really dealing with vagueness at all. As Linda Burns puts it, "Where there is a clearly delimited class of cases to which the term applies, another to which it does not apply, and a third sharply delimited class of neutral instances there seems to be no real uncertainty anywhere."[29] True vagueness arises when there is hesitation or uncertainty about how to establish these three categories or where there is a general uncertainty about whether a given case is a borderline case or not.[30] Undoubtedly jurisprudence made a great leap forward when it was acknowledged that the distinction between easy cases and hard cases was itself hard, so that there could be no rigid separation between the forms of judicial reasoning appropriate to the former and those appropriate to the latter.[31]

In general, as Israel Scheffler and others have argued, we should be wary of responding to vicissitudes like vagueness with changes in the structure of our logic. We should not be so easily persuaded to drop the bivalence of "true-or-false" and adopt the trivalence of "true-or-false-or-indeterminate." Such a move does less than justice to our aspiration to rigor. We hold out to ourselves the possibility of diminishing the vagueness of our predicates as well as the reduction of other forms of verbal and semantic indeterminacy. As long as we have this aspiration, we surely need bivalent logic to embody the results of the diminution of vagueness. To paraphrase Scheffler's point: Why select certain vicissitudes—such as vagueness—for enshrinement in a new logic, rather than holding classical logic constant as a framework to accommodate any reduction in the hesitations or indeterminacies that afflict our use of words?[32]

---

29. BURNS, *supra* note 18, at 25.
30. Burns shows that only this form of vagueness will generate the Sorites paradox. *Id.* at 24.
31. *See* DWORKIN, *supra* note 12, at 265-66.
32. SCHEFFLER, *supra* note 10, at 71-78; *see* W.V. QUINE, PHILOSOPHY OF LOGIC 85 (1970).

V
CAN VAGUENESS BE ELIMINATED?

As a normative doctrine, "void-for-vagueness" implies that vagueness can be reduced in statutes and regulations. But can it be done away with totally? Certainly, logicians have dreamt of an ideal language for science that would eliminate vagueness altogether. In such a language, as Gottlob Frege put it,

> A definition of a concept ([i.e.,] of a possible predicate) must be complete; it must unambiguously determine, as regards any object, whether or not it falls under the concept ([i.e.,] whether or not the predicate is truly assertible of it). Thus there must not be any object as regards which the definition leaves in doubt whether it falls under the concept . . . . We may express this metaphorically as follows: the concept must have a sharp boundary.[33]

The questions we face are these: How could such a language be achieved? What sort of predicates would it have to use?

It is sometimes sloppily said that what is needed is for everyone to use terms that are more *specific*. In fact, it is a mistake to think that vagueness varies inversely with specificity: the opposite of "specific" is "general," and there is no assurance that a reduction in generality corresponds to a reduction in vagueness. The term "tree" is more specific than the term "living thing," but it may be much easier to say whether a given object is a living thing (as opposed to inanimate) than whether it is a tree (as opposed, for example, to a bush). It may be easier to determine that something is a human community (a very general term) than to determine whether it is a city (more specific). However, the correlation does not always go this way: the specific term "chair" is less vague than "piece of furniture." Vagueness therefore seems to be independent of generality and specificity. In terms of the core/penumbra model that we were discussing earlier, vagueness has to do not with the size of the category in question, but with the determinacy of its borders.

A number of philosophers have speculated that vagueness is in principle ineliminable because it is possible to envisage puzzling borderline cases for every predicate we define. This possibility was labelled "open texture" by Friedrich Waismann.[34] Others have suggested that vagueness is at least ineliminable from terms whose application involves the use of the human senses, partly because of the continuum/classification tension noted earlier.[35]

---

33. GOTTLOB FREGE, *Grundgesetze der Arithmetik*, *in* TRANSLATIONS FROM THE PHILOSOPHICAL WRITINGS OF GOTTLOB FREGE, 159 (Peter Geach & Max Black eds., 2d ed. 1960).

34. Friedrich Waismann, *Verifiability*, 19 PROC. ARISTOTELIAN SOC'Y 119, 121 (1945) (supp. volume).

35. MAX BLACK, LANGUAGE AND PHILOSOPHY 28-29 (1949).

So far as open texture is concerned, it is not entirely clear to what the ineliminability claim amounts. Is it that, for any predicate *P*, there are in fact borderline cases? Or that there may, for all we know, be borderline cases? Or that we can always imagine borderline cases? The latter version seems to be the one that Waismann had in mind:

"But are there not exact definitions at least in science?" Let's see. The notion of gold seems to be defined with absolute precision, say by the spectrum of gold with its characteristic lines. Now what would you say if a substance was discovered that looked like gold, satisfied all the chemical tests for gold, whilst it emitted a new sort of radiation? "But such things do not happen." Quite so; but they *might* happen, and that is enough to show that we can never exclude altogether the possibility of some unforeseen situation arising in which we shall have to modify our definition.[36]

Waismann's case may seem fanciful as a basis for arguing for the ineliminability of vagueness in the real world.[37] But I take his point to be this: if we attempt to pin down a precise meaning for a term like "gold," we do so usually on the basis of some physical theory we have of the chemistry of the elements, etc. That theory confronts a traditional field of informally distinguished items and carves it up in a determinate and scientifically useful way. We must remember, however, that such classificatory theories are neither arbitrary or a priori: they are our best response to experience. If our experience began presenting us with new objects that behaved in different ways, we should have to construct a different classificatory theory. While we were in the process of such construction, the hitherto determinate terms given by the old theory would become vague again. This has happened many times in the history of science, and we can surely expect it to recur. The situation arises particularly in the human sciences where theoretical determinacy is orders of magnitude less developed than in the physical and biological sciences.[38]

Followers of Thomas Kuhn sometimes suggest that each new scientific theory brings its own terms and its own meanings, and that *between* theories key terms are largely incommensurable.[39] Experience, however, does not seem to bear this out. Sometimes new theoretical terms are introduced ("neutrino") and others abandoned ("phlogiston"). But often what happens is that the same words are retained with something like their old meaning,

---

36. Waismann, *supra* note 34, at 122-23.

37. Though not as fanciful as other cases he mentions, would we apply the predicate "cat" to a cat-shaped animal that grew to gigantic size? *Id.* at 121-22.

38. See generally the excellent account of the history of taxonomy in MICHEL FOUCAULT, THE ORDER OF THINGS: AN ARCHAEOLOGY OF THE HUMAN SCIENCES (1970).

39. *See generally* THOMAS S. KUHN, THE STRUCTURE OF SCIENTIFIC REVOLUTIONS (2d ed. 1970). For a discussion along the lines intimated in the text accompanying this note, see RICHARD J. BERNSTEIN, BEYOND OBJECTIVITISM AND RELATIVISM: SCIENCE, HERMENEUTICS, AND PRAXIS 52-108 (1983).

but with a new grid of organization and a new sort of tightness around the edges.[40] Moreover, it seems important to the way science develops that we maintain a large stock of such terms and classifications—terms whose meaning can be subtly varied from theory to theory. Since this is so, it is unlikely that open texture, of the sort discussed in the previous paragraph, can or should be eliminated.

Is it not possible to put an end to this simply by stipulating determinate meanings for some predicates? If necessary, we could make our stipulations arbitrary, so that they were not at the mercy of possible scientific change along the lines just indicated. Is it not enough to simply designate two points on the spectrum of visible light and say, "anything at or between these points is to count henceforth as blue"? Similarly, can we not just agree to call any community of 50,000 or more inhabitants a city? Can we not stipulate that a shared belief in a supernatural deity who takes an interest in human affairs is a necessary and sufficient condition for the use of the term "religion"?

In fact, it is unlikely that arbitrary stipulation would lead to the elimination of vagueness. First, in at least some of these cases, drawing the line itself involves the use of vague terms. Consider the suggested stipulative definition of a meaning for "city." What is it to be an inhabitant? To have one's legal residence in the community in question (like George Bush's "residence" in Houston during the time of his Presidency) or to physically be there? If the latter, then for how much of every year? And how stable must the population level be? Suppose the population of a community in the Northeast dips below 50,000 in the winter, as the residents head for Florida. Is it still a city?[41]

Secondly, such stipulations would make prodigious demands on memory and measurement among users of the language that was made determinate in this way. Particularly if the stipulations were arbitrary, there would be no alternative but to learn by rote where the line was to be drawn for every predicate.[42] It seems, in other words, quite unlikely that any such stipulations would succeed as linguistic conventions.

Thirdly, it is plausible to suppose that people will always have a need to communicate informally, using predicates whose application can for most cases be determined at a glance.[43] Either they will invent new terms to perform this function—and thus reintroduce the inherent vagueness that goes with it—or they will subvert the newly stipulated meanings by continuing to use the terms in the old and thus potentially vague way.

---

40. Think of the familiar chemical elements, or the familiar names for animals, that have survived quite startling paradigm shifts in physics and biology.

41. *See supra* note 21, at 220.

42. And if they were nonarbitrary, they would be subject to exactly the changes in our sense of what was a scientifically well-founded distinction that were discussed earlier.

43. *See* Burns, *supra* note 18, at 178-79.

In any case, the idea of pure stipulation is sociologically and linguistically naive. If there is a widespread feeling that the vagueness of an expression is a problem, and if the stipulation to solve that problem is supposed to be arbitrary, then there will likely be many competing stipulations.[44] Most natural languages have no Academy to resolve the disputes and confusion that will result. Once people become aware of a plurality of arbitrarily stipulated delimitations of a previously vague term, they will find themselves at a loss as to which one to use. Interpersonal communication will then become vague or ambiguous all over again, for each listener will be unsure about which of the competing stipulations (if any) his interlocutor is relying on when he uses a given word.

In law as in science, meanings for terms are sometimes stipulated for specific purposes and among a specific community. However, if the terms are natural language terms and are used in a variety of contexts, then people will again be aware of a variety of stipulated meanings, and they will not be able to rule out the possibility that two or more of them may confront one another in a given instance. We can stipulate a precise meaning for "adult" for the purposes of the suffrage, and another precise meaning of "adult" for the purposes of marriage, and yet another precise meaning of "adult" for the drinking age. But these usages will be insufficient to fix a general meaning for the term—i.e., one that gives us a determinate predicate to confront a new sort of case in which adulthood seems to be at stake.

One should not exaggerate the problem. If vagueness is in general ineliminable, it does not follow that it is irreducible in a given area, or with respect to a given speech community. The most successful endeavors in this regard have involved the comparativization and the quantification of descriptions. If we insist on dividing people into those who are *short* and those who are *tall*, our terminology is going to remain vague. But we could classify people on the basis of the predicate "shorter than Clinton." Alonzo Church has argued that this sort of move is capable of eliminating vagueness altogether:[45] he believes that, given sufficiently precise instruments, all individuals can be classified as either shorter than Clinton or not shorter than Clinton. The key to this proposal is, of course, "sufficiently precise instruments." As Scheffler argues, with a given set of instruments, it is always possible to imagine an undecidable case.[46] We know, however, that the concept of vagueness is already relative to some purpose that informs the differentiations that someone is trying to make, and I assume Church's proposal is that, relative to any given purpose, we can always procure

---

44. Think of what happens among moral philosophers who insist on getting clear about the technical meanings of terms like "rights" or "deontology." There are as many competing stipulative definitions, each offered stridently in the name of analytical clarity, as there are practitioners of this dubious art.

45. Alonzo Church, *Relative, in* THE DICTIONARY OF PHILOSOPHY 269 (Dagobert D. Runes ed., 1942).

46. SCHEFFLER, *supra* note 10, at 60.

instruments that enable us to eliminate vagueness in the use of comparative terms like "shorter than." Indeed, this is precisely the basis of measurement in the modern world. "Less than one meter tall" is just another way of saying "shorter than the standard meter rod preserved in Paris."

The other way of reducing or eliminating vagueness from a certain sphere of application is to renounce the use of classificatory predicates altogether. Scientific laws, for example, are increasingly not formulated in terms like "everything which is P is Q" or "an event of type P will always be followed by an event of type Q." Instead, predicates are used simply to designate continua, or dimensions of continuous variation, and laws are stated that make variations in one continuum a function of variations in another: "change in $p = f$(change in q)."

Occasionally, though more crudely, we do the same sort of thing in law. We do not just say, "The rich should pay a greater proportion of their income in tax than the poor." Instead we define a complex function f and legislate: "tax payable $= f$(taxable income)." The example illustrates, however, two residual sources of indeterminacy. First, it is still necessary to define the relevant continua: we all know how difficult that is with regard to "taxable income." Second, in working with these continua, there are fine discriminations that we simply stipulate away, ignoring pennies or rounding up to the nearest dollar.

VI
CONTESTABILITY

I now want to move to the third kind of indeterminacy that I defined: contestability. A phrase becomes contestable when it is clear that it embodies a normative standard, but different users disagree about the detailed contents of that normative standard.

Let me begin with a couple of examples. The Eighth Amendment to the United States Constitution says the following:

Excessive bail shall not be required, nor excessive fines imposed, nor cruel and unusual punishments inflicted.[47]

What counts as excessive bail or an excessive fine? Presumably a sum that is larger than it ought to be. But what ought to be the level of fines and bail bonds? This is something that people disagree about, and those disagreements will shape their quarrels about the meaning of "excessive." What makes a form of punishment cruel? It is, presumably, the point of punishment to be unpleasant; so a cruel punishment would seem to be one that is more unpleasant than it ought to be. But again people disagree about how unpleasant punishment ought to be.

Similar issues arise with regard to the Fourth Amendment:

---

47. U.S. CONST. amend. XIII.

> The right of the people to be secure in their persons, houses, papers, and effects, against unreasonable searches and seizures, shall not be violated . . . .[48]

What counts as an unreasonable search or seizure? It is difficult to say much more, on the basis of the meaning of the words themselves, than this: an unreasonable search or seizure is one for which there is insufficient justification either as to the occasion or as to the manner in which it is conducted. Once again, disagreement in the community about when and how it is appropriate for the police to search for evidence of wrongdoing will surface in disputes about the meaning of "unreasonable."

In other words, it looks as though these constitutional provisions invite us to make value judgments about appropriate levels for financial penalties and other punishments, and about appropriate levels of justification for police actions. The problem is that we disagree about such value judgments. The mere fact that terms like "unreasonable" or "excessive" invite us to make value judgments does not in itself undermine the determinacy of their meanings. On the contrary, it is part of the meaning of these words to indicate that a value judgment is required, a function which the words perform quite precisely. To dramatize the point, we might rephrase the amendments in question as follows:

> The right of the people to be secure in their persons, houses, papers, and effects, against searches and seizures which are [make value-judgment here], shall not be violated . . . . Bail which is [make value-judgment here] shall not be required, nor shall fines which are [make value-judgment here] be imposed, nor shall punishments which are [make value-judgment here] and unusual be inflicted.

So the terms do have a clear meaning: the rule for their use is to elicit a value judgment from anyone applying or implementing the proposition in which they appear. The fact that they do not in addition tell us which value judgments to make does not detract from their univocality. It does make it likely, however, that in a society torn by value conflicts, different people will apply the provisions in different ways.

In fact, words like "unreasonable" and "excessive" give us a little more help than is indicated in the account just given. Some normative terms pin things down more specifically than others do, and different normative terms will do so in different ways. "Bad," "unreasonable," "wicked," "excessive," "undeserving," "wrong," "malicious," and "a violation of rights" are all fraught with negative connotations of value, but they carry those connotations in different ways. "Excessive," for example, indicates that we are to make a value judgment about amount or quantity; it does not invite us to make a value judgment about the beauty of the judicial rhetoric that accompanies the imposition of a fine. "Unreasonable" looks to the justifications

---

48. U.S. CONST. amend. IV.

there might be for an action; it does not invite us to consider whether the action is, for example, shocking or unprecedented, except as relevant to the issue of justification. In these ways, each of the terms we are considering pushes us in the direction of a particular dimension of evaluative significance and away from other dimensions.

One way of putting this is that each of the various terms has a quite specific evaluative meaning, even though people disagree about the criteria for the term's application.[49] Two judges may agree that the phrase "excessive bail" requires them to make a value-judgment about the amount of bail required, but they may disagree about the cut-off point at which the amount of bail for any particular charge becomes excessive. In addition, the specific evaluative meaning may be disputed, or change over time. An instruction to sentence people in accordance with their "desert" gives the judge a different and more specific evaluative task than one which empowers her to impose whatever sentence is appropriate. Two judges may recognize that difference even though they disagree about whether desert is purely a function of past conduct or should encompass a defendant's future prospects for rehabilitation.

So far I have concentrated on strict evaluative meaning. In addition, an evaluative term may have an element of relatively fixed descriptive meaning. A prohibition on cruel punishment, for example, is not an all-purpose invitation to make a value-judgment about punishment. A light sentence may not be struck down under the Eighth Amendment because it violates a victim's rights; nor does the provision allow the state to appeal against the costs of administering a particular penalty imposed by a court. In ordinary language, the descriptive meaning of "cruel" invites us to focus our evaluation specifically on the degree or quality of the suffering experienced by the prisoner and perhaps on the disposition and attitude of those inflicting it.

Beyond that, "cruel" remains indeterminate. We know that it has negative and condemnatory connotations, and we know that it tells us something about the gravity of the suffering experienced. However, people will differ as to whether cruelty is simply a matter of the intensity of the suffering, or whether it also refers to the malice, inhumanity, or disrespect with which the suffering was inflicted.

Either of these positions, considered in itself, might be a plausible account of the descriptive meaning of the term. But when "cruel" is also used as an evaluative term, particularly in a constitutional context, the possibility of these alternative accounts introduces something called "political contestability" into the word's meaning. For now, we are not merely saying (as a semantic matter) that "cruelty means the malicious infliction of pain" or "cruelty means the experience of extreme suffering." By ascribing one

---

49. For discussions of meaning and criteria, see R.M. HARE, THE LANGUAGE OF MORALS 94-110 (1952).

or other of these meanings to a term that is used in a legal or constitutional context, we are saying, in effect, "do not allow pain to be inflicted maliciously" or "do not allow the infliction of extreme pain." Since we may disagree substantively about the merits of these latter principles—particularly in a penal context—the word "cruel" is bound to become an arena for our wider moral and political disagreements.

VII
ESSENTIAL CONTESTABILITY

About thirty-five years ago, W.B. Gallie introduced the idea of "essentially" contested concepts.[50] This idea, which has been quite influential in political theory, bears some discussion in the present context. What does "essential" add to contestability as defined above? It is not just an intensifier. To call a concept essentially contested is not merely to say that its meaning is very, very controversial. Nor is it to say merely that the disagreements which surround its meaning are intractable and irresolvable.[51] Interpreted strictly, "essentially" might indicate any one or more of three notions.

First, it indicates that the dispute about the meaning of the concept in question is a dispute that goes to the heart of the matter. It is not merely a dispute about marginal or penumbral cases between persons who are clear about the concept's core. It is a dispute that can generate rival paradigms because it is a dispute between differing accounts of the essence or central meaning of the concept. Thus "democracy" is essentially contested because people do not just disagree about evidently marginal cases like Kuwait, but also about whether a direct, participatory system like ancient Athens should be taken as a paradigm, relegating the representative system of the modern United States, say, to a penumbral position, or whether the paradigm should be a modern representative system like the United States or like the Westminster system, with Athens dismissed as an historical peculiarity.

Second, the idea of "essential" contestability can be taken to indicate that contestedness is part of the very meaning of the expression in question: it is part of the essence of the concept to be contested. Someone who does not realize that fact has not understood the way the word is used. This does not prevent a person from putting forward a firm view about the concept or taking sides in the controversy about its meaning. But anyone who says that "freedom," for example, has a perfectly clear meaning and that he cannot see why so many people get it wrong, shows that he himself does not understand the most striking rule for the use of "freedom" in the modern

---

50. W.B. Gallie, *Essentially Contested Concepts,* 56 PROC. ARISTOTELIAN SOC'Y 167 (n.s. 1955-56).

51. *Cf.* STEVEN LUKES, POWER: A RADICAL VIEW 9, 26 (1974) (evaluating power as an "essentially contested concept").

world—namely, that it is a verbal arena in which we fight out our disagreements about the nature of human agency and autonomy.

It is true that we often think of meanings as things that are necessarily agreed: the meaning of a term is simply a consensus among its users to deploy it in a certain way. However, in his article, Gallie explored the possibility that, for certain terms, meaning may be tied (conventionally) to the existence of a controversy (or a range of controversies) rather than to the existence of a consensus. There may, as he said, be "concepts the proper use of which inevitably involves endless disputes about their proper uses on the part of their users."[52]

Together, those two elements define the basic meaning of essential contestability for Gallie.[53] Additionally, "essential" can indicate a third idea: that the disagreement is in some sense indispensable to the usefulness of the term, that it serves some purpose associated with the contested expression. This was the main thesis of Gallie's article: he argued that we should not assume that something has gone wrong necessarily when people disagree about the meanings of words. A controversy from aesthetics may serve as an illustration.

Art critics sometimes argue about whether advertisements, rock music, photographs, and Ninja Turtle cartoons should be regarded as forms of *art*. In the course of these debates they must ask themselves questions, not only about the objects at issue (their nature, complexity, qualities, authorship, audience, cultural prominence, and circumstances of production, for example), but also about what *art* is, what makes something *a work of art*, as opposed, say, to a mere commercial artifact. What they find is that they

---

52. Gallie, *supra* note 48, at 169.

53. Gallie specifies five basic criteria for a concept to be considered "essentially contested":

(I) Value-Concept: The concept must be an evaluative or appraisive concept—"in the sense that it signifies or accredits some kind of valued achievement." *Id.* at 171.

(II) Complexity: "This achievement must be of an internally complex character, for all that its worth is attributed to it as a whole." *Id.* at 171-72. To judge something as art or democracy, for example, is to make a complex judgment about it that will involve many aspects. It is different from judging something to be "red."

(III) Variously describable:

Any explanation of its worth must therefore include reference to the respective contributions of its various parts or features; yet . . . there is nothing absurd or contradictory in any of a number of possible rival descriptions of its total worth, one such description setting its component parts or features in one order of importance, a second setting them in a second order, and so on.

Id. at 172.

(IV) Openness: "The accredited achievement must be of a kind that admits of considerable modification in the light of changing circumstances; and such modification cannot be prescribed or predicted in advance." *Id.*

(V) Aggressive argumentation:

[N]ot only [do] different persons or parties adhere to different views of the correct use of some concept but . . . each party recognizes the fact that its own use of it is contested by those of other parties, and . . . each party must have at least some appreciation of the different criteria in the light of which the other parties claim to be applying the concept in question.

Id.

cannot agree about the definition of "art." For some, art is essentially a formal and intellectual achievement, an essay in the configuration of relatively detached elements or ideas undertaken for its own sake. For others, the essence of art is its contribution, direct or indirect, to the representation of reality and possibility, and so to the practical powers of the human imagination. For still others, art is essentially expressive either of the striving or virtuosity of some individual creator, or of the moving spirit of some community in which the artist participates. Thus the debate about the classic Coca Cola bottle, or Jagger and Richards' "Satisfaction," or Donald Duck quickly becomes at least in part a debate about the meaning of the concept of *art*.[54]

Although rival conceptions[55] of art are put forward in these debates passionately and fervently, as though the issue mattered, as though it were not simply a verbal disagreement, there seems to be little prospect of resolving such definitional disputes. Everyone argues as though her own conception were the right one, but everyone knows there is no authoritative dictionary that could settle the true meaning in a way that all the contestants would acknowledge. It is a debate in which it is impossible to imagine anyone having the last word.

Even so, any suggestion that the dispute is futile and that the contestants should disengage by simply abandoning the contested term and coining new words (art, schmart; art_1, art_2; and so on) to embody their respective definitions is likely to be met with derision. The contest continues to be seen as important and unavoidable, even while it is acknowledged to be irresolvable. Indeed, not only does the contest continue but as Gallie points out, "each party continues to defend its case with what it claims to be convincing arguments, evidence and other forms of justification,"[56] though each party knows very well that what it claims to be convincing does not in fact convince.

According to Gallie, this shows that certain terms are important and valuable not despite their contestedness but because of it. Far from contributing to semantic confusion, the disagreements occasioned in the use of *art* play a worthwhile role in social, intellectual, and cultural life.[57] No doubt there are cases in which a debate between rival definitions of a term would simply muddy the dialectical waters, confusing discussion and facilitating talk at cross purposes to no good effect. Often, however, the definitional dispute enriches the wider debate in which the disputed concept is

---

54. "In part" because even if a definition of "art" were agreed, there would still be enormous debate about whether such objects in fact satisfied criteria as abstract as those which the agreed definition would inevitably embody.

55. Different uses of a contested concept are sometimes called "conceptions." For the distinction between concept and conception, see RONALD DWORKIN, TAKING RIGHTS SERIOUSLY 134-36 (1977). *See also* DWORKIN, *supra* note 12, at 70-72.

56. Gallie, *supra* note 48, at 168.

57. *See id.* at 180-83.

deployed, and in many cases the contestants themselves are able to grasp the benefit of the polemic, even while they remain unregenerate partisans of their own respective points of view. Would anyone deny, for instance, that an understanding of art is enhanced, rather than impoverished, by the continuing debate among artists, art critics, and aesthetes about what art "really" is? The dynamics of that debate—putting forward views, citing and assembling examples, responding to rival views with arguments and counter-examples, modifying one's view to meet exceptions, explaining why it is still coherent even after modification, developing schools of thought which evolve partly in response to internal dynamics and partly in response to rival pressures, locating each view in a history and heritage of disputation, opening one's aesthetics in various ways to contributions from other spheres of life and thought, relating one's aesthetics to rival conceptions of the good life for those endowed with talent, and so on—results in any modern claim about the nature of art being considerably richer and more subtle than it would have been if the claim had issued straightforwardly from an historically unchallenged consensus.

Many political concepts are also important for their contestedness. Our earlier example of *democracy* is a good illustration. What is the true meaning of "democracy"? Can the judicial review of representative or plebiscitary legislation be described as democratic if it is done in the name of individual rights? Is the concept of "one-party democracy" a contradiction in terms or can there be democracy without divisive political factions in a society? Are representative institutions really democratic, or are they, as the Athenians believed, either oligarchic because they concentrate power in the hands of the few or aristocratic because voters take themselves to be choosing the "best" candidate? Can there be democracy under conditions of economic inequality? Does political democracy require social democracy? And so on. It is idle to pretend that there are definitive answers to these questions—answers given in the Gettysburg address or in Webster's Dictionary. But the debate continues vigorously and fruitfully, despite the absence of guaranteed answers.

For these reasons, these are not debates we should seek to bring to an end by stipulating more precise or less contestable meanings for our terms. Few of the parties to the American debate about democracy and constitutional adjudication would settle for a resolution that defined two distinct meanings for the word "democracy"[58] and separated the antagonists on the ground that they were talking at cross purposes. Their debate is about what democracy really is, and it is arguable that understandings on all sides of this vexed area of political theory are enriched rather than confused by the persistent disagreement.

---

58. Democracy could be defined as 'democracy$_1$' which allows judicial review, and 'democracy$_2$' which does not.

In Gallie's original exposition, the usefulness of conceptual disagreement was understood in terms of the development of some original exemplar or paradigm. A concept is essentially contested (as opposed to "radically confused"), he said, when the rival conceptions refer back to some original exemplar of the concept "whose authority is acknowledged by all the contestant users" and whose achievement is sufficiently complex to be describable in various ways.[59] For example, disagreements about the meaning of "the Christian way of life" are held together by reference to the Gospel accounts of the life of Jesus of Nazareth; each conception purports to provide the best account of what that complex exemplar stands for. The usefulness of the contestability is then expressed in terms of the plausibility of supposing that the heritage of the exemplar's original achievement will be promoted rather than undermined by ongoing disagreement about the meaning of the concept.[60]

But reference back to an exemplar may be too narrow an account of what makes a contested concept nevertheless a shared concept. In legal contexts, it may be that the authoritative specification of a term is what matters.[61] Given the source, we may have no choice but to conduct our battles of principle about punishment, for example, on the ground defined by the phrase "cruel and unusual." In other contexts, it may be that there is just a history of disputation in which a given term has played a major role, so that continuing in that quarrelsome tradition means, again, fighting on that particular verbal ground. This is certainly a more accurate account of the contestedness of "democracy" than any reference back, for example, to Athens as an exemplar. For these disputes, an exemplar and (or) a paradigm may emerge in the course of discussion as, in Ronald Dworkin's words, "a kind of plateau on which further thought and argument are built,"[62] rather than as a foundation that makes the argument possible in the first place. Their emergence and the fact that they "help to sharpen argument and . . . improve the community's understanding of its intellectual environment" are *signs* that a conceptual contestation is fruitful, rather than explanations of its fruitfulness.[63]

Someone might object that this idea of an essentially contested concept is incoherent, for it moves equivocally between a participant's and an observer's point of view. To a participant, nothing seems to matter more than that his definition be sustained and his opponent's refuted. He is not saying simply, "Here's one more view about democracy to put in the catalogue." Surely each proponent is saying, "This is what democracy really is.

---

59. Gallie, *supra* note 48, at 180.

60. *Id.* at 180-81.

61. One example would be the use of an expression by the framers in the original text of the Constitution.

62. DWORKIN, *supra* note 12, at 70.

63. *Id.* at 71. See generally *id.* at 68-76, 90-101, 424-25, for Dworkin's excellent discussion of these matters.

This, and not those other views, captures the true essence of the concept." An observer, however, will say: "J.W. thinks he's going to win, but he must know in the back of his mind that the discussion is unwinnable. So why is he making so much fuss? There are no right answers here: democracy is an essentially contested concept." Can these perspectives be combined? Is it possible to engage in one of these debates as a partisan of a particular view but also as a theorist who knows why disputes of this kind are valuable as well as intractable? Can one acknowledge that a concept is essentially contested and still claim that one's own view is right and one's opponent's view wrong?

The answer is a cautious "yes." One cannot expect to prevail comprehensively—that is, to have one's opponents say, "But of course! J.W.'s definition of 'democracy' is correct. Why didn't we all see that before?" One understands the ideological and philosophical sources of persistent controversy. Realistically to hope to prevail in such a dispute is to believe, first, that one can convince others to take more seriously the considerations one has been advancing; second, that one can explain why alternative views are less persuasive than they have been thought to be; and third, that though one expects a continuation of the debate in both familiar and novel forms, one thinks one will have something to say about any alternative view or argument that might imaginably come up. Someone who has these hopes will acknowledge that he is engaged in a debate whose richness and usefulness stems only partly from his own contribution; but he will aim to show that this rich and useful fabric of argumentation culminates in the desirability of according greater recognition to his view.

VIII
ARE VAGUENESS AND CONTESTABILITY UNDESIRABLE IN LAW?

It is often assumed that vagueness and contestibility are undesirable in the law—and this is certainly the impression given by the "void-for-vagueness" doctrine. To the extent that the meaning of a term used in a statute, a regulation, or a constitutional amendment is indeterminate, the person to whom it is addressed may not know exactly what is required of her. To that extent, she does not know how to discharge her duty of fidelity to the law.[64] In addition, if she expects the provision to be enforced, she may be left unsure as to how, exactly, the enforcement powers of the state will be used against her. She therefore does not have a clearly defined realm of personal or economic freedom that she can count on.[65]

---

64. This consideration is almost always overlooked in discussions of the subject. Proponents of "The Rule of Law" assume that predictability of the use of power, *see infra* note 63, is the only thing at stake. Some of us, however, take fidelity to law seriously as an issue in its own right, quite apart from worries about enforcement.

65. *See* F.A. HAYEK, THE CONSTITUTION OF LIBERTY 152-53 (1960).

However, these concerns are easily exaggerated. Nothing that has been said so far shows that if a term is vague, it is comprehensively vague, or that if a term is contested, all instances of its use are contested. Though color predicates are vague, we pass information about colors to each other all the time. Though a term like "cruel" is contested, no one doubts that burning people alive in an auto-da-fé would be a cruel mode of execution. Faced with a provision that says "no act of type P shall be performed," we may be perfectly clear about its application to a given act (x_1) even though P is in other cases indeterminate: we will say to ourselves "Of course x_1 would be P." The considerations adduced in the previous Parts do show that we are often not in a position to articulate a comprehensive or uncontroversial meaning-rule from which this statement would follow along with all other applications of P. However, we do not need such a rule to see that x_1 would be P. Indeed, as Wittgenstein has stressed, it may be only because we understand that x_1 is certainly P, and x_2 is certainly P, and so is x_3, that we regard P as vague. It is because we cannot formulate a rule specifying what x_1-x_3 have in common that we have difficulty applying P to a problem case such as x_4. Think how much easier it would be to pin down a definition for "game" if the term did not include ring-around-the-rosy, solitaire, and baseball. Thus, vagueness anywhere presupposes determinacy somewhere else; only the determinacy it presupposes cannot in the nature of things be articulated as rule-governed determinacy.

For many cases, then, the vagueness of the terms used in a legal provision may be of little concern to the citizen or the official. Furthermore, one who is instructed to avoid actions of type P may be disposed to avoid actions that are even arguably of type P. For example, the vagueness and contestedness of "homicide" are issues for most of us only in extraordinary circumstances. Only if we have an independent reason to be pushing up as close as possible against the limits of the provision will we be concerned about its vagueness. A doctor serving terminally ill patients may be in this situation with "homicide"; so may an official whose job it is to draft heavier and heavier penalties in the war on crime, in relation to the contestedness of "cruel." But most people are not placed in such a situation with regard to numerous legal provisions. The citizen needs to know what the law requires of him, but that is not necessarily the same as needing to know exactly how far he can go before his behavior becomes an infraction. "How close can I get to coercing a woman before it counts as rape?" "How active does my assistance in a person's death have to be before it counts as murder?" "How much may I mislead a business partner before it counts as fraud?" A legal profession which poses these and similar questions as crucial for the ordinary citizen's understanding of the law is already in ethical difficulty.[66]

---

66. The same may be said of slippery-slope and bright-line arguments against the redefinition of various offenses such as sexual harassment. Someone for whom the important question is "How much

There are, of course, provisions for which such inquiries are reasonable. "How fast may I drive before I am guilty of excessive speed?" "What is the minimum number of years I need to have been in the country before I can become a citizen?" "How much must I pay in sales tax?" But it is striking that for these cases we specify reasonably precise measures: "Fifty-five miles per hour," "Five years," and "Eight percent of the purchase price." This suggests that in some of the cases where we do not specify numerical limits, cases where we employ instead a relatively vague concept, it may be because we do not think it appropriate for citizens to be finely calibrating their action in very close proximity to legal boundaries. These may be cases where we think it a mistake for us, as a community, to get into the business of specifying rules too precisely.

In defense of the view that I have been criticizing, it has been said that vague provisions are unfair. If a citizen sails close to the limits, he is likely sometimes to be found guilty of an offense by a court which stipulates a different arbitrary boundary from the one he chooses to observe. When this happens, the complaint goes, the citizen is a victim of retroactive legislation. No doubt there is some justice to this complaint.

We need to remember, though, how different this is from the case in which the citizen is suddenly faced with a new statute criminalizing past behavior that was perfectly and uncontroversially lawful when it was performed. The latter is the case to which our intuitions about the injustice of retroactivity are formed. By contrast, in the case of the vague provision, the citizen is not completely blindsided. The fact that there is a law and the fact that it uses a predicate the vagueness of whose meaning is well understood by everyone provide some sort of notice. The citizen knows that he is in a delicate situation and is taking a risk. He may have a particular complaint in regard to a particular provision: maybe a more determinate expression was available and ought to have been used, so as to give him clearer notice. But since determinacy is not always available, since legislation is nevertheless necessary, and since it is of course only arguable cases that are going to come before a court, it would be simplistic to say as a matter of course that courts are guilty of the evil cf retroactivity whenever they make a decision one way or the other about vague provisions that come before them.

On the other hand, the case for vagueness is also sometimes exaggerated. It is said that we should value the open texture of the language used in legislation: since a human legislator cannot possibly contemplate all the cases relevant to his concerns, the vagueness of the expressions gives courts a chance to be flexible in regard to new and unanticipated applications. H.L.A. Hart puts the argument this way:

---

may I flirt with my student before it counts as harassment?" is already poorly positioned with regard to the concerns underlying harassment law.

It is a feature of the human predicament, not only of the legislator but of anyone who attempts to regulate some sphere of conduct by means of general rules, that he labours under one supreme handicap—the impossibility of foreseeing all possible combinations of circumstances that the future may bring. . . . This means that all legal rules and concepts are "open"; and when an unenvisaged case arises we must make a fresh choice, and in doing so elaborate our legal concepts, adapting them to socially desirable ends.[67]

In fact, however, many unanticipated cases where flexibility is desirable have nothing to do with vagueness. Consider the old problem of "No vehicles in the park." Someone has a heart attack in the park and an ambulance is called in: has the prohibition been violated? Clearly the case is one where we should want flexibility, but it has nothing to do with vagueness. An ambulance is not a borderline case of a vehicle; if anything it is a paradigm case of vehicle. We call for an ambulance precisely because we need a *vehicle* to transport the sick person. There are some imaginable instances where the need for flexibility and the existence of borderline cases go together. Lon Fuller's example of the veterans who want to place a Second World War jeep on a plinth as a monument in the park is an example of this, inasmuch as we may hesitate about whether to call the immobilized shell of a jeep a vehicle.[68] But we must not make the mistake of assuming that the vagueness of natural language predicates matches our pragmatic uncertainty about what should be done in future or unanticipated cases. Vagueness may be an indication of *classificatory* uncertainty, but that is not always the same as political or moral uncertainty about what ought to be done in a given case.[69]

Let us return to the original objection about the use of vague terms in the law. Perhaps the complaint is not about "retroactive" decisions as such, for of course, courts have to reach some sort of decision in the cases that come before them, but about decisions that go against the interests or liberty of the citizen. It is sometimes suggested that, in criminal statutes at any rate, all doubts about indeterminate meanings ought to be resolved in favor of freedom: the presumption should be that conduct is not an offense unless it is clearly prohibited. However, the utility of this suggestion is limited in two ways. First, it applies at most to criminal law. In civil law actions, it is

---

67. H.L.A. HART, *Jhering's Heaven of Concepts and Modern Analytical Jurisprudence, in* ESSAYS IN JURISPRUDENCE AND PHILOSOPHY 265, 269-70 (1983). See also my *Critical Notice* of that collection, in 94 MIND 281 (1985).

68. Lon L. Fuller, *Positivism and Fidelity to Law—A Reply to Professor Hart,* 71 HARV. L. REV. 630, 663 (1958).

69. Some loose uses of the term "pragmatic" are often appealed to in order to blur this distinction. Our classificatory uncertainty is, in a sense, pragmatic; so is our political uncertainty. But our purposes do not all run together. The point of classifying things, generally, with a range of natural language predicates, is seldom the same as the point of classifying things in law as "to be done" and "not to be done."

by no means clear that a *defendant* should always be the one to get the benefit of any indeterminacies in the relevant provision, any more than it is clear that agencies should receive the benefit of such a presumption in administrative law.[70] Secondly, it applies best in regard to those expressions for which there is a reasonably bright line between clear applications and borderline applications. But as we saw in Part V, that boundary is often not clear. To the extent that the boundary is disputed, is a defendant to receive the benefit of that doubt also? And then what about the borderlines of this second level of indeterminacy?

Is it never unfair, then, to impose vague rather than precise requirements on a person? One example in which it is not fair is the case of a legal provision which actually requires a person to meet a positive standard: for example, an official may be required to ensure a "speedy" trial for a defendant. In that case, the vagueness of the concept may leave the official unsure about his exact duty. It will not be enough for him to steer well clear of the more flagrant types of delay. The same is true of a requirement that a person stopped by the police must produce "credible and reliable" identification:[71] a good-hearted citizen may steer well clear of obviously spurious forms of identification (library card, New Zealand driver's license, self-addressed envelopes, and so forth), but still be unable to work out what he is actually required to carry with him.

Another case in which vague requirements are unfair involves forms of vagueness and contestedness that do not exhibit anything like a core/penumbra structure. A piece of strict sabbatarian legislation that forbids "the playing of games" on a Sunday may be burdensome if we have no idea what are regarded as paradigm cases and what are considered as borderline cases. Is the purpose of the legislature to prevent noise on Sundays, or exertion, or entertainment, or frivolity, or gambling, or competitiveness, or outdoor pursuits, or pleasure? In this case, the vagueness of the term, without more, leaves even the pious citizen with no idea how to orient herself in regard to the provision.

Even in this last example, however, there may be some point to the use of the vague expression "game," rather than some more determinate phrase such as "team sports played competitively outdoors." Suppose there existed a traditional biblical text that proscribed "the playing of games" on the Lord's Day, much as the Fourth Commandment proscribes "laboring." No doubt, various biblical scholars would argue back and forth on the true meaning of the expression and give reasons for one interpretation rather than another. A Judaic or Christian fundamentalist might think it worthwhile to insert that biblical proscription directly into our law without further

---

70. See also the excellent discussion of "Conventionalism" in DWORKIN, *supra* note 12, at 114-50, especially the section on "Fairness and Surprise," at 140-44.

71. *See* Kolender v. Lawson, 461 U.S. 352, 353 (1983) (holding such a requirement unconstitutionally vague).

clarification, for his aim may be, not to regulate conduct, but rather to turn a theological debate into a legal debate. Even though he has not pinned down a precise meaning for "game," his purpose may still be to make our society a more devout society. For him, that might mean less the prohibition of any putative "game" in particular, and more the institution of a public political practice of arguing about the proper meaning of the prohibition. He may think a society may or may not be devout if it permits children to jump rope on a Sunday, but a society is certainly not devout if the status of jump rope on a Sunday is not even an issue for that society. The religious example is an implausible one, for us at any rate. Still, an analysis like this may be important for our understanding of the dialectical role that contested terms can play in constitutional jurisprudence.

Consider again the Eighth Amendment: "cruel and unusual punishments" shall not be inflicted. The meaning of "cruel," we know, is contestable, and for some jurists that is a flaw: if only the framers had specified whether capital punishment was permissible or not, then we would know where we stand. But knowing where we stand may not be the point of the provision. Instead, the point may be to ensure that certain debates take place in our society: this should not be a society which simply imposes punishments without regard to whether or not they are cruel. Maybe execution is cruel, maybe it is not. But a society which executes criminals without hesitation and without public debate on that question is arguably a poorer society, from the point of view of the ethical theory underlying the Eighth Amendment, than a society which makes it an issue.

Another example: it may be contestable whether flag-burning is to count as "speech" or not for the purposes of the First Amendment. In the middle of a tedious constitutional law class, we may wish that the framers had used a more precise expression than "speech." But that, too, may be a mistake. The point of restraining Congress from abridging freedom of speech may have been to make it an issue—a big deal, a Federal case (in the vernacular sense of that term)—when spoken dissent, or anything arguably like it, is restrained. In other words, the point of the First Amendment might be as much to facilitate a debate about "speech" as to secure a bottom-line of legislative restraint.

Perhaps, then, we sometimes try too hard to determine a precise prescriptive meaning for legal and constitutional provisions. Our urge is to get into a position where we can always answer the question, "Well, *is* this prohibited or is it not?" However, sometimes the point of a legal provision may be to start a discussion rather than settle it, and this may be particularly true of the constitutional provisions that aim at restricting and governing legislation.[72] The purpose of these provisions may be to have an impact on

---

72. In some countries, this is the explicit function of constitutional provisions. The New Zealand Bill of Rights Act of 1990, for example, specifically precludes the courts from striking down Acts of Parliament (§ 4), but § 7 requires the Attorney General to "bring to the attention of the House of

the process of legislating rather than merely on the validity of legislation conceived as some sort of finished product. The rule of law, under this account, involves not just the production of determinate norms, but respect for a certain heritage in the subject matter and style of our legal and political debates.

If this is true, then the use of contestable terms should not necessarily be regarded as a flaw in a legal provision. Particularly if the term in question is "essentially" contested in Gallie's sense—i.e., if continuing debates about its proper meaning are understood to serve some important function associated with the employment of the term—then its use (rather than the use of a more determinate surrogate) may be crucial for the style of politics that we want to foster in our community. It follows, also, that the Critical Legal Studies exposé of the "contradictions" and "indeterminacy" inherent in our legal language is neither surprising nor damning.[73] Of course, some words and concepts that we use in our law will reflect a heritage of fundamental disagreement and facilitate the protraction of such controversies. But far from undermining the legitimacy of the law, that is the whole point of their deployment. We do not agree on many things in our society, but perhaps we can agree on this: that we are a better society for continuing to argue about certain issues than we would be if such arguments were artificially or stipulatively concluded.

Representatives any provision in the [piece of proposed legislation] that appears to be inconsistent with any of the rights and freedoms contained in this Bill of Rights." New Zealand Bill of Rights Act § 7(b), 109 N.Z. Stat. 1687, 1689 (1990).

73. For a more general argument to this effect, see Ken Kress, *Legal Indeterminacy,* 77 CALIF. L. REV. 283 (1989).

Acknowledgments

Frankfurter, Felix. "Some Reflections on the Reading of Statutes." *Columbia Law Review* 47 (1947): 527–46.

Goodhart, Arthur L. "Determining the Ratio Decidendi of a Case." *Yale Law Journal* 40 (1930): 161–83.

Hart, H.L.A. "The Ascription of Responsibility and Rights." *Proceedings of the Aristotelian Society* 49 (1949): 171–94. Reprinted by courtesy of the Editor of the Aristotelian Society. Copyright 1949.

Hutcheson, Joseph C., Jr. "The Judgment Intuitive: The Function of the 'Hunch' in Judicial Decisions." *Cornell Law Review* 14 (1929): 274–88.

Llewellyn, Karl N. "Remarks on the Theory of Appellate Decision and the Rules or Canons About How Statutes Are to be Construed." *Vanderbilt Law Review* 3 (1950): 395–406. Reprinted with the permission of Vanderbilt University.

Miller, Geoffrey P. "Pragmatics and the Maxims of Interpretation." *Wisconsin Law Review* (1990): 1179–1225. Reprinted with permission of the *Wisconsin Law Review*. Copyright 1990 by the Board of Regents of the University of Wisconsin System.

Posner, Richard A. "Legal Formalism, Legal Realism, and the Interpretation of Statutes and the Constitution." *Case Western Reserve Law Review* 37 (1986–87): 179–217. Reprinted with the permission of *Case Western Law Review*.

Radin, Max. "Case Law and Stare Decisis: Concerning *Präjudizienrecht in Amerika*." *Columbia Law Review* 33 (1933): 199–212.

Ross, Alf. "Tû-tû." *Harvard Law Review* 70 (1957): 812–25. Copyright 1957 by the Harvard Law Review Association.

Salmond, John W. "The Theory of Judicial Precedents." *Law Quarterly Review* 16 (1900): 376–91.

Scalia, Antonin. "The Rule of Law as a Law of Rules." *University of Chicago Law Review* 56 (1989): 1175–88. Reprinted with the permission of the University of Chicago Law School.

Schauer, Frederick. "Exceptions." *University of Chicago Law Review* 58 (1991): 871–99. Reprinted with the permission of the University of Chicago Law School.

Simpson, A.W.B. "The Analysis of Legal Concepts." *Law Quarterly Review* 80 (1964): 535–58. Reprinted with the permission of Sweet & Maxwell.

Stone, Julius. "Fallacies of the Logical Form in English Law: A Study of *Stare Decisis* in Legal Flux." In *Interpretations of Modern Legal Philosophies: Essays in Honor of Roscoe Pound*, edited by Paul Sayre (New York: Oxford University Press, 1947): 696–735.

Traynor, Roger J. "Reasoning in a Circle of Law." *Virginia Law Review* 56 (1970): 739–54. Reprinted with the permission of the University of Virginia, School of Law.

Waldron, Jeremy. "Vagueness in Law and Language: Some Philosophical Issues." *California Law Review* 82 (1994): 509–40. Reprinted with permission. Copyright 1994 by the California Law Review, Inc.